T0367139

TREASON

in Roman and Germanic Law

TREASON
IN ROMAN AND GERMANIC LAW

Collected Papers

by FLOYD SEYWARD LEAR

PUBLISHED FOR RICE UNIVERSITY · HOUSTON

UNIVERSITY OF TEXAS PRESS · AUSTIN

Library of Congress Catalog Card No. 65–11151
Copyright © 1965 by Floyd Seyward Lear
All Rights Reserved
ISBN 978-0-292-72960-5

TO ELSIE

PREFACE AND ACKNOWLEDGMENTS

The papers collected in this book consist of reflections and speculations indulged in during interludes in nearly forty years of teaching in the History and Political Science Department of Rice University. All these studies relate to Roman and Germanic public law; most of them bear directly on the concept of treason. Treason is an ugly subject at best. Its purpose is to achieve the death of states through violence or craft as distinguished from the insidious internal disease of degeneration and decay. Treason is that aspect of *stasis* that seeks the murder of a body politic. It is the deadly reverse of that coin of politics of which allegiance, fidelity, and loyalty are the obverse.

Although it is among the most repugnant facets of man's political nature, treason is a fundamental concept of political theory. Its vital significance was impressed upon me first when, as a graduate student at Harvard, I had the good fortune to enroll in Charles Howard McIlwain's History 9 course on the Constitutional History of England to 1485. Later he consented to direct my work for the doctorate on a subject dealing with the background of the Statute of Treasons 25 Edward III (1352). It became clear that the basis of this statute led ever farther back into the dim antecedents of Germanic custom and the intricate background of the Roman law. My doctoral plan changed gradually into a dissertation on the *Early History of Treason*. I owe a large debt to Professor McIlwain for encouragement in the study of this nebulous area as well as for his numerous suggestions regarding avenues of approach to be explored and hypotheses to be considered. The seminars of Charles Homer Haskins in Mediaeval Sources and of William Scott Ferguson in Roman Constitutional History also contributed to an enlarged scope of my research. Their wisdom and judgment have been an unfailing source of light in all my subsequent teaching and study.

It is impossible to express one's full obligation to others over so long a span of years, and it is difficult to find fitting words for so many now long since passed from among us. However, I must mention Professor

Henry Fairfield Burton and Professor Charles Hoeing of the University of Rochester, who made the Latin language a living instrument without which mediaeval study is impossible and who instilled in me an enduring love of the ancient classics, and to Professor Laurence Bradford Packard of Rochester and later of Amherst, who directed my steps into the paths of mediaeval history. I must mention the unfailing encouragement and interest of President Edgar Odell Lovett during the twenty years in which I had the privilege of serving under him in the old Rice Institute. He was always interested to know what I was doing and understood the difficulties of humanistic study confronting educational pioneers.

There are also many generations of my students at Rice who have borne with me in lecture courses and who have helped me to clarify my thoughts, if only by observing the courtesy of listening. A few graduate students in occasional seminars have translated several Germanic codes and, as far as my knowledge serves, these humble efforts still constitute the only English translations of these codes. Indeed, the critical translations of German scholars are only now appearing in the *Germanenrechte*. I must mention also the aid of the Rice Library staff, especially Miss Alice Dean, Miss Pender Turnbull, and Miss Sarah Lane, who helped me to obtain the basic tools of research in the days when library funds were limited. It was an exciting event when we procured the *Monumenta Germaniae Historica*, Migne's *Patrologia Latina*, and the *Rolls Series*. Previously such sets were readily available in the Southwest only in Professor Frederic Duncalf's mediaeval collection in The University of Texas Library at Austin. I felt sometimes in the 1920's and 30's that we experienced something of the isolation of the monastic scriptoria of Merovingian Gaul. But we knew we were building on the frontiers of American education.

I must express my deep appreciation of the aid of my former student and present colleague, Professor Katherine Fischer Drew, whose sharp editorial eye has saved me many a slip of clarity in meaning, sentence structure, and punctuation, and whose knowledge of the barbarian codes is comprehensive and detailed. Also my thanks to the development and administrative offices of Rice University for aid, secretarial and financial, and to the Rice History and Political Science Department for its material assistance, especially to its chairman, Professor R. John Rath. Further I wish to acknowledge the gracious permissions to publish the papers in this book, which were given by the late Dr. Charles R. D. Miller, editor of *Speculum*, by Dr. S. Harrison Thomson, editor of *Medievalia et Humanistica,* and by the Harvard University Press, the *Northwestern Law Review,* and Rice University.

In general these papers remain, with slight revision, as they were first published. The amount of recent publication in this area of Roman and Germanic public criminal law or offenses against the state is not large, and in my opinion expresses no new judgments that would invalidate my original position as set forth in these essays. It is my hope that by bringing them together in this manner the unity of subject matter and continuity of trends in this field will be made more apparent than would have been the case had they remained scattered through a number of journals.

FLOYD SEYWARD LEAR

Houston, Texas

CONTENTS

INTRODUCTION

Treason is not easy to define. No single sentence or paragraph will suffice to clarify and elucidate the essential nature of its concept. The idea of treason possesses many phases and may be viewed from many angles, and its basic character may be appreciated only if studied from the point of view of the history of ideas. It is one of those abstract conceptions of political philosophy that are evolved gradually in the course of man's effort to create and develop public authority. And, as the idea matures, specific legal definitions of treason appear that are applicable to particular situations and cases. However, as an element in political philosophy it may be resolved into certain ethical and moral values involving breach of obligation and bad faith that rest ultimately on the general idea of betrayal. The traitor is one who has betrayed some pledged troth or some confidence rested in him. The Germanic *troth* implies an obligation actively assumed by an individual; the Latin *fides* implies trust and confidence reposed in an individual. The violation of contract and the violation of confidence may be equally treasonable.

Perhaps the most difficult question of all involves determining who shall have the right to judge when a treason has been committed, for treason is a relative matter in particular situations and depends largely on the individual point of view. Thus the tyrant may look upon all revolution and *stasis* as treason, while his people may consider the tyrant to be a traitor hostile to the general welfare of the land. Minorities may speak of the "tyranny of the majority" and hold the larger number to be subverters of the common weal. Individuals may claim revolution as a right, thus making the commission of treason impossible for them. However, it is doubtful whether they would logically extend to others the immunity they claim for themselves. This relativity of the abstract conception of treason as an element in political theory makes necessary its concrete definition in specific statutes. The general idea must be subjected to legal analysis so that the law may set up some absolute standard to serve practical ends. The result is that, as the family, state, and other agencies for exercising authority appear, the history of treason becomes a study of laws that men have devised for the specific purpose of repressing and punishing those who would obstruct the exercise of authority. Therefore the character of the legislation is always adapted to the character of the authority it seeks to uphold. In a sense, then, the history of treason can be related only in terms of the evolution of the state and the development of public authority. The function of the law is the analysis of the general philosophical conception of treason, the application of rules in concrete cases, and the orderly classification of these rules in their proper relations one to another—all of this being done in an effort to establish an absolute standard that will render the most complete justice possible in every particular case. The function of history is to indicate what this standard has been among different peoples at different times, preserving the continuity of the idea as well as indicating the changes that time has wrought in it.

The earliest organic group with which the study of government deals is the family, and this is not a state but a society under such authority as the Roman *patria potestas* and the Germanic *Hausvater* or *Altermann*. This patriarchal authority must be considered private in its origins; yet there is also under way the process of "becoming public." There is authority, but it is not yet state authority. Where there are no state and no public offenses it is clear that there could be no treason as technically defined by modern law, although the basic conception of betrayal and broken faith would exist. One of the most widely accepted and satisfactory theories regarding human society bases the origin of the state on compact or contract. This suggests the protective nature of early society and implies the obligation of the individual to promote the interests of the group, although this obligation may not always have been consciously recognized. Treason would, then, consist of all criminal acts that could threaten the safety and existence of the family as a social unit. A homicide within the early family could well be as treasonable as the murder of the king in an absolute monarchy, since such a crime might deprive that early social group of a warrior essential to its protection or of a child-bearing woman needed for its continuance. Under such circumstances it is not strange that parricide retained a character of particular heinousness among primitive peoples. Such a crime was far more vital in the simple society of early men than in the complex modern social fabric, wherein homicide is merely the wrongful infringement of an individual's right to his life, a right in which the state guarantees to protect him. Modern society has relieved mutual dependence within the family by substituting the higher sanctions of public state authority. Similarly adultery was an offense that would destroy the foundations of heredity and parental responsibility in the early family, although today it is considered primarily a moral delict. Thus, while homicide and adultery were treasonable in the early family, they have no direct connection with treason in modern society. These examples illustrate how the early generalized conception of treason differed from the narrower modern legal definitions. Indeed, from the technical point of view treason was only in process of "becoming treason" during the period prior to the state. These early forms of treason must be regarded primarily as private offenses, weakening the solidarity of the family as a social group, although rudimentary public elements are present. Usually under these conditions of the early family organization it may be said of treason that as a concept it is general; as an act it is private; and its significance is social.

The general idea of treason in a state, as opposed to specific legal definitions, embodies all attempts by an individual or individuals to injure the state. The state is conceived as an instrument for protecting the individual that the individual has bound himself to support, so long as the state meets its obligations. This theory of the state presupposes allegiance and contract of some sort. And, when such a state appears, treason becomes a public crime and acquires political significance, being an act directed against the "life of the state." Treason, thus, loses the diversified character it possessed in a family regime of private law and ceases to include all the large variety of crimes that are inimical to the social common weal. Society has become so stabilized that isolated crimes fail to shake its solidarity. Furthermore, the state has organized special agencies for exercising a governmental authority that can regulate the entire social order. When this change has taken place one may designate this new special agency as a public agency possessing public authority. It is, then, the function of the law to define specifically what acts are sufficiently subversive of this public authority as to endanger the existence of the state. Among these acts are commonly listed such crimes as attacks upon public officers and insubordination in the army, or, more broadly, "lending aid and comfort to the enemy." Vital differences clearly distinguish this situation from the earlier age when homicide might be called a sort of treason. In general treason ceases to consist of individual cases of direct assault on the members of society, but rather becomes attack upon the special instrument society has devised for the regulation and administration of society. Of course, in many instances the functions of the state so permeate the entire social structure that it becomes difficult, if not impossible, to tell whether attacks upon the state can be committed without endangering the general welfare of society as a whole. This is particularly true in pure democracies of the type of the ancient Greek *polis* or city-state, where the state is a "common life" and where the state and society are one. Treason is, then, obviously an act of broad social as well as political significance.

Under a contract theory of the state the position of the individual in his relation to treason is not always easy to define, since the individual may interpret the terms of his contract in a manner different from that of the public officers. He may sincerely believe that he is acting within his rights and still have his action called into question as treasonable by the agents of the state, or he may with equal sincerity believe that the state has violated the contract and that he is no longer bound. Thus the questions arise: Who may judge the right of individual action? When do the mutual obligations between state and individual become void? Clearly the tyrant who rules his people for his own advantage and recognizes no obligation to them can rightfully expect nothing in return. His only sanction must be force; he appears as an anarchical individual outside society and the state who dominates his people wrongfully. Yet even in his case who may judge whether he rules well or ill? A people may consider its monarch a traitor to the general welfare, while the monarch may consider his people traitors to the established agencies of government. Inevitable differences arise between the society subject to regulation and the persons who regulate, administer, and act in society's behalf. Neither should be allowed to be judge in its own cause. Existing governments tend to view any vital change in government as treasonable. Among the Greek city-states the *dēmos* was often held a tyrant and like other tyrants it feared change or *stasis*. Thus the typical treason among Hellenic democracies was the *katalysis tou demou*, or overthrow of the democracy. In general such theoretical propositions are insoluble: as whether it may be treasonable for a democracy, even when using constitutional processes, to declare itself otherwise, as a monarchy. Changes of this sort are accompanied by factional strife, and absolute standards for the determination of treason tend to disappear.

It was the great service of Rome, through formal legal definitions, to resolve this chaos of political theories prevailing in ancient Greek thought. In the later Roman empire the distinction between the governing agency and the society it regulated was plainly drawn. The state tended to concentrate in a single individual, the emperor, who became the symbol of public authority, and the gravest treason became certain specified acts directed against the emperor. However, in monarchy the individual who symbolizes public authority is in no practical danger of being confused with the society he regulates, unlike the situation in a pure democracy where state and society are identified. The monarch is a visible token of the separation of governor from governed. As a result, it becomes possible to classify treason into two types and provide suitable legislation for each type. The treason against society, as constituted, is the Greek *prodosia* and *katalysis tou demou,* the Roman *perduellio* and *seditio,* and the Germanic folk treason (*Landesverrat*)—all of which may be called, in English, types of "treason against land and folk." The treason against the symbolic monarch per se is called high treason or in Latin the *crimen laesae maiestatis* (in its more limited connotation). When the monarch extends his interests in society beyond his symbolic person he tends to fuse the two varieties of treason, as for example among the Romans *perduellio* came to be included among the crimes against majesty. Nevertheless, the basic distinction between these two types of treason remains clear. Complicating factors enter with monarchy in cases where the ruler asserts his divinity as among the "God-kings" of the Hellenistic world and the Roman empire, and where the ruler claims some special divine sanction or dispensation as among the "Godly princes" of the sixteenth century or the "divine right" theorists of the seventeenth century. Here treason becomes confounded with sacrilege or heresy.

Finally there are points of difference between an absolute and a constitutional monarch in their relation to treason. A constitutional monarch is under a contract that he may nullify through his own non-observance. Failure to respect his contractual obligations may bring a loss of his public character with the result that subsequent attacks upon him could not be considered treasonable. Among such monarchs a sharper distinction is likely to be drawn between the office and the person so that injuries directed against the office only may be deemed treason. The appearance of royal wergelds among the Anglo-Saxons tends to support this theory. But the absolute monarch may identify the office with the man, declare himself to constitute the state and to be a living law, or even announce that he is divine, outside the state, and above the law. In such a case he may construct the definition of treason by fiat. However, regardless of theory, the ultimate practical sanction of such government is commonly force, resting on military power or on religious fear and superstition. Allegiance loses its contractual character and becomes mere deference to authority.

This general consideration of the nature of treason indicates that treason is primarily a crime affecting social groups and directed toward the destruction of corporate interests. There must be a common weal that the treason attempts to destroy, and the gravest treason is that directed against the best organized and most comprehensive corporate group, which is usually the state. However, it is possible for states to be combinations of lesser political entities, each retaining some share of sovereign power. In such cases one may doubt whether treason can be committed against one unit of the confederation without offending and injuring every other unit as is frequently exemplified in confederations and leagues. Also, states may form federal unions wherein each of the combining units delegates a share of its sovereignty that a new authority may be created superior to and independent of its components. Curious problems may arise here as to whether there can be treason against the federal or central authority without treason against each subordinate unit, or whether the situation may be reversed.

These problems are more nearly contemporary than those for the most part considered in these studies. Hence there is no attempt to examine these later questions, but allusion is made to them so that attention may be called to the intricacies inherent in the corporate aspects of treason. It is more germane to the subject considered here, however, to note that special corporate groups may appear in a sovereign state, having no political attachment to the state and often having special private interests inimical to the general welfare. The appearance of such corporations in the Roman *collegia* gave much concern to the imperial government, for, when men divide their allegiance between their state and some special group within the state, these new corporations may be a grave menace to the government in case of a clash of interests. Such great apprehension was felt that it became equivalent to treason for an individual to join these special groups. Christian congregations labored under this disability because of their special character. With the decline of central government in the early Middle Ages and the rise of the barbarian kingdoms ecclesiastical groups gradually acquired peculiar privileges in the form of local "peaces" (*paces*) that established them in a semipublic position. Other *paces* or *Frieden* protected the popular assembly (*Landesding*), the army, the home, and the public highways, and finally there evolved the king's peace, which embraced all others, expanded into a general peace of the land, and was administered under a

common law. Breaches of such *paces* became treasonable in the degree
that the groups had been able to assert their corporate character and assume public governing functions. These matters are considered here in
connection with Germanic law. Finally, in cases of the complete break-
down of central authority sovereignty may be almost entirely divided
among these special local interests. Government is administered locally,
as was the case in the feudal period, and treason is reduced to offenses
against a local lord. Upon the restoration of the central power these injuries done to a lesser lord are distinguished as petty treason from the
high treason against the king or emperor.

Another phase of treason that cannot be left entirely aside touches
the matter of sacrilege. This involves religious factors and is most significant among early or ancient peoples where the deities are regarded
as essential members of society. Thus the Romans considered serious
violations of the divine law (*fas*) to be sacrilege or a kind of treason
against the gods. This is obviously quite outside ordinary conceptions
of treason, based upon jurisprudential ideas of the human *ius*. The
Greeks associated impiety (*asebeia*) with treason (*prodosia*) very
closely so that he who betrayed or abandoned his state committed a
sacrilege just as he who outraged the national gods was guilty of treason.[1] It is noteworthy that impiety and treason are made the subjects of
related procedures (*graphai*) in Athenian law, while the Roman *Digest*
states that the crime which is nearest to sacrilege is called the crime of
majesty (*Digest* 48, 4, 1). The Greek thinkers with their exaltation of
human dignity extended a sacred character to man, so that homicide or
parricide became both sacrilegious and impious. Plato likens the human
body to a temple that may not be desecrated through violence. It is also
probable that certain religious sanctions were attached to the family
and home, so that parricide became both a sacrilege and a treason,
while among the Germanic peoples a similar attitude is observable
toward attacks upon a man's home and toward breaches of the peace
of the home (*Hausfrieden*). As has been noted, treason against the
Hellenistic and Roman divine monarchs tended to be held sacrilege as
well. With the advent of Christianity insubordination to the divinely
appointed ruler approximates heresy and becomes a kind of *crimen
laesae religionis*, and sacrilege loses its connection with treason, save
for its incorporation in the ecclesiastical *paces*. Nevertheless, it is hard to

[1] J. J. Thonissen, *Le droit pénal de la république athénienne* (Brussels: Bruylant-Christophe, 1875), p. 178.

see how sacrilege can be dissociated from treason in a social system such
as is implicit where the spheres of church and state (*sacerdotium* and
regnum) are mutually interrelated. There the religious and political
aspects of human activity are organically fused together, and the man
who commits the one crime must logically thereby commit the other.
These are some of the central concepts which will be analyzed in
greater depth in the studies in Roman and Germanic law which follow
these general remarks.

TREASON

in Roman and Germanic Law

I

The Crime of Majesty in Roman Public Law*

A. Under the Republic

The early history of Rome supplies much evidence supporting the theory that treason has evolved gradually from an offense against the family in its primitive origins to an offense against the state regarded as a matured sociopolitical structure. Very important changes in the content of the crime occur during this transformation from its early private and familial beginnings through the long process of becoming public and its final emergence as the ultimate offense in public law. Rome appears as a state very early, being no mere aggregate of families or clans, nor yet a mere nation or *ethnos*, but the historical details of this early time are difficult to establish. In fact, dates, names, and events must be considered legendary or be accepted with the greatest caution at least until the later part of the fourth century B.C., in the period sometimes called the age of Appius Claudius. Even institutions such as laws and the governing machinery of the state, in the forms in which they have been recorded by later Roman writers, must be treated with caution and suspicion. In an extreme degree of scepticism some have doubted the existence of the traditional early kings while many have questioned the possibility of establishing more than the roughest sort of historical sequence for this early time.

The two crimes connected with treason that may be associated assur-

* Reprinted with corrections and additions from *The Rice Institute Pamphlet*, XLII (1955), 5–42 and nn. 111–129. Sections A and C of this study were presented in a public lecture sponsored by the departments of history and classical languages of The University of Texas at Austin, Texas, on December 10, 1953.

edly with this period are *parricidium* and *perduellio*. The parricide who
kills his parent or other near relative may be found in the earliest human
society, where punishment was inflicted according to the judgment of
the *pater familias*. However, such killings and rebellions against the
patriarchal head of the family were probably uncommon in an age
when family ties were strong.[1] The *patria potestas* is an outstanding
institution in the family government of the primitive Romans. The
power of the father represented authority of a semipublic nature, and
was almost certainly extended in these early days over the family re-
tainers, who may have been unrelated by blood ties but were nonethe-
less in very close association. Indeed, it seems altogether likely that the
semipaternal relation of patron and client originated in such manner,
and that any violation of the mutual obligations imposed by this relationship was considered in much the same light as a violation of the
family bond. Under such circumstances homicide became parricide and
treasonable. And all such treasons are analogous to the mediaeval "petty
treason," being "an aggravated degree of murder, where the murderer
owed some special private or domestic allegiance to the murdered."[2]

The oldest legislation relating to parricide is set forth in fragmentary
form by Dionysius and Festus and constitutes a part of the so-called
Leges Regiae. Thus, in the portion of the "Royal Laws" attributed to
Romulus and Tatius it is provided that "If a son's wife . . . [here there
is a lacuna in the text] let her be devoted to the deities presiding over
parents."[3] That the lacuna covers some sacrilegious act of violence may
be inferred from a parallel law of similar structure attributed to Servius
Tullius: "If a lad beat a parent and the parent cries out, let the lad be
devoted to the deities presiding over parents."[4] Next, in the law com-

[1] Cf. E. C. Clark, *History of Roman Private Law* (Cambridge: University Press,
1919), Part III: Regal Period, pp. 588–593, 604–607, for relation of parricide to
treason.

[2] Cf. *Ibid.*, pp. 262–263.

[3] P. F. Girard, *Textes de droit romain* (3rd ed.; Paris: A. Rousseau, 1903), for
Leges Regiae, 1, 7: "si nurus . . . sacer divis parentum estod," and Riccobono,
Fontes iuris romani antejustiniani (Florence: Barbèra, 1941), I, 11, trans. by Johnson *et al.*, *Ancient Roman Statutes* (Austin: University of Texas Press, 1961), Doc.
1, I, 11, and n. 6: "If a daughter-in-law strikes her father-in-law she shall be dedicated as a sacrifice to his ancestral deities." Cf. *Leges Regiae*, Riccobono, *Fontes*,
VI, 6, and Girard, *Textes*, 4, 1; also Festus (F. 230) *Plorare* in Clark, *Roman Private Law*, p. 589, n. 34, and C. G. Bruns, *Fontes iuris romani antiqui* (7th ed. by
Otto Gradenwitz; Tübingen: Mohr, 1909), Part I: Leges et Negotia, p. 7, n. 6.

[4] Girard, *Textes*, for *Leges Regiae*, 4, 1, and Riccobono, *Fontes*, VI, 6 (Johnson,
Statutes, Doc. 1, VI, 6, and n. 47): "Si parentem puer verberit, ast olle plorassit,
puer divis parentum sacer esto."

monly designated the "law of Numa" it is stated that "If anyone has intentionally slain a free man uncondemned, let him be as one who has smitten a parent," that is, let him be outlawed (*paricidas esto*).[5] In its original sense the word *paricidas* is believed to mean a "smiter," if not a "killer," of a parent. Thus, a progressive expansion of parricidal action is suggested by the meager legal fragments. First one finds smiting a parent, next killing a parent, probably followed by killing any member of the family or any client, and finally the slaying of any freeman not under condemnation. The murderer is not called a parricide, but he is treated as a person who has incurred the penalty for insult or outrage to a parent.[6] E. C. Clark remarks in this connection: "We have here, as it seems to me, an interesting step in the development of Roman criminal law. It is the employment of a primeval and well-established religious penalty directed against violence within the family, for the prohibition of malicious homicide within the community."[7] Hence murder became a religious offense, violating sanctions which had attached originally to the family. Finally, special permanent public officers, designated *quaestores parricidii*, were created to track down murderers,[8] and their functions were extended eventually until they seem to have had as their object the apprehension of all kinds of criminals.[9]

[5] Girard, *Textes*, for *Leges Regiae*, 2, 12, and Riccobono, *Fontes*, II, 16 (Johnson, *Statutes*, Document 1, II, 16): "Si qui hominem liberum dolo sciens morti duit, paricidas esto." Cf. Festus (F. p. 221) *Parrici* in Clark, *Roman Private Law*, p. 590, n. 35. For a detailed examination of this problem see Franz Leifer, " 'Paricidas Esto'," in *Studi in onore di Salvatore Riccobono* (Palermo: Arti grafiche G. Castiglia, 1936), II, 101–145, where the sacral, religious connotation of this law is stressed. The observation has been made that *paricidas* may mean "an avenger of blood" and so reflects the existence of the blood feud among the early Romans. Cf. H. F. Jolowicz, *Historical Introduction to the Study of Roman Law* (Cambridge: University Press, 1932), p. 324. Jolowicz suggests that parricide came to refer to the murder of relatives only at a later time in connection with the horrible punishment of the sack. Cf. *Digest* 48, 9, 9 pr *De Lege Pompeia de Parricidiis*, which cites the Twelfth Book of the *Pandects* of Modestinus as follows: "According to ancient practice it has been established as the penalty for parricide that the guilty person be scourged until bloody with rods, then sewed in a leather sack with a dog, cock, viper, and monkey, and finally cast into the depths of the sea." Jolowicz thinks that "the original meaning of *parricidium* [as blood feud] was forgotten, and its supposed connection with *pater* gave it the narrower significance" (*Study of Roman Law*, p. 324). Cf. *Institutes* 4, 18, 6 *De Publicis Judiciis*; Paulus *Sententiae* 5, 24, 1 *Ad Legem Pompeiam de Parricidiis*.

[6] Clark, *Roman Private Law*, III, 604, quoting Plutarch *Romulus* 22.

[7] *Ibid.*, III, 591; A. W. Zumpt, *Das Criminalrecht der römischen Republik* (Berlin: F. Dümmler, 1865–1869), I (Abtheilung I), p. 372 and notes.

[8] See Bruns, *Fontes*, p. 35, for *XII Tab.*, 9, 4, and *ibid.*, p. 10, n. 1 for Festus (F. p. 221) *Parrici*.

[9] Clark, *Roman Private Law*, III, 591–592.

It is clear that parricide contains rudimentary elements of treason in an age when the family was the chief agency for maintaining authority. Under such conditions killing or injuring the *pater familias* would endanger social stability. But when the state appears and parricide has been extended in meaning to include a variety of homicides the treasonable aspects of the crime are lost, for the state is a complex organism, the existence of which is not commonly shaken by isolated homicides. Indeed, the state becomes an instrument to limit family self-help by making the punishment of crime a matter for public authority. In this new situation treason becomes a crime directed against the state, and among the Romans this crime was designated *perduellio*.[10] Since a Roman state existed prior to the earliest historical record, no documentary proof can be cited to show that *parricidium* must have existed before *perduellio*. "It is on intrinsic grounds of progressive juridical development" that *perduellio* must be placed later than *parricidium*,[11] and this evolutionary conception of treason is accepted as a fundamental postulate in this study. The *perduellis* is the "bad warrior," that is, an enemy of the country in general, especially the enemy within, as opposed to *hostis* designating an outside enemy.

It must be noted that the word *hostis* loses its original meaning of stranger and is transformed into an expression referring to the enemy without. Thus, the crime *perduellio* is an act hostile to the state or country (*patria*), particularly from the military point of view, and involves the ideas of treason and desertion.[12] It includes all culpable dealings with the enemy and all incriminating acts dealing injury to the state, considered in relation to an external enemy.[13] Among such acts may be mentioned:[14] (1) *Desertion*, which begins from the moment one leaves the camp.[15] Furthermore, any citizen who goes over to an enemy of Rome or even to a country not allied with Rome must be con-

[10] Cf. Festus (P. p. 102) *Hostes*, with incorrect explanation in Festus (P. p. 66) *Duellum*, in Clark, *Roman Private Law*, p. 595, nn. 3–4.

[11] Clark, *Roman Private Law*, III, 597. Cf T. Mommsen, *Römisches Strafrecht* (Leipzig: S. Hirzel, 1899), p. 527, which relates these crimes from a procedural point of view.

[12] Mommsen, *Römisches Strafrecht*, pp. 537–538.

[13] *Ibid.*, pp. 546–549.

[14] See Daremberg et Saglio, *Dictionnaire des antiquités grècques et romaines*, article "Maiestas" by G. Humbert and Ch. Lécrivain (Graz, Austria: Akademische Druck-u. Verlagsanstalt, 1963), III (2), 1557, for analysis which is followed here in the main.

[15] Note the various circumstances under which the military crime of desertion is defined in *Digest* 49, 16, 3 *De Re Militari*.

sidered a deserter, whether or not he be a soldier in the military service. All such offenders are liable to prosecution for *perduellio*.[16] Both in the time of the Republic and of the Empire these cases came under the jurisdiction of a military court.[17] In both periods the penalties for desertion were extremely severe: the condemned were crucified in republican times; the Empire delivered them over to the stake or wild beasts.[18] Forfeiture of citizenship and loss of civil rights extended to deserters who abandoned the person under whose command (*sub imperio*) they were, and to individuals placed under interdiction of fire and water. All such persons suffered a change of condition (*capitis minutio*) through their loss of status as citizens.[19] (2) *Proditio* is a distinct type of *perduellio* and may be defined as the delivery to the enemy of any city, territory, or military force belonging to Rome. It may even involve the handing over of the person of a Roman citizen.[20] (3) *Aid and comfort*. It is an act of *perduellio* to make any agreement whatsoever with an enemy relative to furnishing information, advice, or such materials as iron, weapons, and food.[21] This heading covers both vital information and strategic materials in modern parlance. (4) *Incitation*. When one incites an enemy to begin a war or an ally to revolt he is guilty of *perduellio*.[22] (5) *Breach of ban of exile*. It is probably a form of *perduellio* to break the ban of exile by returning to Italy. This ban involves the legal prohibition of food and shelter under the formula

[16] *Digest* 48, 4, 2 *Ad Legem Iuliam Maiestatis*; 49, 15, 19, 8 *De Re Militari*; Paulus *Sententiae* 5, 29, 1 *Ad Legem Iuliam Maiestatis*.

[17] Cf. *Digest* 49, 16, 3 pr *De Re Militari*, in which the governor of a province is ordered to send back a deserter to his own commander.

[18] *Digest* 49, 16, 3, 10 *De Re Militari*; 48, 19, 38, 1–2 *De Poenis*.

[19] *Digest* 4, 5, 5, 1 *De Capite Minutis*.

[20] *Digest* 48, 4, 3 *Ad Legem Maiestatis* contains what is probably the earliest reference to *perduellio* in Roman Law. Here Marcian cites from the *Twelve Tables* as follows: "Lex XII tab. iubet eum, qui hostem concitaverit quive civem hosti tradiderit, capite punire." Cf. Bruns, *Fontes*, p. 35. Also see *Digest* 48, 4, 4; 48, 4, 10 *Ad Legem Iuliam Maiestatis*; Paulus *Sent.* 5, 29, 1. Cf. Riccobono, *Fontes*, XII *Tabulae*, IX, 5 (Johnson, *Statutes*, Doc. 8, IX, 5, and n. 103), and see *Fontes, Leges Regiae*, III, 3 (*Statutes*, Doc. 1, III, 3).

[21] *Digest* 48, 4, 1, 1; 48, 4, 4; *Codex Justinianus* 4, 41, 2 *Quae Res Exportare Non Debeant*, for a late prohibition against sales to the barbarians (Marcian, a. 455–457), providing them with weapons; 4, 63, 2 *De Commerciis et Mercatoribus* (Valentinian, Valens, and Gratian, a. 374?), which prohibits the furnishing of gold to barbarians; *Codex Theodosianus* 9, 40, 24 *De Poenis* (Honorius and Theodosius, a. 419), trans. by Clyde Pharr (Princeton: University Press, 1952), p. 258, which prohibits the building of ships for barbarians (*C. Just.* 9, 47, 25).

[22] *Digest* 48, 4, 1, 1; 48, 4, 3; 48, 4, 4; 49, 15, 7, 1 *De Captivis et De Postliminio et Redemptis et Hostibus*; Paulus *Sent.* 5, 29, 1.

of *aquae et ignis interdictio*.[23] This interdiction of water and fire suggests the primitive Germanic outlawry procedures, which declare the
offender outside the law (*exlex*), forbid all forms of assistance to the
criminal, and usually permit him to be killed on sight like a wolf by
anyone who happens upon him.

However, it must not be imagined that *perduellio* was limited to external treason, that is, to dealings with an external enemy. In fact, during the early years of the Republic this term seems to have been applied
promiscuously to several varieties of internal treason. The murder of a
magistrate and the intent to murder a magistrate were among the gravest cases of *perduellio*.[24] Assaults on magistrates and possibly usurping
the powers of magistrates may have been similarly considered.[25] This
seems all the more likely since true magisterial powers such as those
held by a consul or praetor were based on the grant of *imperium*, a concept approximating sovereign power.[26] Also, at a very early time it appears probable that the client who failed in his duties to his patron was
held guilty of *perduellio* and suspended from the "unlucky tree" (*arbor
infelix*) by the secular authorities, while the patron who had treated his
dependent fraudulently was devoted to the infernal gods through religious sanctions imposed under the divine law or *fas*, which ever accompanies or parallels the human law or *ius*.[27]

In general, attempts to alter the constitution, corresponding to the
Athenian *katalysis tou demou* or overthrowing the democracy, did not
involve *perduellio* since Roman political theory held that the modification or changing of an existing form of government is legitimate per se,
although the means employed in achieving that object may violate the
laws.[28] This subject involves a most interesting distinction between the
Greek and the Roman concepts of sovereign power, and so leads necessarily to a brief digression.

[23] Mommsen, *Römisches Strafrecht*, p. 549; J. L. Strachan-Davidson, *Problems of
the Roman Criminal Law* (Oxford: Clarendon, 1912), II, 31–33, 39; A. H. J.
Greenidge, *Roman Public Life* (London: Macmillan, 1911), pp. 55, 140.

[24] *Digest* 48, 4, 1, 1.

[25] *Digest* 48, 4, 3.

[26] See Greenidge, *Roman Public Life*, p. 8, and Mommsen, *Römisches Strafrecht*,
p. 566, with n. 1; also Max Radin, "'Imperium',"" in *Studi di onore di Salvatore Riccobono*, II, 21–45, for an important interpretation of the concept of *imperium*, including a philological examination of the origin of the expression.

[27] Cf. Bruns, *Fontes*, for *Leges XII Tab*; 8, 31: "Patronus si clienti fraudem fecerit, sacer esto"; see Greenidge, *Roman Public Life*, pp. 51–56, on nature and significance of *fas* in Roman legal thinking. Cf. Riccobono, *Fontes*, 8, 21 (Johnson,
Statutes, Doc. 8, VIII, 21, and n. 94).

[28] Cf. Mommsen, *Römisches Strafrecht*, p. 550.

Thus, Aristotle's doctrine of Lordship (*to kyrion*) implies an organic body politic which cannot be changed save by the destruction of its very fabric and intrinsic nature. Here the state is a life and sovereignty is the source of life. If the *politeuma* or bodily structure defined and identified by the domination of a particular ruling class, such as democracy or oligarchy, is changed and one class replaces another, the constitution of the *polis* itself is thereby changed or, indeed, terminated. The source of democratic life is not the same as that of oligarchic life. Hence, the constitution or *politeia* makes the state what it is and determines its nature, and in turn the *politeuma* or ruling class determines the nature of the constitution.[29] This explains why *stasis*—violent change, revolution—is the most deadly disease of states according to Greek modes of political thought, deadly because it destroys that Lordship or vital principle which lends the particular living impulse that identifies a state for what it is. Destroy it and substitute another Lordship and you have another state. For the Greek, sovereignty is almost the personality of the state. But the Roman legal mind finds its source of sovereign power outside the state organism in a rule of law. The *imperium* remains sovereign power and ultimate authority regardless of the faction that controls the state for the time being and that bestows this *imperium* on its magistrates. The state and sovereign power are continuous apart from the men who constitute it and exercise its power. McIlwain puts the matter succinctly:

> The Greek political notion of a *politeuma* was utterly foreign to the legalistic thinking of Rome. To a Greek, thinking politically, an oligarchy or a king *was* the state; to a Roman, thinking in terms of law, it was "the proper business of the magistrate"—a king, even, as well as others—"to understand that he impersonates the state."[30]

This reference to the *De Officiis* of Cicero, upon which Jean Bodin could later base his modern theory of legalistic sovereignty, reveals the source of Roman thinking on this vital political subject. The state of Cicero rests upon the bond of law (*vinculum juris*) arising from common consent—it is the common-bond state, the commonwealth, the republic (*res publica*). Sovereignty is no longer a matter of social and economic control determined by a ruling class, but a legally binding

[29] See C. H. McIlwain, *The Growth of Political Thought in the West* (New York: Macmillan, 1932), pp. 76–81, for a splendid discussion of this subject.

[30] *Ibid.*, pp. 117–118. Note especially the analysis of Cicero *De Officiis* 1, 34, on p. 118, n. 1.

authority under whatever constitutional form.[31] Two exceptions to this
principle of the legitimacy of existing forms of government have been
handed down in legal tradition from the early Republic. These declare
that any attempt to re-establish the kingdom or to create a magistracy not
permitting appeal to the people in the popular assembly (*provocatio ad
populum*) shall be deemed *perduellio*.[32]

Thus, the crime embraces a wide variety of offenses directed against
the safety and welfare of the state; also, its scope varies at different
periods of Roman history. Under the Empire it is usually limited to external treason, whereas in the early beginnings of the Roman state it
contained all public offenses entered before the *duumviri perduellionis*.
These officers do not seem to have been detectives who tracked down
offenders like the *quaestores parricidii*, but were judges who decided all
charges of a treasonable nature.[33] Livy states: "The *duumviri* are to decide on the charge of *perduellio*. If the accused appeals from their decision, he is to fight them on the appeal. If they win, let his head be
veiled; let him be suspended by a halter to a barren tree, and let him
be scourged either within or without the sacred bounds of the city
[*pomerium*]."[34] These stringent penalties with religious overtones suggestive of the divine law (*fas*) remind one of similar punishments imposed on comparable offenders among the early Germanic peoples, for
Tacitus tells us in the *Germania* that traitors and deserters were hanged
from trees, while the cowardly, unwarlike, and infamous were cast into
the marshes, submerged, crushed, and suffocated beneath a *cratis*.[35] The
close association of infidelity and infamy in primitive societes is noteworthy and persistent in their legal traditions. However, in later times,
when *perduellio* had been incorporated into the *crimen laesae maiestatis* the penalties for this crime became widely diversified, differing according to circumstances. Hanging on the "accursed tree" gave way to
crucifixion, casting to the beasts, and other ingenious punishments of a
horrid nature. In general, *perduellio* must be considered the treason

---

[31] *Ibid.*, pp. 132–133, on Bodin and legislative sovereignty.

[32] Cf. Mommsen, *Römisches Strafrecht*, p. 550 with notes, and Daremberg et
Saglio, *Dictionnaire*, III (2), 1557 and nn. 33–38.

[33] Cf. Clark, *Roman Private Law*, III, 596–599.

[34] Livy, 1, 26, for the case of Horatius: 'duumviri perduellionem iudicent; si a
duumviris provocarit, provocatione certato; si vincent, caput obnubito; infelici arbori
reste suspendito; verberato vel intra pomerium vel extra pomerium." Cf. Riccobono,
Fontes, III, 4 (Johnson, *Statutes*, Doc. 1, III, 4, and nn. 32–37).

[35] Cf. Tacitus *Germania*, c. 12. The word *cratis* refers to a contrivance resembling
a basket or crate made of woven interlaced flexible branches—perhaps osier.

typical of early Rome whose identity is eventually lost and merged into the broader field of the crimes against majesty.

The conception of treason dominating the great Roman legal codes is bound up in the word *maiestas*. This word, probably derived from *maius*, the comparative form of the adjective *magnus*, denotes an elevated, higher position and a certain pre-eminence of which inferiors must take account—not so much superior power, perhaps, as a most exalted prestige, although the suggestion of force, even military might, commonly lies in the background.[36] The view of the origin of *maiestas* adopted here is primarily that of Mommsen, but it should be noted that his theory is not universally accepted among authorities and should be considered a conjecture lacking definitive proof.[37] Nevertheless, the Mommsen theory carries a high degree of probability within the limits set and is criticized in the main on the ground that it fails to consider all the factors involved and stops considerably short of the final conclusions reached by Erich Pollack in 1908 in an elaborate study on the idea of majesty in Roman Law.[38]

According to Mommsen the concept of majesty entered the criminal procedure of Rome as a result of political conditions restricting the plebeian leaders, or, at least, the group of political leaders who did not belong to the patrician nobility. These leaders were not classed as magistrates in the Roman community although they resembled these officers. The violation of fundamental plebeian rights and the offenses against political leaders of the *plebs* could not be included within the scope or under the name of *perduellio,* just as a plebiscite could not be a *lex publica* and tribunes could not be magistrates since they lacked the sovereign attributes of *imperium.* In other words, plebeian officials were not protected by the law of *perduellio,* whose sanctions supported the patrician magistracies. The plebeians then demanded for their constitution and their leaders, the tribunes, the same dignity and the same status as belonged legally to the entire Roman community and its mag-

---

[36] Cf. Mommsen, *Römisches Strafrecht*, p. 538; B. Kübler, article "Maiestas" in Pauly-Wissowa-Kroll, *Realencyclopädie der classischen Altertumswissenschaft* (Stuttgart: Metzler, 1928), XXVII, 542–544.

[37] See Mommsen, *Römisches Strafrecht*, pp. 538–540, and notes. Also observe differing views of Humbert and Lécrivain in Daremberg et Saglio, *Dictionnaire*, III (2), 1556, and P. M. Schisas in *Offences against the State in Roman Law* (London: University of London Press, 1926), pp. 6–15. The general subject of the concept of *maiestas* in political theory is explored in Essay II.

[38] E. Pollack, *Der Majestätsgedanke im römischen Recht: eine Studie auf dem Gebiet des römischen Staatsrechts* (Leipzig: Verlag von Veit, 1908).

istrates who possessed the *imperium*. It is commonly agreed that these ends were achieved at the time of the great revolt of the plebs in 287 B.C. through the Hortensian legislation. And it was in the attempt to secure this equality under the law that one first hears the phrase "diminishing the tribunician majesty." This became eventually the *crimen imminutae maiestatis*, and when the tribunes of the plebs became the actual dominant officers of the community the expression persisted, although in an expanded sense. *Maiestas* became associated with the *tribunicia potestas*, and the *crimen imminutae maiestatis* came to stand in the same relation to plebeian officers that *perduellio* did to the patrician holders of the *imperium*.[39]

Thus, by origin *maiestas* is opposed to *imperium* despite the fact that in time both words came to be used more or less interchangeably. Hence, ultimately, not only attack upon the rights of the plebeians but every injury done the prestige of the Roman state resulted in a criminal prosecution as an offense against the majesty of the Roman people. When this stage in the development of the crime had been reached *perduellio* could be distinguished from the "crime of diminishing the majesty of the Roman people" only from a single point of view: namely, every hostile act could be termed *crimen laesae maiestatis*, whereas on the contrary not every crime against majesty could be called a hostile act. For example, *lèse-majesté* included insult as well as injury, whereas *perduellio* seems to have been limited to harmful acts producing a readily recognizable material hurt. Indeed, *crimen laesae maiestatis* included *perduellio* eventually but had a more extended domain, permitting the use of different rules of procedure and less severe penalties than *perduellio*.[40] This distinction is set forth clearly by Ulpian in the *Digest* as follows:

He, who dies accused, dies with unimpaired status: for a crime is a closed incident upon the death of the accused. Unless perchance, one shall be accused of majesty: for, unless he shall be cleared of this crime by his heirs, his hereditable property shall be confiscated by the treasury. However, it is clear that all accused in accordance with the *lex Julia maiestatis* are not in that

[39] See Hugh Last in *Cambridge Ancient History* (Cambridge: University Press, 1932), IX, 160–161, on the relation of *minuta maiestas* to *perduellio*. Also cf. Radin, "Imperium," II, 24, 43, 45, on the interchangeability of *imperium* and *maiestas*, and the relation of *maiestas* to the *magister* or magistrate; Livy, 38, 11, 2 *imperium maiestatemque populi Romani*.

[40] See Kübler, "Maiestas," pp. 544–545, on relation of *crimen perduellionis* to *crimen laesae maiestatis* and his analogy of the circles.

situation, but only those accused of *perduellio* which is an act directed with
hostile intent against the public welfare or the life of the prince: and if anyone
be accused under any other section of the *lex Julia maiestatis,* let him be
cleared of this crime at death.[41]

It is evident from the preceding analysis that the history of treason in
the Roman state divides naturally into three distinct periods. First, there
is the period antedating written legal records and marked by family government wherein the typical treason is parricide. Following the emergence of the state *perduellio* becomes the principal treasonable offense
and so remains until the decline of the patrician magistracies, when it
merges into the *crimen imminutae maiestatis.* Thirdly, the crimes against
majesty appear during early republican times before the age of accurate
chronological record, and *maiestas* probably originates as a protection
for plebeian officials. Its field of application becomes widely extended
under the Empire, and the crimes are variously designated: *crimen imminutae maiestatis, crimen laesae maiestatis,* or simply *maiestas.*

There is no other general expression in Latin denoting crime against
the state, and the Greek language has no word corresponding exactly
to *perduellio* and *crimen maiestatis.*[42] In fact, the Greeks refer to the
most important crimes embodied in *perduellio* through special individual descriptive names, as, for instance, *prodosia* or external treason.
The *crimen laesae maiestatis* is consistently called *asebeia* in the Greek
sources although that is an expression properly corresponding to the
Latin word *impietas.* The use of *asebeia* illustrates and belongs to an
epoch when crimes against the state were, under the influence of religious ideas, considered as crimes against a monarch placed under divine protection. The introduction of the "god-king" idea from the East
attached to the crimes against majesty elements of sacrilege and impiety which were quite foreign to the early native Roman conceptions,
and these religious factors further increased the elevation and remote-

[41] *Digest* 48, 4, 11: *"Ulpianus libro octavo disputationum.* Is, qui in reatu decedit,
integri status decedit: extinguitur enim crimen mortalitate. nise forte quis maiestatis reus fuit: nam hoc crimine nisi a successoribus purgetur, hereditas fisco vindicatur. plane non quisque legis Iuliae maiestatis reus est, in eadem condicione est, sed
qui perduellionis reus est, hostili animo adverus rem publicam vel principem animatus: ceterum si quis ex alia causa legis Iuliae maiestatis reus sit, morte crimine
liberatur." Cf. N. Lewis and M. Reinhold, *Roman Civilization* (New York: Columbia
University Press, 1955), Vol. II: The Empire, pp. 29–31, for translation and comment; *The Civil Law,* trans. by S. P. Scott, (Cincinnati: Central Trust Co., 1932),
XI, 27–28, with n. 1 extending across pp. 33–38, which is an essay on treason containing much curious data not readily accessible elsewhere.

[42] Cf. Mommsen, *Römisches Strafrecht,* pp. 539–540.

ness of the imperial position, raising the ruler above ordinary social obligations and legal responsibilities, separating him immeasurably from
his subjects, and surrounding him with an invincible divine authority.

Owing to the lack of authentic legal records throughout the earlier
part of Roman history, an account of treason cannot be written in a fully
detailed chronological sequence. A number of trials for treason are cited
by late Roman annalists and attributed by them to a very early day, but
recent study suggests that most of these tales are legendary or are the
projection of late custom back into the distant beginnings of the Republic, although the tradition of casting from the Tarpeian Rock seems
well established. On the other hand, if one views Roman institutional
development in its larger aspects he will be struck by the prevalence of
faction or *stasis* emerging in seditious activities under the general legal
designation of *seditio*. Governmental changes were not accomplished
by a gradual, easy evolutionary process but were commonly instituted
through violence and rebellion, so that the history of republican Rome
is, to a large degree, a history of treasonable attempts against the established order. The moderate and balanced constitutional processes
that are sometimes assumed by contemporary scholarship are in fact
only an idealized view suggested, for example, by the philosophy of
history advanced by Polybius and by the political theories of Cicero.
Actually republican Rome affords an abundance of evidence in support
of the validity of the doctrine of the "relativity of treason" as a fundamental principle in political theory. Treason is treason only when it fails,
and even then the treason is seldom acknowledged by the loser, or conversely

> Treason doth ne'er succeed; and what's the reason?
> When it succeeds, no man dare call it treason.[43]

Since this principle is so obvious, Strachan-Davidson believes that
tyrannicide is implicitly authorized in the Roman law. It is interesting
to note that according to tradition the first great change in Roman government followed a revolt against a tyrannical king. This legend asserts
that the Etruscan despot, Tarquin, was overthrown and expelled in 509
B.C., whereupon a single tyrant then seems to have been succeeded by
a group of tyrannical military magistrates called praetors, who were
elected from the body of patrician citizens and possessed the *imperium*,
a sort of commission giving supreme military command. Later, the *imperium* was limited to the military sphere (*militiae*) outside the *po-*

---

[43] Cf. Strachan-Davidson, *Roman Criminal Law*, I, 18.

merium or sacred boundary of the city. These praetors possessed a summary jurisdiction with the right of *coercitio* or arbitrary arrest,[44] and were protected by the law against *perduellio*. The abuse of their powers and the refusal to recognize the rights of the plebeian leaders led to a second revolt, assigned by Livy to 494 B.C. and by Diodorus to 466 B.C. At this time the plebeian officers, designated tribunes, were safeguarded by the laws of *maiestas*, if Mommsen is correct. In addition, their authority was based on religious sanctions provided under the *leges sacratae*, and their person was declared sacrosanct, so that violators were held to be *sacer* or accursed and were devoted to the infernal deities. *Maiestas* gave them secular protection; *sacrosanctitas*, religious protection. It should not be forgotten, however, that the concept of *maiestas* in its ultimate origins, like *sacrosanctitas,* derives from the sacred order of the divine law or *fas*.[45] In any case, as a practical consequence of these political changes the tribune who began as an exceptional officer of the plebs with extraconstitutional powers now gained increasing authority over all classes in the Roman state.

The most important body of Roman law demonstrably possessing considerable antiquity is contained in the *Law of the Twelve Tables*. These appear to have been codified in order to stop the arbitrary definition of the law at the caprice of the patrician magistrates. One cannot assert positively that the technical term *perduellio* was used in the *Tables,* but they did contain the substance of this crime against the state, if the statement attributed to Marcian in the *Digest* of Justinian be correct. This affirms that "according to the *Law of the Twelve Tables,* he shall be punished capitally who arouses an enemy or surrenders a city to an enemy."[46] These laws are commonly assigned to the middle of the fifth century B.C. (*ca.* 450) and are considered the work of the famous decemviral commission. The traditional accounts of the long period between 450 and 287 B.C. contain evidence relating to a number of revolts but the information is most untrustworthy. Many questions remain to be solved in connection with the alleged legislation of 449 B.C. and 367 B.C. More credence may be placed in the events associated with Appius Claudius about 310 B.C. This age appears to have been marked by the emergence of factions based on economic friction. Finally, in 287 B.C., a well-authenticated struggle is connected with the last great revolt of the small-farming class. The ensuing epoch extend-

---

[44] *Ibid.,* 97–98; Greenidge, *Roman Public Life,* p. 95.

[45] See Essay II.

[46] *Digest* 48, 4, 3. Cf. Mommsen, *Römisches Strafrecht,* p. 540 and notes.

ing from 287 to 133 B.C. is distinguished by the long series of struggles with Carthage and the development of the senatorial oligarchy. A number of traditional cases of treason are associated with the Punic wars, but no legislation on the subject is available for this period unless one finds an exception in the *senatus consultum de Bacchanalibus* of 186 B.C., which made it essentially a violation of majesty to hold membership in the proscribed Bacchanalian associations.[47]

One notable result of these years of war was the development of an imperial policy and the organization of the provincial system. Furthermore, after the destruction of Corinth in 146 B.C. the Greek city-states were brought face to face with Rome and were compelled to devise some means of entering into a constitutional relationship with her if they were not to remain mere conquered subjects. And it is probably about this time that they widely adapted Alexander's old expedient of deification to the Republic to which they now owed allegiance, although the cult of Roma seems to have been established at Smyrna as early as 195 B.C.[48] Henceforth the Greek cities deified the city-state, Rome, instead of an individual king or emperor and in this way arose the worship of the goddess Roma in the Hellenistic world. In consequence, the Oriental veneration and deference, so distinctive of *maiestas* in the time of the Empire, now attached itself to the native Roman concept of majesty.[49] When W. S. Ferguson remarked to the effect that the deification of kings involved the subjection and humiliation of cities as symbolized by the Persian custom of *proskynesis*, he might well have added that emperor worship under the Roman Empire marked the beginning of the fusion and combination of the concepts of *maiestas* and *proskynesis*,

[47] See remarks in *C.A.H.*, VIII (1930), 351–352, by Tenney Frank, and 453–454, by Cyril Bailey; Daremberg et Saglio, *Dictionnaire*, III (2), 1559; also Bruns, *Fontes*, pp. 164–166, and Riccobono, *Fontes*, I, 240–241 (Johnson, *Statutes*, Doc. 28 and 28a), for the text of the *Senatus consultum de Bacchanalibus* of 186 B.C., and the extended account in Livy trans. by E. T. Sage, Loeb Series: Vol. XI (London: Heinemann, 1936), 39, 8–19, which is the chief historical record of the episode of the Bacchanals. Note further F. H. Cramer, *Astrology in Roman Law and Politics*, Memoirs of the American Philosophical Society: Vol. 37 (Philadelphia: The Society, 1954), p. 47, with nn. 23–30; Jolowicz, *Study of Roman Law*, p. 323. For the later restrictions and proscriptions of the Egyptian (Isiac) cult, see Cassius Dio, 40, 47, 3–4; 42, 26, 2; 53, 2, 4; 54, 6, 6. For the repression of both Egyptian and Jewish sectaries, see Tacitus *Annals* 2, 85; and Suetonius, Tiberius, 36. Also note Cicero *De Legibus* 2, 8, 19: "Separatim nemo habessit deos neve novos neve advenas nisi publice adscitos; privatim colunto, quos rite a patribus cultos acceperint."

[48] Cf. David Magie, *Roman Rule in Asia Minor* (Princeton: University Press, 1950), I, 501; A. D. Nock, *C. A. H.*, X (1934), 485.

[49] See Essay II.

and of that marriage of Roman and Oriental political theories which caused Mommsen to observe that Egypt, mistress and slave, had become the conqueror of her master, Rome.[50]

Also, in the course of the second century magistrates and provincial governors tended to exceed their authority with the result that attempts were made to limit their independent action, as indicated by the creation of the *quaestiones rerum repetundarum* in 149 B.C. The *lex Cornelia de repetundis*, which had the object of requiring an accounting from malfeasant and dishonest provincial governors, must be regarded as a law directed against maladministration of office rather than treason, although these two crimes have many elements in common and an inevitable tendency to converge. The line that separates the defaulting officeholder and the internal traitor is frequently all too thin when considered from the point of philosophic, if not of legal, treason. Besides, it is during this century that the Roman senate became increasingly tyrannical so that in the words of Pelham it "forfeits its right to govern by its failure to govern well" and so encouraged treasonable, or at the least seditious, attacks upon its authority. The gravest of these assaults were fostered by the Gracchi between 133 and 121 B.C. and may be considered violations of *maiestas* since they involved the illegal usurpation of power by the tribunes. The senate retaliated by voting the "last decree" or *senatus consultum ultimum*, which authorized the arbitrary and perhaps illegal arrest of those whom it considered subversive of the general welfare.[51] Senate and tribunes looked upon each other as traitors, each interpreting the general welfare in the light of his own special interests. Such a plight was occasioned by the prevalence of faction and, the lack of a common public authority competent to define the interest of the whole. In turn, this lack made it impossible to define and apply

[50] Nock (*C. A. H.*, X, 489) says: "Augustus would have smiled in a puzzled way if he had been informed that he had introduced Pharaonic divine monarchy at Rome."

[51] Cf. Strachan-Davidson, *Roman Criminal Law*, I, 240–245, where Cicero is cited to show that the senate acted legally in issuing a *senatus consultum ultimum*. The senate declared its enemies to be *perduelles*, and "the *perduellis* has by his own act placed himself in the position of a foreign enemy, and so has ceased to be a citizen." Then the senate "simply passed a decree 'that the consuls were to see to it that the state took no harm, and the consuls thereupon put in full exercise their full power against those who had constituted themselves *hostes*." But Greenidge (*Roman Public Life*, p. 281) refutes this argument, stating that "though common sense might interpret certain overt acts as a sign of war against society, no degree of treason could *ipso jure* make a citizen into an enemy unless that treason had been proved in a court of law." Cf. Daremberg et Saglio, *Dictionnaire*, III (1), 652–653; III (2), 1556.

general treason laws that would equally safeguard all interests within the Roman state.

Probably the first *lex de maiestate* was the *lex Appuleia* (*ca.* 103 B.C.).[52] This was voted in connection with the crimes committed during the Gallic War and, in particular, with the seizure of the treasures of Toulouse. It established the special *quaestio auri Tolosani,* and indicated that such offenses as injuring the tribunes or exciting to disorder should be considered *laesa maiestas.*[53] However, it was an exceptional law creating no permanent *quaestio maiestatis,* and, in this respect, resembled the earlier *lex Mamilia,* which repressed the acts of treason of the ambassadors and generals sent against Jugurtha in 110 B.C.[54] The trial of Norbanus in 95 B.C. was a trial for *laesa maiestas,* seemingly instituted according to the *lex Appuleia.*[55] In 91 B.C. the *lex Varia* declared guilty of *laesa maiestas* those who, by their advice or assistance, had aroused the *socii* to take up arms against Rome during the Social War. But it was Sulla who established definitively a permanent *quaestio maiestatis,* by the *lex Cornelia judiciaria* of 81 B.C., that he might guarantee the maintenance of his new constitution. The law of treason was probably not yet exactly defined, although an extension of *laesa maiestas* to some new cases is apparent. Humbert and Lécrivain have reconstructed this law as follows:

This law is directed against the citizen who deals a blow to the power of the magistrates, and, in particular, to the right of intercession of the tribunes; against the magistrate who compromises the dignity of the Roman people, who does not maintain the prerogatives of his functions, or who renders himself guilty of assuming excessive powers by making war without the authorization of the people, by leaving his province without authorization of the Senate, or by appropriating another province; against the general who permits the escape of or pardons enemy leaders or pirates taken prisoners; against the person

---

[52] On the history of the majesty legislation under the Republic, see Kübler, "Maiestas," pp. 546–550; also Last in *C. A. H.,* IX (1932), 296–298; and Cramer, *Astrology,* p. 252.

[53] Note Cicero *De inventione,* trans. by H. M. Hubbell, Loeb Series (London: Heinemann, 1949), 2, 17, 52–53, for the case of the father of Gaius Flaminius who did violence to his son who was a tribune: "Intentio est: 'Maiestatem minuisti, quod tribunum plebis de templo deduxisti'," and observe further the definition: "Maiestatem minuere est de dignitate aut amplitudine aut potestate populi aut eorum quibus populus potestatem dedit aliquid derogare." Cf. differing view on the *lex Appuleia* in Last, *C. A. H.,* IX (1932), 160–161.

[54] Cicero *Brutus,* trans. by G. L. Hendrickson, Loeb Series (London: Heineman, 1939), 33, 127; 34, 128.

[55] Cf. Cicero *De oratore,* trans. by E. W. Sutton, Loeb Series (London: Heinemann, 1942), 2, 107, which refers to the trial of Norbanus under the *lex Appuleia* and the necessity for strict definition of the crime of *maiestas minuta.*

who incites troops to revolt or delivers an army to the enemy or usurps the powers of a magistrate. The penalty shall be perpetual exile outside Italy and the *aquae et ignis interdictio,* but there shall be no torture of witnesses.[56]

This law was often applied during the period of anarchy that followed the death of Sulla, in particular against the tribune Cornelius in 67 B.C. for having violated his tribunician right of intercession and for having attacked the Senate,[57] and against Gabinius in 54 B.C. for having left his province with his troops and waged war on his own account.[58] This entire period, leading to the First Triumvirate, was an age of unconstitutional procedure, tyranny, faction, and treason. It was the time of the extraordinary commands when power had passed definitely into the hands of the military leaders.[59]

From 60 B.C. onward until the founding of the principate the constitutional history of Rome becomes so tangled and uncertain that no safe inferences concerning treason may be drawn through a study of the nature of the authority wielded by those claiming to be public officers. Julius Caesar cannot be overlooked, however, because of his introduction of personal rule and the idea of god-kingship. This marked a further step in the Orientalization of the Roman concept of *maiestas,* attaching more firmly to it elements of veneration and deference to supreme authority. Even so it is unlikely that Julius Caesar issued any special *lex Julia maiestatis.* The legislation referred to under that title in the *Digest* was probably the work of Augustus.[60] The outstanding characteristic of all treason legislation well down into the Empire is its lack of clear definition and delimitation. This resulted in prodigious extensions of the *crimen laesae maiestatis* under the emperors. The crime became not

---

[56] Cf. Daremberg et Saglio, *Dictionnaire,* III (2), 1557; Last, *C. A. H.,* IX, 297. The reconstruction of this law is based in part on Cicero, *In Pisonem,* trans. by N. H. Watts, Loeb Series (London: Heinemann, 1931), 21, 50: "mitto exire de provincia, educere exercitum, bellum sua sponte gerere, in regnum iniussu populi Romani aut senatus accedere, quae cum plurimae leges veteres tum lex Cornelia maiestatis, Iulia de pecuniis repetundis planissime vetat."

[57] Daremberg et Saglio, *Dictionnaire,* III (2), 1557, n. 12, which cites Asconius, *In Cornelio,* pp. 59–60.

[58] Cicero *In Pisonem,* 21, 50.

[59] See A. E. R. Boak, "The Extraordinary Commands from 80 to 48 B.C.: A Study in the Origins of the Principate," *American Historical Review,* XXIV (1918), 1–25. This significant study is a definitive contribution to this subject and has never been supplanted.

[60] Cf. Daremberg et Saglio, *Dictionnaire,* III (2), 1557, and C. G. Starr, *Civilization and the Caesars* (Ithaca: Cornell University Press, 1954), p. 75. W. W. Buckland in *C. A. H.,* XI (1936), 841, says that "The Lex Julia Maiestatis brought within the field of the *quaestio* not only facts approximating to *perduellio,* but also facts actually amounting to *perduellio,* previously tried by the Assembly."

merely an offense directed against the person of the emperor but was susceptible of the widest interpretations, embracing not only the deed but also the mere word and thought or intent. The instigation of the act as well as its execution were alike culpable.[61]

Such legislation was a terrible weapon in the hands of the bad emperors since it was employed as an instrument of their vengeance and since it gave rise to delation, surveillance, and unrestricted accusation with all their attendant evils. Suspicion ran rampant and resulted in rigid enforcement of the laws against illicit associations or any group that might prove to be a hotbed of conspiracy. Thus, in the early Empire persons suspected of disloyal and subversive intentions or acts were placed under strict surveillance,[62] while in the later Empire of the Dominate the Christians were considered a disloyal element who would not pay allegiance to the divine emperor and who would consequently bear watching. *Maiestas* ceased to denote primarily the dignity and power of the Roman people and became a conception peculiarly associated with the person of the emperor. The introduction of Eastern cults at the

---

[61] This principle is established under the formula *dolo malo*. Cf. *Digest* 48, 4, 1, 1; 48, 4, 3; 48, 4, 7, 3; Tacitus *Annals* 3, 38, 2 *bellum adversus nos volverat*. See F. Schulz, *Principles of Roman Law* (Oxford: Clarendon, 1936), pp. 45–46, on *actio de dolo*, in which *dolus* may be defined as malicious misrepresentation, malicious deception, and "every kind of malicious act to the disadvantage of another person." See Starr, *Civilization and Caesars*, pp. 75–77, on extension of *maiestas* in the early Empire; pp. 122–124 on the continuation of these trials under Tiberius; and p. 127 on their abolition by Claudius.

[62] See the detailed examination of this problem for the reign of Tiberius in R. S. Rogers, *Criminal Trials and Criminal Legislation under Tiberius* (Middletown, Conn.: American Philological Association, 1935). It must be concluded that violations of *maiestas* were not primarily acts of the republican faction according to F. B. Marsh, *The Reign of Tiberius* (London: Humphrey Milford, 1931), pp. 63, 116, 166, n. 2, which refers to Tacitus *Annals* 4, 9. However, see Cassius Dio *Roman History* (Loeb Series, Vol. VII [1922]), 57, 24, 1–4, on Cremutius Cordus, who wrote a history of the achievements of Augustus, but was charged with praising Cassius and Brutus therein without due regard to Caesar and Augustus; also Tacitus *Annals* 4, 34, for a longer account of the same incident; and Cassius Dio, 67, 12, 4, on Mettius Pompusianus who was put to death by Domitian because "he had excerpted and was wont to read the speeches of kings and other leaders that are recorded in Livy," besides having a map of the world painted on the walls of his bedchamber. Such incidents would seem to indicate grave concern regarding interest in republican ideals and heroes, and the significance of the Roman past generally. Also note C. E. Smith, *Tiberius and the Roman Empire* (Baton Rouge: Louisiana State University Press, 1942), pp. 166–181, for "Lèse Majesté Prosecutions under Tiberius" (Ch. VIII). Advocacy of the republican ideal also seems to have played a part in the persecution of the philosophers. Cf. Starr, *Civilization and Caesars*, pp. 129–130, on the Pisonian conspiracy and Thrasea Paetus, and p. 141 on Junius Rusticus and Herennius Senecio.

time of Elagabalus and of an Oriental court by Aurelian pointed the way
to the full triumph of Hellenistic despotism in the Roman government.
A ruler who was "both lord and god-born" (*dominus et deus natus*), as
well as *Praesens et corporalis deus*, became an object of reverence to his
subjects and could demand their unquestioning allegiance to his supreme authority. It was an authority recognizing no obligations and
transcending all laws, under which the ruler tends steadily to become
sole *legis lator* and the embodiment of the Eastern concept of a "living
law" or *lex animata*. Such a monarch must be both worshipped and
obeyed, and treason to him is sacrilege as well.[63]

However, it must not be forgotten that Roman thought involved two
conflicting and essentially contradictory principles in the matter of the
legal rights and political powers of government. This mingled and confused current runs to some extent from the earliest beginnings in the
powers and restraints of the *patria potestas* to the collisions between republican and imperialist lawyers in the later Middle Ages and early
modern period. We face the problem of limitation versus unrestrained
power. The republican tradition of constitutional limitation is crossed
by an imperial tradition of absolute monarchy. Ernest Barker stated
the matter succinctly nearly forty years ago when he said: "We may
argue with almost equal cogency that Roman Law implies absolutism,
and that it implies constitutionalism."[64] Earlier Erich Pollack had refused to associate his theory of *maiestas* with the dominate since he regarded it as a principle of constitutional law that could not be viewed
as an aspect of unconstitutional despotism.[65] Still earlier A. H. J. Greenidge had held that the early Roman kings were doubtless bound by no
statutory authority in the form of *leges* but that "they could not have
been free from the limitations imposed by custom and constitutional
usage."[66] The history of the republic is replete with examples of limitations upon the arbitrary action of magistrates with *imperium*, until at
length the republican theory of constitutional limitation is established
under natural law in the common-bond state or commonwealth of
Cicero with its *vinculum juris*.[67]

The legal theory of such limited government has been argued co-

[63] H. St. L. B. Moss, *The Birth of the Middle Ages, 395–814* (Oxford: Clarendon, 1935), p. 250.
[64] Ernest Barker, "The Conception of Empire," in *The Legacy of Rome* (Oxford: Clarendon, 1923), p. 71.
[65] Pollack, *Der Majestätsgedanke*, p. 141.
[66] Greenidge, *Roman Public Life*, p. 58.
[67] Cf. McIlwain, *Political Thought in the West*, pp. 117–118.

gently and well-nigh incontrovertibly by Fritz Schulz as firmly established in the writings of the Roman jurists and even in the imperial *constitutiones*; yet in his masterly analysis of the concept of *auctoritas* he
points out that in the early Roman familial structure the *pater familias*
possessed sovereign, unrestrained disciplinary powers in his household.[68]
This authoritarian principle is never relaxed in the maturing of Roman
political theory. It remains essential in the functioning of the imperial
magistracies and underlies the very being of the principate. *Auctoritas*
and *maiestas* combine in a new order of sovereign power; yet the *auctoritas* or *maiestas* of Augustus is based more on Augustus as *augustus,*
the revered one, than as the holder of an *imperium.* Clearly what is
true in legal theory is not necessarily true in political theory, to say
nothing of administrative practice.[69] Even the legal theory is tinctured
with certain political overtones, when viewed in the light of the imperial exemptions, which reached back to the republican extraordinary

[68] See Fritz Schulz, "Bracton on Kingship," *English Historical Review,* LX
(1945), especially pp. 153–162. He distinguishes explicitly between the Roman
legal theory of constitutional limitation and the Hellenistic political theories of absolute monarchy and the doctrine of animate law. Also cf. Kurt von Fritz, *The Theory of the Mixed Constitution in Antiquity* (New York: Columbia University Press,
1954). He states that "there was no authority above the law" or "unchecked and
unlimited political power in Rome from the middle of the fifth century to the conquest of Rome by Sulla" (p. 219), whereas "The historians who write after Alexander in the monarchies of the successors . . . emphasize loyalty to a sovereign and
not the law" (p. 323). The contrast between the Roman republican constitutional
theory and the Hellenistic imperial absolutist theory is also explicit here. For the
auctoritas of the *pater familias,* see F. Schulz, *Principles of Roman Law* (Oxford:
Clarendon, 1936), p. 166. Cf. Greenidge, who makes the point that legislation was
always subordinate to judicial interpretation in Roman thinking. Hence it was the
judicial capacity of the emperor, not a constitutional theory, "which made the
Princeps the highest of all legislative, because the greatest of all interpreting,
authorities" *Roman Public Life,* p. 381.

[69] Political theory must not be identified with legal theory. Certainly it is a primary function of the state to maintain the legal order, nevertheless, the basic legal
theory may not of necessity coincide with the controlling political theory. It is interesting to note that nowhere does law enter into the definition of *political* in the
Oxford Dictionary. Cf. *A New English Dictionary on Historical Principles* (Oxford:
Clarendon, 1909), VII (2), 1074–1076: *Political* is defined as "1) Of, belonging
to, or pertaining to the state or body of citizens, its government and policy . . .;
public, civil; of or pertaining to the science or art of politics; 2) Having an organized government or polity." *Polity* is defined as "1) a. civil organization; civil
order; b. Administration of a state; 2) a. A particular form of political organization, a form of government . . .; 3) Mode of administering or managing public or
private affairs—Policy." The civil order and administrative policy in particular
may be guided by principles inconsistent with legal tradition. This dichotomy
emerges in the course of Roman governing experience.

commands, expand in the *maius imperium* of the Augustan Principate, and eventuate in imperial absolutism. The crossroads at which we turn from the older predominantly republican principle of limitation to the later imperial highway is primarily a chronological question. This point is grasped by Mason Hammond in his recent work on the *Antonine Monarchy* when he notes that "by the beginning of the second century, the doctrine was well established that the prince was above the law." He bases his conclusion on Pliny's *Panegyric* on Trajan whose rule is contrasted sharply with Domitian's autocratic rule, which apparently "extended imperial superlegality beyond any restraints" recognized by previous emperors.[70]

Earlier this shift in emphasis and major turning point was discovered in the *lex de imperio Vespasiani*, in which the *populus* was believed to have bestowed its full *imperium* and entire sovereign power upon the emperor in perpetuity. However, it is now clear that the import of this law, probably enacted as a decree by the senate, was to confirm certain prerogatives, exemptions, and immunities already recognized in connection with previous emperors of the Julio-Claudian dynasty.[71] It is Hammond's further conclusion that the emperor becomes master of the laws enjoying a general exemption by the opening of the third century as expressed in the *legibus solutus* principle of Ulpian, that the constitutional and absolutist doctrines continue to exist contemporaneously, and that even as late as Justinian "there survived some idea of a self-imposed constitutional monarchy."[72] The age of the Antonines reflects a monarchical political theory that has departed far from the constitutional republican theories to which at least lip service was rendered in

---

[70] Mason Hammond, *The Antonine Monarchy* (American Academy in Rome, 1959), p. 39. Also see Lewis and Reinhold (*Roman Civilization*, II, 103), who remark that by the second century the position of the Roman emperor had reached an intermediate stage between *primus inter pares* and absolute monarch by divine right. Von Fritz (*Mixed Constitution*, pp. 304–305) also establishes the chronology of this shift of emphasis and sets it even earlier. He notes "the disappearance of a general respect for constitutional law" from Augustus onward, that thereafter "political power . . . rested no longer on constitutional law," and that Seneca in *De clementia* refers to Nero's "absolutely unlimited powers."

[71] Hammond, *Antonine Monarchy*, pp. 38–39; also see Lewis and Reinhold, *Roman Civilization*, II, 88–90; Ernest Barker, *From Alexander to Constantine* (Oxford: Clarendon, 1956), p. 272, for translated texts of the *lex de imperio;* McIlwain, *Political Thought in the West*, p. 136, for interpretation; and Greenidge, *Roman Public Life*, p. 350. Cf. Riccobono, *Fontes*, I, 154–156 (Johnson, *Statutes*, Doc. 183).

[72] Hammond, *Antonine Monarchy*, pp. 39–40.

the early Augustan Principate. And it is significant that this process of imperial exemption is paralleled by increasing extensions of *laesa maiestas* to even larger areas of application.[73]

Finally, the role of the doctrine of Animate Law must be considered in analyzing this shift of emphasis in Roman political theory. Some thirty years ago E. R. Goodenough directed attention to this aspect of the matter in a study of Hellenistic Kingship which indicated that Persian and other Oriental concepts were impinging on Western thought and importing ideas that the ruler is the state and incarnate law.[74] These views reinforced the ancient ceremonial of the *proskynesis* reaching back to the politico-religious expedients of Alexander the Great and pointing the way to the *adoratio* of Diocletian.[75] Such fragments as those attributed to Diotogenes and Ecphantes ("Ecphantus") must not be disregarded in reconstructing the intellectual milieu receptive to absolutism. Here political ideas long congenial to the East are supported by Western Neo-Pythagorean habits of thought. Barker describes these writers as mystic royalists and panegyrists of Empire, and, while their date is disputed, he would regard them presumably "as exponents of the ideas of Kingship current in the Roman Empire before the triumph of Christianity" of about the second or third century A.D.[76] Even more specifically these views would appear to represent ideas regarding the nature of kingship that were accepted in the reign of Aurelian. In fact, it would seem that the later third century marks the final turn of the road into the despotism of the Dominate, for Mommsen notes that Aurelian is the first emperor described as *dominus* on his coinage.[77]

This transformation is completed long before the One Hundred and Fifth Novel of Justinian refers to the emperor as the sole legislator and a living law.[78] The republican constitutional tradition of limited magis-

[73] Cf. Starr, *Civilization and Caesars*, p. 76.
[74] See E. R. Goodenough, "The Political Philosophy of Hellenistic Kingship," *Yale Classical Studies* (New Haven: Yale University Press, 1928), I, 55–102. Cf. Harold Mattingly, *Roman Imperial Civilisation* (New York: St. Martins, 1957), pp. 40–41, on the concept of authority under the Dominate with emphasis shifted from law to religion, and its consistency with Persian ideas.
[75] Cf. Barker, *Alexander to Constantine*, p. 354.
[76] See *ibid.*, pp. 361–373, for translated extracts and comment; also Lewis and Reinhold, *Roman Civilization*, II, 103–104.
[77] Greenidge, *Roman Public Life*, p. 352, quoting Mommsen, *Römisches Staatsrecht*, II, 760; also Barker, *Alexander to Constantine*, pp. 353–356, on Aurelian; and Mattingly (*Roman Imperial Civilisation*, p. 32), who says in speaking of Diocletian: "There was no longer a 'Prince,' or 'Imperator' even, but a 'Lord and God' "; *ibid.*, p. 36, on Constantine and Christian influence.
[78] *Novellae*, CV. 4.

tracy lives on in juristic legal theory, although it is hard to discover it in the savage attainder provisions of the terrible *lex Quisquis* in which one hears the voice of despotism. The political theory of absolute monarchy has subordinated the ancient legal principles, and their life lingers on in an attenuated form to be resurrected by the republican lawyers of the early modern age. Yet, while the rulers of the Dominate are at last above the law to make the law, it does not follow necessarily that they are above the law to break the law. The moral obligation to observe the law is never submerged completely and does not disappear. Nevertheless, the time-honored principles of *libertas* are gradually fading away.[79] Hence, when one surveys the entire range of Roman thought, political and legal, institutional and administrative, it is with conflicting feelings but with some faith that the considered judgment of C. H. McIlwain in his essay on Roman constitutionalism is correct: "The fundamental doctrine underlying the Roman state, its true guiding spirit, is constitutionalism, not absolutism."[80]

B. Under the Empire

At this point it becomes necessary to analyze the legal codes of the Empire to determine the basic nature of the crime of *maiestas* in its matured form.[81] We are less concerned here with the theory of the con-

---

[79] Cf. Ch. Wirszubski, *Libertas as a Political Idea at Rome during the Late Republic and Early Principate* (Cambridge: University Press, 1950), pp. 169–171, on the incompatibility of autocracy and constitutional freedom even under the enlightened despotism of the Antonine monarchy. In addition, note Ernst Kantorowicz, *The King's Two Bodies* (Princeton: University Press, 1957), pp. 102–107, on the late mediaeval collision between these conflicting principles among the lawyers of Emperor Frederick II. Kantorowicz discusses the apparent antinomy between the maxims of the *lex regia* and the *lex digna*, and between the maxims *legibus solutus* and *legibus alligatus*, and also the eventual reconciliation that the emperor is *legibus solutus*, but *ratione alligatus*.

[80] C. H. McIlwain, *Constitutionalism: Ancient and Modern* (rev. ed.; Ithica: Cornell University Press, 1947), p. 57.

[81] This section of the essay constitutes in the main a revised analysis of portions of the article on *Maiestas* by Humbert and Lécrivain in Daremberg et Saglio, *Dictionnaire*, III (2), 1557–1561, together with a detailed re-examination of the documentation. Humbert's article covers much the same ground as the exhaustive treatment of this aspect of Roman public law found in Mommsen, *Römisches Strafrecht*, pp. 538–594, which is also extant in a French translation in T. Mommsen, J. Marquardt, and P. Krüger. *Manuel des antiquités romaines* (Paris: E. Thorin 1907), (A. Fontemoing), XVIII (2), 233–302 (*Le droit pénal romain* by T. Mommsen). Both Mommsen and Humbert should be reviewed in the light of the excellent independent study, "Maiestas" by B. Kübler in Pauly-Wissowa-Kroll, *Realencyclopädie*, XXVII, 542–559. Also see P. Bisoukides, *Der Hochverrat: eine historische und dogmatische Studie* (Berlin: Carl Heymanns Verlag, 1903), pp. 20–33; and especially Mason

cept *maiestas* than with the content of the crime.[82] Six general subdivisions of *maiestas* may be distinguished in Roman political thought: (1) *perduellio*; (2) acts contrary to the constitution of the state, resembling the *katalysis tou demou* found in Athenian law; (3) acts of maladministration by magistrates; (4) violation of civic duties; (5) personal injuries done to a magistrate or to the emperor; and (6) violation of civic religious duties. *Perduellio* has already been examined and discovered to be the primary form of treasonable offense in republican times. However, it does not lose its identity or disappear in the imperial legislation but is now associated with other offenses under the broader scope of *maiestas,* of which it forms an essential part—almost a central core as it were. The definition of *perduellio* remains embedded at the very heart of the imperial *maiestas* legislation although the actions for *minuta maiestas* and *perduellio* are henceforth comprehended under the new *maiestas* procedures.[83] The second group of offenses is not definitely mentioned in the legal codes, probably because the legal and constitutional status of the Principate itself was long a matter open to question. However, it is clear from the *Annals* of Tacitus that attacks upon the imperial authority, intent to destroy the Principate, and plots to substitute another for the reigning emperor were considered high treason.[84] The third group included all acts whereby magistrates tended

---

Hammond, *The Augustan Principate in Theory and Practice during the Julio-Claudian Period* (Cambridge: Harvard University Press, 1933), pp. 172–176, with detailed references in nn. 11–33. These data are notably valuable and complete for the reigns of Augustus and Tiberius.

The most recent treatment of *maiestas* may be found in Cramer, *Astrology,* pp. 251–253. Although this is only a brief summary it represents an interesting and, in some respects, unique analysis of the crime, especially identifying "second degree" *maiestas* for ordinary cases as distinguished from high treason. I think, however, high treason should be classified as *perduellio* rather than *proditio,* which is a more restricted term. Rogers (*Criminal Trials,* p. 207), in his classification of the various types of *maiestas* actions in the reign of Tiberius, uses the term "quasi-maiestas" in the borderline case of Clutorius Priscus. Starr (*Civilization and Caesars*) is exceptional in respect to the considerable attention devoted to *maiestas* and treason cases in imperial Rome.

[82] On the majesty legislation in the imperial period see Kübler, "Maiestas," pp. 550–558.

[83] See *Digest* 48, 4, 11, and 48, 4, 3, for Marcian's definition attributed to the *Twelve Tables. Digest* 48, 4, 1, gives the basic definition of *maiestas* but the particulars specified relate for the most part to the republican *perduellio* legislation.

[84] Cf. Mommsen, *Römisches Strafrecht,* pp. 549–555. Note Tacitus *Annals* 4, 34–35, for the above-mentioned case of Cremutius Cordus, who incurred the displeasure of Tiberius for preserving his fidelity to the ideals of the Republic; 12, 42, on the plot of Agrippina and Vitellius against Claudius; also Juvenal *Satires* 7, 204;

to exceed their legal powers, to endanger the laws of the state, or to exhibit contempt for the dignity of the state.[85] Specifically it embraced such crimes as raising troops or directing a war without authorization,[86] aiding the escape of a confessed criminal, placing the magistrate's name on public edifices to the exclusion of that of the emperor,[87] and spreading and disseminating false news by inserting it in the public records.[88] It may also be noted that according to Ulpian's *Disputations* the usurpation of power by a provincial governor was held to be *laesa maiestas*, as, for example, when he left his province with his troops[89] or when he remained there and retained his command after the arrival of his successor.[90] In the fourth place, the violation of civic duties involved a wide variety of offenses.[91] Failure in military duties and desertion from the military service were commonly adjudged to be violations of majesty.[92] The absence of a citizen at the time of the census or recruiting might entail a penalty as severe as death with confiscation of goods.[93] *Seditio* was considered *laesa maiestas* under the Empire, and was especially aggravated in the case of meetings by night (*coetus nocturni*).[94] "Instigators of sedition and of tumult, which result in an uprising of the people, shall, according to their rank, either be hanged upon a gallows, thrown to wild beasts, or deported to an island."[95] The use of the oath (*coniuratio*) to bind the conspirators,[96] the use of weapons,[97] and the fomenting of sedition and riots among the soldiers[98] were likewise pro-

---

Cassius Dio *Roman History*, trans. by E. Cary, Loeb, Vol. VII (London: Heinemann, 1924), 59, 20, 6–7.

[85] Cf. Mommsen, *Römisches Strafrecht*, pp. 555–560.

[86] *Digest* 48, 4, 3 *Ad Legem Iuliam Maiestatis; Paulus Sent.* 5, 29, 1; Cassius Dio *Roman History* (Loeb, Vol. VI [1917]), 54, 3 for case of Marcus Primus.

[87] *Digest* 48, 4, 4; 50, 10, 3, 2 *De Operibus Publicis;* 50, 10, 4; *C. Th.* 15, 1, 31 *De Operibus Publicis* (Pharr, p. 426). Cf. the case of the poet Cornelius Gallus noted in Cassius Dio, 53, 23, 5–7.

[88] *Digest* 48, 4, 2.

[89] Cicero *In Pisonem* 21, 50.

[90] *Digest* 48, 4, 2.

[91] Cf. Mommsen, *Römisches Strafrecht*, pp. 560–567.

[92] *Digest* 48, 4, 3.

[93] Cf. Daremberg et Saglio, *Dictionnaire*, III (2), 1558 with n. 18.

[94] Cf. reference in Livy, 39, 15, 12, to nocturnal gatherings of the Bacchanalian worshippers for republican antecedents.

[95] *Paulus Sent.* 5, 22, 1 *De Seditiosis; Digest* 48, 19, 38, 2 *De Poenis; C. Just.* 9, 30, 2 *De Seditiosis et His Qui Plebem Audent contra Publicam Quietem Colligere.*

[96] *Digest* 48, 4, 4 (*iureiurando*); 48, 19, 16 pr. (*coniurationes*); *C. Just.* 9, 8, 5 pr *Ad Legem Iuliam Maiestatis* (*sacramenta*).

[97] *Digest* 48, 4, 1, 1.

[98] *Digest* 48, 4, 1, 1; 49, 16, 3, 19–20 *De Re Militari; C. Just.* 9, 8, 5 pr.

hibited. Such crimes were repressed summarily and the penalties were
applied with particular force against the ringleaders. Other aspects of
laesa maiestas falling in this category were: usurpation of the powers of
a magistrate[99] and, by extension, the crimes of counterfeiting[100] and of
keeping private prisons;[101] also, injurious or defamatory writings (*famosi
libelli*), for which the punishment was exile, deportation, or death.[102]

Many of the most typical manifestations of *laesa maiestas* may be
found among the injuries done to the emperor or to magistrates.[103] The
principle of the inviolability of a magistrate, whether patrician or plebeian passed from the Republic to the Empire, and was naturally extended
to the emperor. The murder of or the intent to murder a magistrate has
been noted previously as one of the gravest cases of *perduellio*.[104] Thus,
assaults and injuries of all kinds done to the monarch naturally became
high treason under the Principate. And, by extension, even utterances
concerning the emperor were held treasonable. Furthermore, the sacred
character of the emperors contributed to transform every injury into the
crime of *laesa maiestas* by making it an impiety.[105] It is noteworthy that

[99] *Digest* 48, 4, 3.
[100] *C. Th.* 9, 21, 9 *De Falsa Moneta* (Valentinian, Theodosius, and Arcadius,
a. 389, 392 [Pharr, p. 243]).
[101] *C. Th.* 9, 11, 1 *De Privatis Carceris Custodia* (Valentinian, Theodosius, and
Arcadius, a. 388 [Pharr, p. 235]).
[102] Paulus *Sent.* 5, 4, 15 (*carmen famosum in iniuriam alicuius*), 16 (*in alterius
infamian compositum et publice cantatum*), 17 (*famosos libellos in contumeliam
alterius*); *C. Th.* 9, 34, 1 *De Famosis Libellis* (Constantine, a. 319 [Pharr, p. 249]);
Digest 47, 10, 1 pr., and 1–2 *De Iniuriis et Famosis Libellis*, on insult as an aspect
of injury. Cf. *The Civil Law*, trans. by Scott, X, 305, n. 1, for a detailed discussion
of this problem. See Cassius Dio *Roman History* (Loeb, Vol. VII [1924]), 56, 27,
1–3, and Suetonius *Augustus* 55; also Dio, 58, 24, 3–4, for the charge that Mamercus
Aemilius Scaurus had written the scurrilous drama *Atreus* after the model of Eu-
ripides, directed against Tiberius. See F. H. Cramer, "Bookburning and Censorship
in Ancient Rome," *Journal of the History of Ideas*, VI (1945), 157–196, for a detailed account of slander and criminal libel in relation to *maiestas*; C. A. Forbes,
"Books for the Burning," *Transactions of the American Philological Association*,
LXVII (1936), 114–125; also Starr, *Civilization and Caesars*, pp. 83–85, on cases
of Titus Labienus and Cassius Severus, pp. 215–218 on Cremutius Cordus, and p.
221 on Mettius Pompusianus, relative to freedom of speech.
[103] Cf. Mommsen, *Römisches Strafrecht*, pp. 580–586.
[104] *Digest* 48, 4, 1, 1.
[105] See Kübler, "Maiestas," 551. Cf. Paulus *Sent.* 5, 29, 1: "quod crimen non
solum facto, sed et verbis impiis ac maledictis maxime exacerbatur"; also Tacitus
Annals 2, 50 (case of Appuleia Varilla charged with having spoken irreverently of
Augustus), and 6, 47 (case of Albucilla impeached of impiety toward Caligula);
1, 73; Cassius Dio *Roman History* (Loeb, Vol. IV [1916]), 44, 5, 3, stating that if
anyone insulted Caesar by deed or word, that man should be an outlaw and accursed. Tacitus (*Annals*, 1, 73) cites the famous case of Falanius or Faianius (see
Appendix B) who was charged with having admitted an infamous mimic, named

many of these injuries involved no bodily hurt to the emperor but were merely insults or offenses against the imperial dignity. Among these special offenses may be mentioned wearing the imperial insignia, such as clothing of silk and gold dyed with the imperial purple;[106] counterfeiting money bearing the effigy of an emperor;[107] consulting the future in all matters regarding the state and the imperial family by employing divination, soothsayers (*haruspices*), or horoscopes;[108] displaying lack of respect for the images of the emperor, including unseemly acts, real or alleged, committed in the presence or in the proximity of an imperial image; and the act of defacing, melting, or destroying a statue of the prince which had been consecrated.[109] Certain rescripts of Severus

---

Cassius, to a *collegium* in his house dedicated to the cult of Augustus, and with having transferred a statue of Augustus in the sale of his gardens. These acts were regarded as impious insults to the divinity of Augustus. Cf. Rogers, *Criminal Trials*, pp. 8–9.

[106] *C. Just.* 1, 23, 6 *De Diversis Rescriptis et Pragmaticis Sanctionibus* (Leo, a. 470), on the illegal possession of purple dye for parchment use; 11, 9, (8), 4 *De Vestibus, Holoveris et Auratis, et de Intinctione Sacri Muricis* (Theodosius, a. 424), declaring it *laesa maiestas* for anyone to have possession of clothing dyed with the Imperial purple; Cassius Dio *Roman History* (Loeb, Vol. V [1917]), 49, 16, on Caesar's orders that no one should wear the purple dress except the senators who were acting as magistrates.

[107] Paulus *Sent.* 5, 25, 1 *Ad Legem Corneliam Testamentariam: C. Th.* 9, 21, 5 and 9 *De Falsa Moneta* (Constantius, a. 343; and Valentinian, Theodosius, and Arcadius, a. 389, 392 [Pharr, p. 243]).

[108] Paulus *Sent.* 5, 21, 3 *De Vaticinatoribus et Mathematicis;* 5, 23, 17 *Ad Legem Corneliam de Sicariis et Veneficis; C. Th.* 9, 16, 3–4 and 7 *De Maleficis et Mathematicis et Ceteris Similibus* (Constantine, a. 321–324, 317–319; Constantius, a. 357; and Valentinian and Valens, a. 364 [Pharr, pp. 237–38]; Cassius Dio *Roman History* (Loeb, Vol. IX [1927]), 79, 4, 7, on the prophecy of an African seer (*mantis*) that Macrinus would replace Antonine (Elagabalus) on the imperial throne (A.D. 217); Tacitus *Annals* 4, 52, on the charge levied by Domitius Afer against Claudia Pulchra of "witchcraft and spells" against the emperor, Tiberius; also 12, 52; 16, 14. See Rogers, *Criminal Trials*, p. 16, on Libo's plot against Tiberius; Clyde Pharr, "The Interdiction of Magic in Roman Law," *Transactions of the American Philological Association*, LXIII (1932), 269–295, which analyzes the religious background of this type of public offense. The definitive treatment of these crimes as an aspect of *maiestas* legislation is Cramer, *Astrology*, pp. 232–283, Part II: "Astrology in Roman Law until the End of the Principate." This study gives a detailed discussion of all the more notable cases, drawing heavily on the literary records, especially the *Annals* of Tacitus, the *Lives* of Suetonius, and Dio's *Roman History*. It does not interpret the juristic literature as fully.

[109] Cf. Tacitus *Annals* 1, 74, on the case of Granius Marcellus who was charged under Tiberius with placing his statue higher than those of the Caesars and with removing the head of Augustus from a statue even though it was replaced with the head of Tiberius; 3, 70, on the case of Lucius Ennius who was charged with converting a silver effigy of Tiberius to other purposes; Cassius Dio (Loeb, Vol. VIII), 67, 12, 2, on the case of a woman who was put to death for undressing in

and Caracalla made it necessary for a number of persons to hide away from proceedings started against them because they had by mischance thrown a stone which struck a statue of the prince, or because they had sold a statue of the prince even though it had not yet been consecrated.[110] Other related offenses were the refusal to swear by the *genius* of the emperor or by his name,[111] violation of an oath taken in the name of the emperor, or swearing falsely to such an oath, although penalties for this type of offense were generally lighter than for most infractions of *maiestas*.[112] Still other offenses involved adultery committed with a princess of the imperial family,[113] and violation of the right of sanctuary attaching to the imperial cult and, later, to the Christian churches.[114]

---

front of an image of Domitian; and especially Suetonius *Tiberius* 58, which repeats the charges about removing the head of Augustus from his statue, adds charges concerning beating a slave or changing clothes near a statue of Augustus, and makes further amazing charges against carrying a coin or signet ring bearing the emperor's effigy into a comfort station or brothel ("nummo vel anulo effigiem impressam latrinae aut lupanari intulisse."). Gothofredus in n. 64 (*violatis statuis*) on *Digest* 48, 4, 7, 4 (Elzevir's Amsterdam edition of the *Corpus Juris Civilis* [1663]), cites a comparable instance under Caracalla: "Quidam etiam damnatus fuit ab Antonio Caracalla, quod urinam eo loco fecisset, in quo statuae et imagines Principis erant." Cf. Antoninus Caracalla, V, 7, in *Scriptores Historiae Augustae*, trans. by D. Magie, Loeb Series, Vol. II (London: Heinemann, 1924), which adds that men were condemned to death for removing garlands from the busts of the Emperor or for wearing such garlands about their necks as a fever preventive. Similar extravagances may be multiplied which suggest the tone of circumstances under which the *maiestas* legislation was executed. One final extraordinary example is cited in Seneca, *De Beneficiis*, trans. by J. W. Basore, Loeb, Vol. III of Seneca's *Moral Essays* (London: Heinemann, 1935), 3, 26, 1–2. In this case a devoted slave hastily removed from his master's finger a ring bearing the portrait of Tiberius upon noting that his master had taken up a chamber pot and was being observed by an informer.

[110] *Digest* 48, 4, 5–6; 47, 10, 38; 48, 4, 1, 1. See Kübler, "Maiestas," p. 552. Cf. Suetonius *Tiberius* 58, for various related offenses associated with statutes and effigies of Augustus.

[111] Cf. Suetonius *Gaius* 27; Cassius Dio *Roman History* 44, 6, 1, requiring that oaths be taken by Caesar's Fortune (*Tyche*); 44, 50, 1 on oaths by Caesar's Health and Fortune (*Hygeia* and *Tyche*).

[112] *Digest* 12, 2, 13, 6 *De Iureiurando, sive Voluntario, sive Necessario, sive Iudiciali*. Cf. Tacitus *Annals* 1, 73, 3, 36; Cassius Dio *Roman History* (Cary, Vol. VII [1924]), 57, 9, 2, on perjury after swearing by the Fortune of Augustus.

[113] Cf. Tacitus *Annals* 1, 53 (case of Sempronius Gracchus under Augustus); 3, 24 (case of Decius Silanus under Augustus): "nam culpam inter viros ac feminas vulgatum gravi nomine *laesarum religionum ac violatae maiestatis* appellando clementiam maiorum suasque ipse leges egrediebatur"; 4, 44 (case of Jullus Antonius under Augustus); Cassius Dio *Roman History* 58, 24, 5, for charge of adultery with Livilla; Suetonius *Augustus*, c. 27, for case of Quintus Gallius.

[114] *C. Just.* 1, 12, 2 *De His Qui ad Ecclesias Confugiunt, vel Ibi Exclamant*

Violation of civic religious duties under the Empire was closely associated with personal injuries done to the emperor inasmuch as the monarch himself was deified.[115] Strange religions were prohibited if they threatened the public peace and safety by creating disorders, or if their devotees refused to participate in the rites of the imperial cult. This anxiety to maintain public order led to the promulgation of laws establishing the severest penalties for introducing new gods and new cults into the Roman world: death for *humiliores,* exile for *honestiores.*[116] Later the progress of the foreign religions, especially of Judaism and of Christianity, led the emperors to recognize, repress, and punish a new crime—that of violation of the national religion. The profession of Christianity was in itself considered inherently a crime, regardless of the allied crimes with which the Christians were charged, such as debauchery, magic, and the possession of evil and dangerous books (*famosi libelli*). In the crime of Christianity Tertullian distinguishes two essential elements: *crimen laesae maiestatis* and *crimen laesae romanae religionis.*[117] The denial of the state gods brought with it as a consequence, in the case of the Christians, the refusal to participate in the ceremonies of the public cult, to sacrifice to the *genius* of the emperor, and to recognize the divinity of the emperor. And since the Christians would not subscribe to the national religion of Rome and could not establish a national state of their own, they were considered *atheoi,* declared guilty of *perduellio,* and were treated as public enemies (*hostes publici*) whether they were Roman citizens or not.[118] Conversion to Judaism was, likewise, opposed by the Roman state, while Diolectian issued a decree punishing the Manichaeans with severe penalties. Their leaders were burned at the stake, and their disciples suffered death or were sent to the mines according to their station.[119] The Roman government was par-

---

(Honorius and Theodosius, a. 409): "si quisquam contra hanc legem venire temptaverit, sciat se ad maiestatis crimen esse retinendum."

[115] See Mommsen, *Römisches Strafrecht,* pp. 567–580.

[116] Paulus *Sent.* 5, 21, 2; also cf. *Digest* 48, 19, 30 *De Poenis;* Cassius Dio, 52, 36, relative to strange religions, magicians, and false philosophers.

[117] See Mommsen, *Römisches Strafrecht,* p. 567 with n. 2, citing Tertullian, *Apologeticus* 10, 24, 27, 28, 35.

[118] Humbert, "Maiestas," III (2), 1559; McIlwain, *Political Thought in the West,* pp. 145–146; Starr, *Civilization and Caesars,* pp. 322–323; Mommsen, *Römisches Strafrecht,* pp. 575–576 and notes. Also cf. Edward Gibbon, *Decline and Fall of the Roman Empire,* ed. by J. B. Bury (London: Methuen, 1896), II, 16, 19, 74–75.

[119] Cf. Mommsen, *Römisches Strafrecht,* p. 576.

ticularly interested in stamping out the leaders of these religious sects
and the apostasy of converts usually procured for them a remission of
the penalty. After the complete victory of Christianity, the Christian
emperors forbade the pagans, in turn, all public exercise of their cult,
including sacrifices and meetings, and pronounced the penalty of death
with confiscation of goods upon those who refused to forsake their pagan
gods.[120] Finally in A.D. 392 Theodosius and Arcadius declared such offenders guilty of *laesa maiestas*,[121] as well as those Christians who went
over to Judaism.[122] And in 386 Valentinian threatened to impose the
penalties of violated majesty upon Catholics who disturbed the public
peace by their quarrels with the Arians.[123]

The *crimen laesae maiestatis* necessarily presumed guilty intent (*dolus malus*)[124] and drew little distinction between the intent and the
deed. It was left for the judge to examine the circumstances and to estimate the exact degree of guilt.[125] Accomplices, embraced under the formula *cuius ope consilio*, were punished as well as the prime instigators,[126]
although generally with less severity. Sometimes failure to reveal plots
was punished as complicity, but that was probably not the general rule
until the later Empire.[127] The penalty was more severe when the guilty
person was a soldier,[128] and, in the later period at least, solicitation in

[120] See Humbert, "Maiestas," III (2), 1559.
[121] Note in general *C. Th.* 16, 10, 12, 1 *De Paganis, Sacrificiis, et Templis* and
especially *C. Th.* 16, 10, 12, 1, issued by Theodosius, Arcadius, and Honorius on
Nov. 8, 392, for *laesa maiestas* (Pharr, pp. 472–475); also *C. Just.* 1, 11, 7 *De
Paganis, Sacrificiis et Templis* (Valentinian and Marcian, a. 451).
[122] *C. Th.* 16, 8, 19 *De Iudaeis, Caelicolis, et Samaritanis* (Honorius and Theodosius, a. 409 [Pharr, p. 469]).
[123] This would appear to be the purpose of *C. Th.* 16, 1, 4 *De Fide Catholica*
(Valentinian, Theodosius, and Arcadius, a. 386 [Pharr, p. 440]).
[124] *Digest* 48, 4, 1, 1: "quo tenetur is, cuius opera dolo malo consilium initum
erit"; 48, 4, 3: "quid sciens dolo malo gesserit"; 48, 4, 4, and 10. Cf. Starr, *Civilization and Caesars*, pp. 159–160, for general remarks on accusation and procedure.
[125] *Digest* 48, 4, 7, 3 where judges are named: "Hoc tamen crimen a iudicibus
non in occasionem ob principalis maiestatis venerationem habendum est, sed in
veritate" (cf. Paulus *Sent.* 5, 29, 2 for similar principle); 49, 16, 3, 12–13 *De Re
Militari* for examples of judicial discretion; *C. Th.* 9, 14, 3 *Ad Legem Corneliam
de Sicariis* (Arcadius and Honorius, a. 397) involves degree of attainder (Pharr,
p. 236), as does *C. Just.* 9, 8, 5 *Ad Legem Iuliam Maiestatis*.
[126] *Digest* 48, 4, 1, 1–3; *C. Just.* 9, 8, 5, 6 (Arcadius and Honorius, a. 397): "Id,
quod de praedictis eorumque filiis cavimus, etiam de satellitibus consciis ac min-
istris filiisque eorum simili serveritate censemus."
[127] Cf. *C. Just.* 9, 8, 5, 7; *C. Th.* 9, 14, 7 (Pharr, pp. 236–237).
[128] *Digest* 48, 4, 7, 4: "Crimen maiestatis facto vel violatis statuis vel imaginibus
maxime exacerbatur in milites."

favor of the guilty was punished.[129] The *lex Julia* permitted accusations to be lodged and allowed the actions to be instituted by persons of ill repute, soldiers, and women, while slaves might accuse their masters and freedman their patrons.[130] In fact, the right of accusation was denied to slaves and freedmen only at rare intervals, as by the emperors Nerva, Tacitus, and, on occasion, Constantine.[131] *Delatores* and accusers were frequently encouraged by a considerable bounty levied on the confiscated property,[132] but those who could not prove their accusation were submitted to torture and given the severest punishments.[133] Also, torture was freely permitted against the accused without distinction of rank,[134] against the slaves of the accused at times,[135] and, at least in the late Empire, even against the witnesses.[136]

Under the Republic the penalty for treason was very diversified[137]

---

[129] C. Th. 9, 14, 3, 1 *Ad Legem Corneliam de Sicariis* (Valentinian, Valens and Gratian, a. 397 [Pharr, p. 236]).

[130] *Digest* 48, 4, 7, 1–2: "Servi quoque deferentes audiuntur et quidem dominos suos et liberti patronos"; 48, 4, 8: "In quaestionibus laesae maiestatis etiam mulieres audiuntur"; C. Th. 9, 6, 2 *Ne Praeter Crimen Maiestatis Servus Dominum vel Patronum Libertus vel Familiaris Accuset* (Valens, Gratian, and Valentinian, a. 376 [Pharr, p. 230]). Cf. Tacitus, *Annals* 2, 30, on torture of Libo's slaves. (Also see *The Works of Tacitus*, Oxford Translation (London: Bell, 1914), I, 73, n. 1. Tacitus *Annals* 3, 22, on the refusal of Tiberius to permit the torture of the slaves of Aemilia Lepida; 3, 67, on the delivery in sale of the slaves of Gaius Silanus to the city steward so that they might be examined by torture.

[131] Cf. C. Th. 9, 5, 1, 1 *Ad Legem Iuliam Maiestatis* (Constantine, a. 314; 320–323 [Pharr, p. 230]). Cassius Dio, 68, 1, 2, on Nerva's prohibition against slaves and freedmen lodging complaints against their masters.

[132] C. Just. 9, 8, 5,; Tacitus *Annals* 4, 20; 4, 30, on rewards to informers.

[133] C. Th. 9, 5, 1; C. Just. 9, 8, 3.

[134] Paulus *Sent.* 5, 29, 2: "Nulla dignitas a tormentis excipitur"; C. Th. 9, 5, 1; 9, 35, 1 *De Quaestionibus* (a. 369 [Pharr, p. 250]); C. Just. 9, 8, 4. Tacitus *Annals* 11, 22, on torture of the Roman *eques* Cneius Novius; 15, 56, on the threat of torture made to Antonius Natalis in Piso's conspiracy; 16, 20, on the death of the ex-praetor Numicius Thermus, and the torture of his freedman under Nero; Suetonius *Domitian*, c. 8, on torture of witnesses in a case involving the charge of incontinence against Cornelia, the head Vestal.

[135] C. Just. 9, 8, 6, 1, in *Corpus Juris Civilis*, ed. by Mommsen-Krüger-Schöll-Kroll (Berlin: Weidmann, 1954); 9, 8, 7, 1, ed. by Gothofredus: "In hoc item crimine, quod ad laesam maiestatem imperatoris pertinet, etiam in caput domini servos torqueri"; 9, 41, 1 pr *De Quaestionibus*. Cf. C. Th. 9, 5, 1, 1; C. Just. 9, 8, 3. In addition, see C. Th. 9, 6, 2; *Digest* 48, 4, 7, 2; Paulus *Sent.* 5, 13, 3 *De Delatoribus*: "Damnati servi, sive post sententiam sive ante sententiam dominorum facinora confessi sint, nullo modo audiuntur, nisi forte reos deferant maiestatis"; also Humbert, "Maiestas," III (2), 1560.

[136] *Digest* 48, 18, 1, 1–2 *De Quaestionibus*.

[137] On penalties see Mommsen, *Römisches Strafrecht*, pp. 590–594.

since it was dependent on whether the magistrate classified the crime as capital or noncapital. The tribunes had the authority to inflict fines, and the death penalty quite disappeared in the procedure of the *quaestiones perpetuae*. The penalty of the *lex Cornelia* and of the *lex Julia* was *aquae et ignis interdictio,* that is, perpetual exile outside the territory of Italy,[138] with death in case the ban was broken.[139] Whoever received an exile on forbidden territory also exposed himself to death under the Republic, and to the penalties of the *lex Julia de vi privata* under the early Empire.[140] The condemned regularly preserved his civic rights and his fortune in republican times but during the imperial era there were considerable changes in the penalties since they could be arbitrarily applied by the emperor, the Senate, and the new imperial magistrates.[141] From Julius Caesar and Augustus onward *aquae et ignis interdictio* was rendered more severe by adding partial or total confiscation.[142] Tiberius added loss of possessions and civic rights and deportation or internment in a designated place.[143] In addition to simple fines and exile,[144] the death penalty was inflicted under Augustus and Tiberius by the courts of the emperor and of the Senate.[145] From then on death was the common penalty, being used and abused by the bad emperors, especially to decimate the senatorial aristocracy.[146] After the

---

[138] Paulus *Sent.* 5, 29, 1. Cf. Tacitus *Annals* 3, 38, for case of Antistius Vetus; 3, 50, for case of Clutorius Priscus.

[139] *Digest* 48, 19, 28, 14 *De Poenis:* "Ita et in custodiis gradum servandum esse, idem princeps [Hadrian] rescripsit, id est ut, qui in tempus damnati erant, in perpetuum damnarentur, qui in perpetuum damnati erant, in metallum damnarentur, qui in metallum damnati id admiserint, summo supplicio adficerentur." Cf. Cassius Dio, 38, 17, 7, on decree of exile against Cicero.

[140] Paulus *Sent., Ad Legem Iuliam de Vi Publica et Privata.*

[141] Cf. Cassius Dio, 57, 22, 5, on Tiberius' prohibition of the right to make a will in cases of persons interdicted from fire and water.

[142] Tacitus *Annals* 3, 50: "cedat tamen urbe et bonis amissis aqua et igni arceatur: quod perinde censeo ac si lege maiestatis teneretur" (oration of Manius Lepidus against Clutorius Priscus); Cassius Dio, 53, 23, 7, on forfeiture of goods in the case of Cornelius Gallus.

[143] Tacitus *Annals* 3, 28; 4, 21 (case of Cassius Severus under Tiberius); 42 (case of Votienus Montanus under Tiberius); 6, 18 (case of Considius Proculus and his sister, Sancia, under Tiberius), cited by Humbert, "Maiestas," III (2), 1560.

[144] Suetonius *Augustus* 51; Tacitus *Annals* 1, 72; 4, 21; 6, 18. *Digest* 48, 19, 24 *De Poenis*, requires that statues of those who have been relegated or deported for violations of majesty shall be removed.

[145] These were mostly cases involving adultery with women of the imperial family. See Note 113 *supra*.

[146] Paulus *Sent.* 5, 29, 1; *C. Just.* 9, 8, 5 pr.; *Institutes* 4, 18, 3 *De Publicis Iudiciis:* "cuius poena animae amissionem sustinet, et memoria rei etiam post mortem

time of Septimius Severus violations of majesty incurred death by the sword in the case of *honestiores,* while the *humiliores* were burned at the stake or delivered over to wild beasts in the arena.[147] This punishment was accompanied with such ignominious consequences as denial of burial, prohibition of mourning to the parents and friends, and damnation of the offender's memory.[148] Also, confiscation of property always existed as an accessory penalty, so that not only the will of the condemned became void but all his acts of alienation and manumission made after he took his criminal resolve were retroactively annulled;[149] even the dowry of a woman guilty of *maiestas* was confiscated.[150] Furthermore, trials for *laesa maiestas* could not only continue after the death of the accused, but, in the gravest cases, could also begin at that time and entail damnation of memory and confiscation of property.[151]

---

damnatur." Note also Tacitus *Annals* 16, 21–35, for the famous case of Thrasea Paetus and his son-in-law, Helvidius Priscus, under Nero.

[147] Paulus *Sent.* 5, 29, 1: "his antea in perpetuum aqua et igni interdicebatur; nunc vero humiliores bestiis obiciuntur vel vivi exuruntur, honestiores capite puniuntur."

[148] *Digest* 11, 7, 35 *De Religiosis et Sumptibus Funerum et Ut Funus Ducere Liceat,* associates those who would destroy their country with those who would kill their parents and children (i.e., parricides): "eum, qui ad patriam delendam et parentes et liberos interficiendos venerit," while *Digest* 3, 2, 11, 3 *De His Qui Notantur Infamia,* associates mourning for enemies and traitors with mourning for suicides—not those who kill themselves because they have a bad conscience. Cf. *Digest* 28, 3, 6, 7 *De Iniusto Rupto Irrito Facto Testamento,* which states that if anyone takes his life because he is tired of living or because his health is poor or because, like certain philosophers, he seeks popular applause and notoriety, such persons' wills shall be in effect. The reference to the sensation-creating philosophers suggests the type illustrated by the death of Peregrine recounted in Lucian (*The Works of Lucian,* trans. by H. W. and F. G. Fowler [Oxford: Clarendon, 1905], IV, 79–95). Also see Suetonius *Tiberius* 61, on the prohibition of mourning in the case of Sejanus.

[149] *Digest* 28, 3, 6, 6–11; 40, 9, 15 pr *Qui et a Quibus Manumissi Liberi Non Fiunt; C. Just.* 9, 8, 5 pr, and 4 (Arcadius and Honorius, a. 397); *C. Th.* 9, 42, 2, and 4 *De Bonis Proscriptorum seu Damnatorum* (Constantius and Julian, a. 356 and 358 [Pharr, pp. 259–260]). *Digest* 31, 76, 9 *De Legatis et Fideicommissis,* states that a legacy may be received from a legatee if the testator was convicted of treason after the legacy had been paid and if the memory of the deceased has become infamous.

[150] *Digest* 48, 20, 3 *De Bonis Damnatorum:* "Quinque Legibus damnatae mulieri dos publicatur: Maiestatis, vis publicae, parricidii, venefici, de sicariis."

[151] *C. Just.* 9, 8, 6, of the Gothofredus edition, based on *Basilics* 6, 36, and omitted as not authentic in the Mommsen-Krüger edition, is explicit on these points. It states that a man may be declared guilty of majesty after his death and his property confiscated. Action may be taken after a man's death; the memory of the deceased may be damned; his property may be seized from his heirs. He who is involved in this crime can neither sell nor manumit nor alienate nor release a debtor.

However, confiscation was deferred if the heir proposed to demonstrate the innocence of the deceased.[152] Damnation of memory was but a step removed from attainder of treason, since the latter is created by extending infamy from the memory of the deceased to his living decendants.[153] Sulla had such an extension of infamy made to the descendants of the proscribed, and had them excluded from the magistracies;[154] Caesar put an end to this injustice, and it did not reappear in the early Empire, save during certain intervals in the reigns of Tiberius, Nero, and Commodus.[155] In the later Empire a *constitutio* of Arcadius in 397 abrogated the Theodosian law, permitting children and grandchildren a sixth of the confiscated property, and re-established confiscation of the whole.[156] It also imposed penalties on the offender's sons—infamy, confiscation of the son's property, and the incapacity to receive or pass on any inheritance. Daughters retained a fourth of their mother's property, while a

---

His slaves may be put to the torture that they may testify against him. And from the time that he began to plot (*subiit cogitationem*) he shall be deemed worthy of punishment on account of the plot. This post-Justinian statute would appear to be an accurate summary of the earlier legislation, notably as set forth in *C. Just.* 9, 8, 5.

[152] *Digest* 48, 4, 11; 49, 14, 22 pr. *De Iure Fisci; Institutes* 4, 18, 3 *De Publicis Iudiciis.*

[153] Cf. extension of this principle to inheritances in *C. Th.* 9, 42, 6 (Pharr, p. 260).

[154] This more sophisticated legal connotation of infamy is treated in detail by Ernst Levy, "Zur Infamie des römischen Strafrechts," in the *Riccobono Studies,* II, 77–100. Thus, *Digest* 3, 2, 22 *De His Qui Notantur Infamia,* states that blows with rods do not constitute infamy, but rather it is the reason (*causa*) for which the punishment is merited that determines infamy. This reason is explained in *Digest* 48, 1, 7 *De Publicis Iudiciis:* A sentence for every crime does not render a man infamous but only such as involve public prosecutions and judgments. Infamy does not result from condemnation for a crime which is not the subject of a public prosecution, save for certain specified offenses as theft, robbery with violence, and injury. Even here we are not completely removed from the primitive relation of infamy to infidelity, since the public significance of the offense bears on the problem of the offender's allegiance to the state. The citizen or subject owes obedience and allegiance to the law of the state; he has broken the law; he is unfaithful and hence infamous.

[155] Cf. Humbert and Lécrivain, "Maiestas," III (2), 1560–1561. See Tacitus *Annals* 5, 9 (6, 4 ed. by Furneaux), on capital punishment of the children of Sejanus under Tiberius; Suetonius *Tiberius* 61, on the attainder of relatives in the case of Sejanus; Nero, 36, on the banishment and death of the children of the conspirators in the plots of Piso and Vinicius under Nero. The general statements of the law prohibiting such attainder may be found in *Digest* 48, 19, 20 and 26 *De Poenis.*

[156] *C. Just.* 9, 49, 10 *De Bonis Proscriptorum seu Damnatorum* (Theodosius and Valentinian, a. 426), and *C. Th.* 9, 42, 23 (Honorius and Theodosius, a. 421 [Pharr, p. 263]), which abrogate *C. Th.* 9, 42, 8, 3 (Gratian, Valentinian and Theodosius, a. 380 [Pharr, p. 261]). See Appendix A on *C. Just.* 9, 5, 5 *Ad Legem Iuliam Maiestatis.*

wife received her dowry and, under certain conditions, gifts given by her husband. Finally, according to a *Novel* of Justinian, in cases of the crime of conspiracy against the emperor, the husband of the guilty woman was authorized to repudiate her and keep her dowry, while the wife of the guilty husband was directed to divorce him and to keep her dowry and gifts.[157]

C. In the Barbarian Kingdoms

The next step in the history of Roman public law involves the transmission of Roman legal concepts to the new states arising from the wreckage of the Empire as Roman authority diminished in the provinces and gave way to the rising new barbarian kingdoms. By the beginning of the sixth century a substantial portion of the Roman law, especially the imperial legislation derived from the *Theodosian Code*, emerges in the Visigothic compilation commonly known as the *Breviary of Alaric*, of A.D., 506.[158] Here appears a brief yet fairly comprehensive statement of the Roman law of *maiestas*, based on the *Sentences* of Paulus, which runs as follows:

I. According to the *lex Julia maiestatis* he shall be held by whose aid and counsel arms have been taken up against the emperor or public authority, or the armies of the emperor have been betrayed: or who has waged war without the lawful consent of the emperor, or levied troops, or stirred up disturbance within the army, or deserted the emperor. All such persons shall be perpetually interdicted from fire and water; the more humble [*humiliores*] shall be cast to the beasts or burned alive while those of higher rank [*honestiores*] shall be punished capitally. Also this offense rests not on overt act alone but is particularly aggravated by impious [disrespectful] words and maledictions.

II. In any accusation of *maiestas* inquiry must first be made with what resources, with what faction, and with what agents this crime was committed: for a person accused [guilty] of so great a crime must be punished not because of the pretext of adulation on the part of anyone but on account of the actual deed [acknowledged guilt]. Hence, when a judicial investigation of this crime is conducted, no dignity is exempt from torture.[159]

Thus, one finds that a substantial portion of the republican law of *perduellio* is retained though adapted to the peculiar role of the emperor as the symbol and personification of the state. In addition, the law of accusations contained in the *Theodosian Code* is included in the *Breviary*

---

[157] *Novellae* 117, 8–9.
[158] See essay on "*Crimen Laesae Maiestatis* in the *Lex Romana Wisigothorum.*"
[159] See Appendix B on Paulus *Sent.* 5, 29, 1–2 (*Lex Romana Visigothorum*, *Paulus*, 5, 31, 1–2) *Ad Legem Iuliam Maiestatis*. Cf. Barker, *Alexander to Constantine*, p. 271.

and bears the caption that "no slave shall accuse his master nor any freedman or household servant his patron save for the crime of majesty."[160] The essential features of this law are best summarized in the *Interpretatio* of its second section and read as follows:

> If a slave accuse his master or inform against him in the matter of any crime whatsoever or if any follower or servant or freedman shall do likewise in the case of his patron, let the sword be his punishment immediately at the very beginning of his accusation, since we wish to cut off such a voice, not listen to it: unless perchance his master or patron shall prove to have been involved in the crime of majesty.[161]

From these two basic laws it is clear that the characteristic and fundamental features of the Roman crime of majesty were preserved and transmitted to the later Middle Ages, and very importantly the expression *maiestas* itself appears in these legal statements.

However, a peculiar circumstance emerges when one turns to the Visigothic legislation of the seventh century which is contained in the collection of laws termed the *Forum Judicum.*[162] Here both the idea of majesty and the word *maiestas* have vanished within the space of a century and a half. Indeed, when the German legal historian, Karl Zeumer, undertook to reconstruct the treason law that had presumably existed in the *Code of Euric* (ca. 481), which antedates the *Breviary,* he made a similar omission in recognition of the dominant Germanic influence in the public law of the new barbarian kingdoms.[163] This new Germanic element represents a great turning point in political and legal theory and a reversion to customary law of a level comparable to the *Twelve Tables* in Roman law. This return to customary law brings an entire revolution in the concepts of sovereignty and allegiance. Among the Germanic peoples allegiance is regarded as contractual in the sense of involving bilateral rights and obligations which rest in turn

---

[160] *C. Th.* 9, 6, 3 (*Lex Romana Visigothorum, Code,* 9, 3, 2) *Ne Praeter Crimen Maiestatis Servus Dominum vel Patronum Libertus seu Familiaris Accuset* (Arcadius and Honorius, a. 397? [Pharr, p. 231]). Cf. *C. Just.* 9, 1, 20 *De His Qui Accusare Non Possunt.*

[161] *C. Th.* 9, 6, 3 (*L. R. V., C.* 9, 3, 2) *Interpretatio:* "Si servus dominum aut amicus vel domesticus sive libertus patronum accusaverit vel detulerit cuiuslibet criminis reum, statim in ipso initio accusantionis gladio puniatur, quia vocem talem exstingui volumus, non audiri: nisi forte dominum aut patronum de crimine maiestatis tractasse probaverit."

[162] See essay on "The Public Law of the Visigothic Code."

[163] See *Lex Visigothorum,* ed. by K. Zeumer in *Monumenta Germaniae Historica, Leges* (Hanover and Leipzig: Hahn, 1902), Sectio I, Tomus I, *Praefatio,* p. xiii.

upon a pledged troth between a ruler and his people.[164] On the other hand, the Roman concept of majesty involves a deferential allegiance to and the veneration of the divine monarch, or in Christian terms a monarch who is the appointed vicar of God to rule mankind, and, hence, *legibus solutus*.[165] Such a ruler is recognized to be either outside the state or a symbol of the state, and to repose above the law. Among the Germanic peoples the king is but one of the folk though *primus inter pares*, whereas the emperor of the Dominate is a living law enveloped by the nimbus of majesty. As a result, in the imperial law of Rome treason is a supreme violation of majesty but among the Germanic invaders it is breach of troth, *infidelitas*, not *maiestas*. Furthermore, sovereignty, which it is treason's purpose to attack, resides according to Roman political thought in the *legis lator*—under the Republic in the *populus*, under the Dominate in the monarch to whom the people have granted their full *imperium*. Here sovereignty is legislative and to that extent modern; it is Bodin's power to make the law.[166] But in Germanic thinking sovereignty rests in the immemorial custom of the folk, which can be found or determined only by a judicial process. Here sovereignty belongs to the Law rather than the Legislator and hence is judicial. The law has been made, now it can only be interpreted. Consequently, it is not surprising to discover that in the portion of the Visigothic legislation which is based on Germanic principles and includes the public law there is a complete omission of the majesty laws. In their stead one finds such expressions as *scandalum*, *conturbatio*, and *intendisse proditus*, or such descriptive clauses as "to stir wicked thoughts and raise the avenging hand against the person of the prince," "to be involved in the crime of infidelity," and "speaking or acting in anywise against king, folk, or native land" (*contra regem, gentem vel patriam*), culminating in the crime of *bausia* in the Catalonian *Fueros*.[167] Only that aspect of *maiestas* which approximates high treason appears in Germanic law, but there is no evidence to show that there is any derivation from the Roman concept of majesty. Instead, the supreme treason in Germanic

[164] See essay on "Contractual Allegiance vs. Deferential Allegiance in Visigothic Law."

[165] See essay on "The Idea of Majesty in Roman Political Thought"; Moss, *Birth of Middle Ages*, p. 250.

[166] For the text of this enactment see McIlwain, *Political Thought in the West*, p. 118; Last in *C. A. H.*, XI (1936), 404–408; Girard, *Textes*, pp. 106–108.

[167] See essay on "Blasphemy in the *Lex Romana Curiensis*." Cf. Usatici of Barcelona, c. 40–50, for the offense of *bausia* with its typically Iberian fusion of Roman and Germanic elements in *Altspanisch-gotische Rechte*, trans. by E. Wohlhaupter (*Germanenrechte*, Band 12 [Weimar: Böhlaus 1936]), pp. 200–205.

thinking is essentially a private breach of faith pledged by man to man. The gravest of treasons is broken troth, *Treubruch, infidelitas.*[168] In the code of the Ripuarian Franks one reads: "If a man shall be unfaithful [*infidelis*] to his king, he shall pay with his life, and all his property shall be forfeited to the treasury."[169] There is no inconsistency here since the royal office in its public character is made secure by personal contract with the subjects. This principle operates upon both ruler and subject and is no one-way arrangement as is evidenced in that famous dictum of limited monarchy of the Visigoths which states: "Thou shalt be king if thou dost right; but, if thou dost not right, then shalt thou not be king."[170] Here is a definite precursor of the feudal *diffidatio* whereby a vassal could withdraw his pledge and allegiance from a faithless lord.

The Almannic legislation, probably of the early seventh century, seems to reflect some contact with the Roman law as in an enactment bearing the caption *De eo, qui mortem ducis consiliatus fuerit,* which reads: "If any man shall have plotted the death of the duke and it shall have been proved against him, he shall forfeit his life or redeem it in such manner as the duke or the leaders of the people shall consider suitable."[171] Pollock and Maitland, referring to the evidence of the Anglo-Saxon Dooms, state that the idea of conspiracy probably "does not represent any original Germanic tradition, but is borrowed from the Roman law of *maiestas.*"[172] Certainly the conspiratorial principle is denounced in the *Digest* under the formula penalizing him "through whose activities a plot shall be entered upon with evil intent" (*dolo malo*).[173] Yet despite some evidence of Roman influence, perhaps through ecclesiastical sources, the general tenor of this legislation makes it clear that this is not *maiestas* resting on a basis of territorial law and

[168] See essay on 'The Public Law of the Ripuarian, Alamannic, and Bavarian Codes."

[169] *Lex Ribuaria,* ed. by Sohm, *M. G. H.* (Legum Tomus V), 67, 1: "Si quis homo regi infidelis exsteterit, de vita componat, et omnes res suas fisco censeantur."

[170] Cf. St. Isidore, *Etymologiae,* ed. by Lindsay (Oxford: Clarendon, 1911), 9, 3, 4–5; Moss, *Birth of Middle Ages,* p. 250 n. 3, referring to the Roman origins of this aphorism. Cf. Horace, *Epistles,* 1, 1, 59–60.

[171] *Leges Alamannorum,* ed. by Lehmann, *M. G. H.* (Legum Sectio I, Tomi V, Pars I), 23.

[172] Pollock and Maitland, *The History of English Law before the Time of Edward I* (2nd ed.; Cambridge: University Press, 1923), I, 51–52.

[173] See essay on "Treason and Related Offenses in the Anglo-Saxon Dooms." Cf. *Digest* 48, 4, 1, 1: "quo tenetur is, cuius opera dolo malo consilium initum erit . . .; cuiusve opera consilio [dolo] malo consilium initum erit."

state sovereignty. The Bavarian laws of the eighth century reveal the same personal bias which is reflected in breaches of fidelity, such as cases where a son attempts to depose his father through a plot devised by evil men (*vel patrem suum dehonestare voluerit per consilio malignorum*).[174] The element of plotting and machination has Roman overtones, but the concept of royal or ducal office is distinctly personal. Thus in the parallel Alamannic legislation reference is made to the son's seeking "to possess the realm through theft" (*raptum*).[175] Majesty cannot be stolen; it can only descend upon the holder as a bearer of sovereign authority and that authority must accord with law. The Lombard laws, which are in the main disappointingly scant in matters of public law, reflect a similar combination of Roman veneer overlaying the Germanic core. Thus, in the *Edict of Rothar* of A.D. 643 it is stated that "If any man has planned by himself or plotted with others against the life of the king [*contra animam regis cogitaverit aut consiliaverit*], he shall be in peril of his life and his property shall be confiscated,"[176] and "If any man has invited or introduced enemies within the province, he shall suffer the loss of his life and his property shall be confiscated."[177] The first of these laws suggests *maiestas* in the sense of high treason, and the other *perduellio* or treason against land and folk. But supplementary provisions dealing with *scandalum* or riot reveal the personal and customary character of the Lombard law since the seriousness of the offense is dependent upon the presence or proximity of the king and is thus determined by the degree of personal insult or affront.[178] One new conception of some interest is suggested in the verb *cogitaverit* which appears to make high treason out of mere "cogitating," thinking about or planning the king's death in the mind of the accused, yet accompanied by no overt act.[179] This trend is symptomatic of a development which culminated in English law with the literal "imagining the

---

[174] *Lex Baiuvariorum*, ed. by Beyerle 2, (Munich: Hueber, 1926), *De Filiis Ducum Si Protervi Fuerint.*

[175] *L. Alam.* 35, 1 *De Filio Ducis, Qui contra Patrem Suum Surrexerit: aut per raptum regnum eius possedere.*

[176] Edictus Rothari, ed. by Beyerle (Weimar: Böhlaus, 1947) 1. Cf. *Ed. Roth.* 9.

[177] *Ed. Roth.* 4: "Si quis inimicus intra provincia invitaverit aut introduxerit, animae suae incurrat periculum et res eius infiscentur."

[178] Cf. *Ed. Roth.* 35–40.

[179] Bisoukides, *Der Hochverrat*, p. 43: "Der Gegensatz des 'cogitare' zum 'consiliare' besteht offenbar darin, dass das erstere die von einer *einzelnen* Person ausgehenden, das letztere dagegen die von *mehreren* geplanten Angriffe gegen das Leben des Königs umfasst."

king's death" as a form of high treason.[180] Parallels for this can probably
be found under such emperors as Tiberius and Caligula in the extreme
extensions of *laesa maiestas* to the prophecies of astrologers and soothsayers (*mathematici et haruspices*) adverse to the imperial health and
fortunes.

Not until one reaches the restored empire of Charlemagne does he
again encounter the term *maiestas* and then but infrequently.[181] Thus,
in the *Capitulare Ticinense* of A.D. 801 it is stated that those who disobey
and desert the army and return home without the command or permission of the king shall be accused of the crime of majesty (*reus maiestatis*), shall be in peril of their lives, and shall have their property
confiscated to the royal treasury.[182] This is the offense described in
Frankish terminology as *herisliz* or flight from the host.[183] However, the
context of this enactment suggests the usual Germanic breach of troth
rather than typical Roman *crimen laesae maiestatis*. The primary stress
is still laid on infidelity, although a more detailed study of the Carolingian capitularies is needed to determine the exact scope of a possible
reception of Roman legal and political concepts accompanying the
revival of the Roman *imperium*. There is even a possibility that the
consistent omissions of the expression *maiestas* in the Germanic codes
resulted from a more or less conscious recognition that the new barbarian kingdoms were mere *regna* outside the Roman *imperium*.

One last bit of evidence supporting the theory of the conscious omission of *maiestas* in barbarian legislation is found in a curious legal
source, a corrupt compilation of the late eighth century based on the
Breviary of Alaric and known as the *Epitome Sancti Galli* or *Lex
Romana Curiensis*. Here the excepting clause in the law of accusations
derived from the *Theodosian Code*, which states that no slave may
accuse his master nor any freedman his patron save for the crime of
majesty, is transformed to read thus: "If any slave shall wish to accuse

---

[180] Cf. Statute 25 Edward III (1352): "quant home fait compasser ou ymaginer
la mort n̄re Seigneur le Roi," and Bracton, *De Legibus et Consuetudinibus Angliae*,
ed. by G. E. Woodbine (New Haven: Yale University Press, 1922), II, 334 (f.
118b): "Si quis ausu temerario machinatus est in mortem domini regis." The Statute
is probably derived in part from this passage in Bracton. See Sir James Fitzjames
Stephen, *A History of the Criminal Law of England* (London: Macmillan, 1883),
II, 248–249; 266–267; Pollock and Maitland, *History of English Law*, II, 503–504.

[181] See M. Lemosse, "La Lèse-Majesté dans la Monarchie Franque," *Revue du
Moyen Âge Latin*, II, (1946), 5–24, which lends support to the views expressed in
this study regarding the omission of *maiestas* in the Germanic legislation.

[182] *Capitulare Ticinense* (a. 801), c. 3.

[183] Frankish *herisliz* in the equivalent of NHG. *Heer zu lassen*.

his master or any freedman his patron, unless, perchance, he can prove
that the master himself or the patron himself has blasphemed against
God, or unless he can prove said master or patron to be pagans, the
persons charged shall be free of his accusation."[184] However, in this
case the basic influences are probably ecclesiastical and not specifically
Germanic. In this remote Alpine district of Rhaetia the Christian adapt-
er of the Roman law seems to have substituted blaspheming the Christian God for malediction against the divine emperor, which had been
an important aspect of *laesa maiestas*. The ecclesiastical Latin word
blasphemare replaces the legal expression *maledicere*.

What final conclusions can we draw? Clearly the *crimen laesae maiestatis* exercised an important influence in the development of the Germanic law of treason by casting the Germanic ideas in Roman form and
at times adding Roman content, although the essentially Germanic
spirit is preserved. One cannot admit, however, the presence in strict
political theory of a genuine *laesa maiestas*, since majesty implies a
deferential allegiance to public authority that is incompatible with the
contractual idea implied in *Treubruch*, which persists as a unifying
principle throughout Germanic customary law. Furthermore, broken
troth remains a personal matter whether it be between subject and king
or between man and lord. The special interest of the king as leader of
his folk and first among his peers is the general welfare of the land,
and whatever harms the folk injures the monarch. In a certain sense the
process of legal evolution has come round the full circle and returned
to the more primitive concepts that characterized the early customary
beginnings of the royal laws and the *Twelve Tables*, yet with profound
differences, for, while history repeats itself, it never repeats itself in
precisely the same way.[185]

---

[184] *Lex Romana Raetica Curiensis* 9, 3; *Lex Romana Visigothorum, Codex,* 9, 3, 2
Interpretatio (Zeumer) M. G. H., *Legum Tomus* V: "Si quis servus dominum suum
aut libertus patronum suum acusare voluerit, nisi forsitan probare potuerit, quid
ipse dominus aut ipse patronus contra Deum blasfemasset, aut paganus eos probare
potuerit, de tale acusatione licenciam habeant."

[185] Shortly after the original preparation of this essay two articles that deserve
mention appeared in the *Journal of Roman History*. These are C. W. Chilton, "The
Roman Law of Treason under the Early Principate," *J.R.H.*, 45 (1955), 73–81, and
R. S. Rogers, "Treason in the Early Empire," *J.R.H.*, 49 (1959), 90–94. Cf. E. Koes-
termann, "Die Majestätsprozesse unter Tiberius," *Historia,* 4 (1955), 72–106.
Although they deal primarily with procedure and penalty, both papers have impli-
cations for political theory. In effect Chilton attacks the Rogers thesis that the Roman
Empire was a state under law. He argues that Roman law changed continually, that
Augustus and Tiberius extended the scope of the law of treason and intensified the

APPENDIX

A. *Codex Justinianus* 9, 8, 5 *Ad Legem Iuliam Maiestatis.*

C. Just. 9, 8, 5, is an enactment of Arcadius and Honorius issued in
A.D. 397. (Cf. *C. Th.* 9, 14, 3 *Ad Legem Corneliam de Sicariis* [Pharr,
pp. 236–237].) This *constitutio* is commonly referred to as the *lex
Quisquis,* so called from the first word of the preface of the law. This
preface states that any person who enters into a criminal conspiracy
with soldiers, civilians, or barbarians and does this under oath shall be
put to the sword as one guilty of *maiestas;* also, his property shall be
confiscated to the *fiscus,* whether he has plotted the death of a member
of the Imperial Council and Consistory, or of the Senate, or of any
other person in the Imperial service. The Emperor is not mentioned
specifically but it can scarcely be doubted that the enactment would
also cover such acts directed at the Imperial person.

Section One adds the concept of attainder or corruption of blood
since the sons of such an offender will be spared their lives although
they merit the fate of their father because the inclination to commit his
crime is inherited. The infamy of their father will accompany them
always. They will always be debarred from holding public office or
performing public duties. Their lot in life will be perpetual want; death
will be a solace and life a punishment.

The later sections of this constitution place detailed and severe restrictions upon the inheritance and disposition of property. Thus, the
fourth section declares that emancipations granted after the commission
of the crime are invalid. Dowries, donations, and all alienations, whether
fraudulent or legal, are null and void from the time that the person

---

penalties in an arbitrary and discriminatory manner, and that it is futile to argue
"the rule of law where no such rule existed." To this Rogers replies that the Roman
law was relatively fixed and conservative although it did "occasionally innovate,"
that Augustus and Tiberius were not arbitrary with respect to the law of treason, and
that "The Empire *was* a reign of law." Both papers gain added significance in the
light of a recent study by H. W. Benario, "Tacitus and the Principate," *Classical
Journal,* 60 (1964), 97–106. This close study of Tacitus forces the conclusion that
some features of the Dominate emerged as early as the emperors of the first century,
and that certain aspects of arbitrary rule antedate by more than two centuries the
eastern influences that come with Aurelian and Diocletian. It indicates that the
Dominate is already incipient in the early Principate, and that the dichotomy between *principatus* and *dominatio,* between constitutional government and unlimited,
arbitrary personal power, appears early within the Roman-Italian frame of reference.
The *principatus* of the earlier years of Tiberius contrasts with the *dominatio* of
Domitian. Benario concludes that "there is no doubt that one of Tacitus' themes was
the change from *principatus* to *dominatio.*"

implicated decided to join the conspiracy. The *dolo malo* principle is basic here, and in this connection one must not overlook the parenthetical statement introduced into the preface: "eadem enim severitate voluntatem sceleris qua effectum puniri iura voluerunt." ("The laws are determined to punish the intent to commit the crime with the same severity as the perpetrated act itself.")

Of this declaration Kübler says:

Here we find something entirely new and unheard of, for the law of Honorius punishes as high treason not only the completed act, the attempt, and the preliminary acts but the mere intent itself. Neither before nor since has the sentence been laid down with such stark nakedness in any laws of the civilized world. The penalties of the *lex Quisquis* permit the most innocent man in the world to be brought to the scaffold.

Kübler adds ironically that another new feature consists in the declaration that the beginning of the incompetence of the alleged criminal with respect to the disposition of his property reaches back to the precise point of time at which the idea of committing high treason first came to the traitor's mind, "surely a legislative finesse of the highest order."

So harsh and unjust was this legislation that Heineccius, a German jurisconsult of early modern times (1681–1741), said that it was written in blood, not in ink. Certainly this unfortunate enactment of the later Empire provides the background from which those dangerous concepts of attainder and corruption of blood in treason cases were transmitted to the English Common Law at the time of the revival of the Roman Law in the later Middle Ages. Compare B. Kübler, "Maiestas," pages 554–558, for a detailed examination of this legislation.

B. Paulus *Sententiae* 5, 29, 1–2 *Ad Legem Iuliam Maiestatis.*

1. Lege Iulia maiestatis tenetur is, cuius ope consilio adversus imperatorem vel rem publicam arma mota sunt exercitusve eius in insidias deductus est; quive iniussu imperatoris bellum gesserit dilectumve habuerit, exercitum comparaverit, sollicitaverit, deseruerit imperatorem, his antea in perpetuum aqua et igni interdicebatur; nunc vero humiliores bestiis obiciuntur vel vivi exuruntur, honestiores capite puniuntur. quod crimen non solum facto, sed et verbis impiis ac maledictis maxime exacerbatur.

2. In reum maiestatis iquiri prius convenit, quibus opibus, qua factione, quibus hoc auctoribus fecerit: tanti enim criminis reus non obtentu adulationis alicuius, sed ipsius admissi causa puniendus est, et ideo, cum de eo quaeritur, nulla dignitas a tormentis excipitur.

This text is contained in Huschke-Seckel-Kübler, *Iurisprudentiae anteiustinianae reliquiae* (Leipzig: Teubner 1911), II (1), 156–157.

These two statements concerning *maiestas* in Paulus *Opinions* (*Sententiae*) 5, 29, 1–2, represent an extremely interesting summary of the essential elements of the crime as reflected in the Roman law of the Imperial period. The first section lists the basic treasonable acts of the late Republic as set forth in the *lex Iulia maiestatis* and condensed from Ulpian, Marcian, and Scaevola, now incorporated in *Digest* 48, 4, 1–4. The phraseology is transcribed with little change save that the earlier jurists define the crime to be against the Republic and *populus romanus*, whereas Paulus makes the emperor the prime objective of *maiestas*. There is a significant shift from republican to imperial emphasis in Paulus. A comparison of the several phrases in the first section of Paulus with their counterparts in the *Digest* reveals these striking parallels, illustrating similarity of content but divergence of emphasis:

Paulus *Sent.* 5, 29, 1	Adversus imperatorem vel rem publican arma mota sunt
Digest 48, 4, 1	quove quis contra rem publicam arma ferat (Ulpian *De officiis proconsulis*, Book VII)
Paulus *Sent.* 5, 29, 1	exercitusve eius in insidias deductus est
Digest 48, 4, 4	cuiusve dolo malo exercitus populi Romani in insidias deductus hostibusve proditus est (Scaevola *Rules*, Book IV)
Paulus *Sent.* 5, 29, 1	quive iniussu imperatoris bellum gesserit dilectumve habuerit, exercitum comparaverit
Digest 48, 4, 3	eadem lege tenetur et qui iniussu principis bellum gesserit dilectumve habuerit exercitum comparaverit (Marcian *Institutes*, Book XIV)
Paulus *Sent.* 5, 29, 1	sollicitaverit
Digest 48, 4, 1	quive milites sollicitaverit concitaveritve (Ulpian *De officiis proconsulis*, Book VII)
Paulus *Sent.* 5, 29, 1	deseruerit imperatorem
Digest 48, 4, 2	aut qui exercitum deseruit (Ulpian *Disputations*, Book VIII)
Digest 48, 4, 3	quive imperium exercitumve populi Romani deseruerit (Marcian *Institutes*, Book XIV)

It may be noted further that the *cuius ope consilio* formula of Paulus replaces the usual *cuius dolo malo* formula of the *Digest* for expressing malicious and evil intent. In addition, Paulus introduces the *aquae et ignis interdictio*, the distinction between *humiliores* and *honestiores* with the differing penalities, and the declaration that the offense must be considered not merely in terms of the overt act but of impious maledictions as well which enhance the heinous nature of the crime.

The second section involves a critical question of translation and interpretation that has proved most troublesome, centering on the clause: "tanti enim criminis reus non obtentu adulationis alicuius, sed ipsius admissi causa puniendus est." This passage in Paulus should be considered in connection with *Digest* 48, 4, 7, 3, quoting from Book XII of the *Pandects* of Modestinus: "Hoc tamen crimen iudicibus non in occasione ob principalis maiestatis venerationem habendum est, sed in veritate." ("This crime must not be considered as an opportunity for the veneration of the majesty of the emperor; on the contrary, it must be considered in the light of the truth.") S. P. Scott (*The Civil Law*, Vol 11, p. 27) renders *in veritate* with the clause "for this should only be done where the charge is true," which gives a very different meaning to the entire statement.

That this passage has long created difficulties is apparent from the commentary of Dionysius Gothofredus on *Digest* 48, 4, 7, 3 (p. 722, n. 60, in the Amsterdam edition of 1663 of the *Corpus Juris Civilis*) in which he quotes Haloander, a German jurist and legal interpreter: "Non in occasione, id est, non obtentu adulationis." In other words this great jurist definitely associates the expression in Paulus *Sententiae* 5, 29, 2, with that found in *Digest* 48, 4, 7, 3. He then proceeds with the following illustration: In response to a certain man accusing Falanius (cf. Tacitus *Annals* 1, 73) of admitting a certain infamous person among the worshippers of Augustus, Tiberius stated that his father had not been elevated among the gods so that his worship might be turned to the ruin of citizens. And for this reason he gave an opinion to this effect: Judges should not decide rashly that every deed whatsoever done by anyone, is done against the Prince, nor likewise ought they to seize every opportunity zealously with such eagerness and diligence as would be employed in punishing acts against the Prince, for they should not strive to please the Prince and Republic by instances of that sort and diligence of that kind. Gothofredus concludes that not every word or deed directed against the Prince is the crime of majesty. He also makes it clear that judges must base their decisions on the facts of the case and not with the ulterior motive of flattering the emperor and public authorities.

Finally I wish to acknowledge my indebtedness to Professor Clyde Pharr, of The University of Texas, for assistance in connection with this translation problem. He has further been kind enough to permit me to quote his analysis of the relationship between these passages as follows:

In both these passages, the point is made that no person, either accuser or judge, shall accuse anyone of high treason [*maiestas*] in an attempt to curry favor with the emperor, using the accusation simply as pretext [*obtentus*] whereby the accuser may display his devotion to the emperor, by such an act of adulation. The passage from the *Digest* closely parallels the one from Paulus from which it was probably derived ultimately. *In veritate* of *Digest* corresponds to *ipsius admissi* of Paulus and may be translated variously: "in the light of the truth, according to the actual circumstances, according to the actual facts of the case."

This conclusion convinces me that Scott's translation of *in veritate* (*Digest* 48, 4, 7, 3) is in error and that *ipsius admissi causa* in Paulus refers to the actual deed or crime. It also supports Haloander's identification of *obtentus* with *occasio* in the sense of pretext, opportunity, occasion, which was cited in the commentary of Gothofredus.

II

The Idea of Majesty in Roman Political Thought*

No principles of Roman Law are more fundamental or more characteristic of the Roman legal mind than those which relate to the idea of majesty, since this concept colors and affects directly all aspects of sovereignty and allegiance in the Roman state. In fact, one may say that in Roman political thought allegiance is the obverse and treason the reverse of the coin called "majesty." As we shall see, care must be taken not to confuse the limited modern legal definitions of treason with the broad field covered by *maiestas* in Roman thinking or to allow a narrow procedural approach to the crime of *lèse-majesté* to prevent one from grasping the far-reaching implications of majesty in political theory. Considering the matter from the angle of criminal law, Pollock and Maitland have remarked aptly that "treason is a crime which has a vague circumference, and more than one centre,"[1] while Bisoukides in his admirable monograph on high treason has cautioned that the entire concept of crimes against the state is rendered elusive on account of the difficulty in defining the object of the crime.[2] Obviously treasons and hostile acts against the state generally will vary and assume differing forms suited to the nature of each particular state in question. In the

* Reprinted by permission of the publishers from *Essays in History and Political Theory in Honor of Charles Howard McIlwain* (Cambridge, Massachusetts: Harvard University Press, Copyright, 1936, by the President and Fellows of Harvard College), pp. 168–198.

[1] Pollock and Maitland, *History of English Law before the Time of Edward I*, (2nd ed., Cambridge: University Press, 1923), II, 502.

[2] Bisoukides, *Der Hochverrat* (Berlin: Carl Heymanns Verlag, 1903), p. 3.

Roman state it will be found that treason is circumscribed within the boundaries of majesty and that the violation of majesty is the prime objective of the crime. Furthermore, in the case of our legal and political heritage from Rome the idea of majesty assumes a position of primary importance, since it reflects with especial clarity the native, intrinsic, peculiar character of the Roman state throughout its entire history, while the failure of the Germanic kingdoms, founded upon the ruins of the Roman Empire, to incorporate the theory of majesty in their political structures marks a significant turning point in the evolution of political thought.

Various efforts have been made to account for this unique concept as regards both its origin and its nature. In the *Strafrecht*, published in 1899,[3] Mommsen seeks to establish the matter of origin on a strictly historical basis by ascribing its beginnings to the struggles which resulted in the creation of the tribunate in the early fifth century B.C.[4] According to this theory, the idea of majesty entered criminal procedure as a result of political restrictions placed on the leaders of the Roman plebs. Since these leaders lacked the *imperium* as bestowed upon regular magistrates of the Roman community through a *lex curiata de imperio*, offenses committed against them or, indeed, any violation of fundamental plebeian rights could not be comprehended under the scope of *perduellio*. In other words, plebeian officers were not protected by the law of *perduellio*, whose sanctions supported the patrician magistracies. "The plebeians now demanded for their constitution and their leaders the same dignity and the same rank, as belonged to the community and its magistrates who possessed the *imperium*. And it was in the attempt to secure this equality that one first hears the phrase 'diminishing the tribunician majesty',"[5] Eventually this became the *crimen imminutae maiestatis*, and the expression persisted with a wider meaning when the tribunes of the plebs acquired governing powers effective over all classes

---

[3] T. Mommsen, *Römisches Strafrecht* (Leipzig: S. Hirzel, 1889), pp. 538 *et seq.*, and detailed notes.

[4] *Ibid.*, p. 538, n. 2. Here Mommsen suggests that *potestas* and *maiestas* are correlative terms, the former connected with the beginning of the patrician magistracies and the latter with the new plebeian offices.

[5] *Ibid.*, p. 538, where Mommsen argues in support of his view that a plebiscite was not a *lex publica* and that tribunes were not magistrates. Note that *perduellio* embraced originally any act committed against the Roman state in which the attacker is regarded as a *hostis*, later it was restricted to designate an "interior enemy" or traitor. See E. C. Clark, *History of Roman Private Law* (Cambridge: University Press, 1919), Part III: *Regal Period*, pp. 595–599.

of citizens after the great revolt of 287 B.C. *Maiestas* became associated with the *tribunicia potestas,* and the *crimen imminutae maiestatis* came to stand in the same relation to plebeian officers as *perduellio* stood to the magistrates with *imperium.* Thus, Mommsen holds that by origin *maiestas* is opposed to *imperium,*[6] although after a time both words came to be used more or less interchangeably. And, ultimately, not only attacks upon the rights of the plebeians but every injury done the prestige of the Roman state resulted in a criminal prosecution, as an offense against the majesty of the Roman people.

Shortly thereafter (1904) this view was seriously questioned by Humbert and Lécrivain as a conjecture lacking definite proof,[7] and in 1926, by a careful analysis of the passages in Cicero and Asconius[8] upon which the argument is largely based, Schisas pointed out that Mommsen's evidence was drawn from events of a late date and is entirely inadequate to prove that "the technical term *maiestas* has its origin in the violation of the tribunicial dignity in the early time of the republic, i.e. before the equalization of the classes."[9] Here Schisas leaves the subject without solution and devotes the balance of his monograph to procedural matters without reference to the theory of majesty.

However, in 1908 Dr. Erich Pollack, in a study entitled *Der Majestätsgedanke in Römischen Recht,* attacked the problem from the angle of political theory and comparative institutions. The weakness of his method consists largely in the fact that his documentation is limited to late literary and legal sources and is not strictly historical. Consequently he presents much that is inference and logical deduction rather than proof. Nevertheless, he advances beyond all other investigators, with the possible exception of Mommsen, since he realized that majesty is not merely a technical expression, possessing significance for criminal law alone, but represents a unique concept in political thought and so belongs to the history of ideas as well as to the history of criminal procedure.

Pollack showed that in Roman thought majesty was considered originally an attribute of the gods and that in its application to criminal law

---

[6] Cf. *minuta maiestas* as opposed to *perduellio* in public criminal law.

[7] Daremberg et Saglio, *Dictionnaire des antiquités grècques et romaines,* article "Maiestas" by G. Humbert and Ch. Lecrivain (Graz, Austria: Akademische Druck-u. Verlagsanstalt, 1963), III (2), 1556.

[8] Cicero *De Inventione* 2, 17, 52; Asconius, *Ad Cic. pro Cornelio,* p. 60.

[9] P. M. Schisas, *Offences against the State in Roman Law* (London: University of London Press, 1926), pp. 6–15.

human punishment was regarded as divine revenge.[10] Thus, the authority of the highest deity is the *maiestas* connected with his person; law is established not by the will of the people but by the divine will; punishment is regarded as the justice of the gods; and the criminal is considered a sacrifice in expiation of his crime.[11] *Fas* has its foundation in the will of the gods and places an absolute limitation on popular sovereignty, while the ideas expressed by the terms *sacer, sacratus, sacratio, sacrosanctitas,* and *sacramentum* are founded on the concept of majesty and lie at the background of the earliest Roman criminal law.[12] Human law assumes a fixed form gradually, until, at last, the constitution of the community is constructed on the basis of two parallel systems of law—the human and the divine, *ius* and *fas*.[13]

Next, as a matter of theory without regard to specific historical origin, Pollack points out that the religious principle of expiation is the chief support of the tribunate and through the sanction of divine will gives an appearance of ordered justice to the unlimited tribunician *auxilium*. The civil constitution is *lex publica*; the independent enactments of the plebs, *lex sacrata*. The consuls, chosen by the assembled citizens, are *magistratus populi Romani* and possess the *imperium*; the tribunes of the plebs are not magistrates and lack *imperium*. The *potestas* of the former is *legitima*, of the latter *sacrosancta;* the former are *lege inviolati*, the latter *religione inviolati*. Sacred law underlies secular law, and *fas* is

[10] E. Pollack, *Der Majestätsgedanke im Römischen Recht: Eine Studie auf dem Gebiet des Römischen Stattsrechts* (Leipzig: Verlag von Viet, 1908), pp. 11–21.

[11] A. H. J. Greenidge, *Roman Public Life* (London: Macmillan, 1911), p. 54 and n. 2. He notes that "We cannot, indeed, say that there was a time when the Roman law regarded every crime as a sin"; yet expiation as punishment for sin indicates the deep religious impress of *fas* in the matter of penalties. This general subject is developed at length in an essay on "Religion as a Source of Law" by J. L. Strachan-Davidson in *Problems of the Roman Criminal Law* (Oxford: Clarendon, 1912), I, 1–27.

[12] See *Leges Regiae* 1, 7; 4, 1; also 2, 12 in P. Girard, *Textes de droit romain,* (3rd ed.; Paris: A. Rousseau, 1903), for formula *sacer esto (paricidas esto)* pronounced as penalty of excommunication in cases of impiety which could not be expiated; also in C. G. Bruns, *Fontes iuris romani antiqui* (7th ed., by Otto Gradenwitz; Tübingen: Mohr, 1909), Part I: *Leges et Negotia* (Romulus 13; Servius 6). Cf. *Leges XII Tabularum* 8, 31. Greenidge (*Roman Public Life,* p. 55) states that excommunication replaced immolation of accursed persons. Note later usage of *aquae et ignis interdictio.*

[13] Greenidge, *Roman Public Life,* p. 52: "[Fas] is a law which has hardly any limits, running parallel with civil justice [*ius*] but far beyond its bounds." Note that *maiestas* is carried from *fas* into the field of *ius* through its association with *perduellio* in late republican times, but reverts back to a religious sanction under the "god-kingship" of the Dominate.

the mainstay and chief support of *ius*. Thus, Pollack avoids Mommsen's pitfall of strict historicity and is not too definite. He builds his case on presumptive evidence, indicating that the sanctions of the tribunate rest upon the *maiestas deorum*. Hence *maiestas* as the motive power in divine *fas* is transmitted to men through the *sacrosanctitas* of the tribunes with their concomitant power of a self-help (*auxilium*) and so stands opposed to the *imperium* of the magistrates. Indeed, majesty might almost be conceived as a limitation placed upon the *imperium* to be associated with such other restrictions, as the sphere *domi*, loss of arbitrary *coercitio*, and the popular right of *provocatio*.

However, the problem of the tribunate forms only an incidental part of Pollack's general theory of majesty, which is much too elaborate for analysis here. He finds that the specific concept bridging the gap from the divine society to the organized state (*res publica*) of the corporate *populus romanus* consists in the *maiestas patris*, for "in the *patria potestas* the idea of majesty has received its first material form."[14] The majesty possessed by the individual *patres* is transferred to the corporate body or sovereign people, conceived as a personality endowed with the *maiestas populi Romani*.[15] This corporate majesty receives concrete expression first in the *rex*, later in the magistracies, and ultimately in the Senate and the Principate.[16] Thus far, Pollack's thesis is logically deduced, is supported by myth and tradition and by the testimony of later writers, and is strengthened by analogy.

But, as the principle of the dyarchy weakens and the prince ceases to be merely the first citizen of the state (*primus inter pares*) and its highest magistrate, the fiction of popular sovereignty disappears and majesty becomes a personal attribute of the reigning monarch. "The idea of majesty has here experienced its principal change inasmuch as

[14] E. Pollack, *Der Majestätsgedanke*, p. 25, n. 2: "No fine distinction is consciously drawn between *maiestas patris* and *patria potestas*. *Potestas* indicates rather the legal sphere of the father's power with the master's right of command proceeding from it. Here the father is more *rex* than *pater*. *Maiestas*, on the contrary, means rather the prestige inhering in the father as *parens*; it is an expression for the holy awe felt for the procreator and the respect inbred from earliest childhood on the basis of the practice of sacred rites and observances." Cf. Livy, 8, 7, 8; 4, 45, 8; 8, 17, 15. See Pollack, *Der Majestätsgedanke*, Ch. III (Die gewaltherrliche Majestät). Cf. Edward Gibbon, *History of the Decline and Fall of the Roman Empire*, ed. by J. B. Bury (London: Methuen, 1896), IV, 473–475, on the *patria potestas*: "The majesty of a parent was armed with the power of life and death."

[15] Pollack, *Der Majestätsgedanke*, p. 28.

[16] *Ibid.*, Ch. V (Die Majestas Magistratus), pp. 101–111, and (Die Majestas des Königs), pp. 111–119; Ch. VI (Die Majestas des Senats), pp. 120–125; Ch. VII (Die Majestas des Prinzeps), pp. 125–141.

the personal side of the highest magistracy has now become the keynote of the new era."[17] The individual magistracies seem to be merged into a single office, and the view appears that no more will an officer of the state be selected for the office, but that the office is now created for the officer. "Das *imperium* macht nicht mehr wie einst die Magistratur aus, sondern als *imperator* schafft der Princeps erst das *imperium*."[18] Finally, through the title of reverence, *Augustus,* a religious element, recalling the sacred character of the old kingship, is introduced into an office established by law. The view that the tribunes were originally *religione inviolati,* not *lege inviolati,* has never vanished, and the shifting of emphasis to the veneration implied in *Augustus, sebastos,* belongs to the same religious category.[19] The *tribunicia potestas* and the imperial cult are allied politico-religious expedients. It is only at the end with the shift from the Principate to the Dominate that Pollack refuses to carry his theory to its logical conclusion. For him this change means the end of the development of the idea of majesty, which he regards as the expression of a constitutional principle at law—indeed, substantially a philosophical principle rooted in natural law. "It could not become the symbol for an unconstitutional despotism."[20] At this point some consideration of the source data becomes necessary.

The philological evidence deserves examination, although the derivation of the word reveals relatively little. In many respects the best estimate of these factors may be found in Kübler's recent article on *maiestas* (1928) in Pauly-Wissowa-Kroll's *Realencyclopädie.*[21] Mommsen, and Pollack and Schisas after him, point out that the word *maiestas* comes from the comparative *maior,* reflecting a position of superiority, just as *potestas* is derived from *potior,* meaning more powerful.[22] Thus, *maiestas* denotes an elevated position, a certain pre-eminence demanding respect from inferiors—not so much by virtue of greater power (*Macht*) as

---

[17] *Ibid.,* p. 127.

[18] *Ibid.,* p. 129.

[19] *Ibid.,* p. 140. Many philologists consider *Augustus* derived from the same root as *auctoritas.* See A. D. Nock in *Cambridge Ancient History* (Cambridge: University Press, 1934), X, 483.

[20] *Ibid.,* p. 141.

[21] Pauly-Wissowa-Kroll, *Realencyclopädie der classichen Altertumswissenschaft,* article "Maiestas" by B. Kübler (Stuttgart: Metzler, 1928), XXVII, 542–559.

[22] It is interesting to note that St. Isidore of Seville in the seventh century (d. 636) held this same view regarding the derivation of the word. See *Etymologiae* 10, 238: "Dictus autem reus maiestatis, quia maius est laedere patriam quam civem unum." (Note deviation of *maies* [*tatis*] from *maius.*) His reason for the derivation is characteristic and need not be considered necessarily true.

through higher prestige (*Ansehen*).[23] Kübler, however, notes that the word escapes definition and may perhaps be rendered best as grandeur (*Hoheit*) or sublimity (*Erhabenheit*).[24]

The literary writers of the classical period provide more valuable evidence, since they endeavor to define the term as it was understood among their contemporaries.[25] These definitions give little direct aid in solving the moot problem of the origin of the idea, but they do reflect current opinion at a time when the idea possessed vital significance in legal and political thought. One must bear in mind, also, that these statements are commonly but partial, dealing with certain phases of the idea as related to the gods, the *populus romanus* or its allied peoples, the *pater familias*, and the magistrates or the prince, so that they must be considered collectively if one is to gain a rounded impression. A few significant examples may be cited. Cicero in *De Inventione* states that "to detract in any way from the dignity [*dignitas*] or sway [*amplitudo*] or power [*potestas*] of the people or of those to whom the people have granted power is to diminish majesty [*maiestas*]."[26] In *De Oratore* he says: "If majesty is the sway and dignity of a state, it is diminished by him who surrenders an army to the enemies of the Roman people, not by him who hands over the man who did this into the power of the Roman people."[27] In the *Philippics* he speaks of diminishing the majesty

[23] Mommsen, *Römisches Strafrecht*, p. 538; Pollack, *Der Majestätsgedanke*, p. 3; Schisas, *Offences against the State*, pp. 6–7.

[24] Kübler, "Maiestas," 542. Note W. Knitschky, *Das Verbrechen des Hochverraths* (Jena: Mauke's Verlag, 1874), p. 36. He remarks that the classical jurists do not include all breaches of law, such as *peculatus*, *repetundarum*, and *ambitus*, under majesty, but only those offenses which injure the *Hoheitsrechte* and *Machtstellung* of the state. Cf. Bisoukides, *Der Hochverrat*, p. 14: "alles, was möglischerweise dem Stolze, dem Ansehen, der Würde und Hoheit des römischen Staates Schaden zufügen könnte, ist crimen maiestatis."

[25] Extensive references to citations of the term *maiestas* in classical authors may be found in Pollack, *Der Majestätsgedanke*, footnotes on pp. 4–7, and Kübler, "Maiestas," 542–544.

[26] Cicero *De Inventione*, ed. by R. Klotz (Lipsiae: Teubner, 1851), 2, 17, 53: "Maiestatem minuere est de dignitate aut amplitudine aut potestate populi aut eorum, quibus populus potestatem dedit, aliquid derogare." Cf. Cicero *Ad Her.* 2, 12, 17: "Maiestatem is minuit, qui ea tollit, ex quibus rebus civitatis amplitudo constat . . . qui amplitudinem civitatis detrimento afficit"; *In Verrem* 4, 41, 88: "est maiestatis, quod imperii nostri, gloriae, rerum gestarum monumenta evertere atque asportare ausus est."

[27] Cicero *De Oratore*, ed. by A. S. Wilkins (Oxford: Clarendon, 1892), 2, 39, 164: "Si maiestas est amplitudo ac dignitas civitatis, is eam minuit, qui exercitum hostibus populi Romani tradidit, non qui eum, qui id fecisset, populi Romani potestati tradidit."

of the Roman people by an act of violence (*vis*),[28] and elsewhere he
mentions in a single connection the authority (*auctoritas*) of the Senate
and the majesty of the Roman people.[29] Quintilian quotes Cicero (*Orat.
Part.* 30, 105) to the effect that "*Maiestas* consists in the dignity of the
Roman empire [*imperium*] and the Roman name [i.e., reputation]."[30]
In *De Divinatione* (1, 38, 82) and *De Natura Deorum* (2, 30, 77) Cicero
refers to the *maiestas deorum;* in *Pro Rabirio Perduellionis Reo* to the
imperium populi Romani maiestasque (7, 20) and to *vestrae maiestatis*
(i.e., of the Senate) (12, 35). Livy provides numerous additional examples of the use of this expression in various contexts, especially relative to the majesty of the different magistrates and public officers, such
as consul, dictator, king, and lictor.[31] There are also references to the
majesty of a class (*ordo*) or an office (*honor*) in a more general sense,
as well as of the Senate. Finally he speaks of the Roman majesty itself,
the majesty of the Roman name, the majesty of the laws and of the con-
sular *imperium,* and the majesty of the gods.[32] The testimony of writers

[28] Cicero *Philippics*, ed. by W. C. A. Ker (London: Heinemann, 1926), 1, 9, 21:
"qui maiestatem populi Romani minuerit per vim"; also "de vi et maiestatis
damnati."
[29] *Ibid.*, 3, 5, 13: "auctoritatem huius ordinis maiestatemque populi Romani."
[30] Quintilian *Institutes*, trans. by H. E. Butler (London: Heinemann, 1922), 7,
3, 35: "Ut Cicero dicit, 'Maiestas est in imperii atque in nominis populi Romani
dignitate'."
[31] Selected references from Livy reveal the following usages of the term: *con-
sulum maiestas* (2, 23, 14; 3, 10, 3); *summa rerum ac maiestas consularis imperii*
(3, 6, 9) = supreme control and majesty; *lex minuendae suae* [the consul's] *maiestatis* (3, 24, 9); *maiestatis patrum* (3, 69, 4; 6, 40, 3; 22, 3, 4); *maiestatem dicta-
toriam* (4, 14, 2; 8, 30, 11); *regiae maiestatis* (4, 2, 8); *iuris aut maiestatis* [of the
king's office] (4, 3, 9); *imperatoriae maiestatis* (7, 14, 2); [*lictoris*] *maiestatem* (2,
29, 12); *maiestatis magistratuum* (2, 36, 3; 9, 34, 23); *maiestatem summi ordinis
imminuisse* (3, 63, 9–10); *maieste honoris* (9, 26, 20); *maiestatem patriam* (8,
7, 15); *maiestatem romani nominis* (2, 48, 8); *maiestatis romanae* (3, 69, 3);
maiestatis imperii (3, 48, 2; 8, 34, 5; 8, 35, 4; 21, 63, 10); *maiestatis gentium* (6,
40, 4); *maiestate petentium* [candidates] (5, 14, 5); *et non modo legum aut patrum
maiestatis sed ne deorum quidem satis metuens* (22, 3, 4).
It is interesting to note in this connection that B. O. Foster (London: Putnam,
1919–) translates *maiestas* as dignity eight times (3, 11, 5; 3, 48, 2; 3, 69, 4; 4, 3,
9; 4, 38, 2; 6, 40, 4; 8, 7, 15; 21, 63, 10), as honor twice (6, 30, 9; 7, 14, 2), and
once each as prestige (8, 30, 11), awe (9, 26, 20), greatness (7, 22, 9), and great
position (22, 29, 11). *Maiestas* is associated with *gravitas*, relative to personal appearance (5, 41, 8). *Venerabilem* is rendered as majesty (1, 8, 2); likewise *amplitudinem* (5, 21, 3). In classical Latin *dignitas* has the specific meaning of rank (1,
13, 17; 1, 42, 4 = *gradus dignitatis*), and distinctions (5, 25, 3), but also the
general sense of good reputation (1, 44, 3), dignity (2, 2, 9), and even majesty
(5, 23, 11).
[32] In connection with the majesty of the gods, Livy (1, 53, 3) makes a statement

like Tacitus and Suetonius indicates some change in the usage of the term during the early Empire, limiting its application to expressions of personal regard for the prince (almost a title at times) and to the crime of *lèse-majesté*.[33]

It will be noted in the examples cited that the word *maiestas* is commonly associated with a group of kindred expressions, such as *imperium, potestas, auctoritas, dignitas, amplitudo.* A close study of this terminology cannot be attempted here; yet it should be pointed out that, while nearly or fully synonymous in some cases, certain basic differences do exist. Nevertheless, these relationships appertain to an integrated nexus of ideas, so that *maiestas* shares elements common to the others. Thus, the meaning of the word *imperium* may range all the way from any order or command to its technical legal usages as a special concrete grant of supreme authority or sovereign power[34] by the Roman people to a magistrate through the medium of a *lex curiata de imperio.* Also it may convey the looser and more general ideas of power, dominion, and empire,[35] and is perhaps the nearest Roman equivalent to the modern idea of legal sovereignty. *Potestas*,[36] on the other hand, is a vaguer term,

---

involving an unusual use of the term: "concepit animo eam amplitudinem Iovis templi quae digna deum hominumque rege, quae Romano imperio, quae ipsius etiam loci *maiestate* esset." Yet I am not quite sure that even here Livy has the modern idea of the "majesty of the site" (i.e., a majestic or imposing site), but rather the majesty that will be attached to this location by virtue of its association with Jupiter. I am uncertain which meaning Foster had in mind in his translation. In classical Latin, however, *maiestas* tends to be a specific attribute, not a general descriptive term. Cf. 1, 38, 7: *amplitudinem* (loci) = splendor of the place; 5, 23, 11: *amplitudine templi* = grandeur of the temple.

[33] As an expression of personal regard, note Tacitus *Annals* 1, 42: *sua maiestas*; 1, 46: *maiestatem imperatoriam*; Suetonius, 2, 25: *suae maiestatis*; 5, 17: *maiestati principali*; 7, 10: *ex imperii maiestate.* As a crime, note Tacitus *Annals* 3, 24: *violatae maiestatis*; 3, 38; 3, 67: *maiestatis crimine*; Suetonius 2, 37: *maiestatis eius imminui*; 3, 2: *iudicium maiestatis*; 6, 32: *lege maiestatis.* Of course, the new usage evolved gradually out of the earlier meanings, and it is clear that Suetonius employs the word in various senses. Cf. his reference in 3, 30 to the ancient majesty and power of the Senate and magistrates (*senatui ac magistratibus et maiestate pristina et potestate*).

[34] Cf. H. F. Jolowicz, *Historical Introduction to the Study of Roman Law* (Cambridge: University Press, 1932), pp. 7, 44, on *imperium* as a grant of undefined, unlimited power.

[35] The idea "empire" would probably refer to range of sway rather than a delimited area according to Roman habits of thinking, though it may approximate "realm" in post-Augustan Latin. Cf. *regnum, dominatus, principatus.*

[36] See Pollack, *Der Majestätsgedanke*, pp. 102 and 103, n. 2, on the relation of *imperium* to *potestas*, where he states: "They are both derivatives of the idea of majesty. *Imperium* is the unlimited power of jurisdiction, military command, and,

but, as Greenidge says, "was the only word which expressed the *generic* power of the magistracy."[37] Hence, in a narrow technical sense it refers to the functions, powers, or authority of an office, as the *tribunicia potestas*, but also it has the general sense of dominion, rule, empire, and, like *imperium*, approximates sovereign power. *Auctoritas* connotes mere authorization, or permissive power or right, as in *auctoritas senatus*, as well as the looser sense of personal influence and prestige. *Auctoritas* follows as a consequence of possessing *potestas* and is derived from *potestas*; one has *potestas* and exercises *auctoritas*.[38] For example, Professor McIlwain is undoubtedly justified in translating *potestas* as legal sovereignty or authority and *auctoritas* as actual political power in Cicero *De Legibus* 3, 12, 28.[39] On the other hand, the expression *numen* refers to divine sway, power, or will—even divine majesty—as opposed to human *potestas* or the *imperium*,[40] while *vis* is usually mere force or might without restriction, as opposed to right or *ius*.[41] Such terms as *dignitas, decus,* and *amplitudo* embrace a somewhat different range of

---

accordingly, the highest power of command in general. *Potestas* is simply the power of command [*Befehlsgewalt*] as exercised by offices lacking *imperium*." Cf. Livy, 2, 1, 7 (*imperium consulare* vs. *regia potestate*) and 3, 9, 10 (*consulare imperium* vs. *tribuniciam potestatem*). Also the edition of Cicero *De Legibus*, by C. W. Keyes (London: Heinemann, 1928), p. 467. n. 7: "*Imperium* was the full power of the state, originally held by the king, and exercised by the higher republican magistrates. *Potestas* was a general word for the ordinary power of the magistrate," especially as applied to magistrates without *imperium*, such as *quaestors*. Cf. Cicero *Philippics*, ed. by Ker, who contrasts *imperium* or military command with *potestas* or civil power on the basis of *Phil.* 5, 16, 45. Note Strachan-Davidson, *Roman Criminal Law*, I, 103 (also pp. 25–26). He includes military, judicial, administrative, and religious functions under the same *imperium*, and states: "The *imperium* according to its original idea, though only a derived and magisterial power, conferred not by Heaven but by the will of the sovereign *populus*, is, when once conferred, a single and indivisible power. . . . This *imperium* or supreme magisterial power is from the first the sole basis of criminal jurisdiction."

[37] Greenidge, *Roman Public Life*, p. 152.

[38] Pollack (*Der Majestätsgedanke*, p. 25, n. 2), in speaking of the *patria potestas* observes that "'Potestas' soll mehr die rechtliche Machtsphäre des Vaters mit der aus ihr strömenden Herrscherbefugnis [i.e., *auctoritas*] bezeichnen." P. Bisoukides (*Der Hochverrat*, p. 14, n. 4), remarks that "while the Senate possessed the *auctoritas*, the people had the *maiestas* from long time past."

[39] See C. H. McIlwain, *The Growth of Political Thought in the West* (New York: Macmillan, 1932), p. 135, n. 1, where he translates the phrase *quom potestas in populo, auctoritas in senatu sit,* as "since the sovereignty is in the people, the actual authority in the Senate," thus transposing *potestas* and *auctoritas* in his English rendering. Cf. Pollack, *Der Majestätsgedanke*, p. 79.

[40] Cf. Livy, 5, 23, 11; 8, 6, 1.

[41] Cf. Cicero *Philippics* 1, 9, 21; Livy, 8, 34, 5–7.

concepts—dignity, reputation, glory, splendor, grandeur, and magnificence.[42]

Perhaps Kübler summarizes the matter most nearly correctly when he says that the idea of majesty differs from *imperium, potestas, dignitas,* and *auctoritas,* and criticizes Pollack for suggesting that majesty may be identified with any of these ideas or may be considered the sum or a combination of them. Rather, he contends, majesty is a peculiar and original conception which bestows upon its possessor reverence (*reverentia*), respect (*honor*), and obedience or deference (*obsequium*) from all men collectively and individually. And it is probably not too much to add that there was more of veneration and deference than of power and authority in the idea of majesty.[43] He who is clothed with majesty is ordinarily viewed more as the passive object of reverence, awe, and esteem than as an active agent exercising positive powers or governing functions, which is the role of sovereignty.

Further problems touching the relation of majesty to sovereignty arise in connection with the expression *maiestas populi comiter conservanto* (or *comiter colunto*).[44] This term is indicative of Rome's scrupulous regard for the majesty of the states with which she was allied or came into contact, and is probably connected with earlier ideas regarding the *maiestas deorum.* Each city had its own deities, its own *fas,* its own *maiestas,* and mutual regard for all religious agencies and prescriptions was essential to friendly intercourse between states.[45] *Fas* underlies the archetypal international law (*ius gentium*) and regulates the peace between the divine population of all cities. As a result of the transmutation of the Latin League and the absorption of rival states into the Roman Federation through the fiction of the *foedus aequum,* Rome was enabled to leave these mutual religious relationships unchanged.[46] In

[42] Note that *dignitas* as reputation is an idea allied with *auctoritas* as influence.

[43] Kübler, "Maiestas," p. 542, makes a less strong statement: "Dieses [*Maiestas*] bezeichnet ebensosehr *potestas, amplitudo* wie auch *splendor* und *gloria,* etwa das, was man heute *Prestige* nennt."

[44] Mommsen, *Römisches Strafrecht,* p. 538, n. 3, and T. Mommsen, *Römisches Staatsrecht* (Darmstadt: Wissenschaftliche Buchgesellschaft, 1963), III, 664, n. 1; Kübler, "Maiestas," pp. 543–544, and his references to the Romans as a "chosen people," based on Cicero *Phil.* 6, 19, and *In Cat.* 2, 11.

[45] See Strachen-Davidson, *Roman Criminal Law,* I, 19–29, for the device of the "noxal surrender" in connection with international offenses; also Pollack, *Der Majestätsgedanke,* p. 70.

[46] Kübler's interpretation ("Maiestas," 542) would make subject cities, in reality, sharers of the *maiestas populi Romani* in accordance with the formula *comiter conservanto.* The various subject *maiestates* are absorbed into the *maiestas* of the Roman state.

a sense, the unimpaired *maiestas* of cities was a necessary corollary to independence. Loss of independence brought diminution of majesty. Consequently, the form and appearance of independence were guaranteed to allied cities, while the substance disappeared. Under these circumstances Rome is revealed not as one sovereign state among many equally sovereign states (or even as *primus inter pares*), but as sole sovereign exercising suzerainty over inferior subject cities.[47] Rome alone conforms to the test of external or political sovereignty under the formula *universitates superiorem non recognoscentes.* Clearly *maiestas* was not sovereignty;[48] yet the appearance of sovereignty had to be retained and permitted by Rome in subject states in order that she might respect the majesty of these cities—an action deemed necessary on religious grounds. Rome felt that she must sustain majesty even when she had no compunction in destroying sovereignty; the validity of majesty in Roman thinking made it necessary to preserve the fiction of sovereignty.

It may be argued that the true test of sovereignty is not the test of external independence,[49] but, as Cicero states in *De Officiis* 1, 34, 124: "It is the proper function of a magistrate to understand that he represents [or better, as McIlwain translates this passage, *impersonates*] the state [*civitas*] and that it is his duty to preserve its dignity and honor, to maintain its laws, to declare its rights, and to remember all things committed to his trust." This is essentially the substance of internal or legal sovereignty, though it falls short of explicit definition.[50] However, both Pollack and McIlwain warn against the misconception that the Romans lacked the idea of sovereignty merely because they have left no specific definition of it, and then proceed to show that sovereignty must not be

[47] This type of external sovereignty, indicating a supremacy elevated above the competition which was possible in a universal state of the Roman type, was often described as empire (*imperium*). Cf. Livy, 4, 3, 13; 4, 5, 1 (*dominatio*); Cicero *De Re Publica* 2, 3, 5 (*imperii*); *Phil.* 5, 14, 39 (*imperii*).

[48] Although majesty and sovereignty are not identical, both principles command allegiance and both may be violated by acts of treason.

[49] It is hazardous to build a theory of sovereignty on an external basis only, since in that case it rests on the shifting ground of mere might or power, through which alone states can maintain their political supremacy over other states, and not on the solid foundation of legal principle, which exists as an absolute common to all states. Legislation presumes a sovereign. In general, see McIlwain, *Growth of Political Thought,* pp. 386–394, on legislative sovereignty.

[50] In many respects, Cicero in *De Officiis* I, 34, 124, resembles the Bodin of the *Methodus* more than the Bodin of the *Republica* in his emphasis on the executive rather than the legislative. This comment is suggested by Professor McIlwain's note in his *Political Thought,* p. 390, n. 2.

confused with the mere power of the state (*Staatsgewalt*), as exercised by its higher officers (i.e., *auctoritas*).[51] As has been noted above, modern legal sovereignty is most nearly rendered by the Latin term *potestas* or perhaps *imperium*,[52] while Du Cange states that the word sovereignty itself (Fr. *souveraineté*) is derived from the mediaeval Latin *supremitas*, that is, *suprema potestas*.[53] Finally one may observe that when Bodin published the first complete definition of internal legal sovereignty in his *Republic* in 1576 (Latin version, 1586) he ascribed to the state one unlimited or sovereign power (*maiestas*). "Maiestas est summa in cives ac subditos legibusque soluta potesta." ("Sovereignty is the highest power over citizens and subjects and is free from the laws.")[54] However, he significantly adds the phrases *legem dare* and *legem dicere*, to give the law and to declare the law (*De Republica* I, 10 [p. 153]). *Legem dare* can only represent the new modern conception of legislation or lawmaking, whereas *legem dicere* refers to the old mediaeval practice of declaring what was the custom. The sovereign has the right not only to find the law (*dicere*), as in former days, but to create the law (*dare*) as well. Hence sovereignty is the highest power in the state "free of the law to make the law," and *maiestas* means absolute legislative power, which is a distinctly legal conception. This basic power is described also: *maiestas summa potestas summum imperium*. Thus, Bodin defines his legislative principle in strictly legal terms according to earlier Roman practice, but the use of *maiestas* itself as legal sovereignty stands at wide variance with the antique concept embodying veneration, deference, respect, and dignity. The modern

[51] Cf. Pollack, *Der Majestätsgedanke*, pp. 75–76, and McIlwain, *Growth of Political Thought*, p. 118: "All the elements of the modern legalistic conception of sovereignty seem to be present here in their entirety and present for the first time, though Bodin's claim may be conceded that no philosopher or jurisconsult before him had exactly defined it." Kübler, "Maiestas," p. 542, quotes Jellinek: "Verfehlt ist es, die Bezeichnung der Souveränität, deren Begriff überhaupt dem Altertum fremd ist, in der *maiestas* zu sehen."

[52] See McIlwain, *Growth of Political Thought*, p. 132, where he remarks that *potestas* and *imperium* are technical legal terms which connote "not vaguely conceived power or influence, but a concrete and definite piece of constitutional authority established by law."

[53] DuCange, *Glossarium Mediae et Infimae Latinitatis* (Paris: Firmin Didot Fratres, 1840–1850), VI, 458. Cf. W. W. Skeat, *An Etymological Dictionary of the English Language* (4th ed.; Oxford: Clarendon, 1924), p. 584, and *A New English Dictionary on Historical Principles* (Oxford: Clarendon, 1919), IX, 487–489, where it is said that the word sovereign is derived from the late Latin accusative form *superanum*, meaning principal or chief.

[54] J. Bodin, *De Republica* (Paris: J. Du Puys, 1586), I, 8, p. 78.

habit of thought has severed the religious connotation from an idea
which had reflected sentiment rather than law in Roman times. Bodin
is thinking of Roman *potestas,* not Roman *maiestas.*

This is not the place to review the history of the crime of majesty
since that subject has been treated in detail by Mommsen, Humbert,
Schisas, and Kübler;[55] yet one cannot altogether avoid some consideration of the crime in discussing the development of the idea itself.
Mommsen may have erred in his attempt to establish the origin of the
idea in connection with offenses against the tribunate in the early Republic; Pollack pressed back the origin into the undocumented and devious realms of primitive psychology and religion in connection with the
maiestas deorum. Kübler avoids these pitfalls by centering his attention
at the beginning upon the authenticated *lex Appuleia* (103 B.C. ?),
lex Varia (91–90 B.C.), and *lex Cornelia* (81 B.C.), although there are
earlier instances which seem to prove that the idea had long been
rooted in the popular mind and that legal procedures for the violation
of majesty were already known.[56] However, *Kübler* is mainly interested,
as far as the matter of origin is concerned, in drawing the distinction
between the older *perduellio,* which embraced attempts against the
state by an "internal enemy" or traitor,[57] and this newer crime, which
was regarded as an infringement or diminution of the power and glory

---

[55] In addition to works and articles cited previously, see P. J. A. Feuerbach,
Philosophisch-juridische Untersuchung über das Verbrechen des Hochverraths (Erfurt: Henningschen Buchhandlung, 1798); J. Weiske, *Hochverrath und Majestäts-
verbrechen, das Crimen majestatis der Römer* (Leipzig: Verlag von Georg Joachim
Göschen, 1836); J. Zirkler, *Die gemeinrechtliche Lehre vom Majestätsverbrechen
und Hochverrath* (Stuttgart: Franz Heinrich Köhler. 1836); J. F. H. Abegg, "Zur
Geschichte des römischen *crimen majestatis,*" *Archiv des Criminalrechts [Neue
Folge]* (Brunswick: Schwetschke, 1853), pp. 205–238; G. Geib, *Geschichte des
römischen Criminal-processes bis zum Tode Justinian's* (Leipzig: Weidmann'sche
Buchhandlung, 1842), pp. 50–66; W. Rein, *Das Kriminalrecht der Römer von
Romulus bis auf Justinianus* (Leipzig: K. F. Köhler, 1844), pp. 504–597; A. Zumpt,
Das Criminalrecht der römischen Republik (Berlin: F. Dümmler, 1865–1869),
I (2), 324–338, on *perduellio;* II (1), 226–264, 376–392, on *perduellio* and
maiestas; Knitschky, *Das Verbrechen,* pp. 17–41, on "Das römische *crimen maiestatis";* Bisoukides, *Der Hochverrat,* pp. 6–33, on the Roman Law; Pollack, *Der
Majestätsgedanke,* pp. 144–208.
[56] Kübler, "Maiestas," pp. 546–548; also Humbert, "Maiestas," III (2), 1556–
1557; Hugh Last on *crimen maiestatis minutae* in *C. A. H.,* IX (1932), 159–161,
296–298. Last says the *crimen* was invented in 103 B.C. by the *lex Appuleia de
maiestate,* but he must have in mind the procedure, not the general idea itself.
[57] *Perduellio* reaches back to the time of the Twelve Tables, if we accept the
statement of Marcian in *Digest* 48, 4, 3: "Lex duodecim tabularum iubet eum, qui
hostem concitaverit quive civem hosti tradiderit, capite puniri."

and prestige of the state. *Perduellio* and *minuta maiestas* must be viewed as intersecting circles, parts of the areas of which overlap and are contained in a common segment. Only later in imperial times do the circles become concentric, with *perduellio* the smaller and interior circle whose area is now completely absorbed into the field of *lèse-majesté*.[58] Under the *lex Cornelia judiciaria* a regular permanent *quaestio* was established for cases of majesty, and some provisions of this *lex* have been reconstructed hypothetically by Humbert, mainly on the basis of certain passages in Cicero and Asconius which indicate that the *crimen maiestatis minutae* embraced a wide range of offenses, extending from attacks of citizens upon civil magistrates and the delivery of an army to the enemy and the inciting of revolt among troops, which are essentially *perduellio*, to the acts of refractory and rebellious provincial governors who leave their provinces, cross the frontiers with their armies, and make war on their own initiative, even invading the territories of client princes without orders from the Senate and Roman people.[59] Indeed, Last has gone so far as to say that Sulla "made the *lex maiestatis* the sanction of the constitution of Rome," and that thereafter each new constitution was accomplished by a new law of majesty.[60] Finally, beginning with the *leges Juliae* of 46 B.C. and/or 18 B.C., the crime expanded to include within its scope many of the offenses listed in Mommsen's classification: (1) criminal collusion with an enemy, *proditio* or external treason, desertion, and attacks upon the land and people (*Landesverrat*); (2) overthrow of the constitution, personal attacks upon magistrates, and other acts of sedition which are high treason (*Hochverrat*); (3) violation of duties connected with political or religious offices, and violation of the public and religious obligations of citizenship.[61] However, it must be noted that throughout the Roman

---

[58] See Kübler, "Maiestas," pp. 544–545, for the analogy of the circles. Note *perduellio* as a phase of *crimen laesae maiestatis* in Ulpian's statement in *Digest* 48, 4, 11: "plane non quisque legis Iuliae maiestatis reus est, in eadem condicione est, sed qui perduellionis reus est, hostili animo adversus rem publicam vel principem animatus."

[59] See Humbert, "Maiestas," III (2), 1557, with citations to Cicero *In Ver.* 1, 33; 1, 5; 5, 25, 27; *Pro Cluent.* 35; *De Orat.* 2, 39, 164; *In Pis.* 21, 50, and to Asconius *Ad Corn.*, pp. 60, 182.

[60] Last, "Sulla," *C. A. H.*, IX, 297.

[61] Mommsen, *Römisches Strafrecht*, pp. 546–587. Of course, the *lex Julia* did not include all the detailed crimes listed by Mommsen and mentioned in *Dig.* 48, 4, 1–11 *Ad Legem Iuliam Maiestatis* and Paulus *Sententiae* 5, 29, 1–2 *Ad Legem Iuliam Maiestatis*. Also note Kübler, "Maiestas," pp. 546–550; Knitschky, *Das Verbrechen*, pp. 37–41; Bisoukides, *Der Hochverrat*, pp. 30–32.
Regarding the question of whether the *leges Juliae* were enacted by Julius Caesar

Law—in the juristic literature of the *Digest*, in the *constitutiones* of the Theodosian and Justinian codes, and in the *Sentences* of Paulus—there are categories and types of cases and descriptions of offenses which constitute violations of majesty, but we do not find definitions or interpretations of the idea itself. Kübler summarizes the matter well:

The abstraction, necessary for the definition of legal concepts, requires a level of philosophical attainment which the legislators of Rome reached only in rare instances. The excellence of the Roman jurists consisted mainly in their practical view of matters and in the amazing sureness with which they made the right decisions, not in the development of legal ideas and dogmas or in their constructive codification. They are inductive or analytical, not builders of syntheses. In their legislation, they confine themselves to the enumeration of cases which are listed in connection with the appropriate procedures, and their treatment of the *lex Julia maiestatis* accords with these methods.[62]

When Professor Ferguson says with Tacitus that "the worship of rulers, *specie religionis*, was really an *arx aeternae dominationis*," he reaches the heart of the problem, not only of "divine kingship" in imperial Rome but of majesty as well.[63] Pollack has insisted that the Principate was merely a continuation and synthesis of the republican magistracies in the hands of one man who should be regarded as *primus inter pares*, but he is alive also to the significance which this constitutional change holds for the idea of majesty. "The Principate signifies the hegemony of the magistracy within the comprehensive power of the highest officer, the glorious precursor of the absolute despotism of the divine kingship.[64] . . . 'Majesty' is no more an attribute of public law, but merely the insignia of the personal authority of the first citizen."[65] The changes wrought in the Roman state by Julius Caesar and Augustus caused the mantle of majesty to be removed gradually from the *res*

---

or Augustus, or in part by both see Sir H. Stuart Jones, "The Princeps," *C. A. H.*, X (1934), 147–148, and Kübler, "Maiestas," p. 548. Humbert and Lécrivain ("Maiestas," III (2), 1557) state that the only text (Cic., *Phil.* 1, 9, 23) which mentions the laws of Caesar *de maiestate* is untrustworthy. Mommsen (*Römisches Strafrecht*, p. 541) seems satisfied that Caesar issued no special majesty laws and that the *lex Julia de maiestate* dates from Augustus. Zirkler (*Die Gemeinrechtliche Lehre*, p. 33), Knitschky (*Das Verbrechen*, p. 17), and Bisoukides (*Der Hochverrat*, p. 38, n. 1) accept the view of Caesar's authorship.

[62] Kübler, "Maiestas," p. 549.

[63] W. S. Ferguson, "Legalized Absolutism en Route from Greece to Rome," *American Historical Review*, XVIII (1912), 29. This article is a landmark in research into the difficult problem of the transmission of Hellenistic conceptions of "god-kingship" to the Roman world.

[64] Pollack, *Der Majestätsgedanke*, p. 127.

[65] *Ibid.*, p. 135.

publica and community of citizens in general popular estimation and to be wrapped about the person of the prince, protecting him from all assaults, whether directed against him in his public or in his private capacity, and embracing ultimately the entire *domus Augusta,* so that the ruler moved progressively from servant of the state to symbol of the state and at last under the Dominate became the efficient cause of the state in his own divine person. This process was a gradual one, however, and Nock is quite right, at least for the earlier emperors, when he asserts that "Divinity hedged a *princeps* around but was not inherent in him" and that constitutionally the prince should be regarded as an intermediary standing between the mass of citizens and the gods.[66] The prince could be held responsible for his acts at the bar of public opinion, although both Caligula and Nero tried to join the gods and so lift themselves above restraint.[67] Speaking of the Flavians and Antonines, Rostovtzeff shows that the old basic principles of republican government still endured, although all classes had come to acquiesce in the rule of one man, but this ruler was the supreme magistrate of the Empire in accordance with the Augustan conception, not a combination of military tyrant and Oriental despot. "The Emperor personified, so to say, the Empire, and so his power and his person were sacred and he himself was an object of worship. The majesty of the Empire was embodied in him. He was not the master of the state but its first servant; service to the state was his duty."[68] Nevertheless, *de facto* the Roman state was becoming an absolute monarchy regardless of the theory of the dyarchy.[69] The great shift in emphasis came with the Severi, whose military despotism paved the way for the Dominate despite their nominal adherence to the idea of the emperor as the highest magistrate.[70] The imperial power rested more and more upon the imperial cult, until the example set by Caligula, Nero, Domitian, Commodus, and Elagabalus culminated with Aurelian, who was *dominus et deus natus* and who

[66] A. D. Nock, "Religious Developments from the Close of the Republic to the Reign of Nero," *C. A. H.,* X, 489.

[67] Cf. articles of Nock and M. P. Charlesworth in *C. A. H.,* X, 497, 657, 664, on the direct worship of Caligula at Rome and the tendency toward introduction of the *proskynesis;* pp. 498, 700, on Claudius as *deus noster* Caesar, and his majesty (*tanta maiestas ducis*); p. 501, on the deification of Nero.

[68] See M. Rostovtzeff, *The Social and Economic History of the Roman Empire* (Oxford: Clarendon, 1926), pp. 116–117. The point of view regarding the nature of imperial authority which I have adopted here is summarized briefly from this definitive treatise by Rostovtzeff.

[69] *Ibid.,* p. 130.

[70] *Ibid.,* pp. 348, 352, 355–356, 370, 372.

transformed "the imperial power into a pure military autocracy, based on religious sanction."[71] With Diocletian the emperor's powers became supernatural and sacred, and the emperor himself became the incarnation of God on earth.[72] This was the logical and final result of what Cumont calls "the republican transformation of the doctrine of the divinity of kings."[73]

In fact, it is precisely at this point that most of the older treatments of the subject of majesty are not altogether clear. They fail to show that we are dealing with a stream of thought with two main tributaries: the oft-traversed channel of the earlier investigators, running from republican times—from the *lex Appuleia* (Kübler), from the founding of the tribunate (Mommsen), even from the *maiestas deorum* (Pollack)—and the Hellenistic and Oriental branch, revealed by more recent research, with its dim sources in the practice of the *proskynesis* and the legalized absolutism of Alexander and the Successors.[74] The work of Ferguson, Nock, Tarn, and Lily Ross Taylor makes it possible to view the concept of majesty in the later Empire in a fuller light, as the expression of an idea embodying all the sanctions effective in establishing the sovereign power of an absolutism in a cosmopolitan world state. As such, the majesty of the Dominate represents the culmination of a long process of evolution in political thought—a mature conception characteristic of the state and society which produced it. Neither tributary of the stream can be neglected, and both have political, as well as religious, elements in common. However, the idea of *proskynesis*, symbolizing the complete subjugation of the individual to the ruler as lord and

[71] *Ibid.*, pp. 407–408.

[72] *Ibid.*, pp. 455–456.

[73] F. Cumont, *After Life in Roman Paganism* (New Haven: Yale University Press, 1923), p. 114.

[74] See Lily Ross Taylor, *The Divinity of the Roman Emperor* (Middletown, Conn.: Amer. Philological Ass'n, 1931), pp. 1–34, 256–266 on Persian origins of *proskynesis*, and pp. 247–255 for controversy with Tarn; W. S. Ferguson, *Greek Imperialism* (Boston: Houghton Mifflin, 1913), Chs. IV–VI; W. W. Tarn, *Hellenistic Civilization* (3rd ed., London: Arnold, 1952), pp. 126–209 (Chps. IV–V on Asia and Egypt). The problem of "god-kingship" is a live subject of research with numerous recent books and articles. In general, see the *Cambridge Ancient History*, with its bibliographies, especially VI (1927), 377–378, 389, 398–400, 419, 432–433, on Alexander by Tarn; VII (1928), 13–22, by Ferguson; IX (1932), 718–735, on Caesar's dictatorship by F. E. Adcock; and X (1934), 481–502, by Nock. Note the opposing views of Taylor and Adcock on Caesar's deification. Also Mason Hammond, *The Augustan Principate* (Cambridge, Mass.: Harvard University Press, 1933), pp. 102–109, with valuable notes, pp. 259–265, and McIlwain, *Growth of Political Thought*, pp. 139–144, in relation to political theory.

master, cannot be connected with the *maiestas* of a republican "common bond" state, such as Cicero conceived, which is a *maiestas populi Romani*. Nevertheless, *proskynesis* to a divine or semidivine ruler may be harmonized readily with such religious ideas as the *maiestas deorum*, from which *fas* and later *ius* developed, and the *maiestas patrum*, which was an emanation from this divine majesty. Indeed, Ciaceri holds that the emperor's *maiestas* was connected with his *sacrosanctitas*,[75] and Kübler notes that the person of the prince was protected by the *lex de maiestate* because he possessed the *imperium* and *tribunicia potestas*, and that the protection was reinforced by his personal identification with the state on the one hand and his divine nature on the other.[76] In any case, we must convict Pollack of inconsistency when he denies the validity of *maiestas* under the Dominate on the ground that it could not exist in an unconstitutional despotism. Also one fails to see how he can accept the *maiestas deorum*, establishing majesty upon the religion of myth and tradition, and then withhold majesty from the materialized "god-kings" of the later Empire. Majesty was not a constitutional principle or even "an attribute of public law,"[77] but a politico-religious conception serving as a buttress to sovereignty.

It is, perhaps, no coincidence that the time which produced the various *quaestiones* (*de maiestate, peculatus, repetundarum*) was the time when ambitious governors and generals were being associated with the symbolic goddess Roma as recipients of "divine" rites in the provinces. The old majesty of the commonwealth was being overthrown and transformed by the incipient majesty of the generals and *principes*, such as Sulla and Pompey, which culminated with Augustus seated beside Roma on the *Gemma Augusta*.[78] Neither can the imperial majesty be dissociated from the so-called *lex regia* and the idea of the emperor as a "living law." Ferguson points out that the Greeks of Magna Graecia had familiarized the Romans with the view that "a monarch who created laws and did not have to obey them was a god" and that Augustus did not wish the Romans to set him above the laws "by giving him the homage of a god,"[79] while Goodenough shows Hellenistic Greeks, in turn, inherited the idea of a νόμος ἐμψυχος or *lex animata* from Persia, in

---

[75] See Hammond, *Augustan Principate*, p. 305, n. 17, for references to Ciaceri, and Hammond's review of Ciaceri, "*Tiberio, successore di Augusto*," in *A. H. R.*, XL (1935), 311.

[76] Kübler, "Maiestas," pp. 550–551.

[77] *Ibid.*, 544.

[78] Taylor, *Divinity of the Roman Emperor*, pp. 226–227.

[79] Ferguson in *A. H. R.*, XVIII (1912), 37, 43.

which the ruler is the state and divine law incarnate.[80] The *proskynesis* and doctrine of the "living law" cannot be excluded from any theory of majesty. These are the ideas upon which a ruler who was both *dominus* and *deus* could establish the new absolutism. On the other hand, there stands the constitutional tradition which, despite vast modifications, remains discernible. The centralization of magisterial powers, beginning with the special provincial commands of the last century of the Republic, leads to the grants of the *imperium proconsulare maius* and *tribunicia potestas,* which underlie the Augustan Principate,[81] and later to even more extensive grants of sovereign power as in the famous *lex de imperio Vespasiani.*[82] Whether these grants were irrevocable forms the basis of one of the most fundamental controversies in Roman Law. The principle of the *digna vox*[83] and the somewhat paradoxical qualifying clause of the *quod principi placuit, legis habet vigorem* would indicate, as Carlyle says, that the emperor has "an unlimited personal authority founded upon a purely democratic basis."[84] Yet one reads to the contrary in the *Digest* that "God has entrusted human affairs to the charge of the emperor that he may do all things needful to change, administer, and provide suitable rules and regulations."[85] In one of his *Novellae* Justinian declares that God has made the emperor sole legislator and given him to men as a "living law" (νόμον αὐτὴν ἔμψυχον),[86] while in the *Code* the emperor is described as the *legis lator* as if he,

[80] See E. R. Goodenough, "The Political Philosophy of Hellenistic Kingship," *Yale Classical Studies* (New Haven: Yale University Press, 1928), I, 55–102. Observe (p. 86) that "in Egypt the king was a solar deity incarnate, but not law incarnate"; also p. 86, n. 102, for criticism of Ferguson's article in *A. H. R., supra.* Cf. McIlwain, *Growth of Political Thought,* p. 114, n. 2.

[81] See Hammond, *Augustan Principate,* especially pp. 8–84; also A. E. R. Boak, "The Extraordinary Commands from 80 to 40 B.C.," *A. H. R.,* XXIV (1918), 1–25; Last in *C. A. H.,* IX, 345–349; Adcock, *C. A. H.,* IX, 718–735.

[82] For text, see Girard, *Textes,* pp. 105–106. Cf. McIlwain, *Growth of Political Thought,* pp. 128, 132, 136; also Adcock, *C. A. H.,* X, 589–590, and Jones, *ibid.,* p. 140, n. 3, and p. 135; Gibbon, *Decline and Fall,* IV, 451 with nn. 39–41. See *Dig.* 1, 3, 31 *De Legibus Senatusque Consultis:* "Princeps legibus solutus est."

[83] *Codex Justinianus* 1, 14, 4 *De Legibus et Constitutionibus Principum et Edictis.*

[84] *Institutes* 1, 2, 6 *De Iure Naturali et Gentium et Civili:* "cum lege regia, quae de imperio eius lata est, populus ei et in eum omne suum imperium et potestatem concessit"; *Dig.* 1, 4, 1 *De Constitutionibus Principum.* R. W. and A. J. Carlyle, *A History of Mediaeval Political Theory in the West* (2nd ed.; Edinburgh and London: Blackwood, 1927), I, 64; McIlwain, *Growth of Political Thought,* p. 128.

[85] *C. Just.* 1, 17, 2, 18 *De Vetere Iure Enucleando:* "quia ideo imperialem fortunam rebus humanis deus praeposuit."

[86] *Novellae, CV,* 4. It is significant that this reference to the emperor as a "living law" should occur in the Greek text of the Novels.

instead of the *Senatus populusque Romanus*, were now the basic source of law.[87] Finally there is that significant phrase at the beginning of a rescript from Justinian to Tribonian which reads "Deo auctore nostrum gubernantes imperium, quod nobis a caelesti maiestate traditum est."[88] Here at last we have majesty lifted from the god reigning incarnate among men to God in His Heaven with the Son sitting *ad dexteram maiestatis in excelsis*,[89] so that now allegiance is rendered to majesty through deference and veneration, not for the patriotic purpose of voluntary co-operation in a common weal. The official acceptance of Christianity marks the last step in the evolution of the Roman idea of majesty from the *maiestas deorum* to the *maiestas caelestis*. Roman sovereignty tends to remain a constitutional thing, at least until the *imperium* and *potestas* were assimilated with *maiestas* in the later Empire or until under Christianity sovereignty itself is handed down *a caelesti maiestate* to the emperor, who is God's vicar on earth to rule over men, but majesty was never at any time a constitutional concept. It was the cloud of glory which overhung the people of the *res publica*; it confirmed the *sacrosanctitas* of the tribunes with the sanctions of *fas*; it was an attribute of the goddess Roma and the mantle of Divus Julius; it shone about the person of Augustus and his successors in the Principate; it was the veil that covered the despotism of the Dominate; it was the voice of God declaring the Christian emperors a "living law" among men. And this majesty, associated with the intimate person of the emperor and enhanced by his divine nature of special appointment, overshadows his sovereign power, based in theory, at least, upon constitutional grant.

This point of view may be confirmed further if we turn briefly to the forms assumed by violations of majesty in the imperial period,[90] such as the time of Augustus when that emperor seems to have insisted on the close relation of *laesa religio* to *crimen laesae maiestatis* for personal

[87] *C. Just.* 1, 14, 12, 3–4: "cui soli legis latorem esse concessum est."

[88] *C. Just.* 1, 17, 1.

[89] *Ad Hebraeos* 1, 3.

[90] An adequate treatment of the crime of majesty in the imperial period may be found in Bisoukides, *Der Hochverrat*, pp. 20–33; Kübler, "Maiestas," pp. 550–558; and Humbert, "Maiestas," III (2), 1558–1559. There are excellent discussions, based on specific cases, dealing with the reign of Augustus in Hammond, *Augustan Principate*, pp. 172–176 with nn. 11–33, of *Tiberius* in F. B. Marsh, *The Reign of Tiberius* (London: Humphrey Milford, 1931), especially pp. 289–295, and M. P. Charlesworth, *C. A. H.*, X, 626–632; also see scattered references to Caligula in J. P. V. D. Balsdon, *The Emperor Gaius (Caligula)* (Oxford: Clarendon, 1934).

reasons.[91] Certainly the establishment of the imperial cult emphasized the convergence of treason and impiety, so that insult to the divine ruler became the equivalent of injury to the state, and even utterances concerning the emperor, especially maledictions or slanderous pamphlets (*famosi libelli*), were deemed treasonable and punished arbitrarily.[92] Humbert observes that the sacred character of the emperors contributed to transform every injury into the crime of *laesa maiestas* by making it an impiety.[93] It is noteworthy that many of these injuries involved no bodily hurt to the emperor but were merely insults or offenses against the imperial dignity. Among these special offenses may be mentioned such acts as consulting the future in all matters regarding the state and the imperial family by employing divination, soothsayers, or sorcery (*vaticinatores, haruspices, mathematici*), disrespect for the images of the emperor and unseemly conduct in the presence of or in the proximity of an imperial image, and counterfeiting money bearing the effigy of an emperor.[94] Hence Ulpian states in the *Digest* that "the crime which is related most closely to sacrilege is that called the crime of majesty."[95] However, he is probably not referring to *sacrilegium* in the ordinary legal sense as an act of violence against or the profanation of a temple or consecrated image, but as a lack of reverence, respect, and deference in the sense of *impietas* (ἀσέβεια).[96] Later we reach the logical culmination of these tendencies in the terrible *lex Quisquis* which equated mere intent with the attempt or the overt act and paved the way for the mediaeval attainder laws.[97]

[91] See Mommsen, *Römisches Strafrecht*, pp. 567–580, for the religious offenses. Note that in the imperial period the crime of majesty is no longer described as diminished majesty (*minuta maiestas*) but as injured, violated, attacked, and repulsed or insulted (*laesa, violata, appetita, pulsata*). However, I have made no special study of the terminology of *maiestas* in the legal sources. R. Mayr, *Vocabularium Codicis Iustiniani, Pars prior (Pars Latina)* (Prague: Ceská Grafická Unie, 1923), lists sixty-seven citations of the word *maiestas* from the *Code* alone, while the number in the *Digest* may be even larger.

[92] Cf. *Codex Theodosianus* 9, 4, 1 *Si Quis Imperatori Maledixerit; C. Just.* 9, 7, 1; Paulus *Sent.* 5, 29, 1; Tacitus *Ann.* 1, 74; 4, 21, and 34.

[93] Humbert, "Maiestas," III (2), 1558, quoting from Tacitus *Ann.* 2, 50: "si qua de Augusto inreligiose dixisset"; 6, 47: "Albucilla . . . defertur impietatis in principem"; Paulus *Sent.* 5, 29, 1.

[94] Cf. *C. Th.* 9, 16, 1–2 *De Maleficis et Mathematicis et Ceteris Similibus; C. Just.* 9, 18, 1–9; *Dig.* 48, 4, 5–6. Note the affecting instance of a slave's devotion mentioned by Kübler, 552. Cf. Suetonius, *Tiberius* 58.

[95] *Dig.* 48, 4, 1.

[96] Cf. Kübler, "Maiestas," p. 551. Also Nock, *C. A. H.,* X, 489–490.

[97] *C. Just.* 9, 8, 5. See Bisoukides, *Der Hochverrat*, pp. 26–29; Kübler, "Maiestas," pp. 554–558.

Since violation of civic religious duties, owed to the state deities, was closely associated under the Empire with personal offenses against the deified monarch, the spread of such new Oriental cults as Judaism, Christianity, and the Manichaean sect led to the recognition of a new crime, which Tertullian defines as *crimen laesae romanae religionis*.[98] The mere profession of Christianity was deemed a crime per se, regardless of any allied crimes with which Christians might be charged, such as immorality, magical practices, and the possession of evil or dangerous books; denial of the state gods, objection to participation in the ceremonies of the public cult, and refusal to recognize the divinity of the emperor or to sacrifice to his *genius* were fundamental treasons, threatening not only the state but all organized society. Hence, since Christians would not subscribe to the state cult and could not establish a state of their own, they were considered ἄθεοι, declared guilty of *perduellio,* and were treated as public enemies (*hostes publici*) whether they were Roman citizens or not.[99] The Christians formed a sect drawn from many nations, and being a sect their ranks were recruited from those who had deserted their ancestral religions. The resulting resentment of the pagans led them to accuse the Christians of atheism, so that Gibbon could well say "the most pious of men were exposed to the unjust but dangerous imputation of impiety."[100] However, the resentment was mutual and reciprocal, for Gibbon tells us elsewhere that "the most trifling mark of respect to the national worship, [the early Christian] considered as a direct homage yielded to the daemon, and as an act of rebellion against the majesty of God."[101] In this dilemma the Christians fortified their faith by their protestations and martyrdoms, and "in proportion to the increase of zeal, they combated with the more ardour and success in the holy war which they had undertaken against the empire of the daemons."[102] One will not err if he identifies "the empire of the daemons" with the Roman state, the national cult, and the pagan emperors whose *genius* the early Christians refused to worship. Later, with the complete victory of Christianity and its elevation to the state religion through the famous *constitutio* of Theodosius in 379,[103] the

[98] See Mommsen, *Römisches Strafrecht,* p. 569 with n. 2, citing Tertullian, *Apologeticus,* c. 10, 24, 27, 28, 35.

[99] Humbert, "Maiestas," III (2), 1559; Mommsen, *Römisches Strafrecht,* pp. 575–576 and notes; McIlwain, *Growth of Political Thought,* pp. 145–146.

[100] Gibbon, *Decline and Fall,* II, 74–75.

[101] *Ibid.,* II, 16.

[102] *Ibid.,* II, 19.

[103] *C. Th.* 16, 5, 5 *DeHaereticis:* "Omnes vetitae legibus et divinis et imperialibus

pagans were forbidden to sacrifice or hold meetings publicly and might
be put to death for refusal to abandon their ancient deities.[104] Finally
in 392 Arcadius declared such offenders guilty of *laesa maiestas,* [105] and
in 409 Christians who went over to Judaism incurred the same charge.[106]
A little earlier, in 384 and 385, sacrilege, perhaps in the sense of heresy,
had been declared an unpardonable capital offense.[107] The profession
of Christianity, adherence to paganism, and heresy became, in turn, the
chief form of *laesa religio.* But it did not accord with Christian theory
that *laesa religio* should be, at the same time, *laesa maiestas.* The Christian Church was not identical with the Christian State, and the majesty
of God was not the majesty of the Emperor. Indeed, the earthly State
stood beneath the Visible Church which symbolized the Heavenly
Kingdom, just as the Emperor was subordinate to God from whom he
derived his power to govern.[108] Hence delicts against Christianity ceased
to be considered as treason, although *lèse-majesté* and heresy were
united by bonds of origin.[109] Yet the only true majesty belonged to God;
earthly majesties were derived or fictitious. And so we have come to the
end of a winding path, pursuing the history of an idea which has brought
us, at last, to the vast gulf that separates the *rex tremendae maiestatis,
qui salvandos salvas gratis* from the *immensa Romanae pacis maiestas,*
the majesty of this world from the Majesty on High. In the study of this
unique concept we arrive at the abyss which cleaves the Middle Ages
from the ancient world and realize that antiquity has become incom-
prehensible to the mediaeval mind.

---

haereses perpetuo conquiescant"; *C. Just.* 1, 5, 2 *De Haereticis et Manichaeis et
Samaritis.*
   [104] Humbert, "Maiestas," III (2), 1559 and n. 22.
   [105] *C. Th.* 16, 10, 2 *De Paganis, Sacrificiis et Templis.*
   [106] *C. Th.* 16, 8, 19 *De Iudaeis, Caelicolis et Samaritanis.*
   [107] Mommsen, *Römisches Strafrecht,* p. 600, n. 4, quoting *C. Th.* 9, 38, 7–8 *De
Indulgentiis Criminum.*
   [108] Cf. *C. Just.* 1, 17, 1 *De Vetere Iure Enucleando.*
   [109] Mommsen, *Römisches Strafrecht,* p. 599, n. 1.

III

The Idea of Fidelity in Germanic
Customary Law*

In his monograph on high treason Bisoukides has made the pointed observation that the concept of hostile acts against the state is by its very nature fluid and fluctuating because it is so difficult to ascertain the precise objective of such crimes.[1] Indeed, one notes constantly that treason is hard to define because the idea is an elusive one. The course of history through the centuries presents a bewildering kaleidoscopic series of changes in the content of the idea. Moreover, the genius of every people expressed itself in the development of ideas of treason which are peculiarly characteristic of that people, so that here, if anywhere, substance is lent to the concept of a *Volksgeist*. Similarly the texture of the crime varies with changing times as if in response to a veritable *Zeitgeist*. Just as the vigorous and active political life of the Greek city-state developed at Athens the typical *katalysis tou demou* and the majesty of the Roman people the *crimen laesae maiestatis,* so the Germanic

* Reprinted from *The Rice Institute Pamphlet*, XLII (1955), 43–78 and nn. 129–142. This study is a revised paper read in part under the title of "The Public Law of the Early Germanic Codes" before the Houston Philosophical Society at Houston, Texas, on May 15, 1941.

[1] P. Bisoukides, *Der Hochverrat* (Berlin: Carl Heymanns Verlag, 1903), p. 3: "Der Begriff der feindlichen Handlungen gegen den Staat als solchen, der sogenannten Staatsverbrechen, ist von jeher ein sehr schwankender gewesen, weil das Objekt des Verbrechens ein sehr bestimmbares ist." Also note Pollock and Maitland, *The History of English Law before the Time of Edward I* (2nd ed.; Cambridge: University Press, 1923), II, 502: "treason is a crime which has a vague circumference, and more than one centre."

peoples evolved breach of faith or troth—the German *Treubruch*.[2] Curiously enough one will observe that the Germanic contribution to the general conception of treason adds the last of three vital elements which must be deemed essential in any final classification of treasonable offenses. First in natural historical development came those attempts on the life of the organized group, whether family, community, or state, involving the entire nexus of crimes against land and folk embraced in the German concept of *Landesverrat*. Secondly, the matured product of Roman public life was the *crimen laesae maiestatis*, in which a single individual came to personify public authority. Treason became an offense against a divine ruler and this phase left its permanent imprint in the element of high treason or *Hochverrat*. It remained for the Germanic peoples to add the factor of a violated personal pledge and broken allegiance owed by one man to another. Indeed, it is the Germanic view of personality that enters directly into the modern concept of individual civic responsibility rather than the ancient politico-religious expedient of Alexander and Augustus, which found expression in deference and veneration based on group response.

The old problem of whether treason antedates the state arises at the very beginning of any treatment involving the life of the early Germans, since one deals with a people not yet reduced to settled society but still migrating about under seminomadic conditions. The situation recalls the state of society in prehistoric Greece and Rome, but the historical data are more reliable because the volume of direct evidence is greater, thanks to the early accounts of Caesar and Tacitus and the established record of the barbarian invasions. The general impression which the Germanic peoples convey as they emerge upon the pages of history is that of a people whose political life represents on the one hand a condition of divided authority, shared among the family group or other wider group of relatives, and on the other hand the broader control exercised by military chiefs and possibly by hereditary kings. Also, these early sources indicate a progressive increase in the powers exercised by the holders of the broader authority. Thus Caesar states that when a *civitas* defends itself or wages war a magistrate is chosen to take command who shall possess powers of life and death, whereas in peace authority rests in no single hand (*communis magistratus*), although there are leading

[2] Cf. Hugh Last, *Cambridge Ancient History* (Cambridge: University Press, 1932), IX, 297, who notes that "the nature of treasonable action . . . varies with the nature of the constitution," and that treasonable crimes "differ greatly in gravity according to their constitutional setting."

men in the *regiones* and *pagi* who speak the law among them and settle controversies.[3] Tacitus mentions kings (*reges*) who are chosen according to their degree of nobility, but whose royal powers are by no means unlimited or free of restraint. Also there are leaders (*duces*) chosen because of their valor, but whose military authority depends on the admiration excited by the example they set in battle rather than on any arbitrary powers of command such as inhered in the Roman *imperium*.[4] Finally in the days of the invasions there appear great chieftains, from Alaric to Clovis, who lead their people, vast armed hosts, into the lands of the Roman Empire. These men possessed royal powers which concentrated much public authority in the hands of a single individual. Pre-eminent military ability and the respect it created led in a straight path to political dominance.

Of course, one would like to know more exactly the size and political significance of the *civitas*, *regio*, and *pagus* which Caesar mentions; whether these divisions were peculiar to a single tribe of Germans or were general in nature; whether Caesar has the usual Roman connotation in mind; and to what later geographical and political divisions of the Germanic peoples these areas correspond. Since, because of their lack of concentrated public authority, there was obviously no true state among the Germans such as that with which Caesar was familiar, his term *civitas* may well be general in its implication and refer to a people or tribe without regard to political circumstance. Certainly there were many tribes of Germans, and numerous local differences must be anticipated; yet one discerns various broad general lines of development. In Caesar's day some communities at least had no common public officials in whose hands public authority was concentrated in time of peace. Tacitus 150 years later speaks of kings but is careful to specify that their powers are limited. Possibly they had existed in Caesar's time as well, or again perhaps Tacitus is only speaking of a different tribe of Germans. In any case the central authority has not yet come into existence save

[3] Caesar *Commentarii de Bello Gallico* 6, 23: "Cum bellum civitas aut illatum defendit aut infert, magistratus qui ei praesint, ut vitae necisque habeant potestatem, deliguntur. In pace nullus est communis magistratus, sed principes regionum atque pagorum inter suos ius dicunt, controversiasque minuunt."

[4] Tacitus *Germania*, trans. by William Peterson, Loeb Series (London: Heinemann, 1914), c. 7: "Reges ex nobilitate, duces ex virtute sumunt, nec regibus infinita aut libera potestas, et duces exemplo potius quam imperio, si prompti, si conspicui, si ante aciem agant, admiratione praesunt." Cf. Rudolf Much, *Die Germania des Tacitus* (Heidelberg: C. Winter, 1937), pp. 103–108. See H. St. L. B. Moss, *The Birth of the Middle Ages, 395–814* (Oxford: Clarendon, 1935), pp. 65, 248–250.

for a certain military authority of the *duces*. Nevertheless, it does begin
to assume definite form at some time in the course of the great migrations, perhaps because the tribes were engaged in almost perpetual
warfare as they forced their way into and through the Roman Empire.
As a result the most eminent chieftains came to hold practically permanent positions and to assume a political leadership which was closely
associated with their military command. When the time came for settling down in more stable communities it was only natural that these
great chieftains (*duces*) continued to wield those powers which would
have been considered most exceptional in an earlier period. The people
had become habituated to a special responsible central authority and
there was no demand that the successful *dux* lay down his command
now that military activity was abating. Added to this was a growing fa-
miliarity with Roman ideas of governmental authority now that contact
between the two peoples was established. By the beginning of the sixth
century A.D. a settled social life and concentrated public authority have
appeared, whereas in the first century B.C. neither existed.

If authority is sufficiently scattered and dispersed until it rests in the
hands of a great many individuals or of all, and if all lack a public sense,
there is grave doubt whether there be any public authority whatsoever;
rather, community discipline is then a private matter for individuals or
the family or other private group. Nevertheless, no matter how private
or small the group, if it possesses a group life or corporate consciousness,
it is a germ from which public life may grow. As soon as the individual
is placed under obligations and recognizes, or is forced to recognize, restrictions the field is prepared for public life. Evidently these early Germans of Caesar's day occupied a position somewhat below the level of a
strictly public life. They might co-operate in a common policy under a
common authority in time of war, but each family pursued its own
private policies in time of peace. Family might fight family and tribe
fight tribe without restriction, still they were above the purely private
exercise of unrestrained individualism where man fights man at will.
Here the kinship group might step in and revenge its injured members;
here a group which would be deemed private today intervenes to protect its members and perform a duty of a public character.[5] It was self-

---

[5] G. Waitz, *Deutsche Verfassungsgeschichte* (Berlin: Weidmann, 1880), 1, 70–
72: "die Verpflichtung war eine allgemeine der Familie." Cf. Heinrich Brunner,
Deutsche Rechtsgeschichte (2nd ed.; Leipzig: Duncker and Hamblot, 1906), I,
110–133, on "Geschlecht und Magschaft" for a detailed account of family and
Sippe; also Waitz, *D. V.*, I, 67–80; Karl von Amira, *Grundriss des germanischen*

help but of the same sort as when a modern state seeks possible redress for the grievances its citizens may have against another state.[6] It is only a matter of proportion and perspective. Just so the corporate life of the early Germans was merely in the way of "becoming public" for as Waitz says rightly: "Aus der Familie erwachsen Volk und Staat."[7] The family is not only the biological but the political basis as well, and from it spring both state and nation. It is the physical foundation of a race, and it is also a common life which expands into the political community; yet it retains its individuality and does not actually identify itself with either community or state.[8] Conversely the state is no mere aggregation of families and is not essential to their existence. The act which establishes the family is the real or symbolic purchase, originally of the woman herself, later of the protection (*mundium*) over the woman.[9] And in the private relationship of marriage appears a first step toward a concentrated public authority, for the husband has purchased the right to maintain the protection or *mundium* over his wife. With the coming of children the authority of the husband and father is established in a household. In the fully developed family veneration and respect for wisdom lead to the centralization of authority in the hands of an elder member, the patriarch or *Altermann*: "quanto plus propinquorum, quanto maior adfinium numerus, tanto gratiosior senectus; nec ulla orbitatis pretia."[10] The circle of the family widens and all recognize the common bond of blood relationship, or, as Brunner states succinctly, "Der Geschlechtsverband erwächst aus der Hausgemeinschaft."[11] The only public policy is the general policy of the family affecting all its members, the family is the only state, and the man without relatives is actually without rights or protection and is outlaw.

It is to this wider circle of relatives, to this union of families that attention must next be turned. In general it consisted of the members of

---

Rechts (3rd ed.; Strassburg: Trübner, 1913), pp. 169–177.

[6] See Sir Paul Vinogradoff, *Historical Jurisprudence* (London: Humphrey Milford, 1920). I, 351–353.

[7] Waitz, *D. V.*, I, 53.

[8] *Ibid.*, I, 60. C. H. McIlwain, *The Growth of Political Thought in the West* (New York: Macmillan, 1932), pp. 63–66, on the Aristotelian *koinonia*. This theoretical Greek *koinonia* has a suggestive relevance to the empirical Germanic *Sippe* or family group.

[9] *Ibid.*, I, 61.

[10] Tacitus *Germania*, c. 20: "the more relations a man has and the larger the number of his connections by marriage, the more influence has he in his age; it is unprofitable to have no ties."

[11] Brunner, *D. R.*, I, 111.

several households who were presumed to be descended in the male line from a common ancestor, although the formation of similar unions of relatives on the female side was not precluded. The interest of the maternal kin or *Spindel* kin in an individual was quite as strong as in the case of agnates; this is evidenced by the peculiar intimacy between maternal uncles and nephews.[12] The family group or *Geschlecht* is ordinarily designated *Sippe*, a term which involves the collateral meaning of the special "peace" and friendship that prevail within the group, as well as the protection of its members against enemies and the obligation to revenge their wrongs. The expression was used in two different connections: on the one hand as a union of agnates, and on the other as the assembled blood relatives of a given individual. This latter was evidently a wider circle of relatives than the agnatic union, since each individual derives his blood from different familial sources, and in this latter sense the *Sippe* was constituted differently for each individual.[13] Thus the natural expansion of the family branched outward into a tangled complex of interlocking associations, each of which felt and understood its own peculiar corporate individuality.[14] Further it must be noted that these groupings exercised some sort of authority and represented in certain respects rudimentary states. It seems most probable that the *Geschlecht, Sippe,* or *maegth* in its narrow agnatic connotation is comparable with the Latin *gens* and Greek *genos,* for the limits of all these groups are established at the point where relationship to the deceased ancestor can no longer be established. Still the group is larger than any mere household under the supervision of a single *Altermann.*[15]

The state, which is the modern bearer of authority, is distinguished by fixed geographical boundaries and established tests of citizenship or membership. It is in no sense an ambulatory affair, whereas these Ger-

---

[12] Waitz, *D. V.,* I, 67–69.

[13] Brunner, *D. R.,* I, 112. The blood relatives are designated variously as *Freunde, Holde, Gätlinge, Gesippen, Sippen,* and *Magen* (whence the Anglo-Saxon *maegth*).

[14] See Sir William Holdsworth, *A History of English Law* (4th ed.; London: Methuen, 1936), II, 36, on *maegth.* Paternal and maternal relatives shared rights and duties, as dividing a wergeld or sustaining a feud, in the proportion of two-thirds and one-third respectively. Since there was no blood relationship between husband and wife, each remained in his own *maegth.* It was a recognized association for social purposes and to some extent possessed a "common aim and will." Cf. F. Liebermann, *Die Gesetze der Angelsachsen* (Halle: Max Niemeyer, 1903–16), Glossary in second half of Vol. II, 651–655, on *Sippe* (*sibb, cynn, maeg, maegsib, maegd, maeglagu, magas*).

[15] The curious *Sippe* or *maegth,* containing both *Speer* and *Spindel* kin in the cases of specific individuals, seems to lack any counterpart in antiquity.

manic kingroups were not only vague in composition but had a discon-
certing tendency to wander about and could not be stationed within
fixed limits. They might and probably they did usually remain in the
same general locality for long periods of time. But they were a nomadic
people who were just beginning the process of settling down. The result
is that here and there one finds certain patronymic forms in the names
of villages (*Dörfer, vici*) which would indicate an area occupied by a
certain *Geschlecht* (*genealogia*). Waitz has observed that the village
community (*Dorfschaft*) is in no sense an agnatic circle of relatives
(*Verwandtschaft*) despite the confusion caused by their occasional
designation as *Geschlechter*.[16] This would seem to indicate that some-
where in the settling-down process a change occurred whereby authority
passed from the *Sippe* to a group which recognized a community of interest though not of blood. This must not, however, be considered proof
that the *Sippe* never possessed authority, or, as Niebuhr attempted to
show in the case of the comparable Latin *gens*, that the *gens* was an
artificial organization created by a pre-existing political authority. Political authority was probably evolved in the kin-group, as Brunner and
Mommsen hold, and the kin-group was not an artificial creation of political authority.[17] The first corporate group was the family, later extensions reached to wider circles of relatives, and finally, the sense of
relationship becoming lost and outsiders entering into the group, a community developed without a sense of kin solidarity.[18] Nevertheless, as
long as the sense of common interest and a corporate consciousness were
present the germs of public authority could continue to grow, even

---

[16] Cf. Waitz, *D. V.*, I, 83–84.

[17] See Pauly-Wissowa-Kroll, *Realencyclopädie der classischen Altertumswissenschaft* (Stuttgart: Metzler, 1928), on *gens* and *patria potestas*, for views of
Mommsen and Niebuhr.

[18] Observe Brunner, *D. R.*, I, 119: "Das Geschlecht hatte gewisse öffentlichrechtliche Funktionen, die bei entwickelteren Verhältnissen als Aufgaben der
Staatsgewalt erscheinen. Ursprünglich auf die agnatische Sippe beschränkt, sind
sie schon lange von der Zeit, da unsere Quelle darüber zu sprechen beginnen, auf
andere Blutsverwandte, schliesslich auf die Verwandschaft überhaupt ausgedehnt
worden, . . . Das Geschlecht war der älteste Friedensverband, er verbürgte seinen
Genossen den Frieden, indem er die an ihnen begangenen Rechtsverletzungen
rächte, das angegriffene Mitglied verteidigte." Cf. Waitz, *D. V.*, I, 84; "Doch geht
man zu weit, wenn man auch in späterer Zeit noch die Dorfschaft und die Familie
zusammenfallen lässt, die Dorfgenossen zugleich für Familiengenossen hält, die
Beziehungen dieser zu einander aus dem Zusammenhang der Familien ableiten, wo
von Dorfgenossen oder Nachbarn die Rede ist, Verwandte oder Geschlechtsvettern
annehmen will, etwa das Erbrecht, das jenen beigelegt zu werden scheint, auf solche
Weise zu erklären gedenkt."

within the bounds of a larger public corporation, until in the later Middle Ages one finds the gild in the town and the town in the kingdom.[19] However, at this early time the *Geschlecht* formed no part of a larger corporation. It lay within a tribe to be sure, but the tribe was a racial or ethnic grouping whose identity was generally felt and recognized, yet which acted as a united organic group only in unusual circumstances—somewhat as modern alliances and ententes of national states have united for special purposes, usually defenses against a common danger, real or fancied.[20] Thus one sees the burden of authority passing successively from one social grouping to another by a natural evolutionary process.[21] The household and family (*Hausgemeinschaft, Familie, Geschlecht*) expand into wider circles of relatives (*Sippschaften, Verwandtschaften*) which become communities (*Gemeinde*), and these in turn merge into tribes which combine to form an entire people (*Volk*). The early Germanic peoples were divided into a number of such folk entities, as Visigoths, Alamanni, Franks, and Lombards, and formed a related ethnic group.

In all the foregoing discussion regarding the social and political condition of the early Germanic peoples, it must be borne in mind that we are dealing with questions of great complexity, that the conclusions drawn are in the main inferential and often controversial, and that the subject matter is commonly ethnological and not strictly historical. A great part depends upon deduction rather than documentation. It is against this problematic background that one reverts to the nature of treason in a primitive people who lacked a developed state organization. Obviously, here treason cannot be an act subversive of a public author-

---

[19] Cf. Brunner. *D. R.*, I, 117–118; Waitz, *D. V.*, I, 90, on the *Gilden*. One must also remember that the *Sippe*, like the Greek city-state, is a "life" which is not limited to political activity but which embraces the economic, military, religious, and legal phases of society. The *Sippe* involves functions that lie outside and beyond the political *koinonia*. Thus the *Geschlecht* or *Sippe* becomes the *fara* or *fyrd* when considered as a division of the host or army. It seems likely that considered as an area of residence it becomes the *Dorf* or *vicus*.

[20] Vinogradoff, *Historical Jurisprudence*, I, 353, on contemporary difficulty in the enforcement of international law.

[21] Holdsworth, *History of English Law*, II, 38, 44–45: "As the state gained in strength it suppressed the *maegth* if it attempted to stand against the law [of the state]; and it invented other means to secure the preservation of the peace," but the old idea lived on and, while these primitive principles gave place to others, they were never wholly eradicated but were often recognized and regulated. "Thus . . . it regulated the occasions upon which recourse might be had to the feud. It regulated the amount of the wergeld. It required a man who had no kin to find himself a lord."

ity which is nonexistent, but the general philosophic conception of betrayal and broken faith must be applied to an authority which is in the process of "becoming public." Hence one must seek the life germ whence the state evolved from the family and trace its development through the later expansions of the family into those wider circles which constantly assume more mature political characters until at the end of the period nearly all the Germanic peoples have merged into a single state, the empire of Charlemagne. Corporate life is based on mutual agreement, whether consciously understood or not. The family is the basic corporate group. All are united for a common protection, and the life of the group depends on the faithful co-operation of its members. Any act subversive of the corporate life threatens the safety of the individual. The common protection or *mundium* of the family must be maintained at all costs.[22] Hence acts which assail the corporate life and promise the destruction of the *mundium* are treasonable and constitute a rudimentary form of treason against land and folk (*Landesverrat*).[23] Concretely such offenses would include parricide. Indeed, the killing of the head of the family (*Altermann*), who would personify in varying degrees the authority which supported the *mundium*, might be considered high treason (*Hochverrat*) in its embryonic form.[24] The homicide or murder of any man capable of bearing arms or of any woman capable of bearing children might well be a serious blow to the organic social life of the group. Adultery or incest might cause internal sedition within the group and render the physical constitution of the *maegth* uncertain in the case of offspring of indeterminable paternity. Arson was particularly heinous since it broke up the customary habits of social existence by destroying the home or other essential property. The theft of livestock, especially the horse, and of weapons would leave the individual without means

[22] Note that the earliest Germanic protective group of which there is definite knowledge is more complex than the theoretical simple family. It is the *Sippe* or *maegth* whose membership varies for each individual and which is an empirically established entity based on social experience.

[23] See Bisoukides, *Der Hochverrat*, p. 34: "Wer nun die Verbandssicherheit gefährdet, indem er seine verbrecherische Tätigkeit nach dieser Richtung hin entfaltet, bricht in schimpflicher Weise die geschuldete Treue, er ist Verräter in diesem Sinne."

[24] Parricide of this sort may also well be one of the roots whence the mediaeval petty treason sprang. Cf. W. E. Wilda, *Geschichte des deutschen Strafrechts* (Halle: C. A. Schwetschke, 1842), I: *Das Strafrecht der Germanen*, 984: "In den ältern Zeiten tritt mehr der Verrath an land und Volk hervor, während der Verrath gegen den König erst allmählig als ein gleichsam gegen das Gemeinwesen selbst und mittelbar gerichtetes Verbrechen in bestimmter Weise sich darstellte und gewissermassen an dessen Stelle trat."

to support or defend himself and his group. This early treason was an elementary primal form which assumes more matured and specialized characters in the progressive codifications known as the barbarian codes or *leges barbarorum*. But long before the period of the codes, there appears the custom of holding intercommunal assemblies or *Dinge*, which act authoritatively over a considerable area, and opposition to whose decisions must have constituted a very real sort of treason against land and folk.[25]

However, one will be wholly misled if he supposes that treason among the Germanic peoples was a simple evolution from the broad general concept of crime in the family group to its specific legal definition in the codes of various Germanic peoples in the earlier Middle Ages. The state was no mere mechanical accretion of subordinate units; one must beware of the alluring theory of an "association of associations" articulating with mechanical perfection in all its parts. Just as the *mundium* of the family became complicated by the development of the *Sippe,* so the protective authority of the state becomes complicated by the presence of kings. And the king with his royal family is a figure who reaches back beyond the dawn of Germanic history, for Tacitus mentions kings who are noble though limited in authority. The complete history of the Germanic kingship from the day of Tacitus until the period of the barbarian invasions cannot be traced, but seemingly it becomes involved during this time with the office of *dux* or military chieftain. Yet no matter how weak the king or how fully understood it may be that he is merely the personification of corporate authority, the possibility and even the likelihood is ever present that he may assume for himself and his family a special interest separated from the interest of the community, and under certain circumstances this may become dangerous and opposed to the welfare of the corporate life. Indeed, the presence of a limited king suggests the idea of the lack of such limitation, and the tendency in later times was to transform the suggestion into reality, as evidenced by the *major domus* of Merovingian times, an officer who was not a king in name yet possessed extensive authority in fact. Hence one finds that the sort of treason which was typical *Landesverrat* in the family and in those wider circles represented in the popular assemblies (*Landesdinge*) becomes transformed into high treason when its object is a single individual, the king.[26] The treason which had been the attribute of a cor-

---

[25] Cf. Brunner, *D. R.,* I, 175–180; Waitz, *D. V.,* I, 340.

[26] Cf. Bisoukides, *Der Hochverrat,* p. 37: "Die gegen das Gemeinwessen gerichteten Verbrechen werden in den Volksrechten teils als Verrat an Land und Volk,

porate group now attaches itself to a special interest.[27] The earlier conception had involved the idea of a contract to maintain the *mundium* for each individual. The Germans, however, were strongly impressed with the notion of dual obligation which would bind the king to rule according to law and custom and the subject to render obedience in return for protection, and it is doubtful how far toward the idea of special interest the Germans might have progressed unaided by Roman influence.

The fact remains that during and shortly after the invasions the Roman conception of *maiestas* attached itself to Germanic law. Allegiance to a king surrounded by *maiestas* is no conditional, contractual matter, but consists of deference to absolute authority, or, in other words, a special interest controlling the state but lying outside the scope of the operation of its law and custom. Indeed, the fact that the Germans possessed some sort of kings who might easily develop a special interest led to their acquisitions of as large an amount of Roman *maiestas* as the Germanic temperament would tolerate. Thus Frankish history is scattered with many cases of kings and officials whose authority exceeds the modest limits set by Tacitus. Ducal houses appear whose powers are royal in scope and whose interests are special. When a king per-

---

teils aus dem Gesichtspunkte der Untreue gegen den König bestraft." Also see essay on "The Public Law of the Ripuarian, Alamannic, and Bavarian Codes," for the problem of the transfer of treasonable and other related offenses from the popular to the ducal causes. This represents a further stage in the process of the attraction and absorption of *Landesverrat* into the area of high treason, in part through the medium of a ducal or royal "peace."

[27] Observe the significant conclusion of Wilda, *Geschichte des deutschen Strafrechts*, I, 992: "Die weitere Entwicklung der Gewalt des Königs, welcher gleichsam Träger des in einem Königsfrieden sich verwandelnden Volksfriedens, der Träger der Persönlichkeit des Staates wurde, hatte aber nun die Folge, dass auch alle Arten des Landesverrathes als zunächst gegen den König gerichtete Missethaten angesehen wurden, und unter den verschiedenen Arten des Hochverrathes nun die Nachstellung gegen das Leben des Königs, gleichsam als die erste und schwerste vorangestellt wurde." Cf. Brunner-von Schwerin, *Deutsche Rechtsgeschichte* (2nd ed.; Munich and Leipzig: Duncker and Humblot, 1928), II, 883–884: "Im fränkischen Reiche wurde der König so sehr zum Träger der Staatspersönlichkeit, dass der Landesverrat als Treubruch gegen den König erschien, und zwar als eine Art jener schweren Infidelität, die in fränkischen Quellen crimen maiestatis heisst und als Hochverrat bezeichnet werden darf."

See Rudolf His, *Geschichte des deutschen Strafrechts bis zur Karolina* (Munich and Berlin: R. Oldenbourg, 1928, pp. 113–118), for a good short analysis of the various types of treason (*Verrat*, old Swedish, *forratha*), including the relation of *Landesverrat* (old Norse, *landrad*) to *Hochverrat* and *Herrenverrat* (A-S, *hlafordsearo, hlafordswice*); also the relation of *Verrat* generally to the *Majestätsverbrechen* (*crimen laesae maiestatis*).

sonifies public authority and recognizes his duty of protection he attaches to his special interest the peace of the realm and the king's peace includes all who are in the king's *mundium*. Self-help and corporate authority are replaced by the uniform law of the king who acts as trustee for the corporation. The scope of the state widens until the elemental crimes against individuals so dangerous to society in its earlier stages are no longer mortal to organized state life; hence the concept treason now includes high treason or *Hochverrat* as its most significant form. Just as the family gave way to the *Landesdinge* as the center of authority during prehistoric times, so the peace or *mundium* of the land gives way to the king's peace in the period from Tacitus to Charlemagne.[28] The various manifestations of *Landesverrat* are still treason, but a higher treason now surmounts them and reflects a further development of political organization which may or may not be an advance. The general rule still holds true that the crimes which may constitute treason differ at different periods according to the conditions of social life and political development.

The foregoing discussion of the Germanic kingship may well have served to cause confusion, presenting as it has two contradictory theories supported by contradicting facts. In the first place one finds a theory of limited royal power supported by evidence from the time of Tacitus to the *rois fainéants*. But again one discovers a theory of strongly centralized authority upheld by such examples as Alaric, Clovis, Charles Martel, and Charlemagne. Perhaps an answer may be suggested. Prior to the barbarian invasions the natural Germanic tendency to untrammeled personal liberty maintained limited monarchy or else complete absence of kings. Some tribes were probably wholly democratic and had

---

[28] Note the total lack of the conception of the king's peace in the earlier period pointed out by Schröder-von Künssberg, *Lehrbuch der deutschen Rechtsgeschichte* (6th ed.; Berlin and Leipzig: de Gruyter, 1922), pp. 30–31: "Die ordentliche Rechtspflege war Sache der vom Volk eingesetzten Richter . . . einen vom König verliehenen Frieden gab es noch nicht, der allgemeine wie der besondere Frieden war Volks-, nicht Königsfrieden."

The best survey of the objections to the Wilda-Waitz-Brunner theory of a legal public "peace" and the literature connected therewith may be found in Julius Goebel, Jr., *Felony and Misdemeanor* (New York: The Commonwealth Fund, 1937), I, 7–25. Goebel denies the existence of a primitive folk peace or state of quiet constituting a legal concept of public order, although he apparently admits the growth of special protections and interests which find expression in the special *paces* of the *leges barbarorum*. Cf. *Illinois Law Review*, XXXII (1937), 387 for my review of Goebel on this topic; also essay on "The Public Law of the Ripuarian, Almannic, and Bavarian Codes," for the relation of the popular to the ducal *causae* and the types of *paces* or Frieden involved.

no kings; others elected their kings from certain royal families at their popular assemblies but gave them no real power. However, when danger threatened and it became necessary to concentrate authority in the interests of efficiency the most capable warrior would be chosen to lead the host, whence he was entitled the leader or *dux* (*Herzog*).[29] But the *dux* was not necessarily the king and probably commonly was not. Thus one discovers the appearance of a dual authority: one permanent but largely fictitious, the other temporary though real while it lasted. Obviously the extensive authority of a *dux* would constitute a true royal power if it were rendered permanent over any extended period of time, and would completely eclipse the older but empty kingship, which after all was retained perhaps in large measure for religious reasons, as the *rex sacrorum* at Rome, and represented the survival of an earlier actual power. Lacking direct evidence, one must assume that in the long and confused hostilities which accompanied the breaking of the Roman frontier and the irruption into the Empire able chieftains or generals held an almost permanent control, with the result that at the end of this period the people had, in general, become accustomed to resting vast authority in the hands of a single individual. Schröder supports this view when he states that the constitution of the East Germans differs from that of the West Germans because the former lived under kings upon their entrance into history, whereas the communities (*Völkerschaften*) of the West Germans obeyed no single heads in time of peace, neither a hereditary king nor a chosen prince of the land. This difference, however, loses its basic importance with the passage of time since the new type of kingship gradually became habitual among the West Germans and acquired overwhelming authority in the course of the migrations, whereas the old Germanic kingship reflected only distinction of honor and rank while the center of gravity of the kingdom's constitution had remained in the popular assemblies.[30] Thus while an older

---

[29] Cf. Schröder-von Künssberg, *Lehrbuch*, p. 30: "Überhaupt aber hatte der altgermanische König ein eigentliches machtgebot nur gegenüber seinem Gefolge, dem Volke gegenüber war seine Gewalt sehr beschränkt," and p. 31: "Die Könige der germanischen Urzeit sind regelmässig Völkerschaftskönige." Further note Schröder's solution of how the king may act as *dux*, p. 30: "in seiner Eigenschaft als geborener Heerführer und Haupt der Landesgemeinde besass er [der König] zwar gewisse Hoheitsrechte, aber doch wirkte er, wie der Herzog, in allem *exemplo potius quam imperio*: er hatte die Leitung, aber die Beschlüsse über König und Frieden, über Beamtwahlen und gerichtliche Entscheidungen lagen in der Hand der Landesgemeinde, der König hatte dabei nur mitzureden und mitzustimmen wie andere auch."

[30] See Schröder-von Künssberg, *Lehrbuch*, pp. 26–31, on the popular assemblies

dignity might remain long after it had lost its powers it stood beside a newer office which possessed the substance of that lost authority. Only in this way may the apparent contradiction be resolved.

At this point it may be recalled that the contractual conception implying a mutual obligation has been cited as typically Germanic, and also that the peculiarly Germanic conception of treason involved the idea of a broken personal pledge (*Treubruch, infidelitas*). Any attempt to show why these views are true must direct its attention to the office of *dux*.[31] The curious ideas of troth and faith common to the Germans center about this office and the institution of the *comitatus*, which was closely associated with it.[32] The duties involved in maintaining the *mundium* of the family among the primitive Germans must be regarded in the light of a social contract which was not consciously contemplated by the parties concerned. Violation of the interests of society as a whole appeared typically as *Landesverrat*; it consisted of breaches made internally in organized social life. When the interest of society becomes personified in an individual or when that individual establishes a special interest, attacks upon him constitute typical high treason. Still in both these situations a conscious personal pledge and bond are lacking between authority and its beneficiaries. *Treubruch* implies the personal

---

and the early Germanic kingship; also Brunner, *D. R.*, I, 164–180; Waitz, *D. V.*, I, 294–337; von Amira, *Grundriss*, pp. 149–153, on the general characteristics of the early Germanic kingship; G. von Below, *Der deutsche Staat des Mittelalters* (2nd ed.; Leipzig: Quelle and Meyer, 1925), I, 159–163, on "Der König und die Reichspersönlichkeit."

[31] Cf. Schröder-von Künssberg, *Lehrbuch*, pp. 32–36, on *Gaufürst* (*satrapa, furisto*) and *Gaukönig* (*regalis, subregulus*), who were also probably *Richter* (*iudices*); also on *Herzog* (*dux, herizogo, heretoga*).

[32] Cf. Brunner, *D. R.*, I, 180–195, on "Die Gefolgschaft"; Schröder-von Künssberg, *Lehrbuch*, pp. 36–40, on "Das Gefolge" (*comitatus*); Waitz, *D. V.*, I, 236–293; and von Amira, *Grundriss*, pp. 187–191, on "Gefolgschaft und Vassalität." For a similar theory of this development, note Bisoukides, p. 34: *Der Hochverrat*, "Wenn aber die antiken Staaten ihre Strafberechtigung gegen die ihre Existenz bedrohenden Handlungen aus dem Begriffe der Feindseligkeit ableiteten, so legte man in den germanischen Völkerschaften einen anderen Gedanken zu Grunde. Nach germanischer Auffassung ist der Mensch als Mitglied eines Verbandes, dessen Schutz er geniesst, zur Treue und Anhänglichkeit an denselben verpflichtet. Wer nun die Verbandssicherheit gefährdet, indem er seine verbrecherische Tätigkeit nach dieser Richtung hin entfaltet, bricht in schimpflicher Weise die geschuldete Treue, er ist Verräter in diesem Sinne." See Bede, *Historia ecclesiastica* 5, 10: "Non enim habent regem iidem antiqui Saxones, sed satrapas plurimos suae genti praepositos, qui ingruente belli articulo mittunt aequaliter sortes, et quemcumque sors ostenderit, hunc tempore belli ducem omnes secuntur, huic obtemperant; peracto autem bello rursum aequalis potentiae fiunt satrapae."

element. However, it is impossible to ascertain definitely whether the weak and limited kingship of the early Germans was supported by the contractual allegiance of its subjects,[33] but certainly in the case of the military chieftain men pledged their personal honor in his support in time of war so long as he was valorous and worthy of admiration. What one really has is a contract whereby the leader promises courageous and resolute leadership and his followers pledge to emulate him. Here cowardice and desertion on the field of battle (*herisliz*) are treason of the basest sort.[34] The ethical implications of *Treubruch* are probably to be associated with the aggressive impulses, one might say with the sporting spirit of a battle-eager race. Yet the powers which the *dux* enjoyed were chiefly those of military authority. In times when the tribe was at peace this peculiar personal contractual relationship was maintained through the medium of the institution known as "the following" (*Das Gefolge, comitatus*), wherein a group of warriors pledged loyalty to a prominent chieftain and supported him on his hunting and marauding expeditions, as well as in war. In return the chieftain or lord pledged protection, subsistence, and fighting equipment to his followers. However, when the great invasions began and able *duces* became permanent leaders of their people, such chieftains acquired powers which were royal and were followed by their host, which was in a sense a vast *comitatus*, while within the host were subordinate leaders with their own chosen followers.

Treason was now very much a personal matter of bad faith between follower and leader.[35] Later when the people had settled down, the king would still retain chosen followers to constitute a bodyguard whence evolved the various *antrustiones, gesithcundmen, húskarlar,* and *hagustaldii* of the western Germans. Allegiance here is no mere

---

[33] Cf. Schröder-von Künssberg, *Lehrbuch*, p. 31, on an entire people forsaking its troth to a king who had abused his authority or who had appeared to be accursed by the gods. This view implies a contractual relationship between the primitive Germanic kingship and the people (*Volk*), and is not irreconcilable with the position taken in this study.

[34] See Wilda, *Geschichte des deutschen Strafrechts*, I, 987–988; Schröder-von Künssberg, *Lehrbuch*, p. 164; Waitz, *D. V.*, I, 348; also Tacitus *Germania*, c. 6: "scutum reliquisse praecipuum flagitium"; c. 14: "iam vero infame in omnem vitam ac probrosum superstitem principi suo ex acie recessisse"; Caesar *Comm. de Bell. Gall.* 6, 23; Beowulf, 2885. Cf. Brunner-von Schwerin, *D. R.*, II, 883: "Treubruch gegen das Gemeinwesen ist auch das Verbrechen der Heerflucht, der Desertion, des sogenannten Harisliz" (*Heerschlitz, Spaltung des Heeres*).

[35] This is also the end result of Germanic legal development as reflected in the Carolingian capitularies. See Brunner-von Schwerin, *D. R.*, II, 886.

deference to Roman majesty nor support of a Greek faction, but is the assent of the subject to a contract which is bilateral. Here is no king with all the rights and none of the obligations. Obviously this is a situation looking forward to feudalism, since every *dux* had his followers even though he were less than the king of his tribe or *Volk*.[36] Furthermore every petty chieftain was joined to his followers by personal pledges. Hence treason could be committed against any *dux* or lord, and when the distinction between the *dux-king* and the *duces-lords* has been drawn, one finds a *Treubruch* which is high treason on the one hand, and a *Treubruch* which is petty treason on the other hand.[37] Throughout all this one discerns many elements reminiscent of the Roman relation of patron and client, but here the military element is predominant. In both instances one cannot mistake the personal nature of the pledge and the consciously assumed obligation which the later ceremony of fealty and homage symbolizes. But the combination of land tenure with the *comitatus* nexus, the resolution of the *dux-king* into a *dominus* and of the kingship into an office possessing special interests, and the gradual adoption of the idea of *maiestas* changing allegiance from a contractual to a deferential matter was a process left for the ensuing Middle Ages.

Furthermore, one must observe that *Landesverrat* may also be involved in the idea of *Treubruch*, for treason to the land and folk involves bad faith, though the personal relation is obscured; thus the *Treubruch* in this case is hardly typical.[38] However, when one wishes to evaluate the seriousness of a treason, he must consider the conditions existing between the criminal and the object of his crime. Hence the weightier the obligation the more heinous the offense, but this does not imply that the narrowest and most personal obligations were the most serious, as Epstein suggests.[39] Rather, treasons which affect a wider

---

[36] See Wilda, *Geschichte des deutschen Strafrechts*, I, 984–985.

[37] See Bisoukides, *Der Hochverrat*, 37: "Der Treubruch stellt sich nunmehr tatsächlich als ein Gattungsverbrechen," which includes high treason, treason to the land and folk, and other crimes such as petty treason; also Brunner-von Schwerin, *D. R.*, II, 881: "Was das neuere Strafrecht als Landesverrat bezeichnet, war in älteren Rechte Treubruch gegen das Gemeinwesen."

[38] Compare this theory of the relation of *Treubruch* and *Landesverrat* with that advanced by Bisoukides, *Der Hochverrat*, p. 35. Wilda (*Geschichte des deutschen Strafrechts*, I, 988) speaks of high treason as not only depriving a king of his power and seeking his deposition, but as also separating him from the land and people which have been under his authority. Here there seems to be a certain integration of the concepts of *Hochverrat* and *Landesverrat*.

[39] Cf. Bisoukides, *Der Hochverrat*, p. 34, n. 1, referring to Max Epstein, *Der*

number of individuals, as in the community or state, or which affect more influential persons as the king, would be more serious than breaches of faith against the narrower circle of the family or against a petty lord. Consequently, in the absence of a true king whose authority is generally recognized as superior to that of all other *duces* or lords, one can hardly say there is any real high treason, but instead as many petty treasons as there are crimes against lords. This condition, which may not be altogether hypothetical for this early period, was surely realized later when feudal society had developed.

Finally something must be said about the only references to treason that may be found in writers who are contemporary with the early Germans and who treat of their laws and customs. Caesar mentions treason in connection with the *comitatus* quite specifically in an oft-quoted passage.[40] Here one discovers that when any chieftain in the council offered to act as *dux* those who wanted to follow him declared their wish by rising and approving "the cause and the man" and were applauded by the assembled folk, but any men who had pledged their support and then did not follow the *dux* were counted in the number of deserters and traitors (*in desertorum ac proditorum numero*), and no further confidence was reposed in them. This statement is decidedly interesting since it presents the conditions of typical *Treubruch* at such an early date that one must conceive of the entire matter as characteristically Germanic. Also it represents this early *Treubruch* as a closer approximation to the feudal petty treason than any other form of treason unless it be violations of the Roman relation of patron and client. This is clearly treason to a lord or *dux* who possesses no mark of royal authority; hence there is no high treason here, although elements of *Landesverrat* may enter into the breach of troth insofar as the *dux* is representing the authority of the community and is not acting in a private capacity when he is not engaged in an enterprise of his own. It is the general implication of the passage that traitors are considered as men who cannot be trusted to live up to personal pledges and obligations which they have

---

Landesverrat in historischer, dogmatischer und rechtsvergleichender Darstellung in H. Bennecke *Strafrechtliche Abhandlungen,* Heft 12 (Breslau: Schletter, 1898), p. 18.

[40] Caesar *Comm. de Bell. Gall.* 6, 23: "Atque ubi quis ex principibus in concilio dixit se ducem fore, qui sequi velint profiteantur, consurgunt ii qui et causam et hominem probant suumque auxilium pollicentur, atque a multitudine conlaudantur; qui ex his secuti non sunt in desertorum ac proditorium numero ducuntur omniumque his rerum postea fides derogatur." See M. Haidlen, *Der Hochverrat und Landesverrat nach altdeutschem Recht* Stuttgart: Tübingen Diss., 1896), pp. 4–10.

voluntarily assumed. Perhaps this affords some basis for the remark of Pollock and Maitland that "the close association of treason against the king with treason against one's personal lord who is not the king is eminently Germanic."[41] A curious question arises here as to what attitude would have been taken to an injury done to those early Germanic kings who "reigned but did not govern" in the tribes which possessed kings. One hazards the guess that it would have been less high treason than sacrilege done to a sort of *rex sacrorum*.[42] But the later position of the *duces* as kings was defined by the personal *Treubruch*, and their ducal character as *primus inter pares* was evinced by the fact that high treason against them was still the personal infidelity mentioned by Caesar, which was amendable among some peoples upon the payment of a suitable *wer*.[43] Also it should be noted that this sort of action involves Germanic *infidelitas* but nothing resembling Roman *maiestas*. An overt act against a Germanic ducal king was often a less serious offense than a word whispered or a malediction uttered against a Roman emperor.

In another passage comparable in significance to that cited from Caesar, Tacitus observes in his *Germania* that it is permissible at the popular assembly (*concilium*) to make accusations and place individuals in peril of their lives by bringing capital charges against them.[44] He adds that the death penalty is imposed in different ways according to the nature of the crime. Traitors and deserters are hanged from trees while the cowardly, unwarlike, and infamous or effeminate are cast into the marshes beneath a wicker basket (*cratis*).[45] The reason for this dif-

---

[41] Pollock and Maitland, *History of English Law*, I, 51–52.

[42] Cf. Schröder-von Künnsberg, *Lehrbuch*, p. 30: "Wesentlich gehörte zum nordgermanischen Königtum auch die priesterliche Tätigkeit."

[43] See essay on "Treason and Related Offenses in the Anglo-Saxon Dooms," for the problem of a royal wergeld in Germanic law.

[44] Tacitus *Germania*, c. 12: "Licet apud concilium accusare quoque et discrimen capitis intendere. distinctio poenarum ex delicto. proditores et transfugas arboribus suspendunt, ignavos et imbelles et corpore infames caeno ac palude, iniecta insuper crate, mergunt. diversitas supplicii illuc respicit, tamquam scelera ostendi oporteat, dum puniuntur, flagitia abscondi." For a detailed interpretation of this passage, philological and legal, see Much, *Die Germania*, pp. 146–150.

[45] Regarding this especially horrible form of punishment, see Much, *Die Germania*, p. 149, where he suggests that it was, in the main, considered appropriate for women, and that it was regarded as most disgraceful when applied to men, being used in the cases of effeminates and weaklings. Cf. *Lex Gundobada Burgundionum* 34, 1: "se qua mulier maritum suum, cui legitime est iuncta, dimiserit, necetur in lute." Much cites additional instances from the old Norse laws. However, there are examples of similar punishments and the use of the *cratis* in early Roman history, as recorded by Livy, 1, 51: "novo genere leti, deiectus [Turnus] ad caput

ference in the mode of punishment rests on the principle that the criminal acts of traitors should be punished in a manner exposed to the sight of all. In this way the retribution due the traitor might serve as a warning to others. On the other hand, abominable and infamous crimes should be hidden, thereby concealing what was considered too vile and disgraceful for public knowledge. This curious association of the crimes involving infidelity and infamy hardly seems accidental since a similar relationship emerges in the later barbarian codes.

The greatest difficulty in evaluating the testimony of Tacitus results from the fact that he did not define what he meant by *proditores,* and a certain ambiguity results from that omission. The difference of opinion to which this has given rise is set forth at some length by Bisoukides.[46] Some assert that by *proditio* is meant a crime which is committed through the breach of a special troth and they do not consider it a relatively recent product of Germanic law but a type of criminal act reaching back into a very primitive period.[47] Others, like Knitschky, maintain that *proditio* refers only to the Roman equivalent of *Landesverrat* and that Tacitus has used the word in this Roman sense, urging that he would have appended an explanatory statement had he employed *proditio* in other than its usual Roman connotation. In corroboration of this view Bisoukides adds an original theory of his own. He states that it would be misleading to maintain that the mention of the traitor in connection with the deserter rests on pure accident; furthermore, desertion is a subordinate species of treason and perhaps the oldest type of treason against land and folk.[48] Also he asserts that the breach of troth occasioned by a follower's desertion of his lord had not been punishable in criminal law, but that such traitors were merely held in general contempt without legal consequence. Knitschky has supported this on the basis of the remark in Tacitus that "it brings life-long infamy and shame to have fled the field of battle surviving one's chieftain."[49] It may also be

---

aquae Ferentinae crate superne iniecta saxisque congestis mergeretur"; and 4, 50: "quos necari sub crate iusserat."

[46] This controversy is explained in Bisoukides, *Der Hochverrat,* pp. 34–36.

[47] *Ibid.,* p. 35. However, cf. C. H. Knitschky, *Das Verbrechen des Hochverraths* (Jena: Mauke's Verlag, 1874), p. 4: "Denn unter proditores zunächst nur Landesverräther zu verstehen, ist um so gerechtfertiger, als auch den Römern der Ausdruck in dieser Bedeutung geläufig war."

[48] See Heinrich Zoepfl, *Deutsche Rechtsgeschichte* (Brunswick: F. Wreden, 1872), III, 373: "den Verrath und das Ueberlaufen zum Feinde, welches letztere selbst nur eine Unterart des Verrathes ist."

[49] Tacitus *Germania,* c. 14: "iam vero infame in omnem vitam ac probrosum superstitem principi suo ex acie recessisse"; Knitschky, *Das Verbrechen,* p. 7.

noted that Beowulf says it is better for the coward and traitor to die than
to live a life of disgrace and dishonor.[50] But Bisoukides is unwilling to
go the full distance with Knitschky and thinks the difficulty may be
solved by taking a midway position in the controversy. He thinks it possible that the condition of troth was standard (*massgebend*) for a certain class of crimes, but that the cases which actually occurred were
clearly those now falling under the category of *Landesverrat*, in accordance with Brunner's dictum that what the more recent criminal law
calls treason against land and folk was in the older law breach of troth
against the community.[51] Thus Tacitus meant *Landesverrat* and has used
the word *proditio* accordingly.[52]

However, if one returns to the passage in Caesar concerning treason
he finds that the evidence supports the view that *proditio* is a breach of
a special personal troth which goes back into deepest antiquity, for it
mentions *proditorum* in specific connection with the *dux* and *comitatus*,
and Caesar has the advantage of antedating Tacitus by a century or
more.[53] The only *Landesverrat* that can be construed from Caesar's passage would be in a case where the *dux* represented the authority of the
community. Furthermore, the argument for *Landesverrat* of the Roman
type, drawn from the association of the words *proditores et transfugas*
in Tacitus, loses its force when faced in Caesar by the earlier and almost
identical combination *desertorum ac proditorum*, which is employed in
connection with typical *Treubruch*. On the other hand the punishments
differ, for Caesar mentions only the contempt of their fellows whereas
Tacitus speaks of hanging in one passage and of disgrace in the other.
Again this might indicate two different sorts of treason: one, a clear case
of *Treubruch* where a man deserts his chief in the line of battle and sur-
vives in disgrace and contempt; the other, desertion as well but punishable with death. Seemingly Tacitus either contradicts himself or else
refers to desertion under two different sets of circumstances. A plausible
explanation may be advanced for the second alternative. The first in-

[50] Beowulf, 2885, trans. by Edwin Morgan (Aldington: Hand and Flower Press,
1952), lines 2888–2890: "when hero and nobleman Hear from afar the story of
your flight and inglorious action."

[51] Brunner-von Schwerin, *D. R.*, II, 881.

[52] This theory accords with the general view taken in this study as far as
Bisoukides' "standardized troth" corresponds to that *Treubruch* mentioned above
(n. 38) which was *Landesverrat* and therefore untypical because it lacked the full
personal relation. Cf. Bisoukides, *Der Hochverrat*, p. 35: "es ist wohl möglich, dass
das Verhältnis der Treue für eine Verbrechensgattung massgebend gewesen war."

[53] Cf. Zoepfl, *D. R.*, III, 373–374.

stance may relate to simple breach of the personal pledge where a man deserts his chief in a marauding expedition or other privately conducted warfare, whereas the latter case bearing the death penalty may refer to desertion in an intercommunal or intertribal war, where the *dux* represents the folk and in which case the desertion would constitute *Landesverrat* as well as the modified form of *Treubruch.* In general, however, one cannot feel that Knitschky has found *perduellio*, the Roman equivalent for treason against land and folk (*Landesverrat*), in Tacitus or that Bisoukides has done more than discover a qualified *Landesverrat.* Of course, the latter is quite correct when he says it cannot be maintained with certainty that the matter of troth and *Treubruch* is a specifically and uniquely Germanic institution, for Dionysius reports a somewhat comparable relationship between patron and client existing in Rome as early as the time of the kings.[54]

Also, the ancient Greek *prodosia* had the basic connotation of bad faith, but there was no personal breach of troth of the Germanic type in classical Greek political thought, although something very similar may be found in Homeric times. The later Greek idea of *prodosia* related to the destruction of the form of government of a state over which some tyrant, for example, had secured control; in a democracy it was inherent in any aspect of *stasis* or revolutionary activity that would result in the overthrow of the *demos* (*katalysis tou demou*).[55] Such attacks upon the constitution do not appear in the primitive Germanic legal sources, since the communities of that period lacked a constitutional structure. Likewise they lacked the special protection of a royal criminal law enforced under the king's peace. There is even evidence that if the king attacked another he could be pursued by his fellow countrymen and killed if taken prisoner by them, a situation which leads back to a very early form of customary law.[56] The advanced po-

---

[54] See Dionysius of Halicarnassus, *Roman Antiquities*, trans. by E. Cary, Loeb Series (London: Heinemann, 1937), Vol. I, 2, 10, for a remarkable description of the relation between client and patron among the early Romans. He states that it was impious and unlawful for both patron and client to be found in the number of each other's enemies, and that whoever was convicted of such association was guilty of treason (*prodosia*) according to the law sanctioned by Romulus. Dionysius adds that such a person "might lawfully be put to death by any man who so wished as a victim devoted to the Jupiter of the infernal regions [Dis or Pluto]. For it was customary among the Romans, whenever they wished to put people to death without incurring any penalty, to devote their persons to some god or other, and particularly to the gods of the lower world."

[55] See Bisoukides, *Der Hochverrat*, p. 36, n. 1.

[56] *Frostuthingslög*, 4, 50. This Norse code of the thirteenth century is a basic

litical structures of Greek constitutionalism and Roman absolutism did not fit the simple conditions of the early Germanic communities, but they approached the Greek more nearly than the Roman since the trend of their political theory was in the direction of limitation.

As far as punishment is concerned, treason and desertion belonged to the gravest breaches of the peace and were among the few crimes punished with a capital penalty executed in public.[57] They were generally associated with those offenses which were held especially shameful and dishonorable and in which burial was completed by covering the condemned with mud and dirt.[58] As Tacitus notes, the death penalty was executed through hanging the condemned to trees. In this way the loathing felt for the traitor could be given expression or else linked with certain religious conceptions. Wilda, however, affirms that the death penalty was not inflicted in all cases of *Landesverrat* but only in those where the evildoer was taken in an overt act.[59] Finally, treason against land and folk has always brought an irreparable hostility for the offender and an outlawry which Brunner says must be associated with the death penalty.[60] The outlaw was called Wolf (Gothic *wargs*) and hence was condemned to death; indeed, he was probably consecrated or devoted to death on religious grounds reminiscent of the Roman conception of *sacer*.[61] Schröder explains that the outlaw (*útlegth*) was accursed and unholy because he had failed to respect the sacredness of human rights, and thus he had forfeited the protection which society could maintain over his person.[62] However, it was the Germanic view that whoever broke the peace had forfeited it for himself with the result that the outlaw had no further claim to the protection which he had enjoyed in the state or society of which he had formerly been a member. The idea of the law is clearly apparent: that every man must consider an enemy of the people as his own personal enemy. The outlaw was thrust out of the community and anyone might kill him without fear of punishment.[63] He

---

legal source for early Scandinavian legislation. See note 65.

[57] Cf. Wilda, *Geschichte des deutschen Strafrechts*, I, 986; Zoepfl, *D. R.*, III, 376–378.

[58] See Waitz, *D. V.*, I, 424.

[59] Wilda, *Geschichte des deutschen Strafrechts*, I, 986. Bisoukides states that this is an arbitrary assertion for which he can find no substantiating evidence (*Der Hochverrat*, p. 36, with n. 1).

[60] Brunner-von Schwerin, *D. R.*, II, 882, 57–59.

[61] Schröder-von Künssberg, *Lehrbuch*, p. 81; Brunner, *D. R.*, I, 234–235.

[62] Schröder-von Künssberg, *Lehrbuch*, pp. 82–83; Waitz, *D. V.*, I, 427–428.

[63] Bisoukides, *Der Hochverrat*, p. 37, n. 1.

was forced to flee into the wilderness. No one dared protect him, house him, or feed him (*Speisebann*), much as in the case of the Roman *aquae et ignis interdictio*. Whoever assisted him laid himself liable to punishment or to the possibility of becoming outlaw also. All traitors were outlaw (*exlex*), and outlawry was the inevitable concomitant of a wide variety of detestable crimes. The bond of the *Sippe*, which underlies the authority of the state and which at one stage of social development constituted the sole public authority, would be destroyed completely by failure to check treasons and related offenses.[64] Hence the penalty was of the utmost severity; the wife of the outlaw became as a widow, his children as orphans. His property was unprotected and what he possessed would be partly turned over to the community to serve as restitution for the damage he had wrought and partly given as compensation to those whom he had injured. Later he was denied all rights in property or at law, and finally even his innocent kin were held attainted of his crime.

At this point it may be profitable to turn aside for a brief analysis of certain Scandinavian materials of the later Middle Ages. Although much later in point of time than the general period here under survey, these old Norse sources contain so much that is early from the point of view of ideas that they should not be disregarded, especially since they serve to illustrate many of the political and legal principles now under discussion. Furthermore, the sections dealing with secular law are not greatly influenced by Roman and ecclesiastical traditions; in fact, they represent a very pure Germanic formulation of the customary criminal law. Of these sources the two most important are the *Frostathing* law (*Frostuthingslög*) of the middle thirteenth century and the *Gulathing* law (*Gulathingslög*) which may be as much as a century earlier.[65] In

---

[64] See Schröder-von Künssberg, *Lehrbuch*, pp. 85–86, for the difference between *Volksfeindschaft* and the *faidosus* against a *Sippe*. Cf. in general, Brunner, *D. R.*, I, 221–231, on the feud (*faida*).

[65] Cf. Karl von Amira, *Das altnorwegische Vollstreckungsverfahren* (Munich: I. Ackermann, 1874), pp. 21–25, for a brief survey of the old Norse laws relating to treason; Wilda, *Geschichte des deutschen Strafrechts*, I, 985–986, for selections from these laws; F. P. Brandt, *Forelaesninger over den norske Rethistorie*, Lectures on the History of Norwegian Law (Kristiania [Oslö]: N. W. Damm, 1883), II, 130; Konrad von Maurer, *Altisländisches Strafrecht und Gerichtswesen*, Vol. V: Vorlesungen über altnordische Rechtsgeschichte, (Leipzig: A. Deichert, 1910), pp. 136–174, on *Die Friedlosigkeit*. An invaluable aid to research into the old Norse laws is the translation of the *Gulathing* law and the *Frostathing* law by L. M. Larson in the Columbia Records of Civilization Series, No. XX, entitled *The Earliest Norwegian Laws* (New York: Columbia University Press, 1935). On the age and transmission of these laws, see Larson, pp. 25–31. There are also excellent

both these laws the curious Norse expression, *nithingsvíg, nithingsverk,* is used in connection with such capital offenses as high treason, treason against land and folk, housebreaking, arson, and murder (morth).[66] Such crimes are shameful acts placing the offender outside both legal and religious protection and involving "strict peacelessness" (*die strenge Friedlosigkeit*), which means absolute exclusion from the peace of the land.[67] The man who commits arson with hostile intent has violated the fundamental social sanctions, and consequently the usual protection of society is withdrawn from him. He is termed a *Brandwolf,* deemed unholy and accursed (*úheilagr*), and placed outside the peace of the land (*útlegth*).[68] It is interesting to note that the essence of the idea of *nithing* is shame, and that the *Frostathing* law states that the greatest *nithingsvíg* is committed when one betrays the land and people away from the king.[69] Here treason against land and folk seems to be integrated with high treason. Just as in the time of Tacitus crimes of infamy were associated with the crimes of infidelity, so here treason is declared to be the greatest act of shame. The traditional connection of these crimes has developed in this strictly Germanic custom until, at last, the

---

translations in German in the *Germanenrechte, Schriften der Akademie für deutsches Recht* as follows: *Band 4, Norwegisches Recht: Das Rechtsbuch des Frostothings,* trans. by Rudolf Meissner (Weimar: H. Böhlaus, 1939); *Band 6, Norwegisches Recht: Das Rechtsbuch des Gulathings,* trans. by R. Meissner (Weimar: H. Böhlaus, 1935). In addition there are translations by R. Meissner, *Band 5, Das norwegische Gefolgschaftsrecht* (*Hirthskrá*) (Weimar: H. Böhlaus, 1938); by Baron von Schwerin, *Band 7, Schwedische Rechte: Älteres Westgötalag, Uplandslag* (Weimar: H. Böhlaus, 1935). Andreas Heusler's *Das Strafrecht der Isländersagas* (Leipzig: Duncker and Humblot, 1911) is disappointing in its failure to deal with treasonable offenses as such, although it has significant references to such topics as inviolability (*Unverletzlichkeit*), accursedness (*Unheiligkeit*), "peacelessness" (*Friedlosigkeit*), banishment (*Landesverweisung*), outlawry (*Acht*), blood feud (*Fehde*), and revenge (*Rache*).

[66] Cf. von Amira, *Voll.,* 19; Larson (*Norwegian Laws,* 423) defines *nithing* crime (*nithingsvíg*) as follows: "A crime, usually murder, committed under such circumstances and by such methods as to give the criminal the character of a *nithing* (a mean, infamous, treacherous person). *Nithing* deeds usually led to permanent outlawry." Also see von Amira, *Grundriss,* pp. 233–234, on *Böswilligkeit.*

[67] In general, see von Amira, *Voll.,* pp. 11–45, on *die strenge Friedlosigkeit*; von Amira, *Grundriss,* pp. 229–240, on *Friedensbruch*; Haidlen, *Der Hochverrat,* pp. 10–14.

[68] Haidlen, *Der Hochverrat,* p. 20.

[69] *Frostuthingslög* 4, 4 (Larson, 257): "the worst form of *nithing* crime is plotting to deprive the king of land and subjects"; von Amira, 21: "Das ist das grösste Neidingswerk, wenn man Land und Leute unter dem König weg verrät"; Meissner, 4, 61: "Das ist das grösste Neidingswerk, wenn jemand verräterisch Land und Leute dem Könige abwendig macht"; Brunner-von Schwerin, *D. R.,* II, 882.

ideas of infamy and infidelity are identified in a single crime, treason. The law, then goes on to say that

if the king accuses any man of treason against the land, he shall appoint from his household a man of equal rank with the accused. . . . This man shall have the king's writ and seal and shall press the charge at a shire-meeting [*fylki*] of the folk from which the king is absent. It is, also an act of shame if any man flees from the land in time of war and returns to wage war against his own country without having renounced the peace from which he departed.[70]

Another provision of this law states that

if any man goes away beyond the peace of the land and returns to wage war against his country or against the folk who still remain within the king's peace, whether they be of native or alien birth, such a man shall forfeit his lands and movable property. However, if he wishes to atone for his actions, a helmsman [shipmaster] shall pay forty marks to the king, but each oarsman only three marks. To all those whom they have despoiled they shall pay as much as those who were ravaged can claim under oath.[71]

In general, it is affirmed that if a man is convicted of a shameful crime (*nithingsvíg*) he shall forfeit his real property, "but no man can at any time forfeit more land than he actually owns."[72]

The office of king was placed so distinctly beneath the law among the Norse that it was easier according to their legal thinking for a king to be guilty of treason against the land and folk than for any of the people to be guilty of high treason. The king was merely *primus inter pares* without extraordinary, unlimited authority and care was taken to bind him so that he would respect the law. This end was attained not by placing the king under oath but by pledging the people to avenge any breach of the law made by the king or a lord. Thus it was enacted that

no man shall make an unlawful attack upon another in his home, and, if the king does this, an arrow shall be cut and sent through all the shires [*fylken*] and every man shall rise up and kill him if he can be caught. And, if he escapes, he shall never again return to the land. And whoever will not rise up against him shall pay a fine of three marks, and a like amount shall be paid by any man who fails to forward the arrow.[73]

---

[70] Cf. Larson (*Norwegian Laws*, p. 257), who renders *in time of war* as *in time of unpeace*; von Amira, *Voll.*, 2; Meissner, *Norwegisches Recht*, 4, 61–62; Wilda, *Geschichte des deutschen Strafrechts*, I, 986.

[71] *Frost.* 7, 25 (Larson, 322; von Amira, 23, but here incorrectly cited as *Frost.* 4, 25; Meissner, 4, 151).

[72] *Frost.* 4, 4 (Larson, 258; Meissner, 4, 62).

[73] *Frost.* 4, 50 (Larson, 278; Meissner, 4, 88; Wilda, I, 989). Cf. *Frost.* 4, 51–52 (Larson, 278; Meissner, 4, 89; Wilda, I, 989, n. 2), stating that if a *jarl* commits

An additional illustration of this principle may be found in the *Goda* of
King Hakon of Norway, relating to an occasion when the king issued a
command to the *Landthing* that the entire folk should accept Christianity:

> It is the will of all the countryfolk, spake Asbjörn, to keep the law, that you
> have established here in the *Frostathing* and that we have here adopted; we
> wish to follow you in all things and to keep you as our king, so long as a single
> one of us countryfolk, here present in this *Thing*, remains alive, if you, O king,
> preserve moderation and only ask of us such things as we can grant you, and
> as are not impossible for us. However, if you press these matters with such
> impetuosity and if you try force and violence on us, then we, countryfolk,
> determine to forsake you in all things, and to take for ourselves another lord,
> as is our right, who shall hold in freedom to the faith that is dear to us. Now,
> O king, you shall choose between these alternatives before this *Thing* comes
> to an end.[74]

Although the section of the older *Gulathing* law enumerating the
various *nithingsverke* does not include the crime of treason, several references to this offense may be found in the law.[75] Thus in one place
Landesverrat is associated with murder (*morth*) and breach of oath to
keep the peace, and it is stated that one may clear himself of this crime
through an oath taken by twelve oath helpers.[76] Also it provides that "if

---

such an offense the arrow shall be sent forth through four *fylken*, and if a baron
does this the arrow shall be sent forth through two *fylken*.

[74] Wilda, *Geschichte des deutschen Strafrechts*, I, 989, quoting *S. Hakonar Goda*,
c. 17.

[75] Cf. von Amira, *Voll.*, 21, 24–25. Von Amira notes that *Gulathingslög*, 178,
which lists the *nithingsverke* and corresponds to *Frostuthingslög* 4, 4, contains no
reference to treason, whereas *Frost.* 4, 4, contains no reference to homicides caused
by striking with sticks and stones, to the killing of thieves under certain circumstances, and to the robbing of bodies on a battlefield, all of which are contained in
Gula, 178. Von Amira then says that although the *Frostuthingslög* is more recent
than the *Gulathingslög*, it cannot be maintained from the omissions in the former
law that the old *strenge Friedlosigkeit* was being weakened. Rather the addition of
treason in the *Frostuthingslög* indicates that the circle of *nithingsverke* was widened
in the period between 1150 and 1225. However, when considered from the general
point of view of the history of treason among the Germanic peoples, the failure of
the *Gulathingslög* to list treason among the *nithingsverke* does not imply a recent
extension of the idea of *nithing*, or shame, to treason. The association of infamy with
infidelity is as old as Germanic law itself.

[76] *Gulathingslög* 132 (Larson, 121; Meissner, 6, 97). Cf. *Frost.* 15 (Larson, 399;
Meissner, 4, 248); and *Gula.* 312 (Larson, 198; Meissner, 6, 182); also *Frost.* 2, 46
(Larson, 244; Meissner, 4, 42); and *Gula.* 23 (Larson, 51; Meissner, 6, 20–21),
which involve church law relative to the breaking of a sinful oath if it concerns
treason and to the denial of burial in hallowed ground to traitors (*Königsverräter*).
The Norwegian *Hirthskrá*, or Law of the Following (*Gefolgschaftsrecht*), of the

anyone fares forth from our land . . . he has the right to return whenever he wishes, so long as he is not a member of a band of enemies to our
king."[77] But if a man joined such a hostile band, then he has clearly
forfeited the peace of the land and become *friedlos,* placing himself
outside the law (*utlagr*). In yet another place the *Gulathing* law asserts
that

> if a man who was once sent hence into outlawry returns to the land bringing
> true war tidings, he shall be allowed the right of habitation though he had
> formerly been outlawed. But if a man brings war tidings that are not true, he
> shall be outlawed even though he has already been allowed the right of
> habitation.

Then it adds that if the token arrow sent forth through the *fylken* to
summon the farmers to repel raids shall go out into their homes, all to
whom it comes must muster on shipboard within five days. "But if anyone stays quietly at home, he shall be outlawed, for at such a time both
thegn and thrall shall go forth." Finally it declares: "If a hostile force
invades the land and the king, fearing that men are likely to fail him,
demands hostages from us, we have no right to refuse the demand. But
whoever does refuse is [by that fact] guilty of treason."[78] This legislation suggests a form of treason against land and folk that stresses the
obligation of the folk to defend the land against hostile raids and to
prevent the spread of false reports which might endanger the security
of the land, but it also makes clear the responsibility of the king to lead
and command even if he must take hostages to ensure the successful
defense of the land.

Further, the attachment of the Norse people for the sea colors much
of this legislation and has a bearing on the manner in which treason may
be committed. This is evident in a law concerning treason against land
and folk which runs as follows:

> If anyone makes ready a longship in some part of the countryside and does
> not make known the destination whither he will fare . . . and if [the men who

---

thirteenth century indicates the procedure where the king reproaches a duke (13, 3)
or a *jarl* (17, 3) or a freeman (*Landherr, baro*) (20, 1–2) with treason or faith-
lessness (*Verrat oder Untreue, Landesverrat oder Falschheit*). In any case, the
charge shall be made with circumspection and restraint. Here taking the twelvefold
oath seems to be replaced with the opportunity for the person charged to be judged
according to law with the counsel of responsible men (*mit dem Rate guter Männer
nach dem Gesetz*), twelve in number for the *Landherr.* Cf. *Hirthskrá* 3, 1–2, on
Landesverrat for failure to perform certain requisite duties for the king.

[77] *Gula.* 148 (Larson, 126; Meissner, 6, 97).
[78] *Gula.* 312 (Larson, 197–198; Meissner, 6, 181–182).

sail the ship] renounce the peace and fare forth to ravage this region, then they are *nithing*; but if they harry elsewhere then they are outlaw but not *nithing*. And, if they fare forth and do not renounce the peace, then they are outlaw and *nithing* as well and forfeit every penny's worth of their goods, no matter where they harry.[79]

High treason, as well as *Landesverrat*, is suggested in the law which states:

If you point the ship southward along the shore, and a man deserts the ship while it is faring southward and while the king is fighting to defend the land, then he is outlaw and may regain the peace by the payment of forty marks. If, however, the helmsman [shipmaster] deserts, he is outlaw in every respect.[80]

Approximately contemporary with these laws are the Swedish *Westgötalag* and *Ostgötalag*. The former sets forth that "it is a shameful act for a man to carry his shield across the boundary and wage war upon his own land, and that such a man forfeits his land and peace and shall lose his possessions." It is an irredeemable offense both for him and his followers.[81] The *Ostgotalag* defines the penalties for *Landesverrat* even more exactly:

If one chances upon a man who leads a band of strangers [foreigners] into his own land; and, if he bears his shield across the boundary, if he wages war upon his own land, if he burns, if he binds the people and carries them off, and, if he shall be convicted of these things upon evidence, then he shall forfeit his life and all that he possesses in the land and in the province. And of his property one-third shall go to those who have suffered injury, another third shall go to the king, and the last to the folk.[82]

Similarly one reads in the Danish law of King Erik:

This shall men, also, know, that no man may renounce his land. Furthermore, if one fares forth from the realm and joins an army of strangers in an expedition against his own land and harries that land, then shall that man

---

[79] *Gula.* 314 (Larson, 198–199; Meissner, 6, 182–183).

[80] *Gula.* 302 (Larson, 192; Meissner, 6, 175–176). Cf. von Amira, *Voll.* 22.

[81] See *Westgötalag*, trans. by von Schwerin (7, 22), who renders *landvist* as *Landverbleib* rather than *Frieden*, which is given by Wilda, *Geschichte des deutschen Strafrechts*, I, 985, quoting *Westgötalag*, I, 4, with further reference in I, 985, n. 3.

[82] *Ibid.*, 985–986, quoting *Ostgötalag*, *Ethz.*, c. 30. Also note *Uplandslag*, c. 15 (Von Schwerin, 140), in the section on *Mannheiligkeit*, dealing with matters whose sanctity must be respected, which states that "if any man bears a hostile shield against the all-powerful king or against the realm in which he himself was born, he has thereby forfeited his neck [i.e., his life] if he be captured, and in addition he must lose his land and goods whether he be captured or not." Then follows a statement of the procedure to be followed against such a traitor, including judgment by twelve responsible men.

forfeit to the king every penny that belongs to him in the land, both landed property and other possessions. For men call that the crime of bearing the war-shield against the realm.[83]

Later one hears that the Frisians led those guilty of treason to their land and folk northward to the strand and drowned them in the sea.[84]

In early Scandinavian political thought kings and princes are justified only when they perform the definite service of protecting their people. As is the case among the Greeks, the duty of the ruler is to rule well, and he who rules badly is an incompetent or tyrant whom the people are obligated to remove. But, in addition, the Germans were a people whose political and legal thought expressed itself in terms of "rights." Hence this right to forsake the bad king is defined in the laws themselves, and is frequently set forth in other writings. The skald, Sighvater, sings: "Red gold serves ofttimes to redeem plunderers from the courageous king; but [this time] the monarch refused it; he had the heads of these wicked men cut off with his sword; his trusty warriors hastened the revenge for the robbery: thus should the land be protected"; and then again: "This proved his might best, for, with a sharp sword, the guardian of the land cleft the skull of many a Viking."[85] In the *Fagrskinna* one reads of the jarl Erlingr:

> When Erlingr was in Tunsberg, he learned that they [Vikings] were harrying to the east. Then he went eastward to seek them and captured Fridrek and Bjarni with two ships; and he had Fridrek bound to an anchor and thrown overboard; and Bjarni was hanged and no man troubled himself about it.[86]

[83] *Ibid.*, I, 985, quoting *K. Erichs seeländisches Recht* 2, 31. This enactment is numbered 2, 27, in the translation by Baron von Schwerin in the *Germanenrechte*: *Band 8. Dänische Rechte* (Weimar: H. Böhlaus, 1938), pp. 46–47. Here the clause, *thet callae maen awgskiold førth a rikit*, is rendered merely "Denn das nennt man Landesverrat," although he points out on p. 47, n. 2, that the literal meaning is "das nennen die Leute einen feindlichen Schild gegen das Reich geführt." It is the same expression employed above in *Uplandslag*, c. 15 (Von Schwerin, 140). The theme is extended from traitorous hostile attack (*feindlichen Schild*) to treasonable malicious counsel (*mit üblem Rat*) in Knut's Law of the Following (*Gefolgschaftsrecht*), c. 2 (*Germanenrechte*, Band 8, p. 195). After stating that all men must render their lord full troth and obedience and observe all his commands (c. 1), it proceeds to state: "If it happens that there be a more dangerous and shameful troth-breaker [*Treubrecher*] and if he commits a Judas-act against his lord through evil counsel, then he forfeits his life and all his goods."

[84] Brunner-von Schwerin, *D. R.*, II, 882.

[85] Von Amira, *Voll.*, 24, quoting Snorri, *Olafs s. ens helga* 177.

[86] *Ibid.*, 24, quoting the *Fagrskinna* 205. See *Fagrskinna-Kortfattet norsk Konge-saga*, edited by P. A. Munch and C. R. Unger (Christiania [Oslö]: N. W. Damm, 1847).

Nevertheless, despite this general recognition that the king should be subordinate to the law and should actively maintain the law, examples may be cited of rulers who were quite despotic. The case of King Harold Fairhair of Norway, related in the Icelandic *Egils-saga* recalls the capricious disregard for earlier custom and precedent that may be found among the early Merovingian kings of the Franks. Thus one reads that

> King Harold was very careful, when he had gotten new peoples under his power, about barons and rich landowners, and all those whom he suspected of being at all likely to raise rebellion. Every such man he treated in one of two ways: he either made him become his liege-man, or go abroad; or [as a third choice] suffer yet harder conditions, some even losing life and limb.[87]

High treason immediately assumes greater importance when kings appear who, in large measure, disregard customary "rights." Such rulers are bound to incur much unpopularity and to be held up to the folk as tyrants by the freedom-loving barons. It is true that the king may intend to enforce the peace of the land more thoroughly by consolidating the land in his own hands, but this was what the great barons least desired since it would interfere with their freedom to plunder and harry when and where they pleased. Rights were insisted on even when their loss might mean greater peace, for these Northmen were, in no sense, a peace-loving folk. These kings felt the insecurity of their position and sought to compel fidelity. Thus in the *Egils-saga* King Harold suspects his powerful baron, Thorolf, and says: "Great pity it is Thorolf should be unfaithful to me and plot my death."[88] Thorolf denies that he is a traitor or has shown disloyalty to the king.[89] Later, after the king has caused the death of Thorolf, Thorolf's brother, Grim, comes to the king. But the king has to guard himself against disaffected individuals like Grim and the latter may not come within the hall before the king so long as he or his twelve followers are armed. They must enter weaponless, so six go in while the other six remain outside and keep the weap-

---

[87] *Egils-saga*, c. 4, trans. by the Reverend W. C. Green, under the title of *The Story of Egil Skallagrimsson* (London: Elliott Stock, 1893).

[88] *Egils-saga*, c. 13. The idea of plotting the death of a ruler is probably as old as kings themselves; hence the presence of the terms *consiliatus* and *machinatus* in the *leges barbarorum* does not in any sense constitute absolute proof of the introduction of these conceptions from the Roman Law. It is possible that the Latin words were merely applied to pre-existing Germanic ideas. However, the statements dealing with the Roman concepts of plotting and machination in Roman codes might suggest and so lead to the formulation of their Germanic counterparts in the *leges barbarorum*.

[89] *Egils-saga*, c. 14–16.

ons.[90] Thus here are careful regulations for the prevention of high treason and the punishment of the traitor is death, if one may judge the fate of Thorolf.

In the *Gulathing* law the homicide of parents, children, brother, or sister—all forms of parricide—incurs "strict peacelessness," while in the *Frostathing* law "the slayer, even though demented, shall leave the land as an outlaw and never return to the realm."[91] In ancient times this crime seems to have been almost unknown.[92] King Magnus believed that one who committed such an act must be insane.[93] The killing of a husband by a wife, or of a wife by a husband, was regarded by the church in the same light as parricide, although it must be remembered that from the point of view of Germanic law husband and wife did not stand on the same plane of equality. The woman was in a state of dependence on her husband which gave him the right to punish her or even to inflict the death penalty on her if he had secured the consent of her relatives. The wife pledged faith and fidelity to her husband, so that any crime committed by her against her husband appeared as treason against her lord.[94] It is extremely probable that this early Germanic conception of a wife's allegiance to her husband had much to do with the definition of petty treason in the later Common Law of England where killing, or plotting the death of, a husband by his wife was held petty treason along with killing, or plotting the death of, a lord by his vassal. In regard to this crime the *Frostathing* law states:

> If a wife slays or betrays her husband in a crime that she commits with another man, then may the kinsmen of the slain man accept no redemption-money from her, and let them maim her or slay her as they wish. Her property, however, shall be used to pay a full wergeld if she struck the death-blow, but only half wergeld if she counselled the slaying. From the property of him who struck the deathblow, the kinsmen of the slain man receive a full wergeld, and the king receives what remains both in land and movable property: the slayer, however, becomes an outlaw forever.[95]

Some Norse laws, it is true, do punish the husband, as well as the wife, for such slaying on the ground that they have committed a breach of the pledged troth of wedlock (*Ehebruch*) or have sought to commit it,

---

[90] *Egils-saga*, c. 25.
[91] Cf. *Gula*. 32 (Larson, 60; Meissner, 6, 30); 4, 31 (Larson, 271; Meissner, 4, 79–80).
[92] Cf. Wilda, *Geschichte des deutschen Strafrechts*, I, 714–715.
[93] Cf. von Amira, *Voll.*, p. 31.
[94] Cf. Wilda, *Geschichte des deutschen Strafrechts*, I, 717–718.
[95] *Frost*. 4, 35 (Larson, 272; Meissner, 4, 81).

and this is an inexpiable crime. The *Ostgötalag* states that "if a wife murders her husband, or a husband his wife, then he shall be broken on a wheel or rack [*geradebrecht*] if he has done it, and she shall be stoned if she has done it." But laws relating to *Ehebruch* of this sort provide generally that if the husband can demonstrate that he wished only to correct his wife, he shall not be punished as a "spouse-murderer" (*Gattenmörder*) but shall pay wergeld for her as for any other homicide.[96]

These slayings were envisaged from various angles in Germanic law according to the circumstances: they were considered either petty treason or *Ehebruch* when the wife was the offender, and either *Ehebruch* or homicide when the husband was the offender. It does appear quite certain, however, that *Ehebruch* approximates *Treubruch* only in the case where the wife commits the criminal act. The personal troth which the wife owes the husband lies at the basis of petty treason, just as in the case of the personal troth which the vassal owes to his lord.[97] Petty treason implies a reciprocal relationship involving mutual bonds and obligations; yet here the wife and vassal seem to incur a heavier responsibility of loyalty commensurate with their inferior status, so that the punishment for breach of troth weighs more harshly upon them. The husband and lord seem to have a more favored position though perhaps counterbalanced by greater obligations in the way of protection and sustenance. Probably some comparable equation or proportion between benefits and duties exists in the case of high treason as between king and subject. This aspect of the mediaeval development of the crimes of high treason and petty treason has never been subjected to a systematic and critical examination, but it cannot be disregarded in any consideration of the basic nature of homage and fealty. At this point Germanic law brings us to the frontiers of feudal law.[98]

[96] Wilda, *Geschichte des deutschen Strafrechts*, I, 718, quoting *Ostgötalag, Ethz.*, c. 17.

[97] See Appendix on Petty Treason.

[98] For the examination of problems connected with feudalism and for the relation of the concept of fealty to vassalage, there is no better point of departure than the foundation articles by Carl Stephenson which appeared in the *American Historical Review* as follows: "The Origin and Significance of Feudalism," XLVI (1941), 788–812; "Feudalism and Its Antecedents in England," XLVIII (1943), 245–265; "The Problem of the Common Man in Early Mediaeval Europe," LI (1946), 419–438. These articles have been reprinted recently in *Mediaeval Institutions: Selected Essays*, ed. by Bryce D. Lyon (Ithaca: Cornell University Press, 1954), pp. 205–233; 234–260; 261–284. In these truly splendid background studies the late Professor Stephenson analyzes the relevant aspects of the theories of Roth, Waitz,

Petty Treason

The crime of petty treason has never been explored in detail although significant observations on this topic may be found in the great basic histories of English Law. The central importance of this crime becomes apparent when one notes its intermediate position serving as a connecting link between the concepts of broken faith or *Treubruch* inherent in Germanic custom and the feudal concepts of fealty and *ligeance*. Legally it represents the dividing line at which the felonies are distinguished from the treasons. (Sir Matthew Hale, I, 179, notes that "all treasons include felony.") As the power of the state increases and the position of the king is enhanced by his becoming lord of the realm, the king is set apart from all lesser lords. The relation of lesser lords to him is that of subject, not of vassal; offenses against him become breaches of allegiance rather than of homage; and the treasons against lesser lords are carefully differentiated as petit treason from high treason against the king. Petty treason becomes an archaic survival from a day when broken troths or faith with all lords (*domini*) were alike treasons until at last it is abolished as a special offense in 1828 by Statute 9 George IV, c. 31, 2, being reduced to a felony of the rank of murder.

Nevertheless, this trend of distinction between the treasons was already apparent in the twelfth century, as Pollock and Maitland point out (II, 504, with nn 1 and 2):

In the twelfth century another wave of Romanism was flowing. The royal lawyers began to write about *laesa maiestas*, to paint in dark colours the peculiar gravity of the crime, to draw a hard line between the king and mere lords. But they could not altogether destroy the connexion between vassalship and treason; men were not yet ready to conceive a "crime against the state."

Brunner, Guilhiermoz, Dopsch, von Below, and many others. In the opinion of the writer the evidence of the public law set forth in the *leges barbarorum* supplements and confirms the conclusions which were reached by Stephenson through an evaluation of factors, chiefly social and economic. It seems certain that Stephenson has charted the course which will prove most fruitful for subsequent research in this area. One must also consider the views advanced in Charles E. Odegaard, *Vassi and Fideles in the Carolingian Empire*, Harvard Historical Monographs, XIX (Cambridge: Harvard University Press, 1945), which gives much consideration to semantic features involving the meaning of the terminology. See Gaines Post, *Studies in Medieval Legal Thought* (Princeton: Princeton University Press, 1964), for subsequent development of public law in the Middle Ages.

Petty treason perpetrated against a lord was but slowly marked off from high treason perpetrated against the king; and in much later days our law still saw, or spoke as if it saw, the essence of high treason in a breach of the bond of "ligeance."

Although he discusses *laesa maiestas* in some detail, Bracton does not specifically mention petit treason in his *De Legibus et Consuetudinibus Angliae* of the mid-thirteenth century. However, in f. 105 (ed. by G. E. Woodbine. [New Haven: Yale University Press, 1922], II, 299) he does state that "those who plot against the lives of their lords shall be burned with fire," which is an adaptation from *Digest* 48, 19, 28, 11 *De Poenis*. Pollock and Maitland (II, 504, n. 2) cite Britton, 1, 40, as perhaps "the first writer who talks expressly of *high* (or rather, *great*) and *petty* treasons; with him to 'procure' the death of one's lord is great treason, and one is hanged and drawn for forging one's lord's seal or committing adultery with his wife." Therefore, with Britton the distinction between *graund treson* and *petit treson* is not between crimes against the king and those against a lord, but between differing types of offenses against lords.

However, Sir Matthew Hale in his *Historia Placitorum Coronae* (*The History of the Pleas of the Crown* [1st Amer. ed.; Philadelphia: R. H. Small, 1847], I, 378–379) notes that falsifying the lord's seal and committing adultery with his wife or daughter (Fleta, 1, 22; Britton, c. 8) are omitted from the great statute of treason, 25 Edward III (1352), Stat. 5, c. 2, 10, which now defines the crime as "when a servant slayeth his master, or a wife her husband, or when a man secular or religious slayeth his prelate to whom he oweth faith and obedience." The independent identity of petty treason is still maintained, but a significant change has occurred, for, as Hale sets forth, "The killing of a master or husband is not petit treason, unless it be such a killing, as in case of another person would be murder," that is, it must be no mere case of manslaughter; and again, "if a wife conspire to kill her husband, or a servant to kill his master, and this is done by a stranger in pursuance of that conspiracy, it is not petit treason in the servant or wife, because the principal is only murder, and the being only accessory, where principal is but murder, cannot be petit treason." Pollock and Maitland stress that henceforth (after 1352) treason against any person other than the king is petty treason, that "servant" does not mean "vassal" nor does "master" mean "lord," and that the killing must be actual and not merely compassing to kill. High treason against the king is now sharply distinguished from petty treason against masters and husbands. By the fourteenth century Holdsworth, III, 287, declares four distinct ideas have emerged in the statute of Edward III to constitute the basis for the offense of high treason: "a) the idea of treachery; b) the idea of a breach of the feudal bond; c) the idea that the duty to king as king is higher than the feudal duty to a lord; d) an admixture of ideas taken from the Roman law of *laesa majestas*."

In general, see Sir Matthew Hale, *Historia Placitorum Coronae* (*The History of the Pleas of the Crown*, with notes by Sollom Emlyn), I, 376–382 (Ch. XXIX concerning Petit Treason); William Hawkins, *Treatise of the Pleas of the Crown* (London: Eliz. Nutt for J. Walthoe, 1716–1721), I, 87–88 (Ch. XXXII, "Of Petit Treason"); Sir James Fitz-James Stephen, *A History of the Criminal Law of England* (London: Macmillan, 1883), III, 34–35, on petty treason as a special aspect of homicide; Pollock and Maitland, *History of English Law before the Time of Edward I*, II, 502–505; Sir William Holdsworth, *A History of English Law*, II, 48, 449–450; III, 56, 287 291; see essay in this volume on "Treason in Anglo-Saxon Dooms," for the Anglo-Saxon background with references to Alfred, Introd., 49, and Cnut, 2, 26 (*Leges Henrici Primi* 75, 1–2, with which cf. Pollock and Maitland, I, 300).

For Scandinavian parallels in this connection, see *Uplandslag*, c. 15, 1 (von Schwerin, p. 140) which states that if a man kills his rightful lord, whether the lord be rich or poor, that man shall be brought before the *thing* or assembly and racked on the wheel, and his land and goods shall be divided into thirds and shared among the king, the accusers, and the hundred (*Hundertschaft*). On the personal relationship between husband and wife relative to petty treason, see Pollock and Maitland, *History of English Law*, II, 436.

IV

Crimen Laesae Maiestatis in the Lex Romana Wisigothorum[1]

The crimes of *lèse-majesté* and treason under the Roman Law have been investigated with care by Theodor Mommsen in his *Römisches Strafrecht* (Leipzig: S. Hirzel, 1899), while some additional evidence has been brought forward in the articles on *Maiestas* and *Perduellio* by G. Humbert and Ch. Lécrivain in Daremberg and Saglio's *Dictionnaire*

---

[1] Reprinted by special permission of the Editors of *Speculum* and the Mediaeval Academy of America from *Speculum*, Vol. IV No. 1 (1929), 73–87.

The standard edition of the *Breviary* is *Lex Romana Visigothorum*, ed. by G. Haenel (Leipzig: Teubner, 1849). In the present study I refer to the provisions of the *Breviary* in Haenel's edition under the abbreviation *L. R. V.*, while other references to this work will be designated simply Haenel. A valuable aid to research is M. Conrat, *Breviarium alaricianum: römisches Recht im fränkischen Reich in systematischer Darstellung* (Leipzig: J. C. Hinrichs, 1903), which provides a systematic topical arrangement of the material in the *Breviary*. For the various texts and redactions of the *Breviary* and its epitomes, see the *Prolegomena* (Vol. I, part 1) of the Mommsen-Meyer edition of the *Theodosian Code* (Berlin: Weidmann, 1905), pp. lxv–cvi.

For essential secondary works, see R. Schröder-von Künssberg, *Lehrbuch der deutschen Rechtsgeschichte* (6th ed. by E. von Künssberg; Berlin and Leipzig: de Gruyter, 1922), pp. 252–253, with nn. 5–6 (Bibliography); H. Brunner, *Deutsche Rechtsgeschichte* (2d ed.; Leipzig: Duncker and Humblot, 1906), I, 510–516; O. Karlowa, *Römisches Rechtsgeschichte* (Leipzig: Veit, 1885), II, 976–982; M. Conrat, *Geschichte der Quellen und Literatur des römischen Rechts im früheren Mittelalter* (Leipzig: J. C. Hinrichs, 1891), I, 41–46; 89–90; 218–252; P. Krüger, *Geschichte der Quellen und Literatur des römischen Rechts* (2d ed.; Leipzig: Duncker and Humblot, 1912), pp. 308–316, in *Systematisches Handbuch der*

des antiquités grècques et romaines.[2] More recently a brief treatment of these offenses has appeared in Part I of a monograph by Pandias M. Schisas of the University of London, entitled *Offences against the State in Roman Law.*[3] This study is incomplete but represents independent research. However, Mommsen still remains our standard authority, and it seems unlikely that the near future will add greatly to his definitive contribution in the field of Roman public criminal law. Unfortunately, Mommsen did not carry these studies into either the *Breviary*[4] or the

---

deutschen Rechtswissenschaft; R. de Ureña y Smenjaud, *La Legislación góticohispaña* (Madrid: I. Moreno, 1905), pp. 296–323; F. C. von Savigny, *Geschichte des römischen Rechts im Mittelalter* (2d ed.; Heidelberg: J. C. B. Mohr, 1834), II, 37–67; Haenel, pp. v–xl; A. Tardif, *Historie des sources du droit français, origines romaines* (Paris: A. Picard, 1890), pp. 129–143; H. O. Taylor, *The Mediaeval Mind* (4th ed.; New York: Macmillan, 1925), II, 272–273, 278; *Select Essays in Anglo-American Legal History*, compiled and edited by a Committee of the Association of American Legal Schools (Boston: Little, Brown, 1907), I, 15 ff.; H. D. Hazeltine, "Roman and Canon Law in the Middle Ages," *Cambridge Medieval History* (Cambridge: Macmillan, 1926), V, 721–722.

[2] Mommsen was by no means the first scholar to deal with this phase of Roman Law, as one may observe if he scans through the lists in the various editions of the *Bibliotheca realis iuridica* (post F. G. Struvii, with Supplement by G. A. Jenichen (Lipsiae: Wendler, 1743–1746), an extensive bibliography of legal literature widely used in the eighteenth century and compiled by M. Lipenius, but rather Mommsen's *Strafrecht* represents the culminating accomplishment of modern study in this field. Also the writers of the sixteenth, seventeenth and eighteenth centuries were, as a rule, commentators or legal theorists, whereas Mommsen determined facts in accordance with modern scientific methods of research. Note the works of Mommsen's immediate predecessors: G. Geib, *Geschichte des römischen Criminalprocesses bis zum Tode Justinian's* (Leipzig: Weidmann, 1842), pp. 50–66; W. Rein, *Das Kriminalrecht der Römer von Romulus bis auf Justinianus* (Leipzig: K. F. Köhler, 1844), pp. 504–597; A. Zumpt, *Das Criminalrecht der römischen Republik* (Berlin: F. Dümmler, 1865–1869), especially I (2), 324–338 on *perduellio*; II (1), 226–264; 376–392 on *perduellio* and *maiestas*; II (2), 62–78 on *crimen falsi.*

[3] P. M. Schisas, *Offences against the State in Roman Law* (London: University of London Press, 1926), pp. 3–15.

[4] Various names have been applied to this compilation. The confusion in terminology seems to have arisen mainly because of the variations of the manuscript sources. The following list gives several titles, which I have chanced upon in the course of the preparation of this study, and does not exhaust the possibilities: *Lex Romana, Lex Romana Wisigothorum, Liber Legum Romanorum, Liber Legum Romanarum, Lex Romanorum, Liber Aniani, Liber Legum, Liber Legis, Liber Legis Doctorum, Originalia Legum, Corpus Legum, Liber Iuris, Liber Iuridicus, Lex Theodosii, Corpus Theodosii, Corpus Theodosianum, Liber Breviatus, Breviarium, Breviarium Alarici,* and *Breviarium Alaricianum.* See H. Brunner, *D. R.,* I, 512; P. Krüger, *Quellen und Literatur,* p. 309; Haenel, p. vi, n. 6.

The *Lex Romana Wisigothorum* belongs to the group of laws designated *leges romanae* and must be distinguished carefully from the *Leges Wisigothorum* or *Forum Iudicum* of later date, which are properly termed *leges barbarorum.*

Papianus, and an analysis of these bodies of law must be made if we are to know what provisions of the Roman Law dealing with offenses against the state were carried over into the *leges romanae* when the Visigothic and Burgundian kings turned to the task of providing codes for their Roman subjects. Of the two, the *Lex Romana Wisigothorum,* or *Breviarium Alarici (Breviary),* is by far the more significant and far-reaching in its influence.

The history of the *Breviary* has been dealt with at length by a number of accepted specialists in legal history and historical jurisprudence, and requires no detailed discussion. It was compiled for the use of the *provinciales* of southern Gaul by a commission of jurists who were appointed by King Alaric II to examine such Roman laws as were in current use in his dominions.[5] The resulting code was approved in 506 at an assembly at Aire in Gascony and was promulgated by the king as the sole code for his Roman subjects. Constructed directly upon the foundations of Roman Law, it is a curious collection of materials drawn in large part from the *Theodosian Code* and *Sentences* of Paulus.[6] The text of the Roman Law is quoted *verbatim,*[7] and many provisions are accompanied by an interpretation (*interpretatio*) which usually expresses in briefer form the sense of the text.[8] These *interpretationes* do not reflect a Visigothic attempt to restate the Roman Law in terms which they could better understand, but, as Henry Osborn Taylor remarks, probably represent "the approved exposition of the *leges,* with the exposition of the already archaic *Sentences* of Paulus, current in the

---

[5] Brunner believes that Alaric's sudden interest in his Roman provincials was caused by no altruistic impulse but by the threat of impending attack at the hands of Clovis and his Franks. Cf. H. Brunner, *D. R.,* I, 511.

[6] These are the only portions of the *Breviary* containing material bearing on treason and related offenses. The texts derived from the *Novellae* of Theodosius and succeeding emperors, the Gregorian and Hermogenian Codes, the *Resposa* of Papinian, and the *Liber Gaii* yield nothing of importance.

[7] Save for the *Institutes* of Gaius, which appear in the corrupted form of the *Liber Gaii.*

[8] Cf. *Codex Theodosianus* 7, 1, 1 (*L. R. V., Codex* 7, 1, 1) with its *interpretatio.* The invidious relation between *barbari* and *Romani* in the *constitutio* disappears in the *interpretatio* and epitomes. Marauding barbarians give way to plundering brigands, that is, the *interpretatio* generalizes the law. Cf. another similar case in *C. Th.* 15, 14, 14 (*L. R. V., C.* 15, 3.1). The omissions of the *interpretationes* are sometimes suggestive; however, all evidence of this sort is, in the main, negative. The Visigothic *interpretationes* are not complete analyses and commentaries with some reformulation or restatement comparable to portions of the Lombard *expositiones.* They are "often not so much explanatory of the text as qualificative or corrective." Cf. H. Goudy, "Roman Law," *Encyclopaedia Britannica* (11th ed.; Cambridge: University Press, 1911), XXIII, 572.

law schools of Gaul in the fifth century."[9] Maitland says in his helpful article in the *Select Essays in Anglo-American Legal History:* "It is thought nowadays that this 'interpretation' and the sorry version of Gaius represent, not Gothic barbarism but degenerate Roman science. A time had come when lawyers could no longer understand their own old texts and were content with debased abridgments."[10] Little contrast between Roman and Germanic legal ideas may be obtained by comparing the *Interpretatio* with the text which it accompanies. Thus, the *Breviary* possesses little value arising from any originality of its own, but it does serve to indicate what Roman laws bearing on treason and other related public offenses were transmitted to the western Germans, since it remained the great legal compend for those peoples outside Italy as late as the Carolingian period.[11] Between the eighth and tenth

---

[9] H. O. Taylor, *Mediaeval Mind,* II, 272. Cf. O. Karlowa, *Römisches Rechtsgeschichte,* II, 977–979, regarding a basis of earlier commentaries for constructing the *interpretationes* and giving the views of Fitting, Dernberg, and Degenkolb; H. Brunner, *D. R.,* I, 514; P. Krüger, *Quellen und Literatur,* pp. 311–313; M. Conrat, *Quellen,* I, 89–90; Haenel, pp. x–xi especially nn. 37–38. Haenel remarks: "Finis interpretationis duplex potissimum erat: ut explanarentur leges et ad praesentem Romanorum statum accommodarentur, quare complurium legum interpretatio ad verbum facta est, contra aliarum eum in modum, quem praesens Romanorum status et usus provinciae postulavit. Ad hoc genus interpretationes pertinent, quibus leges correctae rebusve aliunde sumtis amplificatae sunt, aut in quibus aliorum librorum similes leges commemorantur. Eae moverunt doctos, ut a Wisigothis factam esse interpretationem existimarent, et hunc quidem in finem, ut ius Gothorum ad Romanos deferretur, quam sententiam veram esse nego." For the older contrary view, see F. von Savigny, *Geschichte des römischen Rechts,* II, 54–55.

[10] *Select Essays in Anglo-American Legal History,* 1, 15.

[11] Cf. O. Karlowa, *Römisches Rechtsgeschichte,* II, 977: "Sie (Savigny, Haenel, Fitting) haben gezeigt, dass sie als eine wichtige Erkenntnisquelle für die damaligen Zustände des westgotischen Reichs zu betrachten ist, ferner aber auch, wenn sie auch keinen Wert hat für die Kenntnis des klassischen römischen Rechts, doch Aufschluss giebt über den Rechtszustand in weströmischen Reich um die Scheide des 5. und 6. Jahrhr. nach Chr."

H. Brunner (*D. R.,* I, 515) discusses the later history of the *Breviary* and shows that it remained the chief book on Roman Law in France, Germany, and England as late as the twelfth century. It was retained in the Frankish lands, although its use in Spain had been discontinued by Recceswinth. Cf. H. O. Taylor, *Mediaeval Mind,* II, 272.

In determining precisely what contributions the *Breviary* made to subsequent legislation, no student of mediaeval law should overlook the highly detailed analysis of Alfred von Wretschko in Vol. I, Part 1, of the Mommsen-Meyer edition of the *Theodosian Code,* pp. cccvii–ccclx (*De Usu Breviarii Alariciani Forensi et Scholastico per Hispaniam, Galliam, Italiam Regionesque Vicinas*).

The influence of the *Lex Romana Burgundionum* (*Papianus*) and of the *Edictum Theodorici* was much more circumscribed, and the possible influence of a Roman

centuries it was reduced to epitomes making the work less bulky and combining the *lex* and the *interpretatio*.[12] In general, however, little new light is cast upon the provisions relating to public criminal law by either the *interpretationes* or the epitomes. New ideas are rarely added, while alterations and excisions seldom modify the original meaning in a vital manner.[13] The chief exceptions to this rule may be found in the *Epitome Sancti Galli*.

Following the classification of the Roman Law, the most serious offenses against the state are included under the provisions of *laesa maies-*

---

vulgärrecht, wherein Roman law became debased to a kind of popular custom among the Gallo-Roman provincials, must be subjected to special study before one reaches positive conclusions. Cf. Taylor, *Mediaeval Mind,* II, 268, 275, 277, on Romanesque or popular Roman law; also C. H. Haskins, *The Renaissance of the Twelfth Century* (Cambridge: Harvard University Press, 1927), pp. 195–196. He says: "For most people [in parts of Italy and in Southern France] the Roman law came to rest upon local custom, a popularized and, in some respects degenerate form of law, which bore somewhat the same relation to the classical jurisprudence as the Vulgar Latin of the provinces bore to the classical speech."

Also it should be borne in mind that there were other channels, less obvious than the *Breviary,* whereby Roman legal ideas might find their way into the *leges barbarorum.* Cf. M. Conrat, *Quellen,* I, 3, with nn. 8–9, 13–14, regarding elements in the Bavarian and Lombard laws derived from the *Corpus Juris Civilis* and ecclesiastical legislation.

[12] As a rule, the epitomes tend to be based upon the *interpretationes* rather than the original text of the Roman *lex* and *ius.* Cf. H. Brunner, *D. R.,* I, 515–516. The best discussions of the epitomes and glosses are Haenel, pp. xxiii–xl, Conrat, *Quellen,* I, 222–252, 286–292, with notes, and Tardif, *Histoire des Sources,* pp. 136–142. Haenel, Conrat, and Tardif agree, in the main, on problems concerning the date and place of origin of the epitomes, as here listed: *Epitome Aegidii* (8th century, southern France); *Scintilla* or *Epitome Codicis Parisiensis 10753,* formerly Suppl. Lat. 215 (8th century, France); *Epitome Monachi* (8th century, France); *Epitome Codicis Guelpherbytani* (8th century, France?); *Epitome Codicis Lugdunensis* (7th–9th century, France); *Epitome Codicis Seldeni* (12th-century English MS., based on earlier Frankish sources?); and *Epitome Sancti Galli,* variously known as *Lex Romana Utinensis, Lex Romana Curiensis, Lex Romana Raetica,* and *Lex Romana Raetica Curiensis* (ca. 8th century, Switzerland). The exact place of origin of the *Epitome S. Galli* has long been disputed. Various places have been suggested, including Lombardy, Istria, southern Germany, and the region of Switzerland (Rhaetia), which is generally accepted at present. See Conrat, I, 288, n. 6; 289, n. 1; 290, n. 4; 291, n. 1. The *Epitome S. Galli* alone possesses any large significance for this study inasmuch as it markedly displays the influence of Germanic elements: "*Die Lex Romana Curiensis*—von germanischrechtlichen Einflüssen stark durchsetzt ist" (Conrat, I, 238); "[La *Lex Curiensis*] nous fournit des renseignements précieux sur le droit romain vulgaire de cette époque" (Tardif, p. 141).

[13] This statement is by no means true of the provisions relating to matters in private law, and must not be accepted too narrowly in any case. For the relation of the epitomes to the development of a Roman *Vulgärrecht* under the influence of German law, see H. Brunner, *D. R.,* I, 516, especially n. 26.

tas,[14] and in the *Breviary* the crime of *laesa maiestas* is defined in the terms of the well-known passage from the *Sentences* of Paulus:[15]

I. According to the *lex Julia maiestatis* he shall be held by whose aid and counsel arms have been taken up against the emperor[16] or public authority,[17] or the armies of the emperor have been betrayed:[18] or who has waged war without the lawful consent of the emperor, or levied troops,[19] or stirred up dis-

---

[14] Note other offenses against the state listed in the *Breviary*, which are closely related and sometimes involved with *maiestas*: *C. Th.* 9, 10, 1 and 3–4 (*L. R. V.*, *C.* 9, 7, 1–3) *Ad Legem Iuliam de Vi Publica et Privata*; Paulus *Sententiae* 5, 26, 1–4 (*L. R. V.*, *P.* 5, 28, 1–4) *Ad Legem Iuliam de Vi Publica et Privata*; *C. Th.* 9, 27, 1 and 4 (*L. R. V.*, *C.* 9, 21, 1–2) *Ad Legem Iuliam Repetundarum*; Paulus *Sent.* 5, 28, 1 (*L. R. V.*, *P.* 5, 30, 1) *Ad Legem Iuliam Repetundarum*; *C. Th.* 9, 19, 1 and 4 (*L. R. V.*, *C.* 9, 15, 1–2) *Ad Legem Corneliam de Falso*; Paulus *Sent.* 4, 7, 1–6 (*L. R. V.*, *P.* 4, 7, 1–6) *De Lege Cornelia*; 5, 25, 1–2 and 4–13 (*L. R. V.*, *P.* 5, 27, 1–12) *Ad Legem Corneliam Testamentariam*; *C. Th.* 9, 34, 1 and 9 (*L. R. V.*, *C.* 9, 24, 1–2) *De Famosis Libellis*; 9, 39, 1–3 (*L. R. V.*, *C.* 9, 29, 1–3) *De Calumniatoribus*; Paulus *Sent.* 5, 27, 1 (*L. R. V.*, *P.* 5, 29, 1) *Ad Legem Iuliam Peculatus*; 5, 30a, 1 (*L. R. V.*, *P.* 5, 32, 1) *Ad Legem Iuliam Ambitus*.

[15] Paulus *Sent.* 5, 29, 1–2 (*L. R. V.*, *P.* 5, 31, 1–2) *Ad Legem Iuliam Maiestatis*: "1. Lege Iulia maiestatis tenetur is, cuius ope consilio adversus imperatorem vel rempublicam arma mota sunt, exercitusve eius in insidias deductus est: quive iniussu imperatoris bellum gesserit, dilectumve habuerit, exercitum comparaverit, sollicitaverit, deseruerit imperatorem. His antea in perpetuum aqua et igni interdicebatur: nunc vero humiliores bestiis obiiciuntur vel vivi exuruntur; honestiores capite puniuntur. Quod crimen non solum facto, sed et verbis impiis ac maledictis maxime exacerbatur. 2. In reum maiestatis inquiri prius convenit, quibus opibus, qua factione, quibus hoc auctoribus fecerit: tanti enim criminis reus non obtentu adulationis alicuius, sed ipsius admissi causa puniendus est. Et ideo quum de eo quaeritur, nulla dignitas a tormentis excipitur."
Cf. *Digest* 48, 4, 3 (*Ad Legem Iuliam Maiestatis*): "*Marcianus libro quarto decimo institutionum . . .* lex autem Iulia maiestatis praecipit eum, qui maiestatem publicam laeserit, teneri; qualis est ille, qui in bellis cesserit aut arcem tenuerit aut castra concesserit, eadem lege tenetur et qui iniussu principis bellum gesserit dilectumve habuerit exercitum comparaverit: quive, cum ei in provincia successum esset, exercitum successori non tradidit, quive imperium exercitumve populi Romani deseruerit: quive privatus pro potestate magistratuve quid sciens dolo malo gesserit: quive quid eorum, quae, supra scripta sunt, facere curaverit."
It should be noted that neither *C. Th.* 9, 4, 1 *Si Quis Imperatori Maledixerit* nor *C. Th.* 9, 5, 1 *Ad Legem Iuliam Maiestatis* was taken over into the *Breviary* (cf. *Codex Justinianus* 9, 7, 1 and 9, 8, 3). Hence most positive statements in the *Breviary* defining *maiestas* are drawn from the juristic literature, as indicated above, and not from the *constitutiones* of the emperors. Cf. Ulpian in *Dig.* 48, 4, 1–2, and Scaevola in *Dig.* 48, 4, 4.

[16] Cf. Mommsen, *Römisches Strafrecht* (Leipzig: S. Hirzel, 1899), pp. 549–555.

[17] Cf. *Dig.* 48, 4, 1 and 3; *C. Just.* 9, 8, 5 *Ad Legem Iuliam Maiestatis*.

[18] Cf. Mommsen, *Römisches Strafrecht*, pp. 546–549; *Dig.* 48, 4, 3–4 *Ad Legem Iuliam Maiestatis*; 48, 4, 10: "Maiestatis crimine accusari potest, cuius ope consilio dolo malo provincia vel civitas hostibus prodita est"; 49, 16, 6, 4 *De Re Militari*.

[19] Cf. *Dig.* 48, 4, 3.

turbance within the army,[20] or deserted the emperor.[21] All such shall be perpetually interdicted from fire and water,[22] the more humble [*humiliores*] shall be cast to the beasts or burned alive while those of higher rank [*honestiores*] shall be punished capitally.[23] Also this offense rests not on overt act alone but is particularly aggrevated by [impious, disrespectful][24] words and maledictions.[25]

II. In any accusation of *maiestas* it should be asked through what resources, by what faction, and through what agents this act was performed: and the person accused of so great a crime must be punished not as a pretext for fawning flattery [*non obtentu adulationis*] but on account of acknowledged guilt.[26] Hence when evidence is sought in such cases, no dignity shall be exempted from torture.[27]

It is noteworthy that this statement of the crime, which is one of the most comprehensive in Roman Law, should have been incorporated into the *Breviary*. The authorities of the *Digest* expand and amplify the subject, but they adhere in a general way to the categories by Paulus. His rather bare outline preserved the essential features of the Roman theory of treason for the Latin West.[28]

---

[20] Cf. *Dig.* 48, 4, 1; 49, 16, 3, 20 *De Re Militari; C. Just.* 9, 8, 5.

[21] Cf. Mommsen, *Römisches Strafrecht*, pp. 537–538; *Dig.* 48, 4, 2–3; 49, 15, 19, 8 *De Captivis et de Postliminio et Redemptis ab Hostibus*; 49, 16, 3 *De Re Militari*; 4, 5, 5, 1 *De Capite Minutis. Epitome Aegidii* says: "vel ipsum imperatorem in exercitu deseruerit." Does this convey the Germanic idea of deserting the army when the king is present or suggest the Frankish offense of *herisliz*? Cf. Ethelred, c. 5, 28; 6, 35; Cnut, 2, 77–78; *Leges Henrici Primi* 13, 12; 43, 7; *Edictum Rothari*, c. 7; *Leges Alamannorum*, c. 90; *Capitulare Ticinense* (a. 801), c. 2; *Capitulare Bononiense* (a. 811), c. 4.

[22] Cf. Mommsen, *Römisches Strafrecht*, p. 549, for "aquae et ignis interdictio." Cf. *Dig.* 48, 19, 28, 13–14 *De Poenis* for breaking the ban of exile.

[23] Cf. *Dig.* 48, 19, 38, 1–2 *De Poenis*; 49, 16, 3, 10 *De Re Militari*; 49, 16, 6; 3, 2, 11, 3 *De His Qui Notantur Infamia*.

[24] *Verbis impiis* refers in this passage to the addressing of unseemly language to a "god-king" and is not far removed from blasphemy, but among the Visigoths, who were now Christians, and their converted Roman subjects the force of *impiis* must be considered as reduced to "disrespectful" or some similar correlative meaning.

[25] Note that malediction appears a mitigating rather than an aggravating circumstance, at least in certain cases, in *C. Th.* 9, 4, 1 *Si Quis Imperatori Maledixerit; C. Just.* 9, 7, 1. The law can hardly be construed ironically: "eum poenae nolumus subiugari neque durum aliquid nec asperum sustinere, quoniam si id ex levitate processerit, contemnendum est, si ex insania, miseratione dignissimum, si ab iniuria, remittendum." Cf. *Dig.* 48, 4, 7, 3. Note *Dig.* 48, 4, 3: "facere curaverit."

[26] Cf. *Dig.* 48, 4, 7, 3: "Hoc tamen crimen iudicibus non in occasione ob principalis maiestatis venerationem habendum est, sed in veritate."

[27] Cf. *C. Just.* 9, 8, 3–5; *C. Th.* 9, 5, 1 *Ad Legem Iuliam Maiestatis*; 9, 35, 1 *De Quaestionibus*. On the torture of slaves, see *C. Just.* 9, 8, 6, 1 *Ad Legam Iuliam Maiestatis*. Cf. Essay II, n. 159.

[28] Paulus is comprehensive in the sense that his statement includes the most

Under the heading *Ne Praeter Crimen Maiestatis Servus Dominum vel Patronum Libertus seu Familiaris Accuset,*[29] *L. R. V., C.* 9, 3, 1–2, states the Roman Law relative to accusations of *laesa maiestas*[30] and emphasizes the important exception, namely, that information regarding crimes against majesty is not included among the prohibited delations. The best summary is, perhaps, the *Interpretatio* of *L. R. V., C.* 9, 3, 2:

> If a slave shall accuse his master or inform against him in the matter of any crime whatsoever or if any follower or servant or freedman shall do likewise in the case of his patron, let the sword be his punishment immediately at the very beginning of his accusation, since we wish to cut off such a voice, not listen to it: *unless* perchance the master or patron shall prove to have been involved in the crime of majesty.

A most significant difference arises here between the text of the *constitutio* and the *interpretatio* (*L. R. V., C.* 9, 3, 2) on the one hand, and the text of the *Epitome S. Galli* on the other, as may be noted:

> *Interpretatio.* Si servus dominum aut amicus vel domesticus sive libertus patronum accusaverit vel detulerit cuiuslibet criminis reum, statim in ipso initio accusationis gladio puniatur, quia vocem talem exstingui volumus, non audiri: nisi forte dominum aut patronum de crimine maiestatis tractasse probaverit.
>
> *Epitome S. Galli.* Interpretatio. Si quis servus dominum suum aut libertus patronum suum accusare voluerint, nisi forsitan probare potuerint, quid [*sic*] ipse dominus aut patronus contra dominum blasfemasset, aut paganus eos probare potuerit, de tale accusatione licenciam habeant, et si vero dixerint, ipse libertus aut servus sine omne iniuria liberi abscedant; nam si de hoc mentierint, aut si forsitan de alia qualecumque causa libertus patronum aut servus dominum suum ad qualecumque iudice accusaverint, de presente in ipsa ora accusatione iudex eos capite punire faciat.

---

important elements of *laesa maiestas,* but his outline is bare because the separate topics have not been developed in the complete manner of *Digest* 48, 4 *Ad Legem Iuliam Maiestatis.*

[29] *C. Th.* 9, 6, 2–3 (*L. R. V., C.* 9, 3, 1–2). Cf. Paulus *Sent.* 5, 13, 3 (*L. R. V., P.* 5, 15, 3) on delation (*De Delatoribus*). Cf. *C. Th.* 9, 5, 1 *Ad Legem Iuliam Maiestatis,* which states: "In servis qouque vel libertis, qui dominos aut patronos accusare aut deferre temptaverint, professio tam atrocis audaciae statim in admissi ipsius exordio per sententiam iudicis conprimatur ac denegata audientia patibulo adfigatur." This sentence is lacking in *C. Just.* 9, 8, 3 *Ad Legem Iuliam Maiestatis.* Cf. *C. Just.* 9, 8, 4–5; 9, 41, 1 *De Quaestionibus; Dig.* 48, 4, 7, 1–2; 48, 4, 8; 5, 1, 53 *De Iudiciis.*

[30] Cf. *L. R. V., C.* 9, 3, 1, which speaks not of *crimen laesae maiestatis* (crime of injured majesty), but employs the unusual term, closely synonymous, of *crimen appetitae maiestatis* (crime of assailed majesty). Cf. *C. Just.* 9, 24. 2 *De Falsa Moneta* which mentions *crimen obnoxii maiestatis,* but the expression is not found in *L. R. V., C.* 9, 17, 1 *De Falsa Moneta.*

Thus the great exception in the Roman Law is transformed from *maies-tas* to blasphemy and adherence to paganism. The *Epitome Aegidii, Epitome Monachi, Epitome Lugdunensis,* and *Epitome Guelpherbytani* all follow the original *interpretatio* closely and represent the law of Gallo-Romans, but the *Epitome S. Galli* exhibits profound modification under Christian and Germanic influence. This passage offers added evidence concerning the frequent failure of the *leges barbarorum* to adopt the Roman idea of *maiestas* and the very general failure to employ the word *maiestas* itself.[31]

The great exception, likewise, makes its appearance in the laws of inheritance, and that noble principle of the Roman Law which says that "the crime shall perish with its author" is expressly denied application in the cases of the children of those who have been condemned for *laesa maiestas.* According to the *constitutio* IMPP. *Valentinianvs et Valens AA. ad Symmachvm pe. v.* (25 November, 364):[32] "Substantiam damnatorum integram ad liberos pervenire, et in qualibet causa positis parentibus liberos heredes esse praecipimus, excepta sola maiestatis quaestione: quam si quis sacrilego animo assumit, iuste poenam ad suos etiam posteros mittit."[33] The property of a traitor thus withheld from

---

[31] Cf. heading of *Epitome S. Galli* (*L. R. V., C.* 9, 3, 2) which reads *Ne propter Crimen Magistatis Servus Dominum vel Patronum Liberatus seu Familiares Acuset; Epitome S. Galli* (*L. R. V., C.* 10, 5, 4): "Si quis homo in crimine magistatis inventus fuerit"; *Epitome S. Galli* (*L. R. V., C.* 9, 32, 1): "si de crimine magistatis acusatus fuerit." I have found the genitive form *magistatis* three times in the *Epitome S. Galli:* once in a heading, although there lacking in the ensuing *lex,* and twice in the main body of the *lex*—all as indicated in the references above, but I have noted no other declension forms of the word *magistas.* Cf. Brunner, *D. R.,* II, 687–688; G. Waitz, *Deutsche Verfassungsgeschichte* (3rd ed.; Berlin: Weidmann, 1880), II (1), 195–196; Pollock and Maitland, *History of English Law before the Time of Edward I* (2d ed.; Cambridge: University Press, 1898), II, 502; also Fustel de Coulanges, *Histoire des institutions politiques de l'ancienne France* (*La Monarchie franque*) (5th ed.; Paris: Hachette, 1924), Ch. VII: Étendue du Pouvoir Royal, especially pp. 132–135.

[32] *C. Th.* 9, 42, 6 (*L. R. V., C.* 9, 32, 1) *De Bonis Proscriptorum seu Damnatorum.* Cf. *C. Just.* 9, 49, 10.

[33] I think this statement clearly implies attainder of blood. In the *Interpretatio* the force of the passage is weakened to mere disinheritance. If one takes the liberty to combine *lex* and *interpretatio,* he may secure this forceful expression: "Si quis pro crimine suo occidi vel damnari meruerit, crimen cum auctore deficiat: nisi forte maiestatis crimine damnatus sit aliquis" (*Int.*), "iuste poenam ad suos etiam posteros mittit" (*lex*). Cf. *Dig.* 48, 4, 11, quoting *Ulpianus libro octavo disputationum:* "Is, qui in reatu decedit, integri status decedit: extinguitur enim crimen mortalitate. Nisi forte quis maiestatis reus fuit: nam hoc crimine nisi a successoribus purgetur, hereditas fisco vindicatur." The use of *purgetur* implies attainder which must be cleansed away. Subsequently Ulpian limits this harsh rule to those guilty of *perduellio* only. Cf. *C. Just.* 9, 49, 10, 5: "Excepta sola maiestatis quaestione: quam

his children (nisi forte maiestatis crimine damnatus sit aliquis, quorum etiam filios de bonis damnati patris fieri iubemus alienos) was confiscated to the *fiscus*, although the prince reserved the privilege of making unsought gifts of such goods at his discretion.[34]

Keepers of private prisons were subject to the penalties for offended majesty.[35] Also by implication the majesty of the prince was injured if suit was entered through the imperial treasury with the emperor as heir, "*nec enim calumniandi facultatem ex principali maiestate capi oportet.*"[36] Similarly one may infer that *lèse-majesté* was incurred by anyone who consulted astrologers or soothsayers (*mathematici, harioli, haruspices, vaticinatores*) regarding the health or security of the prince or the welfare of the state, and by those who made replies and prophecies in such matters, for these offenses were punished capitally.[37] Whoever was discovered to be in possession of books treating of the magic arts was to be exiled to an island, while his goods were to be seized and burned in public. *Humiliores* were to be punished capitally. "Non tantum huius artis professio, sed etiam scientia prohibita est."[38] Such was the pall of fear and suspicion that overhung the later despots of Rome's declining empire.[39] Even slaves who consulted about the health of their masters were ordered to be crucified, and the offending soothsayer was either condemned to the mines or exiled upon an island.[40]

---

si quis sacrilego animo adsumpserit, iuste poenam ad suos etiam posteros mittit" (*ca.* A.D. 426). However, note *Dig.* 48, 19, 26 *De Poenis:* "Crimen vel poena paterna nullam maculam filio infligere potest"; 48, 19, 20.

[34] Cf. *C. Th.* 10, 10, 15 (*L. R. V., C.* 10, 5, 4) *De Petitionibus et Ultro Datis et Delatoribus: Interpretatio:* "Si quid tamen nullo petente, proprio arbitrio de talibus bonis cuiquam dederimus, donatio huius modi firma permaneat."

[35] *C. Th.* 9, 11, 1(*L. R. V., C.* 9, 8, 1) *De Privati Carceris Custodia.* Note variant reading in *Epitome S. Galli.* Cf. *C. Just.* 9, 5, 1 *De Privatis Carceribus Inhibendis.*

[36] *L. R. V., P.* 5, 14, 4–5 *De Fisci Advocato.*

[37] Paulus *Sent.* 5, 21, 3 (*L. R. V., P.* 5, 23, 3) *De Vaticinatoribus et Mathematicis;* and 5, 23, 17 (5, 25, 11) *Ad Legem Corneliam de Sicariis et Veneficis* states that the punishment for those "magicae artis conscios" shall be the beasts or crucifixion, while the sorcerers (*magi*) themselves shall be burned alive. Cf. *C. Th.* 9, 16, 3–4 and 7 (*L. R. V., C.* 1–3) *De Maleficis et Mathematicis et Ceteris Similibus.*

[38] Paulus *Sent.* 5, 21, 4 (5, 23, 4); 5, 23, 18 (5, 25, 12) *Ad Legem Corneliam de Sicariis et Veneficis.*

[39] Cf. *Lex Wisigothorum,* 6, 2 *De Maleficis et Consulentibus Eos adque Veneficis,* ed. by K. Zeumer, in *Monumenta Germaniae Historica, Leges* (Hanover and Leipzig: Hahn, 1902), Sectio I, Tomus I. Note especially 6, 2, 1 and 6, 2, 4, which were taken over from the *Breviary* and hence indicate the diffusion and continuance of older Roman ideas among the Visigoths of the seventh century.

[40] Paulus *Sent.* 5, 21, 4 (5, 23, 4). In this connection it must be remembered that under ordinary circumstances slaves could not inform against their masters.

Perhaps the parallel should not be forced too far, but it is impossible to escape the suggestion that the *potestas* of the master over the slaves and freedmen within his *dominium* was similar in kind, though more limited in scope, to the *maiestas* of the prince over the subjects beneath his *regnum* or *imperium*. This line of thought links up with parricide, which may originally have been punished as a violation of the *patria potestas* and so have constituted a rudimentary form of treason within the family group in an age when the family group fulfilled functions of a semipublic character.[41] In any case parricide was a heinous offense against the sacred ties of blood.[42] Of this crime, Paulus states: "According to the *lex Pompeia de parricidiis* he shall be held who has killed his father, mother, grandfather, grandmother, brother, sister, patron, or patroness, and although in earlier days all such were cast into the sea bound in a sack [*culeus*], let them now be either burned alive or cast to the beasts."[43]

In the matter of counterfeiting and debasing the coinage, which constitutes a cardinal instance of *lèse-majesté* in Roman Law,[44] two provisions may be found derived from the *Theodosian Code*. The first says that a reward will be given for information concerning an adulterine moneyer (*adulterinus monetarius*), while the accused moneyer if convicted of his crime shall be burned.[45] The second declares that whoever clips *solidi* or offers counterfeit *solidi* (*figuratum solidum adultera imi-*

---

[41] On the relation of parricide to treason, see E. C. Clark, *History of Roman Private Law* (Cambridge: University Press, 1919), Part III: Regal Period, pp. 588 ff., 604 ff.

[42] Parricide seems to have involved the ideas of pollution and sacrilege. Note *Dig.* 48, 4, 1: "Proximum sacrilego crimen est, quod maiestatis dicitur."

[43] Paulus *Sent.* 5, 24, 1 (*L. R. V., P.* 5, 26, 1) *Ad Legem Pompeiam de Parricidiis.* Cf. *C. Th.* 9, 15, 1 (*L. R. V., C.* 9, 12, 1) *De Parricidio*, which fails to list the *patronus* and *patrona* along with the *propinqui*.

[44] The various phases of *crimen falsi* are again associated with treason when one comes to the latter English codes. Cf. H. de Bracton, *De Legibus et Consuetudinibus Angliae,* ed. by G. E. Woodbine (New Haven: Yale University Press, 1922), f. 119b: "Est et aliud genus criminis laesae maiestatis quod inter graviora numeratur, quia ultimum indicit supplicium et mortis occasionem, scilicet *crimen falsi*"; R. de Glanville, *Tractatus de Legibus*, 14, 7; also Britton, I, 41; Fleta, p. 32.

[45] *C. Th.* 9, 21, 5 (*L. R. V., C.* 9, 17, 1) *De Falsa Moneta.* Cf. *C. Th.* 9, 21, 9, where counterfeiting is declared to be *crimen maiestatis*. Also Paulus *Sent.* 5, 25, 1 (*L. R. V., P.* 5, 27, 1) *Ad Legem Corneliam Testamentariam*:
"Lege Cornelia testamentario tenetur . . . quive nummos aureos, argenteos adultaverit, laverit, conflaverit, raserit, corruperit, vitiaverit: vultuve principum signatam monetam, praeter adulterinam, reprobaverit. Et honestiores quidem in insula deportantur, humiliores autem aut in metallum damnantur aut in crucem tolluntur. Servi autem post admissum manumissi capite puniuntur." *Ibid.*, 5, 25, 5 (5, 27, 4).

tatione) shall be punished capitally.[46] The distinction between debased and counterfeit money should be kept in mind though both were regarded in the same light at law. The offense to majesty consisted in the desecration of the image of the divine emperor through making a fraudulent likeness,[47] though the economic consequences of the crime were possibly considered also. In this connection it is interesting to note that the Emperor Constantine opens his *constitutio* on this subject by affirming that "our countenance and veneration are one."[48] The extent to which pagan elements depending upon the conception of "god-kingship" exercised influence among the provincials of the West in the sixth century must have been negligible. At any rate the evidence of the *Forum Judicum* (*ca.* 650–675), which incorporates the legal ideas prevailing in Spain during the previous century, contains no suggestion that would support a contrary view.[49]

As regards sedition and disturbance of the public peace one finds: instigators of sedition and rioting or popular disturbance, according to their station, shall be crucified, cast to the beasts, or exiled;[50] if anyone rouses the people to revolt, let him be subject to the heaviest fines;[51] if anyone shall obtain booty in company with public enemies or shall di-

---

[46] *C. Th.* 9, 22, 1 (*L. R. V., C.* 9, 18, 1) *Si Quis Solidi Circulum Exteriorem Inciderit vel Adulteratum in Vendendo Subiecerit.*

[47] A similar point of view is maintained in legislation regarding the desecration of statues of the emperors. Cf. *Dig.* 47, 10, 38 *De Iniuriis et Famosis Libellis;* 48, 4, 7, 4; 48, 4, 4, 1; 48, 4, 5; and especially 48, 4, 6: "*Venuleius Saturninus libro secundo de iudiciis publicis.* Qui statuas aut imagines imperatoris iam consecratas conflaverint aliudve quid simile admiserint, lege Iulia maiestatis tenentur." Cf. Mommsen, *Römisches Strafrecht,* p. 585, and notes; also T. Hodgkin, *Italy and Her Invaders* (2d ed.; Oxford: Clarendon, 1892), I (2), 470–509, which discusses the insurrection of Antioch in 387 and the overthrowing of the imperial statues. Cf. Tacitus *Annals* i, 73–74; iii, 36, 70, with the notes in the edition of Furneaux (2d ed.; Oxford: Clarendon, 1896), Vol. I.

[48] *C. Th.* 9, 22, 1 (9, 18, 1): "Omnes solidi, in quibus nostri vultus ac veneratio una est, uno pretio aestimandi sunt atque vendendi."

[49] *Lex Wisigothorum* (ed. by Zeumer), 7, 6, 2. This is a law of Recceswinth and Erwig entitled *De His, Qui Solidos et Monetam Adultaverint.* It is based upon *L. R. V., C.* 9, 18, 1 (*Interpretatio*) and *L. R. V., P.* 5, 27, 1.

[50] Paulus *Sent.* 5, 22, 1 (*L. R. V., P.* 5, 24, 1) *De Seditiosis; ibid.,* 5, 3, 1 (5, 3, 1) *De His, Quae per Turbam Fiunt,* provides that those who suffer loss in a case of "res pecuniaria, per turbam seditionemve," shall receive double damages, and personal injuries shall be vindicated at the discretion of the judge, but nothing is said regarding the capital punishment of the offenders. In *L. R. V., P.* 5, 3, 3, however, we read: "Hi, qui aedes alienas villasve expilaverint, effregerint, expugnaverint, si quidem id turba cum telis coacta fecerint, capite puniuntur."

[51] *C. Th.* 9, 33, 1 *Interpretatio* (*L. R. V., C.* 9, 23, 1) *De His, Qui Plebem Audent contra Publicam Colligere Disciplinam.*

vide the booty with brigands, let him be burned.[52] The first two provisions resemble the laws concerning *seditio* and *perduellio*, which had a larger significance in the time of the Roman Republic, while all three are incorporated eventually into the Germanic crime of breaking the peace (*pax*) of the land (*Landesverrat*), or perhaps evolve into *scandalum* or spoliation.[53]

A survey of the evidence given above will indicate the broad scope of Roman legal principles relating to the general subject of treason, which were made accessible to the western Germans through the medium of the *Lex Romana Wisigothorum*. The laws concerning *maiestas* extended the field of high treason beyond the limits of Germanic customary law, since they depended on a different conception of sovereignty.[54] The crime was not limited to such overt acts of violence as would bring personal injury to the ruler, but came to include maledictions as well as mere offensive expressions of opinion. The conception of violated majesty ranged from aggravated assault and attempted assassination of the monarch to counterfeiting, which had long been a form of *laesa maiestas* in Roman Law.[55] The provisions regarding guilty intent (*dolus malus*), which appeared later in the *Digest*,[56] do not seem to have been carried over into the *Breviary*, although one finds no good reason to suppose that these general juristic rules did not prevail among the Roman provincials of Spain and Gaul. The *ius* held the intent equivalent to the deed, while instigators and accomplices, embraced under the formula *cuius ope consilio*, were punished in the same way as the authors of the crime, though perhaps with somewhat less severity.[57]

---

[52] *C. Th.* 7, 1, 1 *Interpretatio* (*L. R. V., C.* 7, 1, 1) *De Re Militari.* Cf. *C. Th.* 9, 29, 2 (9, 22, 1) *De His, Qui Latrones vel Aliis Criminibus Reos Occultaverint.*

[53] Cf. *Edictum Rothari,* c. 8; 35–41, on *scandalum*; also c. 4 ("inimicus intra provincia"), and c.5 ("escamaras intra provinca").

[54] In the earliest and purest Germanic custom treason consists in the main of *Landesverrat* and *Treubruch* (*infidelitas*), and is closely associated with crimes of infamy. See Tacitus *Germania,* c. 12–14; H. Brunner, *D. R.* (Leipzig: Duncker and Humblot, 1892), II, 685 ff.; P. Bisoukides, *Der Hochverrat* (Berlin: Carl Heymanns Verlag, 1903), pp. 34–40; K. von Amira, *Das altnorwegische Vollstreckungsverfahren* (Munich: I. Ackermann, 1874), pp. 21–25; and especially W. E. Wilda, *Geschichte des deutschen Strafrechts* (Halle: C. H. Schwetschke, 1842), I, 21, 989, quoting from the old Norwegian *Frostuthingslög.* Suggestive material may be found scattered through the Icelandic sagas.

[55] Mommsen, *Römisches Strafrecht,* pp. 580–587.

[56] *Dig.* 48, 4, 1, 1; 48, 4, 3; 48, 4, 7, 2; 48, 4, 10; 49, 16, 3, 11.

[57] *Dig.* 48, 4, 1, 1–3. Cf. Daremberg et Saglio, *Dictionnaire des antiquités grècques et romaines,* article "*Maiestas*" by G. Humbert and Ch. Lécrivain (Graz, Austria: Akademische Druck-u. Verlagsanstalt, 1963), III (2), 1559, 1560.

Violated majesty, however, comprehended more than the elements which entered later into high treason since it embraced treason against land and folk (*Landesverrat*) as well.[58] Other components of *Landesverrat* have been derived from the laws concerning sedition, rioting, and breach of the peace, but the military crimes, such as desertion, did not pass extensively into the *Breviary* despite their presence in the *Theodosian Code.*[59] Many factors which have hastened the development of petty treason passed over to the Middle Ages from the laws on accusation and parricide.[60] In each case the sanctity of the bond between patron and client is emphasized. The client may inform against the patron only when the latter is guilty of a violation of *maiestas,* and the murder of a patron by his client is the basest sort of crime. Thus, a certain parallel is suggested here with the later relation of lord and vassal, just as the laws of *maiestas* suggest the later relation of king and subject.[61] Of course, this relation must not be pushed too far and must be considered in its more purely legal bearings.

Finally, it must be added that, in any case, the *Breviary* preserved the characteristic and fundamental features of Roman public criminal law for the Middle Ages, albeit in an excised and fragmentary form. But we still face the solution of certain problems: Was the mediaeval legal mind sufficiently mature to understand and apply the earlier Roman theory of *maiestas*? Did the circumstances attending Germanic cus-

[58] Cf. Paulus *Sent.* 5, 29, 1 (*L. R. V., P.* 5, 31, 1), which represents in the main the earlier law of the Republic and is directed against *perduellio* (*Landesverrat*). The wording has been modified to meet the conditions of the Principate, and the addition of "sed et verbis impiis ac maledictis maxime exacerbatur" refers to high treason against the person of the emperor.

[59] Cf. *C. Th.* 7, 18, 1–17 *De Desertoribus et Occultatoribus Eorum.*

[60] Clark, *Roman Private Law,* pp. 262–263, especially n. 22. Also cf. *ibid.,* pp. 588 ff.; Mommsen, *Römisches Strafrecht,* p. 527, regarding the close association of *parricidium* and *perduellio* in the early Roman Law.

[61] See Pollock and Maitland, *History of English Law,* II, 504: "Petty treason perpetrated against a lord was but slowly marked off from high treason perpetrated against the king; and in much later days our law still saw, or spoke as if it saw, the essence of high treason in a breach of the bond of 'ligeance'." That the relation of client to patron or even of slave to master in the Roman Law was interpreted by the lawyers of the later Middle Ages as bearing upon the matter of feudal allegiance may be inferred from the argument in II, 504, n. 2. Here Pollock and Maitland quote from Bracton, f. 105: "Igne concremantur qui salute dominorum suorum insidiaverint," and point out that he copies with certain omissions from *Dig.* 48, 19, 28, 11 *De Poenis:* "Igni cremantur plerumque servi, qui saluti dominorum suorum insidiaverint, nonnunquam etiam liberi plebeii et humiles personae." "He [Bracton] holds therefore that to plot against one's lord's life is a capital crime. We imagine that this crime would have been punished in England rather by drawing and hanging than by burning."

tomary law admit the application of Roman rules and practice in the matter of offenses against the state? Were the fields of operation of Roman public law and of Germanic customary law mutually exclusive, or did they interact and combine? The answers to these questions await a careful analysis of the public law matter in the barbarian codes and its comparison and correlation with the Roman materials accessible during the earlier Middle Ages.

V

Contractual Allegiance vs. Deferential Allegiance
in Visigothic Law*

No phase of public law affords a more striking contrast between Roman and Germanic ideas than that embracing the sphere of sovereignty, allegiance, and treason. The Roman conception of majesty,[1] established upon deference and veneration, especially in its absolutist aspects under the late Empire, is seen to be squarely opposed to Teutonic notions of contract, as exemplified in the coronation oath and other devices designed to bind the ruler under the law in the respect of public rights. Statutory law, legislative sovereignty, and the absolutist principle are set off sharply against limiting rights or liberties, judicial sovereignty, and immemorial custom. Under such circumstances, it is hardly surprising to discover that the idea of majesty, indeed even the term *maiestas*, disappears almost completely in the barbarian codes. Nevertheless,

---

* Reprinted by special permission of the *Illinois Law Review* (Northwestern University School of Law), Vol. 34, No. 5, 1940, pp. 557–566, with minor corrections. Read in part before the Southern Classical Association (presently designated Classical Association of the Middle West and South: Southern Section) at San Antonio, Texas, on November 30, 1939, under the title of "The Idea of *Maiestas* in Visigothic Law."

[1] See T. Mommsen, *Römisches Strafrecht* (Leipzig: S. Hirzel, 1899), pp. 538–540, and notes regarding the origin of *maiestas*. This view is not universally accepted among authorities and should be considered a conjecture lacking definitive proof. Cf. Daremberg et Saglio, *Dictionnaire des antiquités grècques et romaines*, article "Maiestas," by C. Humbert and Ch. Lécrivain (Graz, Austria: Akademische Druck-u. Verlagsanstalt, 1963), III (2), 1556, and P. Schisas, *Offences against the State in Roman Law* (London: University of London Press, 1926), pp. 3–15, for criticism of Mommsen's view; also Pauly-Wissowa-Kroll, *Realencyclopädie der classischen Altertumswissenschaft*, article "Maiestas" by B. Kübler (Stuttgart: Metzler, 1928), XXVII, 542–559 for a sound, well-considered estimate.

this curious fact appears to have passed quite unnoticed, although important inferences for political theory may be derived clearly therefrom, depending somewhat upon whether the conception of majesty was omitted purposely, or whether the entire idea disappeared because it belonged to an earlier time in a widely differing political and social structure and was accordingly no longer understood by the simpler legal mind of a barbaric age. Also the replacement of older Roman ideas of the state by the new Germanic views lends support to the contentions of those who hold that, contrary to some extreme Romanic theories, the German invaders constituted a positive intellectual force making definite contributions and that they did more than absorb and transform their heritage from antiquity. The precise way in which the older Roman concepts were supplanted or commingled with Germanic ideas is investigated in the essay on "The Public Law of the Visigothic Code."

There is probably no better point of approach or center of investigation for the complex materials of the *leges barbarorum* open to the student of public criminal law than that afforded by the legislation of the Visigoths,[2] since the various Visigothic laws illustrate the transition from a Roman to a Germanic legal basis and the fusion of Roman and Germanic law with greater explicitness and clarity than any of the other barbarian codes. Incidentally, it would be easy to overemphasize the extent and significance of the Germanic elements in these codes, and to avoid this pitfall it may be best to apply the term "Romance law" to the materials of the *Leges Visigothorum*, as perhaps to the *leges barbarorum* generally. These laws are not constituted of pure Germanic custom, but contain many Roman elements, some of which are embodied in the new codes quite unchanged, as in the Visigothic *antiqua*. In the main, they reflect the age for which they have been compiled. There is an organic welding together of Roman theory and practice, some Christian senti-

---

[2] An excellent recent historical account of the Visigothic legislation may be found in A. K. Ziegler, *Church and State in Visigothic Spain* (Washington: Catholic University of America, 1930), especially Ch. III on the "Visigothic Code of Civil Law." Also see a most valuable, though uncompleted, series of articles by K. Zeumer in *Neues Archiv der Gesellschaft für ältere deutsche Geschichtskunde*, entitled "Geschichte der westgothischen Gesetzgebung," XXIII (1898), 419–516; XXIV (1899), 39–122, for analysis of *Leges Visigothorum*, Section II, 571–630 for analysis of Section III; XXVI (1901), 91–149 on Section IV. A good general discussion of the *Leges Visigothorum* may be found in H. Brunner, *Deutsche Rechtsgeschichte* (2nd ed., Leipzig: Duncker and Humbolt, 1906), I, 481–496, and of the *Lex Romana Visigothorum*, *ibid.*, I, 510–516. Also note, especially for bibliography, H. D. Hazeltine, "Roman and Canon Law in the Middle Ages," *Cambridge Medieval History* (Cambridge: Macmillan, 1926), V, 720–29, 743–48.

ment, and a new element which the Germanic invaders contributed from their ancient custom or built up in the course of their experiences during the invasions. Such a mixture or growth surely deserves to be called "Romance" as well as do the languages that were created within the same *milieu*. Thus, Ziegler designates the Visigothic Code "a gradual and discriminating amalgamation of the written code of Rome with Germanic customary law,"[3] and states that it is "not a Germanic code, but Roman, with considerable vestige of German custom" and "with a distinctly Christian tone."[4] Also, the Visigothic laws provide another central focus for the barbarian legislation, since they stand in an especially direct relationship to the great bodies of Bavarian and Lombard law.[5] Finally it must be noted that in many respects the Visigothic laws present characteristically German legal ideas in their most typical forms,

[3] Ziegler, *Visigothic Spain*, p. 23.

[4] *Ibid.*, pp. 54, 75–76, 88, 204. Also see Fustel de Coulanges, *Histoire des institutions politiques de l'ancienne France* (*La Monarchie franque*) (5th ed.; Paris; Hachette, 1926), III, 17–18. He voices a similar point of view: "Le titre de Lois barbares, que leur ont donné les éditeurs modernes, prête à une illusion. Ce ne sont pas des législations vraiment germaniques, c'est-a-dire qu'elles ne sont pas de vielles coutumes a Germanie qui auraient été mises en écrit au septième siècle. Elles sont l'oeuvre propre de l'epoque même ou elles ont été écrites; elles subissent l'influence du pays et du temps ou elles sont rédigees; l'esprit de l'Eglise chrétienne y règne. Loin qu'elles soient oeuvre traditionelle et populaire, ce sont les rois du septiéme siècle qui en sont les auteurs." But with these last remarks we may, in some respects, dissent, and there may be more that is old and Teutonic than Fustel thought. Indeed, Fustel may be considered an outstanding proponent of the *Romanic* view regarding the content and origins of the barbarian legislation, whereas W. E. Wilda maintains the more purely Germanic theory in his *Geschichte des deutschen Strafrechts* (Halle: C. A. Schwetschke, 1842), I: Das Strafrecht der Germanen.

[5] The general resemblance of the *leges barbarorum* in structure and content is a vital matter. See the *Praefatio* of K. Zeumer's definitive edition of the *Lex Visigothorum* or *Forum Iudicum* in *Monumenta Germaniae Historica*, Leges (Hanover and Leipzig: Hahn, 1902), Sectio I, Tomus I, pp. xvii–xviii, where convincing proof is adduced regarding the close relationship of the *Code of Euric* to the *Lex Baiuvariorum;* also see *ibid.*, 28–32, for a critical text of the *Codicis Euriciani Leges ex Lege Baiuvariorum Restitutae.* There is also a well-established relationship between the *Lex Baiuvariorum, Leges Alamannorum*, and *Leges Ripuariorum.* See E. von Schwind, "Kritische Studien zur Lex Baiuvariorum," *Neues Archiv*, XXXI (1906), 399–453. For the influence of the Visigothic legislation upon the Germanic folk laws in general, see Brunner, *D. R.*, I, 423, 488; Schröder-von Künssberg, *Lehrbuch der deutschen Rechtsgeschichte* (Berlin and Leipzig: de Gruyter, 1922), pp. 252, 256, 260, 269, 271; Hazeltine ("Roman and Canon Law," V, 726), who notes that "the *Antiqua* influenced the Salic, Burgundian, Lombard, and Bavarian codes." For the relationship of the *Code of Euric* to the *Lex Burgundionum*, see Brunner, *D. R.*, I, 486–487. The political connections between the Bavarians and Lombards, beginning with the marriage of Theodelinda to Authari, may be responsible for legal contacts and the legal characteristics common to the *Leges Baiuvariorum* and *Edictus Rothari.*

so that by studying them one gains a general impression of the nature of the other compilations.[6]

Early in the fifth century the Visigoths settled in Gaul and Spain in territory which had been Roman for centuries, and in course of time issued a most interesting series of enactments.[7] During this century it appears that the laws used by Visigoths and by Romans were not carefully distinguished or separated into two different codes, although the two races were severely distinct.[8] Prior to the promulgation of the *Code of Theodosius* II in 438 the Roman law may well have been so diffuse and difficult of access as to have been impracticable for wide use among the ignorant judges of these regions which were undergoing barbarization, while the conquerors doubtless clung to their immemorial tribal custom, which may have suffered some modification during the period of invasion for custom is not static and some change might be expected during this dynamic period of social flux. Between 438 and 506 the situation is not clear, although the orderly systematic character of the *Theodosian Code* must have been a strong factor in bolstering the position of the Roman law. Also, the earliest attempts to reduce Gothic custom to written form were made during these years under Roman influence, concluding with the legislation of Euric (466–485). The spheres of Germanic custom and of Roman law may well have overlapped and intertwined together. The law was in process of becoming "Romance." Thus, Zeumer thinks that the *Code of Euric* (*ca.* 481) contained laws enforced upon both Gothic and Roman litigants, although for cases involving only Romans the Roman *ius* and *leges* held.[9] Even in 506, Alaric

---

[6] This is particularly true of the problems associated with *maiestas, scandalum, macinamenta* or conspiracy, and the special *paces*.

[7] The Visigothic occupation of Aquitaine and Septimania resulted in a permanent and pervasive legal influence upon Gaul. This is more true in the case of the *Breviarium Alarici (Lex Romana Visigothorum)* than of the *Forum Judicum (Lex Visigothorum)*; yet for the latter see the *Fragmenta Gaudenziana* in Zeumer, "Geschichte der westgothischen Gesetzgebung," pp. 469–472, a group of fourteen *capitula* intended for use in Septimania under the rule of King Leovigild. Also note Ziegler, *Visigothic Spain*, p. 60, n. 11, regarding the influence of the code of Leovigild upon the *Edictus Rothari*. Cf. Zeumer, *Neues Archiv*, XXIII (1898), 428–429; Schröder-von Künssberg, *Lehrbuch*, p. 243. The Visigothic influence should not be considered to have ceased after the battle of Vouillé in 507 or after the cession of Provincia by Witigis to the Franks in 537, especially as the *Breviary* had not been rejected by the Ostrogoths.

[8] Cf. Brunner, *D. R.*, I, 486, regarding the supremacy of the Goths.

[9] Zeumer, *Praefatio*, p. xiii. Cf. *Lex Romana Visigothorum*, ed. by G. Haenel (Leipzig: Teubner, 1849), p. v, n. 1, and Brunner (*D. R.*, I, 486–489), who discusses the relation of the *Code of Euric* to the Roman Law.

II can speak in the *Commonitorium* or Preface of the *Breviary* "de omni legum Romanarum et antiqui iuris obscuritate," that is, of the obscurity both of the Roman laws and of the ancient custom or *antiqua* of the Goths.[10]

Leaving out of consideration the so-called *Leges Theodoricianae* mentioned by Apollinaris Sidonius,[11] attention must be paid to the *Code of Euric*, issued about 481, of which only fragments of chapters cclxxvi to cccxxxvi have survived.[12] Nothing bearing upon treason or related public offenses may be found in the existing fragments, which are devoted largely to the law of sales and inheritance.[13] Any portion of Euric's legislation that may have dealt with public criminal law is unfortunately lost. However, Zeumer makes an ingenious reconstruction of a hypothetical provision concerning high treason and treason against land and folk (*Landesverrat*)[14] on the basis of survivals in the Bavarian Law and in Rothar's *Edict*.[15] This reconstructed law states that whoever shall plot the death of the king or shall invite enemies to enter the land shall be in peril of his life and shall suffer confiscation of his property. Thus, the elements of *Landesverrat* and *Hochverrat* are contained here, drawing the distinction so sharply presented in Roman Law between *perduellio*

[10] See Haenel, *Lex Romana Visigothorum*, pp. v and 2.

[11] Cf. Zeumer (*Praefatio*, p. xiii), who attributes these laws to Theodoric I, father of Euric, and dates them as prior to 469 or 470. Cf. C. Pfister, "Early Germanic Laws," *Encyclopaedia Britannica* (11th ed.; Cambridge: University Press, 1910), XI, 775. He says "Besides his own constitutions, Euric (466–485) included in this collection constitutions of his predecessors, Theodoric I (419–451), Thorismund (451–453), and Theodoric II (453–466), and he arranged the whole in logical order." Cf. Brunner, *D. R.*, I, 483, nn. 4–5, for detail; also Zeumer, *Neues Archiv*, XXIII (1898), 440.

[12] For the authenticity, dating, and authorship of these fragments and for a discussion of *Codex Parisinus Lat.* 12161 of the Bibliothèque Nationale (Paris palimpsest), see Zeumer, *Praefatio*, pp. xiii, xvi–xviii; also Brunner, *D. R.*, I, 482–489. For a critical edition of the text of the *Legum Codicis Euriciani Fragmenta*, see Zeumer, pp. 3–27.

[13] The leading captions are *De Commendatis vel Commodatis* (278–285); *De Venditionibus* (286–304); *De Donationibus* (305–319); *De Successionibus* (320–336).

[14] Since nearly all the secondary literature relating to the *leges barbarorum* is written in German and since the German term is convenient, I use the word *Landesverrat* when referring to treason against land and folk, as opposed to high treason (*Hochverrat*).

[15] See Zeumer, *Praefatio*, p. 53, n. 1, where he discussed the substitution of *L. Vis.* 2, 1, 8, by Chindaswinth for an earlier law of Euric now lost. He reconstructs this law from *Lex Baiuvariorum* 2, 1–2, and *Edictus Rothari*, c. 1 and 4, to read as follows: "Si quis in necem regis consiliatus fuerit aut inimicos intra provinciam invitaverit, animae periculum incurrat et res eius infiscentur."

and those aspects of *laesa maiestas* representing personal offenses against the emperor. Also present are the ideas of conspiracy and confiscation, which find their counterparts as well in the Roman Law.

The next important step in Visigothic legal history was the compilation of the *Breviary* or *Lex Romana Visigothorum*, which was approved and promulgated by King Alaric II in 506 as the sole code of law for his Roman subjects.[16] Since its provisions were derived from the older materials of the Roman Law, such as the *Theodosian Code* and *Sentences* of Paulus, and were incorporated with little or no change of text, the *Breviary* encompasses the entire range of Roman legal principles available to the barbarians in the West.[17] Also it was destined to remain the basic legal compend of the western Germans outside Italy until the Carolingian era, while it retained a dominant influence in France, Germany, and England as late as the twelfth century; its use in Spain, however, was discontinued by Recceswinth in 654.[18] Accordingly, since it contained all the fundamental matter relating to *maiestas* and allied offenses against the state, a survey of its contents will reveal the most important ideas concerning these subjects which were transmitted to the Middle Ages prior to the recovery of the *Corpus Juris Civilis*. The primary fact to be noted here is that the laws of majesty expand the scope of treason beyond the limits of Germanic customary law, since they were based on widely differing conceptions of sovereignty and allegiance.

Not only overt acts of violence, capable of inflicting injury or death upon the ruler, but also alleged intent and opinion in the form of maledictions, insult, and slander were deemed violations of majesty.[19] In ad-

[16] The relation of the *Breviary* to Visigothic public law is treated in some detail in the essay on "*Crimen Laesae Maiestatis* in the *Lex Romana Visigothorum*."

[17] There are some reservations to this general statement based upon possible influences of the *Vulgärrecht* and also of the *Corpus Juris Civilis* during the period of Byzantine occupation in Spain. Cf. W. K. Boyd, *The Ecclesiastical Edicts of the Theodosian Code*, Vol. XXIV, No. 2 in *Columbia Studies in History, Economics and Public Law* (New York: Columbia University Press, 1905), Ch. VI, especially pp. 113–118, on the influence of Justinian's legislation in Italy, Spain, and the Frankish territory during the sixth and seventh centuries; also Ziegler, *Visigothic Spain*, p. 75 with n. 67; Hazeltine, "Roman and Cannon Law," V, 730.

[18] See O. Karlowa, *Römische Rechtsgeschichte* (Leipzig: Veit, 1885), II, 977; Brunner, *D. R.*, supra note 3, at I, 515; Sir Paul Vinogradoff, *Roman Law in Medieval Europe*, ed. by F. de Zulueta (2nd ed.; Oxford: University Press, 1929), p. 16; H. O. Taylor, *The Mediaeval Mind* (4th ed.; New York: Macmillan, 1925), II, 272; and Alfred von Wretschko in the *Prolegomena* of the Mommsen-Meyer edition of the *Theodosian Code* (Berlin: Weidmann, 1905), Vol. I, Part 1, cccvii–ccclx.

[19] It should be noted that certain offenses listed here were considered *maiestas* in the *Theodosian Code*, although not specifically cited as such in the *Breviary*. See text of Paulus *Sententiae* 5, 29, 1–2 (*Lex Romana Visigothorum, Paulus* 5, 31, 1–2)

dition, the laws of *maiestas* embraced offenses against the land and folk (*Landesverrat*), which had been included under the laws of *perduellio* in the time of the Roman Republic, as well as high treason (*Hochverrat*) or personal attacks upon the ruler. Thus, sedition, rioting, and breach of the peace were punished as *Landesverrat*, while malediction, counterfeiting, and other forms of *crimen falsi* were high treason. Most of these crimes with their appropriate penalties pass unchanged into the *Breviary* by way of the *Theodosian Code* and *Sentences* of Paulus. Finally, the laws on accusation and parricide, which are either incorporated among the laws of *maiestas* or are closely related to them, transmit elements that may bear upon the development of petty treason in the feudal age, for here the sanctity of the bond between patron and client is strongly suggestive of the later relation of lord and vassal, whereas, on the other hand, the majesty laws themselves suggest the later relation of king and subject.[20]

It should be noted, also, that among the Germanic peoples who established the barbarian kingdoms the idea of allegiance is ordinarily rendered into Latin as *fides* in the special sense of a pledged troth. Conversely, treason is *infidelitas* (*Treubruch*).[21] Allegiance among these

---

Ad Legem Iuliam Maiestatis. This passage in the *Breviary* preserved in outline the essential features of the Roman theory of treason for the Latin West. Cf. *Digest* 48, 4, 7, 3: "Hoc tamen crimen iudicibus non in occasione ob principalis maiestatis venerationem habendum est, sed in veritate."

[20] Pollock and Maitland, *The History of English Law before the Time of Edward I* (2nd ed.; Cambridge: University Press, 1923), II, 504. Note also that the sanctity of the bond between patron and client offers a certain parallel to Germanic contractual ideas of a pledged troth. This notion of a bilateral obligation is present in both cases, whereas the majesty laws stress the position of the ruler as against the rights of the subject. This is, however, much less true under the Republic than in the period of the *Theodosian Code*. Also, the Germanic view of *infidelitas* applies consistently to all aspects of treason. Every petty chieftain was joined to his personal followers by personal pledges. Hence treason could be be committed against any *dux* or lord, and when the distinction between the *dux-king* and the *duces-lords* has been drawn, one finds a breach of faith (*Treubruch*) which is high treason, on the one hand, and a *Treubruch* that is petty treason, on the other.

[21] Regarding *infidelitas* (*Treubruch*), see G. Waitz, *Deutsche Verfassungsgeschichte* (3rd ed.; Berlin: Weidmann, 1880), I (3), 236–293; Wilda, *Strafrecht*, I, 984, 988 (*herisliz*); F. Dahn, *Die Könige der Germanen* (Leipzig: Breitkopf and Härtel, 1894), VII (1), 381; Brunner, *D. R.*, I, 185 *et seq.*; Brunner-von Schwerin, *Deutsche Rechtsgeschichte* (2nd ed.; Munich and Leipzig: Duncker and Humblot, 1928), II, 883 (*harisliz*), 886; P. Bisoukides, *Der Hochverrat* (Berlin: Carl Heymanns Verlag, 1903), 37–40; Schröder-von Künssberg, *Lehrbuch*, pp. 32–36, on the *Gaufürst, princeps (satrapa), furisto,* and on the *Herzog, dux, herizogo;* pp. 36–40 on the *Gefolge, comitatus;* p. 31 on an entire people forsaking its troth to a king who has abused his authority or who had appeared to be accursed by the gods. Cf.

early Germans is pervaded with the idea of a contractual relation which is bilateral.[22] No matter how despotic the ruler, allegiance in theory is never mere deference to a higher power which is recognized as being outside the state and above the law, such as was implicit in *maiestas* during the later Roman Empire. The barbarian period remains, by and large, a judicial age, interpreting and determining the ancient custom.[23] The idea of rights was predominant. If the people promised faith to their king which he could claim as a pledge by right, this faithful people understood that it should receive in return the benefit of the royal peace (*pax*).[24] The theory that the promissor is not giving something for nothing always lies just under the surface when an oath of fidelity is taken to the king. The contractual Germanic *sacramentum fidelitatis* is very different from the military *sacramentum* of the Roman soldier.[25]

Brunner-von Schwerin, *D. R.*, II, 881: "Was das neuere Strafrecht als Landesverrat bezeichnet, war in älteren Rechte Treubruch gegen das Gemeinwesen."

[22] Various types of legal obligation and responsibility which contribute to the development of later feudal contractual relations may be discovered in the formulae: *in dominio, in tuitione, in familiaritate, in patrocinio, in precario, in mundio, in truste,* and *in fide.*

[23] See C. H. McIlwain, *The Growth of Political Thought in the West* (New York: Macmillan, 1932), pp. 286, 390, on judicial sovereignty in the Middle Ages; also pp. 190–191 on the contractual nature of customary law.

[24] For the traditional view of the special or higher *paces* (*Frieden*) and of outlawry or "peacelessness" (*Friedlosigkeit*) see Wilda, *Strafrecht*, I, 238–313. These *paces* are essentially special applications of the Germanic concept of a "general peace." This theory of a "general peace," constituting the foundation of public order, has been elaborated in an orthodox form by Wilda, Waitz, Brunner, and Beyerle, but has been attacked vigorously, though not altogether convincingly, by Julius Goebel, Jr., in his recent *Felony and Misdemeanor* (New York: The Commonwealth Fund, 1937), I, 7–25, 37–38; also note 327–335 on the Duke's Peace in Normandy, 423–440 on the King's Peace in England. Cf. Pollock and Maitland, *History of English Law*, I, 44–48; II, 449–455.

[25] For the Visigothic conception of limited monarchy with the king beneath the law and related views of St. Isidore of Seville, see Ziegler, *Visigothic Spain*, pp. 95–98; R. W. and A. J. Carlyle, *A History of Mediaeval Political Theory in the West* (2nd ed.; Edinburgh and London: Blackwood, 1927), I, 172–173. Also note St. Isidore, *Etymologiae* (Oxford: Clarendon, 1911), 9, 3, 4–5, for that famous dictum of limited monarchy: "Rex eris, si recte facias: si non facias, non eris" (Rey seràs si fecieres derecho, y si non fecieres derecho, no seràs Rey). Cf. Horace, *Epistles* 1, 1, 59–60, probably reflecting Stoic doctrine.

Although it would be unsafe to deduce Visigothic conditions in detail by analogy from other Germanic peoples, there is a large amount of collateral evidence of a general nature, based on Frankish materials in the main, that cannot be disregarded. See P. Roth, *Geschichte des Beneficialwesens* (Erlangen: Palm and Enke, 1850), pp. 113–115, 128–136, 142; Schröder-von Künssberg, *Lehrbuch*, p. 117, and n. 27;

On the other hand, the thing that is most notably lacking in Roman public law of the later empire is the element of personal contract. As a result, treason is not described in the *Breviary* as *infidelitas* but as *laesa maiestas*, and crimes against public authority are not represented as breaches of a pledged obligation or *troth*. Sovereignty in Roman political thought is legislative and, to that extent, modern rather than judicial and mediaeval, and must be considered from two angles: religious and temporal. Strong forces were operating under the Dominate to establish the emperor above the law with power to make the law. From the point of view of religion, and later of the Church, *maiestas* depended upon reverence and veneration; from the point of view of the State and of secular society, it was postulated upon an exalted dignity and power resident in the people. This latter conception of majesty reflects a tradition extending back into Republican times. Thereafter the introduction of Oriental ideas of "god-kingship," including the theory of Legalized Absolutism,[26] modified current Republican ideals of a state founded upon supreme respect for law and the popular will and substituted veneration of a deified monarch who moved progressively toward autocracy. Christianity transferred veneration from the divine emperors to God

---

F. Dahn, *Könige* (Leipzig: Breitkopf and Härtel, 1895), VII (3), 382; G. Waitz, *Deutsche Verfassungsgeschichte*, (3rd ed., Berlin: Weidmann, 1882), II (1), 201–202. Regarding negotiations between the king and people, and reciprocal promises and oaths taken by the Frankish kings, see Waitz, II (1), 209–210; Schröder-von Künssberg, p. 118; also Gregory of Tours, *Historia Francorum*, ed. by Arndt and Krusch in *M. G. H. Scriptores Rer. Merov.* (Hanover: Hahn, 1894), Tomus I, Pars 1, 9, 30 for King Charibert, 3, 11 for Theuderich, 4, 9, (14) for Lothar, 7, 8 for Guntram. Cf. oath of allegiance required by Charlemagne from all freemen in his dominions in *Capitulare Missorum Generale* (a. 802), c. 1–2; also *Capitulare Missorum* (a. 789), c. 4.

[26] The Oriental veneration and deference, so distinctive of *maiestas* in the days of the Empire, was first attached to the native Roman concept when Hellenistic city-states deified the city-state of Rome and began the worship of the goddess Roma. Cf. W. S. Ferguson, "Legalized Absolutism en Route from Greece to Rome," *American Historical Review*, XVIII (1912), 29 *et seq.*; W. S. Ferguson, *Greek Imperialism* (Boston: Houghton Mifflin, 1913), c. IV–VI; C. H. McIlwain, *Political Thought*, pp. 139–144. This was really the *proskynesis* of the Eastern cities to the Roman state and marks the beginning of the combination of the idea of the *proskynesis* with the concept *maiestas*. See E. Pollack, *Der Majestätsgedanke im römischen Recht* (Leipzig: Verlag von Veit, 1908) for an extended discussion of majesty as a political and legal idea; see also essay entitled "The Idea of Majesty in Roman Political Thought" which offers a critique of Pollack and adds further suggestions in the light of recent research. Pollack's views require modification and expansion in various respects, especially for the period of the Dominate.

without restoring the autonomy of the popular will.[27] Supreme majesty became an attribute of God while his vicars upon earth were sovereigns in a delegated sense only.[28] Allegiance became a matter of deference, and veneration yielded to supreme authority vested in a higher power. Any contractual elements in early Roman law had become obliterated, for all practical purposes, in the decrees and *constitutiones* of the later absolute monarchs. The faithful servant and subject of the late Roman Empire who receives his due reward not in his own right but by the *grace* of his lord and emperor stands in sharp contrast with the faithful man who, according to Germanic custom, is bound to keep faith only so far as his lord or king does *right* by him. On the one hand lies Roman deferential allegiance, on the other hand Germanic contractual allegiance. The former is the reverence rendered unto others; the latter is a mutually pledged troth. Finally the veneration and respect for Roman majesty has a religious tincture, whereas the contractual fealty of the German invaders is a businesslike relationship entered into with a king who long remains *primus inter pares* in theory only.[29]

[27] This raises the problem of the *lex regia* or *lex de imperio Vespasiani*, which has never been entirely cleared of the obscurities created by imperialist and republican lawyers. Cf. imperialist arguments based on the doctrines of *legibus solutus* and *quid principi placuit, habet legis vigorem* (*Digest* 1, 3, 31; 1, 4, 1; *Institutes* 1, 2, 6) with republican replies resting on the principle of the *digna vox*, established by the rescript of Theodosius and Valentinian to Volusianus in 429 A.D. (*Codex Justinianus* 1, 14, 4; 1, 17, 1, 7), and with the view of God as the source of the *imperium* and of the emperor as a living law (*lex animata*) (*C. Just.* 1, 17, 1; 1, 17, 2, 18; *Novellae*, CV, 4). See Carlyle, *Political Theory*, I, 64, 69, 161–174, 229–234; McIlwain, *Political Thought*, pp. 128, 136; Edward Gibbon, *History of the Decline and Fall of the Roman Empire*, ed. by J. B. Bury (London: Methuen, 1896), IV, 451.

[28] For the significance of this change as regards the relation of treason (*laesa maiestas*) to *laesa religio* (sacrilege, impiety, and heresy), and for the Gelasian theory of the spheres, *sacerdotium* and *regnum*, see Carlyle, *Political Theory*, I, 148–149, 190–192, 256, and c. XXI generally; J. N. Figgis, *Studies of Political Thought from Gerson to Grotius (1414–1625)* (2nd ed.; Cambridge: University Press, 1923), pp. 55, 64, 163; C. H. McIlwain, *The Political Works of James I* (Cambridge: Harvard University Press, 1918), pp. xvii–xxiv (Introduction); McIlwain, *Political Thought*, pp. 163–166.

The principles of pagan "god-kingship" reflect an amalgamation of *laesa maiestas* with *laesa religio*, while the confusion of the two spheres in the Middle Ages tended toward a similar integration. On the other hand, the recognition of two separate vicars, spiritual and temporal, and the preservation of their identity and differing functions was a force tending toward the modern sharp differentiation between Church and State.

[29] Cf. Gregory of Tours, *History of the Franks*, ed. by O. M. Dalton (Oxford: University Press, 1927), I (Introduction), 210–211.

Thus, although the Roman Law regarding *crimen laesae maiestatis* has influenced the laws on treason in the later *leges barbarorum,* it could not make the Germanic crime a true *laesa maiestas,* since the Germanic crime was *Treubruch* and since the Germans did not render deferential allegiance. The term *crimen laesae maiestatis* passes over to the Germans, although it is used very rarely in their legislation. Indeed, it appears so infrequently that one must consider the omission as deliberate and intended. Similarly many of the crimes listed under that caption in the Roman Law pass over into the Germanic codes, but in the process of transmission something is added on the German side of the account—contract—and something deducted on the Roman side—deference and veneration. Thus, killing the king or rebelling against him become most perfidious breaches of faith, and counterfeiting becomes a serious invasion of royal rights, which might be delegated to other lords in a later age of feudal division and local sovereignty but which must never be usurped unlawfully. The talk is always of contract and rights, and these are ideas that form no typical part of majesty.

The outcome of this collision between two opposing principles of allegiance held a decisive significance for subsequent political and legal theory and had a practical effect in determining the governmental form and structure of the later mediaeval states. The idea of the citizen, civil rights, and the commonweal (*res publica*) disappeared when allegiance was rendered through deference and veneration toward a divine monarch in whose person rested the religious sanctions of the ancient Roman *fas,* combined later with the prescriptive rights of Hellenistic *apotheosis,* the Oriental ceremonial of the *proskynesis* (*adoratio*), and the doctrine of the emperor as a "living law" (*lex animata*). Such was the transformation which replaced the common-bond state of Cicero with the absolutism of the Dominate under the later pagan emperors. Nor was the essential sovereign authority of these monarchs impaired by the constitutional tradition that they now enjoyed the fulness of magisterial powers, which had formerly been distributed among many offices and persons. The position of the emperor as a composite magistrate merely gave the semblance of constitutionality to his dominant position. His sovereign powers were supreme, divine, and "above the law to make the law." The theoretical justification of all dictatorship and tyranny is included in our heritage from imperial Rome, and the Christian modification of this principle in the Patristic era, whereby the emperor ceased to be divine but became God's chosen vicar to rule men, does not change the basic theory involved in deferential allegiance. The prototype of the "power state," which clothes the substance of might and force with the forms of constitutionality, emerges in full maturity in the Roman Dominate. In this respect modern dictatorship is the spiritual child of the ancient Caesars.

However, the absolutist principle was not destined to prevail in mediaeval times. It was the function of the Germanic invader to restore those ideas of contract and commonweal upon which the Roman Republic had been established and which had made civic life and civil law possible. In other words, they restore the germ of constitutional government, albeit in the crudely personal forms and procedures of the customary law. The victory of contractual allegiance makes possible the rise of constitutional states. It is significant that individual men are no longer considered as subjects but as free agents and independent entities. They have rights and liberties which they can maintain as against society, state, and monarch. The supremacy of Law is recognized, so that all men, including the rulers of the land, are beneath the law. The Law becomes the true sovereign, and allegiance is rendered to it by observing fidelity to its obligatory bond, which guarantees the integrity of the individual. Contractual allegiance is not the veneration of a divine monarch but the observance of Law, respect for its sanctity, and fidelity to its protective power upon which all rights and privileges depend. Furthermore, the mediaeval king is not a legislator; not even the people at any specific moment of time may be called a legislator. Law is not made, it grows; it is "immemorial custom." Even with the rise of popular assemblies men find the law or state the law (*legem dicere*); they do not give the law or make the law (*legem dare*). Sovereign power is not legislative but judicial. It flows from the inner sense of generations of men whom it has bound for ages; it is not an act of the moment, emanating from a royal or divine will. This great shift in legal perspective begins with the downfall of the Roman Dominate in the West and its replacement by the incipient barbarian kingdoms. It is a long story through the rise of representative institutions and democratic processes to the constitutional republic of modern times, but the appearance of the new contractual allegiance of our Germanic forebears represents no small advance along the road toward constitutionalism. Unfortunately the devious alternative path of deferential allegiance still follows parallel, and many have passed along it through the revival of the Roman Law in the new national states of the later Middle Ages, the absolutism of the Sixteenth Century, the modern advocacy of the "Divine Right of Kings," the despotisms of the Enlightenment, and the end is not yet. Nor can any man foresee the day when these two basic conflicting principles in law and politics shall be resolved. The collision in principle between the constitutional republic resting on democratic processes and the authoritarian dictatorships is merely the current phase of a continuing struggle. The basic question of legal and political philosophy involved in the struggle is this: Shall we have a government of Law or a government of men?

VI

The Public Law of the Visigothic Code*

It has been observed that the student of public criminal law can hardly find a better central point from which to begin an examination of the complex matter in the barbarian codes than the legislation of the Visigoths. There is little doubt that the Visigothic codes illustrate the transition from a Roman to a Germanic legal basis and the fusion of Roman and Germanic law with greater precision and detail than any other examples in the *leges barbarorum*.[1] However, to avoid attributing undue emphasis to the Germanic element, the *Leges Visigothorum*, and indeed much other barbarian legislation, may best be described as "Romance law" and not merely as "barbarian law." It is true that they are Germanic folk laws, but much else is commonly added. These laws do not consist of pure Germanic custom, but contain many Roman elements which at times are transmitted with little change, as in the Visigothic *antiquae*. In general they reflect the legal ideas and intellectual climate of the age for which they were devised. There is an organic combination of Roman theory and practice, Christian sentiment, and a new factor contributed by the Germanic invaders from their ancient custom or established on the basis of their experiences during the invasions. It must be reiterated that the product of such fusion and growth

° Reprinted by special permission of the Editors of *Speculum* and the Mediaeval Academy of America from *Speculum*, Vol. XXVI, No. 1 (1951), 1–23. Read in part at the annual meeting of the American Historical Association in Washington, D. C., on December 29, 1948.

[1] For a more extended discussion dealing with the basic legal and political concepts of the Visigothic legislation, see essay in this volume on "Contractual Allegiance vs. Deferential Allegiance in Visigothic Law."

deserves to be called "Romance" as well as do the languages that were evolved within the same cultural *milieu*. No one has put the matter better than Father Ziegler in his study of *Church and State in Visigothic Spain,* where he terms the Visigothic Code "a gradual and discriminating amalgamation of the written code of Rome with Germanic customary law," and indicates that "it is not a Germanic code, but Roman, with considerable vestige of Germanic custom" and "with a distinctly Christian tone."[2] Also, the Visigothic laws occupy a central position in relation to much other barbarian legislation, especially the great bodies of Bavarian and Lombard law, and in many instances present characteristically German legal ideas in their most typical forms, as in the problems associated with *maiestas, scandalum, macinamenta* or conspiracy, and the special *paces*.[3] Hence a study of the Visigothic Code is an invaluable aid in any approach to and comprehension of the other barbarian compilations.

The basic code, compiled in the seventh century, and known variously as the *Leges Visigothorum, Forum Judicum, Forum Juridicum, Liber Judicis, Liber Judicum,* and *Liber Judiciorum,* presents, then, an organic union of Roman and Germanic elements.[4] It was based in considerable degree upon the earlier legislation of Euric and Alaric, and was reduced to final form in its most essential features during the reigns of King Chindaswinth (642–653) and King Recceswinth (649–672). Despite its diffuse and stilted style, its tedious circumlocution and redundancy of phrase, its didactic sententiousness, its barbaric Latin and elaborate artificial rhetoric, especially in the later enactments, this code has been declared "the most remarkable monument of legislation which ever emanated from a semibarbarian people"[5] and which "incomparably

[2] Cf. A. K. Ziegler, *Church and State in Visigothic Spain* (Washington: Catholic University of America, 1930), pp. 23, 54, 75–76, 88, 204. Also, this is substantially the position assumed in Ernst Levy, "Reflections on the First 'Reception' of Roman Law in Germanic States," *American Historical Review,* XLVIII (1942), 20–29. See Fustel de Coulanges, *Histoire des institutions politiques de l'ancienne France (La Monarchie franque)* (5th ed.; Paris: Hachette, 1926), III, 17–18, for the Romanic view regarding the content and origins of barbarian legislation, and W. E. Wilda, *Geschichte des deutschen Strafrechts,* I *(Das Strafrecht der Germanen)* (Halle: C. H. Schwetschke, 1842) for the Germanic theory.

[3] See essay on "Contractual Allegiance vs. Differential Allegiance in Visigothic Law."

[4] For the history of the *Leges Visigothorum,* see Ziegler, *Church and State,* pp. 60–68 (containing a concise, accurate survey which makes use of recent literature on the subject and to which I am much indebted); H. Brunner, *Deutsche Rechtsgeschichte* (2nd ed.; Leipzig: Duncker and Humblot, 1906), I, 481–496.

[5] S. P. Scott, *The Visigothic Code* (Boston: Boston Book Company, 1910), p. xxiv.

surpassed in excellence the codifications of the other barbarian peoples."[6] The need for a code applicable to Visigoths and Hispano-Romans equally had grown commensurately with the racial fusion of these peoples, so that it was no longer desirable to have one body of law for the Visigothic rulers, consisting in large measure of Germanic custom such as the *Code of Euric,* and another compilation for the descendants of the Hispano-Roman *provinciales,* based upon Roman law as in the *Breviary.* As early as the time of King Leovigild (568–586), the older material of Euric was corrected and modified with additions and deletions in the so-called *Codex revisus,*[7] of which no manuscript is extant but which left its imprint on later legislation, since certain provisions in the *Forum Judicum,* denominated *antiquae,* are generally considered to be derived from this reform of Leovigild. It is not always easy to separate positively the ancient Gothic laws, based on unwritten, immemorial custom, from material descended from Roman sources. Vinogradoff considers that about one-third of the *antiqua* is derived from Roman law and that entire sections of the *Leges Visigothorum* are taken over or adapted from the *Breviary,* the *Novellae,* and the *Vulgärrecht* or customary laws of Roman origin. However, he goes on to utter the caution that even though the Roman content bulks large in Visigothic law still "there was a continuous stream of German legal customs" which are clearly Teutonic and resemble Scandinavian materials.[8]

Certain it is, in any case, that during the period extending from Leovigild to Chindaswinth and including the reigns of Reccared (586–601), who made the momentous decision to adopt Catholic orthodoxy in the place of Arian Christianity, and of Sisebut (612–621) there is a constant tendency toward the amalgamation of Roman law with Germanic custom for the common use of all subjects within the realm.[9] Chindaswinth seems to have been the "Visigothic Justinian" who saw the need for a general code that was applicable uniformly throughout his kingdom, and the work, incomplete at his death, was finally promul-

---

[6] Ziegler, *Church and State,* p. 88; also see *ibid.,* pp. 70–73 and 83–87, for the opinions of various scholars regarding this code: the unfavorable estimate of Montesquieu, the well-balanced judgments of Gibbon and Savigny, the friendly criticism of Zeumer and Ziegler himself, and the enthusiastic appreciation of Guizot.

[7] Cf. Brunner, *D. R.,* I, 489.

[8] Paul Vinogradoff, *Roman Law in Medieval Europe* (2nd ed.; London: Humphrey Milford, 1929), pp. 30–31.

[9] Note Brunner, *D. R.,* I, 489, where he says: "Leovigild's legislatorische Tätigkeit bewegte sich in der Richtung einer Ausgleichung der zwischen Römer und Goten bestehenden Gegensätze."

gated by the *lex quoniam* in 654 under his son, Recceswinth.[10] From this time onward both Goths and Romans were subject to a common uniform law with the result that the *Breviary* was discarded and passed from active use in Spain. And this new law was "Romance law"—neither Roman law nor Germanic custom, but an organic combination of both. The new compilation (*Liber Judiciorum* or *Lex Visigothorum Reccessvindiana*) contained a large number of recent decrees by its authors, together with the *antiqua*. Later, a few *capitula* were added by King Wamba (672–680), and a thorough revision (*Lex Visigothorum renovata*) was made by Erwig (680–687), though not always in the interest of greater clarity and more substantial justice.[11] Erwig's code was promulgated by the *lex pragma* in 681 to supplant the older version of Recceswinth.[12] Subsequently, this code with laws added by Egica (687–702) and later interpolations was transmitted to the Middle Ages in the *Forma vulgata*.[13] The *Forum Judicum* did not perish but survived in Spanish translation in the Castilian *Fuero Juzgo* of the thirteenth century and found its way into the *Siete partidas* of Alfonso the Wise.[14]

At this point it becomes necessary to examine the text of the Visigothic Code itself so that we may discover what provisions it contains relating to offenses against the state, what light these provisions cast upon the ideas of *maiestas* and *infidelitas*, and what results were produced by the fusion of Roman and Germanic concepts in the sphere of public criminal law. A few general statements illustrating the purpose of the law (*lex*) and the nature of the kingship will establish a convenient background, since offenses against public authority are conditioned by the nature of that authority.[15] In a section on the legislator we

[10] *L. Vis.* 2, 1, 5 *De tempore, quo debeant leges emendate valere* (Recceswinth). Cf. K. Zeumer, *Neues Archiv der Gesellschaft für ältere deutsche Geschichtskunde*, XXIII (1898), 511 ff.

[11] In Zeumer's edition of the *Leges Visigothorum in Monumenta Germaniae Historica, Leges*, Sectio I, Tomus I (Hanover and Leipzig: Hahn, 1902), the original code of Recceswinth and the new version of Erwig are printed in parallel columns, with the latter in smaller type save where it differs from the older text. See Brunner, *D. R.*, I, 492.

[12] *L. Vis.* 2, 1, 1 *De tempore, quo debeant leges emendate valere* (Erwig). Cf. Zeumer, *Neues Archiv*, XXIII (1898), 496–497.

[13] Regarding the disagreement between Zeumer and Ureña in the matter of a separate code by Egica, see Ziegler, *Church and State*, p. 67, n. 45.

[14] See *Las Siete Partidas: Translation and Notes* by S. P. Scott and Introduction by C. S. Lobingier (Chicago: Published for the Comparative Law Bureau of the American Bar Association by Commerce Clearing House, Inc., 1931).

[15] The First Book of the Code from which these general statements of political principles have been selected deserves more serious attention than it has been

find that the architect of the laws must provide laws for the welfare of the people.[16] He must establish laws, not for private gain, but for the common welfare and utility of all the people.[17] He who safeguards the security of others should govern by common consent rather than render judgment through his own personal power.[18] A kind of social compact, if not the idea of contract, is implicit in this statement. The lawgiver shall have no favorites and shall deserve the love of all his subjects, even to the lowly, and here Christian influence is evident in the injunction to govern by love rather than by force.[19] Another famous law, urging moderation upon princes, states:

And so moderation in princes results in temperate laws, just as harmony among citizens produces victory over enemies. For well-ordered laws arise from the clemency of princes, the establishment of morals from well-ordered laws, harmony of citizens from the establishment of morals, and triumph over enemies from the harmony of citizens. And so the good prince, ruling within and conquering without, while he possesses peace at home and ends strife abroad, is celebrated both as the leader of citizens and victor over enemies, to have after the rolling years eternal rest, after golden dross the heavenly kingdom, after the diadem and purple the glory and a crown; nay naught shall be lacking to such a king, since, when he has left the kingdom of earth and

---

granted heretofore. As Father Ziegler has observed, it contains concepts of limited government standing in the great tradition of the Magna Carta, the Declaration of Independence, and the Bill of Rights. Cf. Ziegler, *Church and State*, pp. 70–73, who states: "Perhaps the dominant note of the philosophy in the first book is a repeated insistence that laws are for the welfare of the people and not for the peculiar advantage of individual persons" (p. 71). See Charles H. Lynch, *Saint Braulio, Bishop of Saragossa (631–651): His Life and Writings*, The Catholic University of America Studies in Mediaeval History, New Series, II (Washington: Catholic University, 1938), pp. 135–140. He goes so far as to suggest that the probable author of the First Book was St. Braulio, bishop of Saragossa, adviser of King Recceswinth, and the dominant ecclesiastical figure in Spain after the death of St. Isidore. Also cf. Ferdinand Lot, *Les invasions germaniques* (Paris: Payot, 1935), pp. 182–183.

[16] *L. Vis.* 1, 1, 2 *Quo modo uti debeat artifex legum*: "Ab illo enim negotia rerum non expetunt in teatrali fabore clamorum, sed in exoptata salvatione populi legem."

[17] *L. Vis.* 1, 1, 3 *Quid requirendum est in artificem legum*: "qui legislator existet, nullo privatim commodo, sed omnium civium utilitati communi motum presidiumque oportune legis inducere."

[18] *L. Vis.* 1, 1, 5 *Qualis erit in consiliandum artifex legum*: "ut aliene provisor salutis commodius ex universali consensu exerceat gubernaculum, quam ingerat ex singulari potestate iudicium."

[19] *L. Vis.* 1, 1, 8 *Qualis in publicis, qualis in privatis erit artifex legum*: "ut hunc universitas patrem, parvitas habet dominum." Cf. 1, 1, 7 *Qualis erit in iudicando artifex legum*: "Personam tantum nesciat accipere, quanto et contemnet eligere."

acquired a heavenly kingdom, he shall not be deemed to have lost the glory of his realm but to have increased it.[20]

Finally, two laws of Recceswinth must be noted. The first declares that laws are provided for human safety by divine command and indicates that both king and people are equally bound by the laws: "Therefore gladly fulfilling the divine commands, we provide moderate laws for ourselves and our subjects which our clemency, together with all kings who succeed us and the entire general populace of our realm are enjoined to obey, so that no person of whatsoever rank may put himself beyond the custody of the laws."[21] The other law contains the common mediaeval simile of the human body and its members as applied to the body politic, a figure of speech that indicates an organic relation between the ruler and his subjects but emphasizes the primacy of the ruler. Nevertheless, majesty can hardly be attributed to him on the basis of this statement. The king is the head (*caput*) which transmits power and vigor to the limbs;[22] hence the health of the head is the first concern of the skilled physician of the state. "Therefore the affairs of the prince must be considered first; his safety must be insured and his life protected, and thereafter attention may be given to the condition and affairs of the people, so that, when rulers are seen to be safe, the welfare of the people may be maintained the more confidently and vigorously."[23]

Among enactments relating to offenses properly designated as treasonable, we may well begin with an edict of Recceswinth, issued on the occasion of the Eighth Council of Toledo (a. 652) and closely parallel to the tenth canon of that council on sedition.[24] Here the prince is en-

---

[20] *L. Vis.* 1, 2, 6 *Quod triumphet de hostibus lex* (Recceswinth, Erwig): "Sicut ergo modestia principum temperantia est legum, ita concordia civium victoria est hostium."

[21] *L. Vis.* 2, 1, 2 *Quod tam regia potestas quam populorum universitas legum reverentie sit subiecta* (Recc.): "convenit omnium terrenorum quamvis excellentissimas potestates illi [legi] colla submittere mentis, cui etiam militie celestis famulator dignitas servitutis."

[22] Cf. St. Isidore *Etymologiae* 11, 1, 25: "Prima pars corporis caput, datumque illi hoc nomen eo, quod sensus omnes et nervi inde initium capiant."

[23] *L. Vis.* 2, 1, 4 *Quod antea ordinare oportuit negotia principum et postea populorum* (Recc.).

[24] *L. Vis.* 2, 1, 6 *De principum cupiditate damnata eorumque initiis ordinandis, et qualiter conficiende sunt scripture in nomine principum facte* (Recc.). Cf. *Conc. Tolet.* VIII, can. 10: "Abhinc ergo et deinceps ita erunt in regni gloriam praeficiendi rectores, ut aut in urbe regia aut ubi princeps decesserit cum pontificum maiorumque palatii omnimodo eligantur assensu, non forinsecus aut conspiratione paucorum aut rusticarum plebium seditioso tumultu." Note other canons of the Councils of

joined to have regard for the welfare of the people and not merely for his personal advantage. Also, the prince is declared to be under the law: "ut, quia subiectis leges reverentie dederamus, principum quoque excessibus retinaculum temperantie poneremus." In other words, the king must not batten on the woe of his subjects, and is restrained from taking and withholding the properties of his subjects illegally and wrongfully. On the other hand, both in crown properties ("pro regni apice adquisita") and personal properties, the king is guaranteed possession and the right of disposal within the limitations of the law. One should note that the distinction is drawn here between crown properties which pass to the king's successor in the realm and the personal properties inherited by his heirs according to Germanic custom.[25] The king is more than the possessor of personal power and authority; he is becoming a symbol of the sovereignty of the realm. Nevertheless, he is compelled to bind himself under royal oath to respect the provisions of this law, and the contractual element enters at this point, *since the king is bound.*[26]

But whoever is found to have obtained the throne through popular tumults or concealed plots shall forthwith, together with all the accomplices of his wickedness, be declared anathema and deprived of association with Christians, stricken by such a dire revenge, that every follower of the divine order who shall presume to communicate with the offender shall be damned with a like penalty and be destroyed utterly.

Also if any holder of a palatine office shall wish to break the provisions of this law through evil detraction or shall be found to advocate that it be

---

Toledo, cited by Zeumer as follows: *Conc. Tolet.* IV (a. 633), can. 75; *Conc. Tolet.* V (a. 636), can. 3; *Conc. Tolet.* VI (a. 638), can. 17. See Zeumer, *Neues Archiv,* XXIV (1899), 45–57.

[25] The distinction between crown and personal property is an extremely interesting matter and would appear to be a Visigothic innovation in barbarian law, based perhaps on Roman precedent. Thus, Zeumer apparently considers that the separation of personal and crown properties reaches back to a time earlier than *L. Vis.* 2, 1, 6. See *Neues Archiv,* XXIV (1899), 45–46, and Zeumer's notes in *M. G. H.,* *Leges,* Sectio I, Tomus I, 48–52, based on the *Decretum* directed to King Recceswinth by the Eighth Council of Toledo in 652. It is my impression that this situation does not prevail in either Frankish or Lombard law, but it is a subject that will bear further investigation. See P. N. Riesenberg, *Inalienability of Sovereignty in Medieval Political Thought* (New York: Columbia University Press, 1956), for recent views on the origin of the concept of the crown.

[26] See *L. Vis.* 2, 1, 6: "ut non ante quispiam solium regale conscendat, quam iuramenti federe hanc legem se in omnibus implere promittat." Cf. *Conc. Tolet.* VIII, can. 10: "non prius apicem regni quisque percipiat, quam se illam [i.e., legem nostram de successione in res regis] per omnia suppleturum iurisiurandi taxatione definiat."

voided, whether by whispering secretly or by open proclamation, he shall be deprived forthwith of all rank and position of palatine office and forfeit half of all his possessions, and, having been removed to an appointed place, he shall remain secluded from all contact with the palace. Even an ecclesiastic [*religiosus*] who is involved in a fault of this kind shall be subject to a similar loss of his property.[27]

The final provisions of this law are directed against seizure of the throne and overthrow of the king by violence, which is essentially high treason or *laesa maiestas*; yet such crimes are designated as only *tumultus* (*seditio*) and *macinamenta* or conspiracy, or in the canons as presumptuous and tyrannical usurpation, while the penalty of anathematization shows that these basic public criminal acts are being repressed by religious sanctions under ecclesiastical influence. This is far removed from the modes of punishment in Roman law where such offenses would have been declared most serious violations of majesty. Last of all, one cannot fail to observe that the expression *maiestas* itself is significantly absent.

This decree is followed by a novel of Egica, relating to the matter of rendering allegiance to new princes and the penalties for failure to take an oath of fidelity.[28] Every subject must give a pledge of loyalty to a new king immediately upon his election, and if of palatine rank he must present himself in person before the king without delay. If any freeman attempt to avoid swearing allegiance to the king ("ut pro fide regis conservanda iuramenti se vinculo alliget"), or if any palatine officer delay to enter the royal presence, it shall lie wholly within the king's discretion to dispose of the offender's person and property as he wills, save only in cases of illness or the performance of necessary public duties, in which cases the tardy person must contrive to bring the matter to the king's attention at once as proof of his sincere loyalty. This is a most interesting law and raises the question: Why did men seek to avoid this oath and delay entering the royal presence? The answer lies in the contractual nature of allegiance. They did not wish to bind themselves by any personal tie or troth to a ruler to whom they may have objected. As long as they delayed to take the oath they were under no obligation of obedience. These ideas are Germanic and utterly foreign to the Roman

---

[27] *L. Vis.* 2, 1, 6: "Quemcumque vero aut per tumultuosas plebes aut per absconse dignitati publice macinamenta adeptum esse constiterit regni fastigia, mox idem cum omnibus tam nefarie, sibi consentientibus et anathema fiat et christianorum communionem amittat."

[28] *L. Vis.* 2, 1, 7 *De fidelitate novis principibus reddenda et pena huius transgressionis* (Novella of Egica).

conception of majesty. Here there can be no treason unless there be a broken pledge (*Treubruch*), and men were seeking to avoid taking such a pledge. There could be no treason without allegiance, and breaches of allegiance are *infidelitas*, not *laesa maiestas*.

Two earlier laws of Recceswinth in this same second book strengthen these impressions. One [29] serves as a protection to the king against those who would disregard his commands (by urging some fictitious and fraudulent pretext such as ignorance of the order in Erwig's revision) under penalty of fines and the lash, save only in such instances or acts of God as illness, tempest, floods, or blizzards. Valid excuses are accepted on the ground of legitimate cause or manifest necessity.[30] The point to be noted is this: The king is under the law, but the king's law, if right and just, must be obeyed. The purpose of the second law[31] was to prevent judges from causing a miscarriage of justice and rendering decisions contrary to law because of the king's command or their fear of him. Instead, all contracts and judgments not based on justice and due process of law, but created by royal interference, were declared null and void, while judges acting under compulsion should not be penalized. This law constitutes a definite limitation of royal powers, placing the king under the law, since absolutism is so often contrary to the ends of justice. "The heavy hand of power sometimes perverts the justice of an action, and, while it often prevails, it is just as certain always to be harmful."[32] The subject's allegiance is binding only so long as the king does right under the law. And the law is still, in large degree, the ancient custom of the race, although statutory enactments of a novel and a "made" character are clearly emerging on the basis of the new Christian ethics.[33]

The basic treason law of the entire code (*L. Vis.* 2, 1, 8 *De his, qui contra principem vel gentem aut patriam refugi sivi insulentes existunt*)

---

[29] *L. Vis.* 2, 1, 33 *De his, qui regiam contemserint iussionem* (Recc.).

[30] This is the doctrine which Zeumer describes under the formula of *Echte Not.* Cf. *Lex Ribuaria* 6, 5. 1.

[31] *L. Vis.* 2, 1, 29 *Ut iniustum iudicium et definitio iniusta, regio metu vel iussu a iudicibus ordinata, non valeant* (Recc.).

[32] *Ibid.*, "nonnumquam gravedo potestatis depravare solet iustitiam actionis, que, dum sepe valet, certo est, quod semper nocet."

[33] See F. Kern, *Kingship and Law in the Middle Ages*, ed. by S. B. Chrimes (Oxford: Blackwell, 1939), for a new approach to the relation of contract to custom, and the nature and sources of royal authority in Germanic custom. My view of this position is given in the essay on "The Public Law of the Ripuarian, Alamannic, and Bavarian Codes."

was issued by Chindaswinth probably in 642 or 643.[34] The king begins by stating that the realm has been shaken more bitterly by the disaster caused by *émigrés* and deserters (*profugi, dediti*) than by any need for opposing a foreign foe. Accordingly, beginning with the reign of King Chintila, whoever flees abroad to a hostile people or to foreign parts, now or in time to come, with the purpose of doing harm to the Gothic people or the state, and whoever plots or attempts to do these things, is held bound equally by this law. Also, beginning with the first year of Chindaswinth's reign, whoever stirs strife or scandal (*conturbationem aut scandalum*) to the disadvantage of the realm or people, and whoever is found to plot the death or overthrow of the king is, likewise, guilty of violating this law. Throughout, intent and attempt are equated with the overt act in past, present, and future time, save that the crafty monarch who had reached the throne by seditious and treasonable acts removes himself specifically from the jurisdiction of the law by excluding all acts of internal treason prior to the beginning of his reign.[35] Otherwise, both internal and external treason against the land, as well as high treason, are embraced by its provisions. Whoever commits one or all of these offenses shall suffer an irrevocable death penalty, save only that by royal mercy his life may be spared under the condition that he lose his eyes, "so that he may not see the ruin in which he had wickedly delighted, and may grieve ever to lead his bitter life thus." Erwig mitigated death and exoculation to decalvation[36] with one hundred blows of the lash and banishment in close and perpetual exile without possibility of restoration to palatine rank, and decreed that the guilty person must spend his life in chains as a royal slave. The property of such transgres-

---

[34] Zeumer (*Neues Archiv*, XXIV [1899], 57–69) believes that the First Canon of the Seventh Council of Toledo (a. 646) was patterned after this law, since they correspond *ad verba fere* in certain places, and cites proof against the contrary view of F. Dahn, *Die Könige der Germanen* (Würzburg: Breitkopf and Härtel, 1870), V, 195. Zeumer holds also that this superseded the hypothetical provision in the *Code of Euric*, cited above, whose vestiges survive in *Lex Baiuvariorum* 2, 1–2, and *Edictus Rothari*, c. 1 and 4. Since the earlier legislation was not directed specifically against *refugi* or *émigrés* who had fled outside the realm, the better to plot and instigate revolt, and since the ecclesiastical penalties of *Conc. Tolet.* VI, can. 12, did not suffice to check the conspiracies of the *refugi*, Chindaswinth enacted this severe decree. Cf. references in the Chronicle of Fredegar (4, 82 in *M. G. H., S. S. rer. Merov.*, II), who refers to this monarch's cruel suppression of rebels and suspects.

[35] See Ziegler, *Church and State*, p. 102, and Zeumer, *Neues Archiv*, XXIV (1899), 58, regarding this curious inconsistency in the treatment of internal treason relative to external treason, which seems so deliberately designed in the treason law of Chindaswinth and must be accounted for by practical considerations only.

[36] See Appendix B.

sors shall be entirely at the king's disposal, and interesting provisions
are established against fraudulent transfer of property to churches, relatives, and friends in *dominio alieno*. Such transfers were made with the
view of preventing confiscation and keeping the way open for a possible
future return *in suo denuo dominio*.[37] Accordingly all possessions, as of
the time of the criminal act, are taken over by the *fiscus* to be distributed
or disposed at the king's pleasure. But, if the king, moved by the spirit
of mercy, should desire to bestow anything upon the culprit, it must
not be out of the culprit's former property and it must be a sum not ex-
ceeding one-twentieth of his portion as an heir.

It should be noted that this enactment differs from the preceding law
of allegiance (*L. Vis.* 2, 1, 7), since it comprehends precisely the range
of offenses, from *perduellio* to high treason, that are embraced under
the caption of majesty in Roman law;[38] yet even here the expression
maiestas is not found once. The entire tenor of the law has an unmis-
takably Germanic coloring despite the fact that *infidelitas* is not defined
specifically. The law of allegiance (2, 1, 7) rests squarely upon Germanic ideas of a pledge, bond, or troth, whereas the law of treason (2,
1, 8) covers offenses which have their parallels in Roman law. Nevertheless, the idea of majesty in the Roman sense of the word is as lacking
in the one as in the other. Treason is broken faith (*infidelitas*), whether
with the land and folk or with the king, and constitutes the negative
aspect of the political principle of allegiance. Allegiance is the recognition of sovereignty; treason, the denial and destruction of it.

Also a *novella* of Egica, serving as a supplement to *L. Vis.* 2, 1, 6–8,
must be noted.[39] This law is directed against those, who, in violation of
their allegiance, bind themselves under oath in a plot to kill or overthrow the king, and so forbids conspiracy against the royal power or
any similar act of criminal fraud. Zeumer thinks this statute may have
been inspired by the conspiracy of Sisebert, metropolitan of Toledo,
against Egica himself.[40] Certainly these offenses would have constitu-

---

[37] Cf. legal sophistry or fraudulent intent involved in entering suits through the
imperial *fiscus* with the emperor as heir, in *L. R. V., Paulus* 5, 14, 4–5 *De Fisci
Advocato*.

[38] Cf. Paulus *Sententiae* 5, 29, 1–2 (*L. R. V., P.* 5, 31, 1–2) *Ad Legem Iuliam
Maiestatis*, and *Digest* 48, 4, 3 *Ad Legem Iuliam Maiestatis*.

[39] *L. Vis.* 2, 5, 19 *Ut nemo deinceps citra fidem regiam vel propria causarum
negotia in deceptione regii potestatis vel cuiuslibet alterius se iuramenti vinculo
alligare presumat* (Egica).

[40] Cf. Zeumer, *L. Vis.*, p. 119, n. 2; also Zeumer, *Neues Archiv*, XXIII (1898),
507; XXIV (1899), 69. Note *Conc. Tolet. XIIII* (a. 683), can. 2.

ted typical *lèse-majesté* under the Roman law; yet here the crime is *infidelitas* committed by those owing allegiance to the king (*citra fidem regiam*) who prove faithless to their troth by binding themselves in a false and hostile compact against the king.

A somewhat earlier law of Chindaswinth is also of particular interest, because it draws a sharp distinction between the king's jurisdiction in cases of high treason and in cases of *Landesverrat*.[41] Here high treason, like issues connected with the king's personal property, may be decided by the king alone, but the king is bound by the interest of the people in *Landesverrat*, just as in the disposition of crown properties.

However often supplication is made to us in behalf of those who are implicated in some crime in our cases [*causis nostris*], we provide access for lay-
ing those matters before us, and out of mercy we endeavor to release such
offenders from the consequences of their acts so far as we may. But in cases
belonging to the land and folk [*pro causa gentis et patrie*] we deny this freedom. However, if divine pity compels the heart of the prince to show mercy
to such evil persons, he shall have full freedom to extend mercy with the
consent of the bishops and palatine officers [*cum adsensu sacerdotum maiorumque palatii*].

In this decree high treason is *infidelitas*, not *laesa maiestas*, and the king may judge as he wills in breaches of faith owed to himself, but his con-
tract or bond with his land and people withholds him from independent action in cases where their special interest is involved. In this instance, he must consult the other sovereign party to the bond.

Finally, we must analyze the very important enactment of King Wamba dealing directly with treason as well as breaches of military discipline, which has been preserved in Erwig's revision and is referred to in the seventh canon of the Twelfth Council of Toledo (a. 681).[42] Wamba begins by deploring the lack of co-operation and of uniform resistance to the enemies of the realm, and chides those who dwell along the frontiers for abandoning the defense of the land at the slightest pretext. Whereupon he decrees that each officer, ecclesiastical, civil, and military, who dwells or chances to be on the frontiers or within one hundred miles of a threatened point shall come to the aid of the realm forthwith upon the attack of an enemy (*ad defensionem gentis vel patrie nostre prestus cum omni virtute sua*), whether he be summoned

[41] *L. Vis.* 6, 1, 7 *De servandi principibus pietate parcendi* (Chind.). Cf. Zeumer, *Neues Archiv*, XXIV (1899), 57 ff., 64 f.
[42] *L. Vis.* 9, 2, 8 *Quid debeat observari, si scandalum infra fines Spanie exsur-
rexerit* (Wamba).

in person or learn of the danger in any other manner. But if he fails to come to the defense of his land and folk and to contend with all his might against his people's enemies he shall repair the country's losses from his own resources, if a high ecclesiastic. If an ecclesiastic of lesser rank or a layman, *sive sit nobilis, sive mediocrior viliorque persona*, he shall be reduced to servitude, losing all evidence of his rank, while his properties shall be applied to the recovery of the devastated regions, since it is unjust to maintain the cowardly and incompetent in their possessions. It must be noted that all this portion of the law is directed against those who fail to defend their country against external enemies.

The balance of the decree relates to internal treason, especially in the form of *scandalum* which approximates *seditio* and even *perduellio* as defined in the Roman law. This curious crime of "scandal" is more than mere rioting, breach of the peace, or civil disturbance; it is a seditious act, endangering public safety and the welfare of the state, and is also viewed as an act of insult and effrontery toward the royal power.[43] This section of the law may be paraphrased thus:

If anyone within the bounds of Spain, Gaul, Galicia, or all the provinces beneath our sway shall attempt or intend to create scandal at any place, directed against the land and folk or against our realm or the kingdom of our successors,[44] let all persons within one hundred miles of the disaffected places, howsoever they may have learned of the matter, hasten immediately with ready devotion to defend the king, land and folk, and *fideles* of the reigning king against whom the scandal has been raised [*ad vindicationem aut regis aut gentis et patrie vel fidelium presentis regis, contra quem ipsum scandalum excitatum extiterit*]. If such persons do not show themselves ready to aid the loyal in repressing the scandal thus raised, whether they be bishops or clergy of any sort, palatine officers of whatever rank or dignity, or lesser folk, who are involved in this crime of infidelity [*huius infidelitatis implicatus scelere*],

[43] For *scandalum*, see DuCange, *Glossarium Mediae et Infimae Latinitatis* (Paris: Firmin Didot Fratres, 1840–1850), VI, 93, and *The New English Dictionary on Historical Principles*, VIII, Part II, 173–175.

[44] The Latin terminology is interesting: "si quilibet . . . scandalum in quacumque parte contra gentem vel patriam nostrumque regnum vel etiam successorum nostrorum moverit aut movere voluerit." Note the distinction between the *gens* or folk, reflecting the racial or national element, the *patria* or land occupied by and belonging to the people of folk, and the *regnum* or realm, which is the same land viewed in the light of its personal relation to the king. However, the difference between *patria* and *regnum* is clear: the former embodies the ancient idea of the people's own native land, the latter is the sphere of the king's rule. One is tempted to advance a theory associating the idea of the realm with that of the crown, but it seems hardly tenable on the basis of the actual evidence. These are mature conceptions in political theory which are not defined in the Visigothic Code sharply enough for us to reach positive conclusions.

they shall not only be sent into exile but shall suffer their property to be placed at the pleasure of the king.

The only exceptions to these provisions are persons incapacitated by age or illness from accompanying the *fideles* (*in consortio fidelium*), and even these must exert all their efforts and resources sincerely in the aid of their leaders and brethren who are fighting loyally for king and country (*pro utilitate regie potestatis, gentis et patrie fideliter laborantium*).[45] Those who fail in these respects shall be punished in the same manner as the actual transgressors, but those who establish their incapacity by approved testimony shall be deemed guiltless. The ultimate result of the law shall be that "harmony and co-operation may secure peace among the people and protection for the land."

This is probably the most comprehensive treason law in the entire code, though perhaps less fundamental with respect to the theory of the crime than the decree of Chindaswinth (*L. Vis.* 2, 1, 8). It embraces external and internal treason, reflecting aspects of *perduellio* and *seditio*; high treason against the king and realm (*rex et regnum*), which would be comprehended under *laesa maiestas* according to Roman conceptions, and *infidelitas*. The emphasis upon this last idea indicates that these offenses were all viewed in a characteristically Germanic light as breaches of contractual allegiance. Finally, the law contains some elements of military correction and discipline, belonging to the category *De Re Militari* under the Roman law, and possibly related to the Frankish *herisliz*.

The next succeeding law, issued by Erwig as a supplement to *L. Vis.* 9, 2, 8, is entitled: "Concerning those who fail to accompany the army on the appointed day and at the appointed place and time, and those who flee back from the army; also concerning what portion of his slaves each person should take with him on a campaign."[46] However, the treasonable nature of these acts is neither stressed in any statement nor implied clearly in the terminology. Instead, all these offenses are treated

---

[45] See Appendix C on the problem of the Visigothic *fideles* with special reference to the views of Claudio Sánchez-Albornoz and Manuel Torres.

[46] Zeumer (*L. Vis.*, p. 374, n. 1) considers that in this law (*L. Vis.* 9, 2, 9) Erwig mitigated the severity of the preceding law of Wamba *de progressione exercitus*, according to a commitment made to the Twelfth Council of Toledo. However, it may be noted that lesser folk (*inferiores sane vilioresque persone*) who violate this law may be punished with two hundred lashes, decalvation (*turpiter decalvatus fedati*), and a fine of several pounds of gold, with servitude for those who cannot make good the composition—penalties which seem actually more ferocious than those of Wamba's law.

as breaches of military discipline. As in the case of sedition, it is not always easy to determine when military offenses should be deemed treasonable; yet in general the determining factor seems to be the matter of intent, combined with the scope and character of the defection. *L. Vis.* 5, 7, 19, which is a novel of Egica, supplementing *L. Vis.* 9, 2, 9, may be classified also under the caption *De Re Militari*. It requires all royal freedmen to come to the aid of the king in time of war, unless prevented by valid cause, under the penalty of reduction to servitude. Besides the entire group of decrees contained in *L. Vis.* 9, 2, 1–7, *De his, qui ad bellum non vadunt aut bello refugiunt* covers infractions of military discipline. These specify such offenses as the failure of army officers to compel soldiers to leave home, the granting of leave to return home, and the acceptance of bribes in connection with such matters.

Finally, we must summarize briefly the evidence in the *Forum Judicum*, bearing on the problem of majesty, that is contained in the legislation subsidiary to the treason laws. In the first place, the laws on accusation preserve a general parallel with the provisions of the *Breviary* but differ in important points of detail. The "great exception" of the Roman law,[47] permitting *delatores* to give information in accusations of *crimen laesae maiestatis*, is preserved in distorted guise in the *antiquae*, dealing with extortion of evidence from slaves by means of torture. Thus, a slave or handmaid may not be tortured in cases involving their master or mistress, "save only in the crime of adultery, or if he shall have spoken or acted to the disadvantage of the realm, land and folk, or shall have fashioned counterfeit money, or if it be established that the case under investigation involved homicide or sorcery."[48]

---

[47] Cf. *Codex Theodosianus* 9, 6, 2–3 (*L. R. V., Codex* 9, 3, 1–2) *Ne Praeter Crimen Maiestatis Servus Dominum vel Patronum Libertus seu Familiaris Accuset;* Paulus *Sent.* 5, 13, 3 (*L. R. V., P.* 5, 13, 3) *De Delatoribus; C. Th.* 9, 5, 1 *Ad Legem Iuliam Maiestatis.*

[48] *L. Vis.* 6, 1, 4 *Pro quibus rebus et qualiter servi vel ancille torquendi sunt in capite dominorum* (Antiqua): "nisi tantum in crimine adulterii [cf. *L. Vis.* 3, 4, 10], aut si contra regnum, gentem vel patriam aliquid dictum vel dispositum fuerit, seu falsam monetam quisque confixerit [cf. *L. Vis.* 7, 6, 1], aut etiam si causam homicidii vel maleficii querendam esse constiterit." Zeumer thinks this law was issued by Euric and based on Roman Law. Cf. Paulus *Sent.* 1, 12, 4 *De Iudiciis Omnibus; Digest* 5, 1, 53 *De Iudiciis; Codex Justinianus* 9, 41, 1 *De Quaestionibus;* Mommsen, *Römisches Strafrecht*, (Leipzig: S. Hirzel, 1899), pp. 414–18; *L. Vis.* p. 251, n. 2. Note *L. Vis.* 2, 4, 4 *Servo non credendum* (Chind.), with slight changes by Recceswinth and Erwig, which excepts under special permission of the king or in the case of royal servants; *L. Vis.* 5, 7, 10–12 *De Libertatibus et Libertis*, cover-

Zeumer has pointed out correctly that the same crimes which are excepted here (*crimina laesae maiestatis, adulterii, falsae monetae*) are excepted in various sections of the Roman law, but one must not fail to note that the characteristic expression of the Roman law, *crimen laesae maiestatis,* is replaced here with "contra regnum, gentem vel patriam aliquid dictum vel dispositum fuerit."

Similarly, in the case of freemen (*ingenui*) anyone may freely accuse any person equal to himself in nobility or rank in cases involving the royal power (high treason), the land and folk, homicide, or adultery, and may even compel the accused person to submit to torture. But, if the person so tortured proves to be innocent, then the accuser is to be given over in servitude to the accused who may do with him as he wills, save that he may not kill him.[49] A parallel decree by Chindaswinth[50] provides the most comprehensive statement in the *Code,* linking criminal fraud, falsification, counterfeiting, and sorcery with high treason and *Landesverrat* as a related group of offenses under a common procedure in accusations. The pertinent portion of this law states:

> If anyone shall make false accusations to the prince regarding any person, charging that he had plotted something with evil intent or was acting or had acted against the interests of the king, land or folk [*ita ut dicat eum adversus regem, gentem vel patriam aliquid nequiter meditatum fuisse aut agere vel egisse*], or that he had changed something with fraudulent intent in the orders or commands of the royal power or [of] those performing judicial duties, and that he had made or published a forged document or fashioned counterfeit money, and if he shall reveal poisoning or sorcery or adultery, let the accuser of these or similar crimes which pertain to loss of life or property, if they be proved true as charged, sustain no injury in any wise.

It is interesting, however, to note that the enactments dealing specifically with these subsidiary crimes fail, in the main, to make any direct

---

ing accusations by freedmen against their *patroni,* in which the "great exception" of the Roman law does not appear.

[49] *L. Vis.* 6, 1, 2 *Pro quibus rebus et qualiter ingenuorum persone subdende sunt questioni* (Chind.), which is modified in the *renovata* of Erwig so that the accuser is allowed to render composition if he fails to prove his charge, but the accused can set the price according to his own estimate of his injuries incurred under torture. The simpler conception of *talio* in the law of Chindaswinth gives way to the new practice of settlement by means of composition or fine. Cf. Dahn, *Studien,* pp. 282 ff.

[50] *L. Vis.* 6, 1, 6 *Qualiter ad regem accusatio deferatur* (Chind.), which Zeumer believes to have been substituted for an *antiqua* of Euric on the basis of *Leges Euricianae restitutae* 10. Also, it is highly probable that the nexus of crimes listed in this law are derived from an *antiqua,* since they are conjoined in the usual classification of the Roman Law. Cf. *L. Vis.* 6, 1, 4 *supra.*

connection between them and the various treasons, although there are
prohibitions against the incrimination of the king in various offenses:
slander, defamation, and maledictions against the king as well as consulting soothsayers concerning the death of the king.[51] And, of course,
this is precisely the range of offenses that is declared to be *laesa maiestas* in the Theodosian and Justinian codes, the *Digest*, and the *Sentences* of Paulus.[52]

[51] Cf. *L. Vis.* 2, 1, 9 *De non criminando principe nec maledicendo illi* (Recc.,
Erwig); also *Conc. Tolet.* V, 5, and Zeumer, *Neues Archiv*, XXIV (1899), 69–70.
This interesting and significant enactment ("On prohibiting the casting of aspersions
upon the king or uttering maledictions against him") reads: "Just as we forbid all
persons either to plot evil or lift their hands vengefully against him, so we suffer
no one to accuse him of crime or cast maledictions upon him, for the authority of
Holy Scripture enjoins that no one raise his hands against his neighbor and declares that he who curses the prince of his people is guilty of crime [alternative
reading, following Zeumer's text: "who curses his prince is guilty of crime against
the people"]. Wherefore, whoever charges the prince with crime or casts maledictions upon him, or whoever fails to admonish the prince regarding his conduct
humbly and respectfully but instead attempts to insult him with pride and contumely or presumes to utter cowardly, base and harmful words of detraction, shall
forfeit half of all his property, if he be a noble or person of similar rank whether
cleric or layman, as soon as he shall be detected and convicted, and the king shall
have the privilege of disposing of the property at his pleasure. But if he be a person
of lowly and humble state without dignity of place, the prince shall be free to
dispose of both his person and property at pleasure. Also, by a similar precept we
forbid fittingly any audacious act of detraction against a dead prince, for the living
cast the darts of detraction in vain against the dead, since the dead can neither be
affected by slander nor touched by reproaches. But since he is assuredly mad who
heaps detraction vainly upon one who cannot feel or understand, let that con-
temptuous person suffer fifty blows of the lash and lend a fitting silence to his presumption. However, whether a prince be living or dead, it is freely permitted to all
to discuss any matters and affairs pertinent to a case and to contest in court as is
proper and seemly and to obtain the justice due, for thus we strive to establish
reverence for human dignity and maintain the justice of God devotedly."

[52] This table indicates the relation between the subsidiary legislation in the *Leges
Visigothorum* and parallel provisions of the Roman Law:

1) See *L. Vis.* 2, 1, 9 *De non criminando principe nec maledicendo illi* (Recc.)
for malediction. Cf. *C. Th.* 9, 4, 1 *Si Quis Imperatori Maledixerit; C. Just,* 9, 7, 1;
Paulus Sent. 5, 29, 1 (*L. R. V., P.* 5, 31, 1) *Ad Legem Iuliam Maiestatis.*

2) See *L. Vis.* 6, 2, 1–5 *De maleficiis et consulentibus eos adque veneficis,* for
sorcery. Cf. *Paulus Sent.* 5, 21, 4 (5, 23, 4); 5, 23, 17–18 (5, 25, 11–12) *Ad Legem
Corneliam de Sicariis et Veneficis;* 5, 21, 3 (5, 23, 3) *De Vaticinatoribus et Mathematicis; C. Th.* 9, 16, 3–4 and 7 (*L. R. V., C.* 9, 13, 1–3) *De Maleficis et Mathematicis et Ceteris Similibus.*

3) See *L. Vis.* 7, 5, 1; 7, 5, 3; 7, 5, 9 *De falsariis scripturarum* (Recc., Erwig),
for *crimen falsi.* Cf. *Paulus Sent.* 5, 25, 1 (5, 27, 1); 5, 25, 5 *Ad Legem Corneliam
Testamentariam; C. Th.* 9, 19, 1 and 4 (*L. R. V., C.* 9, 15, 1–2) *Ad Legem Corneliam de Falso.*

4) See *L. Vis.* 7, 6, 2–5 *De falsariis metallorum* (Recc., Erwig), for *crimen falsae*

The patron and client relationship which is listed in the law of parricide in the *Breviary* disappears in the *Forum Judicum*, though this special relation of the *libertus* or *manumissus* to his *patronus* and of the slave to his master, retained in some laws on accusation, indicates that legal areas involving special narrow interests within the state still existed.[53] It is possible that the wider development of petty treason in feudal times derives from these earlier ties which bind those *in dominio, in patrocinio, in familiaritate, in truste,* or *in tuitione* to their lords or superiors. Traces of another early special interest appear in a decree defending the peace of the home (*Hausfrieden*) and the ancient idea that "a man's house is his castle,"[54] while the laws of sanctuary in a similar manner guarantee the "peace of the church."[55] These special *paces* deserve special consideration from the standpoint that, to the extent that they are of Roman origin, they provide, in a rudimentary form before the Germanic invasions, some of the conditions out of which contractual allegiance develops. In this respect, these special relationships rest upon bonds or sanctions which it would be essentially *infidelitas* to break. Also, there is legislation against rioting and sedition in the sense of ordinary civil disturbances (*tumultus, turbae*), which are created without such guilty intent against the state as distinguishes *scandalum* or *perduellio*.[56] Mere riot is not to be identified with treason. And lastly, an *antiqua* of the Code retains the ancient maxim of the Roman law that a crime shall perish with its author, and thereby denies the inhuman principle of attainder of blood and makes no reference to any application of attainder in treason cases, whereas in point of fact

---

monetae or counterfeiting. Cf. Paulus *Sent.* 5, 25, 1 (*L. R. V., P.* 5, 25, 1) *Ad Legem Corneliam Testamentariam; C. Th.* 9, 21, 5 (*L. R. V., C.* 9, 17, 1) *De Falsa Moneta; C. Th.* 9, 21, 9; *C. Th.* 9, 22, 1 (*L. R. V., C.* 9, 18, 1) *Si Quis Solidi Circulum Exteriorem Inciderit vel Adulteratum in Vendendo Subiecerit.*

5) See *L. Vis.* 3, 4, 10–11 *De adulteriis (antiqua),* for adultery. Cf. Paulus *Sent.* 2, 26, 9 *De Adulteriis* (not in *Breviary*); *C. Th.* 9, 7, 4 (*L. R. V., C.* 9, 4, 3) *Ad Legem Iuliam de Adulteriis.*

[53] See *L. Vis.* 6, 5, 17 *De parricidiis et eorum rebus* (Chind.), and 6, 5, 18 *De his, qui proximos sanguinis sui occiderint* (Antiqua, revised by Recc. and Erwig). Cf. Paulus *Sent.* 5, 24, 1 (*L. R. V., P.* 5, 26, 1) *Ad Legem Pompeiam de Parricidiis,* and *L. Vis.* 5, 7, 10–12 *De Libertatibus et Libertis.*

[54] *L. Vis.* 8, 1, 4 *Si intra domum vel ianuam suam violenter aliquis includatur* (Chind.); also 8, 1, 9.

[55] *L. Vis.* 9, 3, 1–4 *De his, qui ad ecclesiam confugiunt;* 6, 5, 16 *Si homicida ad ecclesiam confugiat* (Chind.). Cf. *C. Th.* 9, 45, 4 (*L. R. V., C.* 9, 34, 1) *De His, qui ad Ecclesias Confugiunt;* also *C. Th.* 9, 45, 1 and 5. See F. Dahn, *Könige,* VI (2), 374 ff., on right of asylum.

[56] *L. Vis.* 8, 1, 3 *Si ad faciendam cedem turba coadunetur (Antiqua).*

154 Treason in Roman and Germanic Law

both the *Digest* and *Code* of Justinian failed to extend such mercy to the children of those condemned for *laesa maiestas,* and through the extension of the "great exception" to matters of attainder laid the vicious precedent which applied to relatives of traitors and similar heinous offenders in later systems of law.[57]

In closing this study a brief summary of our conclusions may be desirable. In the first place, the *Forum Judicum* displays an organic assimilation of the Roman law, and not a mere reclassification and selection from it, such as occurred in the *Breviary,* for much that is typical of the Roman law in that compilation is omitted or cast into a Germanic mold in the later Visigothic legislation. In the treason laws the most conspicuous change consists of the omission of all specific references to *maiestas.*[58] Instead, the Goths took the trouble to explain at length the character of the crime referred to in each particular law, and ran no risk of a misunderstanding through the application of a general label to an entire category of offenses. The idea that the term was avoided deliberately gains strength when one notes that the word appeared in the *Breviary,* in the *Etymologiae* of St. Isidore of Seville (who died in 636, only about fifteen years before the promulgation of the *Forum Judicum*), in the Visigothic Formularies, and in occasional scattered references in the church literature. Isidore is a prime witness, since he gives short but relatively accurate definitions of *maiestas* in its Roman sense: "They are deemed guilty of *maiestas* who have injured or violated the royal majesty, or who have betrayed the state or made a compact with the enemy,"[59] and again, "A man who is accused of a crime against

---

[57] *L. Vis.* 6, 1, 8 *Quod ille solus culpabilis erit, qui culpanda conmiserit (Antiqua):* "Ille solus iudicetur culpabilis, qui culpanda conmittit, et crimen, qum illo, qui fecit, moriatur." Cf. *Digest* 48, 4, 11: "extinguitur enim mortalitate."

Zeumer points to an interesting modification of this principle in connection with *L. Vis.* 7, 2, 19 *De hereditate et successoribus furis,* which states "crimen cum fure defecit," and so places no penalty (*poena*) upon the heir to a dead thief. No criminal disability is involved, but restitution (*damnum satisfactionis*) is required, since the thief, had he lived, would have been compelled to make good the loss he had occasioned.

[58] The late Professor Summerfield Baldwin has made the interesting suggestion that the reason for the consistent omission of the expression *maiestas* in the Germanic codes lies in the fact that the barbarian states were mere *regna* outside the Roman *imperium*. The implications of this view cannot be dismissed lightly.

[59] St. Isidore *Etymol.* 5, 26, 25 *De criminibus in lege conscriptis:* "Maiestatis reatu tenentur hi qui regiam maiestatem laeserunt vel violaverunt, vel qui rempublicam prodiderunt vel cum hostibus consenserunt." Cf. *Ibid.*, 10, 238: "Reus maiestatis primum dictus qui adversus rempublicam aliquid egisset, aut quicumque hostibus consensisset . . . Postea etiam et ei rei maiestatis dicti sunt qui adversus

majesty is so accused because it is a greater injury to harm the state than an individual citizen."[60] However, unlike the *Breviary* and *Etymologies,* the formularies and theological writings employ *maiestas* in its religious connotations rather than in connection with affairs of state and law.[61] Considering this background it is a matter of some surprise to find such a general omission of the term *maiestas.* Numerous expressions are used to denote treason, such as *scandalum, conturbatio, intendisse proditus.*[62] In other instances longer descriptive phrases appear: "in personam principis omnibus proibemus aut commovere nequitiam cogitationis aut manus inicere ultionis";[63] "si contra regum, gentem vel patriam aliquid dictum vel dispositum fuerit";[64] "huius infidelitatis inplicatus scelere."[65] Of course, the theory that the compilers of the *Visigothic Code* may have considered *maiestas* merely obsolete or indefinite is not entirely eliminated. Working toward clarity and definiteness—ideals which are realized to an unusual degree in these laws despite their grandiloquent language and general verbosity—the compilers succeeded in giving

maiestatem principio egisse viderentur, vel qui leges inutiles reipublicae detulerant, vel utiles abrogaverant."

[60] St. Isidore, *ibid.,* 10, 238: "Dictus autem reus maiestatis, quia maius est laedere patriam quam civem unum."

[61] *Formulae Visigothicae,* ed. by Zeumer in *M. G. H. L L,* Hanover: Hahn, 1886), Sectio V, Formulae, 5: "per divini nominis maiestatem"; 14: "Bonis enim auspiciis divina voluntas adsurgat, et prosperum iter aggredi propria magestas impellit"; 24: "prae divini nominis maiestatem futurumque resurrectionis tremendi iudicii diem atque regnum gloriossissimi domini nostri"; 34: "per Patrem et Filium et Spiritum sanctum, qui est Trinitas inseparabilis et una maiestas"; 39: "per Deum omnipotentem et Jesum Christum filium eius sanctumque Spiritum, qui est una et consubstatialis maiestas. . . . Quod si in falsum tantam Divinitatis maiestatem ac deitatem taxare aut invocare ausi fuerimus, maledicta efficiamur in aeternum." It is generally agreed that the Formularies cannot be earlier than 615, but were collected before the abolition of the *Lex Romana* by Chindaswinth (641–652), probably before 645. Zeumer suggests the compilation was made under Sisebut (615–620).

As to the ecclesiastical materials, DuCange (*Glossarium,* IV, 187–189) remarks under the caption "Maiestas" that this term is commonly attributed to God and cites proof from Prudentius, Symmachus, Arator, Gregory of Tours, and numerous references to later authors. Also, DuCange gives many instances of the use of *maiestas* as a title or term of address in the documentary sources. The only references I have happened to find in the *Historia Francorum* of Gregory of Tours are unique, since they allude specifically to the "crime of majesty" in the legal sense: "ob crimen maiestatis lesi iudicium mortis susceptum" (5, 25, [18 Dalton]); "Pro crimine maiestatis superius vinctum" (9, 13). Cf. Sir Samuel Dill, *Roman Society in Gaul in the Merovingian Age* (London: Macmillan, 1926), pp. 117–18 and 133.

[62] *L. Vis.* 2, 1, 6.

[63] *L. Vis.* 2, 1, 7.

[64] *L. Vis.* 6, 1, 4.

[65] *L. Vis.* 9, 2, 8.

vitality to the Roman foundation by amalgamating it in organic fashion with Germanic legal conceptions. Hence *maiestas* disappeared and its place was taken by *scandalum* and other current expressions; yet, also, one cannot avoid the conviction that the content of the dominant political ideas of the age changed with the changing terminology. However, despite change no one can deny that the atmosphere of the Roman law permeates this legislation. Our danger has consisted rather in the neglect of the Germanic ideas surcharged upon the Roman foundation. Deep-rooted ecclesiastical influences are, likewise, scattered through these laws, and it is possible that the *talio*, appearing in a decree of Chindas-winth on parricide, may be derived indirectly from the Hebrew Scriptures.[66] Also these ecclesiastical interests tend clearly in the direction of limited royal power.[67] The general condition of public authority was unstable, as among the Merovingian Franks; this is evinced by some laws of the code whose tenor is despotic and absolute, whereas others indicate extensive limitations of royal power.[68] However, the idea of limitation is far more prominent than that of unrestricted absolutism.

In consequence, *Landesverrat*, including both internal and external treason, occupies a primary place in the treason legislation and is never subordinated to high treason, a fact indicating that the ancient rights of the land and folk are being maintained without reference to the newer special royal interests.[69] These laws denounce the fomenting of disorders and scandals, acts of rebellion and disrespect against the land, conspiring or intending evil against one's country, sedition, and departing to another nation with hostile intentions, while under certain circumstances such military offenses as failure to heed the summons to arms, insubordination, and desertion on the field of battle approximate *Landesverrat*. High treason, on the other hand, ranges from plotting the death or injury of the king to uttering slander, defamation, and maledictions against him. The ideas of scandal and slander, as well as many

---

[66] L. Vis. 6, 5, 17 *De parricidis et eorum rebus* (Chind.).

[67] On the other hand, however, note Ziegler, *Church and State* Ch. IV, especially pp. 126–133, showing that Visigothic Spain was an Erastian state. Cf. O. M. Dalton, *The History of the Franks by Gregory of Tours*, I, 192, on the despotism of contemporary Merovingian kings in Gaul, an insecure absolutism free from constitutional checks but still absolute as long as they permitted the great magnates or landholders the licence they desired.

[68] Note differences in the tone of L. Vis. 2, 1, 2, and 2, 1, 4.

[69] Dahn, *Studien*, p. 237, notes that high treason is mentioned in the code more frequently than *Landesverrat*, but this must not be interpreted as indicating that treason against land and folk was the less important of the two treasons.

of the other crimes, however, were in all probability more Germanic than Roman in spirit, indicating the intention of personal insult to the ruler rather than of injury to the monarch as a personification of public authority. Forgery and counterfeiting are not specifically named as treason, but following the Roman tradition they are punished with all the severity of that category of crime. Some scholars have professed to see an increasing mildness in Visigothic legislation under the influence of Christianity and the Germanic sense of fair-dealing, thus replacing the stern severity of the Roman law, but in the matter of treason, it is hard to discover much improvement. Interdiction from fire and water, decapitation, burning alive, casting to the beasts, and crucifixation give way to blinding, scourging, mutilation, reduction to servitude, exile, and death. The way of the traitor is hard, whether he be trampled to death under the feet of Manu's elephants in India, stoned to death in ancient Greece, impaled on stakes by the Persians, or hung, drawn, and quartered in the England of Edward III. It is to be noted, however, that the penalty for offenders of noble rank was usually less than for those of inferior station. Practically every sort of treason resulted in confiscation of the traitor's property to the king, and the law stated sometimes that the king might not restore such property by any exercise of royal grace. In cases of high treason the life of a criminal was frequently placed at the king's mercy, while in a mere matter of slander a noble might be penalized by confiscation of half his property. Treasons were not punished one and all alike, but regard was had for the relative heinousness of the offense. Attainder was not allowed. Sanctuary was permitted, though usually the only restriction upon the fate of an offender who had sought sanctuary was that he should not suffer death. His fate might be a worse penalty of blinding or other mutilation.

Finally, we must conclude that the Visigothic law is not altogether typical of the *leges barbarorum*. It comprehends too complete a system; the amalgamation of Roman and Germanic elements is too organic; the sense of justice and equity is too well balanced; the position of royal authority is too limited. On the other hand, certain Germanic features cannot be mistaken: the deferential allegiance of imperial Rome is replaced by contractual allegiance; treason is *infidelitas*, not *laesa maiestas*; the legislative sovereignty inherent in majesty could not find a place in the political thought of an age of customary law when sovereign powers were interpretative and judicial. In the light of these facts, this study would redirect attention to the Germanic contribution in the foundations of mediaeval civilization upon which such exacting labor was performed by the great German and English constitutionalists of the last century.

APPENDIX A

Recent Spanish Publications

Reference should be made to recent Spanish work in the historical field, since the Renaissance of Spanish historical studies beginning about the turn of this century and still continuing has influenced research in Hispanic legal history. This revival of historical interest was inaugurated in considerable degree by the great scholar, Rafael Altamira y Crevea, who expounded his views on the philosophy of history in English in *The Book of the Opening of the Rice Institute* (Houston, Texas: DeVinne Press, 1912), II, 265–346, and produced his distinguished narrative and interpretative work in the *Historia de España y de civilización española*, 4 vols., (Barcelona: J. Gili, 1900). This was followed by the even more comprehensive *Historia de España y su influencia en la historia universal*, 12 vols. (2nd ed.; Barcelona: P. Salvat, 1918–1950) of D. Antonio Ballesteros y Beretta, and the great collaborative *Historia de España* edited by Ramón Menéndez Pidal (Madrid: Espasa-Calpe, Tomo I, Vol. I, 1947; Tomo II, 1935, Tomo III, 1940), and still in progress. One may well begin his investigation of Visigothic law by referring to Ballesteros, *Historia*, I, 55–59 with notes, and Menéndez Pidal, *Historia*, III, 203–264 with notes (Part II, c. IV–VI by Manuel Torres and Ramón Prieto Bances), followed by Altamira, *Historia general del derecho español* (Madrid: V. Suárez, 1908). Other detailed treatises of value are Román Riaza and A. García Gallo, *Manual de historia del derecho español* (Madrid: V. Suárez, 1934–1935); Manuel Torres, *Lecciones de historia del derecho español*, I (Salamanca: G. García, 1933); Juan Beneyto Pérez, *Instituciones de derecho histórico español*, 3 vols. (Barcelona: Bosch, 1930–1931); and the detailed *Historia del derecho español* (4th ed., rev. Barcelona: Editorial Labor, 1953) by S. Minguijón Adrián. To these may be added the studies of the legal sources: J. Beneyto Pérez, *Fuentes de derecho histórico español: Ensayos* (Barcelona: Bosch, 1931), and M. Torres, "Fuentes del Derecho Visigodo," in Menéndez Pidal, *Historia*, III, 251–264, with numerous references to Spanish and German work in the field.

There is little material in English in the Visigothic area, as indeed of Spanish law generally, although a very useful account of the sources and a comprehensive critical bibliography may be found in J. T. Vance, *The Background of Spanish-American Law: Legal Sources and Juridical Literature of Spain* (New York: Central Book Company, 1943). However, one very substantial work must be noted which should be consulted in any study of Visigothic legislation: A. K. Ziegler, *Church and State in Visigothic Spain* (Washington: Catholic University of America, 1930), especially Ch. III on "The Visigothic Code of Civil Law," to which may be added the somewhat slender historical account of the *Lex Visigothorum* contained in Marie R. Madden, *Political Theory and Law in Medieval Spain* (New York: Fordham University Press, 1930). Also Luitpold Wallach has some reference to the Carolingian "Reception" of the *Breviarium Alaricianum* in Ch. VIII of his *Alcuin and Charlemagne*, Cornell Studies in Classical Philology (Ithaca: Cornell University Press, 1959).

Appendix B

Decalvation

The precise nature of decalvation has been disputed by many scholars. Some scholars claim it resulted in physical injury comparable to scalping as practiced by some North American Indian tribes; others that it was a mere shaving of the head or cropping of the long flowing locks in which Gothic kings and nobles took great pride. In the latter case, the punishment consisted in the shame and contumely resulting from the loss of the hair—their badge of nobility and perhaps of racial superiority. It seems to me that the association of the tonsure with decalvation in *Conc. Tolet.* VI (a. 638), can. 17, may argue in favor of shaving the scalp with its accompanying insult and shame: "nullus sub religionis habitu detonsus aut turpiter decalvatus aut servilem originem trahens vel extraneae gentis homo." Also *L. Vis.* 6, 4, 3 *De Reddendo talionis* (Chind.) seems to rate decalvation as less than mayhem. On the other hand, *L. Vis.* 6, 2, 4 *De maleficis et consultenibus eos* (Chind.) speaks of sorcerers *decalvati deformiter* who are compelled unwillingly to go about through ten nearby districts (*convicinas possessiones*) that others may be corrected by their examples. *Deformiter* can mean either "disfigured" or "disgraced," but the psychology of the situation might argue a sight calculated to shock the onlookers rather than merely shame the guilty. Cf. *L. Vis.* 7, 5, 9, which forbids unauthorized persons to proclaim or issue royal orders and which punishes "turpiter decalvatus ac insuper pollice in manu dextra absciso"; and *L. Vis.* 8, 1, 3 *infamia notatur* with its possible relation to *deformiter decalvatus*.

The most recent opinion on this moot subject is contained in an article by Robert S. Lopez on "Byzantine Law in the Seventh Century and Its Reception by the Germans and Arabs" in *Byzantion*, XVI (1945) for 1942–1943, 450. Here, arguing from East Roman sources, Lopez notes that the penalty for forgers of royal charters in *L. Vis.* 7, 5, 9 is mutilation by cutting off the thumb of the right hand, preceded by flogging and shaving—"a degrading punishment which is found very often in later Byzantine law." Also, see A. K. Ziegler (*Church and State in Visigothic Spain*, p. 81, n. 95, on *decalvatio*), who inclines to this view, and much earlier G. A. Davoud-Oghlou (*Histoire de la législation des anciens germains* [Berlin: G. Reimer, 1845], I, 160), who advocates shaving because "on pouvait être décalvé plus d'une fois." The evidence cited in DuCange, II, 751, also points to the conclusion that this penalty consisted in shaving the head (*Tondere, ad cutem caput radere*), and notes that cutting off the hair is employed as a punishment bringing both insult and injury, a vulgar penalty by which the Goths, Spanish, and Franks repressed those guilty of crime. Examples are given from the Visigothic and Lombard legislation, the Carolingian capitularies, decrees of the Councils of Toledo, the *Chronicle* of John of Biclar, the *Historiae Wambae regis*, and others. On the other hand, many German scholars have suggested a more severe penalty, as F. Dahn, *Westgothische Studien*, (Würzburg: Stahel, 1874), pp. 191–192, on tearing out the hair with the scalp—"Ausreissen des Haares (sammt der Schädelhaut)." Also parallel evidence from the Anglo-Saxon Dooms indicates that the more severe penalty was imposed in Germanic law. Thus, Edmund, iii, 4, declares that each member, other than the leader, of a band of slaves committing theft, "shall be scourged three times and have his scalp removed and his little finger mutilated as indication of his guilt" (rendered in the *Quadripartitus* as "aliorum singuli verberentur ter et excorientur [extoppentur], et truncetur minimus digitus in signum"). Also, Cnut, ii, 30, 5, declares that in cases of major crimes and repeated offenses involving the triple ordeal the offender "shall have his eyes put out and his nose and ears and upper lip cut off or his scalp removed" (*hine haettian*, rendered *decapilletur* in the *Quadri-*

partitus). F. Liebermann, *Die Gesetze der Angelsachsen* (Halle: Max Niemeyer, 1903), I, 355, gives the text of the *Instituta Cnuti*: "aut corium cum capillis, quod Angli dicunt behaetian"; and of the *Consiliatio Cnuti*: "aut pilletur." Cf. *ibid.* (Halle: Max Niemeyer, 1916), III, 206–207, for *Skalpieren* (ii Cn., 30, 5, 3).

In general for other references in the Visigothic Code, see *L. Vis.* 2, 1, 8; 2, 2, 7; 2, 4, 6; 3, 3, 8–9; 3, 4, 17; 3, 6, 2; 5, 4, 11; 6, 4, 3 and 5; 6, 5, 2; 7, 5, 9; 9, 2, 9; 12, 3, 2–3; 12, 3, 5; 12, 3, 7–8; 12, 3, 11–13; 12, 3, 17 and 19. Also it should be noted that two significant references to decalvation may be found in the Lombard legislation of Liutprand, and in each instance the context suggests that the penalty consists of the shaving of the offender's head. See *Leges Liutprandi* (*M. G. H., Leges*, Tomus IV) 80 [14th year, A.D. 726, XI]: "decalvit eum," and 141 [22nd year, A.D. 734, III]: "Faciat res decalvare et frustare per vicos vicinantes ipsius loci." The penalty in the latter case bears a striking resemblance to *L. Vis.* 6, 2, 4, owing to the requirement that the guilty (in this instance, women) be shaved and then whipped through the neighboring villages of the region to serve as examples to others. Finally, S. P. Scott states in his translation of *The Visigothic Code* (Boston: 1910), p. 44, n. 1, discussing *Decalvatio*:

The tonsure itself was considered degrading, among a people who attached the highest importance to a luxuriant growth of hair, even when, as a distinctive mark of their calling, it was undergone by ecclesiastics; and shaving the head, in the execution of a judicial sentence, was often regarded as an indelible mark of infamy [cf. *ibid.*, p. xxi]. There were several degrees of this punishment, all of which did not entail the same suffering and disgrace: hair cut in the form of a cross; head entirely shaved; "turpiter decalvatus"—scalping, with skin entirely stripped from the head above the ears—sometimes even part or all of the forehead was included.

These conclusions seem to be unsupported and only represent Scott's personal inferences from the laws. Nevertheless, this threefold division of the penalty is extremely interesting, and I am unable to contradict it with positive evidence to the contrary.

Appendix C

The Visigothic *Fideles*

In Claudio Sánchez-Albornoz y Menduiña, *En torno a los orígenes del feudalismo* (3 vols., Mendoza, Argentina: Universidad Nacional de

Cuyo, 1942), the chapter "Los Fideles Regis Visigodos" (I, 41–76) contains a detailed examination of the expression, *fidelis, fideles,* in Visigothic law. It begins by arguing that all textual evidence throughout Visigothic history affirms the existence of people bound to the king by bonds that appear to be a continuation of those which united the leader to the members of the Germanic *comitatus.* Legal and canonical sources seem to confirm the presence in Visigothic society of a group of men who, with respect to their sovereign, owe a double allegiance: the general allegiance of subjects, and another allegiance, special, voluntary, and personal. This group consists of the *fideles regis* noted in the *Lex Visigothorum* and various conciliar canons (I, 41). As a result, Sánchez-Albornoz throws added light on the contractual nature of allegiance in the Visigothic kingdom and its relation to later feudal practice. He continues further that the word *fideles* is employed with these basic meanings in the legal and canonical texts and in the narrative sources: (1) a member of the Catholic Church, (2) all persons held bound by an oath of loyalty in the general sense, including loyal subjects of the king, and (3) any subjects bound by a special voluntary allegiance (*una fidelidad especial, voluntaria y espontánea*) beyond any general pledge to the king (I, 41–42).

The first meaning is obvious and need not detain us, but the second requires explanation. This idea of general fidelity or allegiance is advanced by Torres and Prieto Bances (Menéndez Pidal, III, 210), who hold that the Visigothic designation "subjects" involves a general bond of all directly with the crown, without reference to any intervening condition of vassalage, and extends to both Goths and Hispano-Romans, and even to the servile classes. This general fidelity, then, is equal among all subjects, as indicated in *L. Vis.* 2, 1, 7 *De fidelitate novis principibus reddenda et pena huius transgressionis.* This general oath of the subjects can only be regarded as the manifestation of a common bond, and finds its counterpart in the king's reciprocal oath of fidelity to his subjects (III, 214). During the Visigothic period this general bond is not severed by the interposition between the crown and subjects of other powers unrelated to sovereign rights. Cf. also W. Schücking, *Der Regierungsantritt* (Leipzig: Veit, 1899), Book I, on the royal oath; Ziegler, *Church and State,* pp. 94, 124, 128, for concept of "kingdom above the king," and my references to Visigothic limited monarchy in the essay entitled "Contractual Allegiance vs. Deferential Allegiance in Visigothic Law."

However, it is the third connotation that involves the specific con-tribution of Sánchez-Albornoz and that especially engages our attention because this special bond is established personally. It is more than a general oath of fidelity to land, folk, and ruler, and represents a per-sonal relation between a reigning king and his subject. Sánchez-Albor-noz builds a very convincing argument on the basis of *L. Vis.* 9, 2, 8 *Quid debeat observari si scandalum infra fines Spanie exsurrexerit*, in which the phrase *fidelium presentis regis* proves, through the adjective *presentis*, that a general allegiance of all the subjects of the realm must be excluded in favor of a special bond attaching the *fidelis* in person to the present reigning king (I, 46). Further, he shows that by the use of the genitive case, *regis* or *regum*, *principis* or *principum*, in whatever application, we are forced to suppose that such *fideles regis* are united to the monarch by a special personal bond much more intimate than the passive loyalty of those who are faithful to the king in the performance of their general duties as subjects. Nothing could be more explicit than this statement which represents the heart of the position of Sánchez-Albornoz (I, 48). In addition, he continues that *L. Vis.* 9, 2, 9, *De his, qui in exercitum constituto die, loco vel tempore definito non success-erint aut refugerint*, refers to the same *fideles* and complements *L. Vis.* 9, 2, 8. Nothing could be more logical than the supposition that this de-cree directs the *fideles regis* to take over the goods of those who fail to perform their military duties as a recompense for their services to the prince (I, 48, 49). Cf. *M. G. H., Leges*, Sectio I, Tomus I, p. 375, line 26. Similarly, Sánchez-Albornoz shows that the canons of the Councils of Toledo and later legislation support his position.

Finally, he points out that the existence of the expression *fideles regis* in Visigothic Spain in this restricted sense as a group of men united to their prince in a relation of personal fidelity distinct from the general allegiance of subjects does not constitute a phenomenon which is pecul-iar to the Gothic kingdom, extraordinary and without parallel in western Europe (I, 71), but rather represents a common trend perhaps best illustrated elsewhere in Merovingian Gaul. This leads to the reflection that the distinction or the confusion between fidelity and vassalage in the feudal epoch is a problem upon which scholars and historians find no common agreement (I, 72). However, a long step toward the resolu-tion of this difficulty has been taken by C. E. Odegaard, *Vassi and Fideles in the Carolingian Empire* (Cambridge: Harvard University Press, 1945), as was indicated in my review in *Speculum*, XXI (1946),

263–265. Nevertheless, this work of Sánchez-Albornoz deserves the careful consideration of all scholars desiring to establish the relation between the Visigothic legislation and early feudalism. The further pursuit of the subject lies beyond the range of this study but may well engage the attention of specialists in feudal origins since the contract factor in Germanic law seems definitely to underlie the feudal bond. (In general, for Sánchez-Albornoz, see the review by R. S. Lopez in *Speculum*, XXIV [1949], 285–289.)

VII

Blasphemy in the *Lex Romana Curiensis**

In 1889 Karl Zeumer published in the *Monumenta Germaniae Historica, Leges* (Tom. V) a critical edition of the *Lex Romana Raetica Curiensis* or *Epitome Sancti Galli*. "This is a statement of legal custom, drawn up for the Romance population of Eastern Switzerland, and used in the Tyrol and Northern Italy as well."[1] It was written between the middle of the eighth and the middle of the ninth century,[2] and was

---

* Reprinted by special permission of the Editors of *Speculum* and the Mediaeval Academy of America from *Speculum*, Vol. VI, No. 3 (1931), 445–459, with minor corrections.

[1] Paul Vinogradoff, *Roman Law in Medieval Europe* (2d ed. by F. de Zulueta; Oxford: University Press, 1929), pp. 21–22. The exact area over which this code was applied has been the subject of much controversy. See M. Conrat, *Geschichte der Quellen und Literatur des römischen Rechts im früheren Mittelalter* (Leipzig: J. C. Hinrichs, 1891), I, 288–291 on place of origin. Also K. Zeumer, *Praefatio* to the *Lex Romana Raetica Curiensis* in *Monumenta Germaniae Historica, Leges* V, fasc. 3 (Hanover: Hahn, 1888), 296–302; and K. Zeumer, "Über Heimat und Alter des Lex Romana Raetica Curiensis," *Zeitschrift der Savigny-Stiftung für Rechtsgeschichte (Germanistische Abtheilung)*, IX (1888), 1–52.

[2] H. Brunner, *Deutsche Rechtsgeschichte* (2d ed.; Leipzig: Duncker and Humblot, 1906), I, 518–525. He says the *Epitome* originated in the later eighth century (perhaps before 766) and was certainly in popular use before 852 or 859. Cf. K. Zeumer (*Praefatio*, pp. 302–303), who believes the law was begun before 751 and completed later. One cannot avoid the idea that the authority of the Bavarian Dukes may have become relatively weak and so created the need for a new formulation of the older Roman Law of the *Breviary* before the time of the Carolingian Capitularies, and that the *Epitome S. Galli* was prepared privately at the behest of the Church to remedy this need before the deposition of Tassilo III and the end of Bavarian independence in 788 (or 794).

probably compiled under ecclesiastical directions.[3] It is "based on a very imperfect abstract of the *Lex Romana Visigothorum,* in which the *Institutes* of Gaius and the greater part of Paulus *Sententiae* are dropped, while the enactments of emperors are generally taken from the text of the 'Interpretation'."[4] Written in Latin, the grammar and mode of expression are most barbarous, while the sense of the Roman Law is often completely misunderstood or changed.[5] Christian and Germanic influences have combined to debase the clear and logical definitions of the Roman *ius* as well as the *constitutiones* of the emperors into Romanesque or Romance customary law.[6] Indeed, this *Epitome* carries us to the very place where the solid highway of the Roman legal system either loses itself amid the pathless swamps and forests of Germanic custom or dwindles into the rough and rut-filled lanes and byways of the *Vulgärrecht.*[7] Vinogradoff cites several instances from the civil procedure that illustrate this point.[8]

There is, however, another passage which the great Oxford scholar

---

[3] M. Conrat, *Quellen und Literatur,* I, 288, n. 5; H. Brunner, *D. R.,* I, 517.

[4] Vinogradoff, *Roman Law,* p. 22. K. Zeumer (*Praefatio,* p. 302) believes it was derived from a recension related to the *Epitome* of Aegidius. H. Brunner (*D. R.,* I, 518) says the compiler did not use the *Breviary* in its official version, but in some denatured, modified form that coincides with none of the known epitomes.

[5] Cf. Introduction to G. Haenel's edition of the *Lex Romana Visigothorum* (Leipzig: Teubner, 1849), p. xxi: "Et quod ad sermonem attinet, non solum verba Breviarii, quae non poterat omittere, ad barbarorum modum et elocutionem mutavit, formavit interque se coniunxit, verum etiam alia aliis substituit et insolita in regionem suam a barbaris demum introducta immiscuit effecitque, ut liber non latina, sed alia quadam lingua scriptus videatur, quae everso romano imperio in Occidentis aliqua parte a barbarorum Romanorumque promiscua multitudine paulatim ficta est."

[6] P. Vinogradoff, *Roman Law,* pp. 23–24: "It is evident that we are in the presence of a rather debased and Germanized form of legal custom, engrafted on fragments of what had been once a system of Imperial law." K. Zeumer (*Praefatio,* p. 289) notes that the law was not issued publicly but, instead, was prepared privately by some person who did not wish to set forth anything new but merely to transform and expound the ancient statutes of the Roman Law in accordance with the needs of his own time.

[7] K. Zeumer, *Praefatio,* p. 289: "Pleraque tamen in hac lege Raetica ita mutata atque ad modum et rationem legum et morum Germanorum redacta esse, ut non modo non genuinum ius Romanorum, sed ne vulgare quidem continere videatur." Also H. Brunner, *D. R.,* I, 517: "Die Abweichungen von der *Lex Romana Visigothorum* beruhen zum Teil auf römischen Vulgarrecht, zum Teil führen sie auf deutsches, insebesondere auf fränkisches Recht zurück." The compiler's misconceptions of Roman Law are often determined and controlled by his knowledge of local Germanic custom. Brunner adds (I, 518): "Für römisches Vulgarrecht ist seine Arbeit die reichhaltigste Fundgrube."

[8] P. Vinogradoff, *Roman Law,* pp. 22–23.

did not touch upon that holds important implications for the fields of political theory and of public criminal law: another passage illuminating the dim area where statute law and popular custom intermingle and modify one another reciprocally. *Lex Romana Curiensis* 9, 3 may be translated as follows:

> Save for the crime of majesty a slave may not accuse his master nor may a freedman accuse his patron or other member of the household.
>
> If any slave shall wish to accuse his master or any freedman his patron, unless, perchance, he can prove that the master himself or the patron himself has blasphemed against God or unless he can prove said master or patron to be pagans, let them be free of his accusation. If these charges are made truly, then the freedman or slave shall depart freely and unharmed; but if they shall lie about these matters, or if, perchance, the freedman shall accuse his patron or the slave his master for any other cause whatsoever before any judge, let that judge have them punished capitally at the very beginning of their accusation.[9]

The disparity between the heading and the body of the law must be evident at once to the most casual observer since the "crime of majesty" is scarcely to be confused with blasphemy and paganism.[10] It is one's first impression that the ecclesiastical compiler of this *Epitome* has either misunderstood the significance of *maiestas* as it is commonly employed in Roman Law or else has introduced into the passage new ideas conforming more closely to the needs and interests of his more Germanic age. Blasphemy and pagan practices were evils that beset clerics and missionaries carrying the Gospel into the rude frontier coun-

---

[9] *Lex Romana Raetica Curiensis* 9, 3 (*Lex Romana Visigothorum, Codex* 9, 3, 2 *Interpretatio*) according to Zeumer's text: "*Ne preter crimen magistatis servus dominum vel patronum libertus seu familiares acuset.* Imp. Valentinus. Data Id. Mar. Interpretatio. Si quis servus dominum suum aut libertus patronum suum acusare voluerit, nisi forsitan probare potuerit, quid [*sic*] ipse dominus aut ipse patronus contra Deum blasfemasset, aut paganus eos probare potuerit, de tale acusatione licenciam habeant. Et si vero dixerint, ipse libertus aut servus sine omne iniuria liberi abscedant; nam si de hoc mentierint, aut si forsitan de alia qualecumque causa libertus patronum aut servus dominum suum ad qualecumque iudice accusaverint, de presentem in ipsa ora acusationis iudex eos capite punire faciat.*" Zeumer notes the correct accusative form, *paganos*, as appearing in MS. 3493 of the Library of the University of Leipzig. The same MS. also employs the spellings, *magestatis, blasphemasset.* Cf. Haenel's Introduction, p. xxxi, n. 103 for numerous examples of the barbarized vocabulary. Also see *ibid.*, p. 177 for Haenel's abbreviated text of this passage.

[10] See the essay "*Crimen Laesae Maiestatis* in the *Lex Romana Wisigothorum*" for text, translation, and comment on *Codex Theodosianus* 9, 6, 3 *Interpretatio* (*L. R. V., C.* 9, 3, 2) *Ne Praeter Crimen Maiestatis Servus Dominum vel Patronum Libertus seu Familiaris Accuset*, the passage in the *Breviary* upon which this provision of the *Epitome* is based.

try of the Saxon, Avar, and Slavic marches.[11] We must remember that such scholars as Haenel, Conrat, and Tardif assign the *Epitome* to the later eighth century,[12] and St. Boniface (d. 755) had been scouring over the Germanic lands in behalf of righteousness not so much earlier.[13] The strong hand of Charlemagne was only beginning to reach across the Rhaetian Alps toward the eastern marches.[14] For such men and for

[11] J. W. Thompson, *Feudal Germany* (Chicago: University of Chicago Press, 1928), p. 171, n. 1. He points out that paganism continued among the Saxons until the twelfth century in some localities. Cf. *ibid.*, Ch. XII, for the conversion of the Slavs and the persistence of paganism among the Trans-Elbean Slavs. The Avars may have been converted toward the close of the eighth century. See C. A. Macartney, "Avars," *Encyclopaedia Britannica* (14th ed.; London and New York: Encyclopaedia Britannica, Ltd., 1929), II, 792.

[12] See *"Crimen Laesae Maiestatis* in the *Lex Romana Wisigothorum."*

[13] See H. O. Taylor, *The Mediaeval Mind* (4th ed.; New York: Macmillan, 1925), I, 197–200 on St. Boniface-Winfried and his part in "The Conversion of the North," and *The Life of Saint Boniface* by Willibald, trans. by G. Robinson (Cambridge: Harvard University Press, 1916), with Introduction, pp. 11–20. Cf. J. W. Thompson, *Feudal Germany*, pp. 393–396 on missionary work in early mediaeval Germany; p. 583 on the organization of the church in Bavaria by Boniface; pp. 467 and 473; also J. W. Thompson, *The Middle Ages, 300–1500* (New York: Knopf, 1931), I, 236–237.

[14] K. Zeumer (*Praefatio*, p. 290) says that the *Lex* speaks of a king (*rex*) frequently, whereas an emperor (*imperator*) is never mentioned and that for this reason such authorities as Haenel, Stobbe, Planta, and Pertile have concluded that the law was compiled toward the close of the eighth century. Cf. Brunner's contention in *D. R.*, I, 520 that the *Lex* must have originated either before or after the period, 800–843: "Da an verschiedenen Stellen vom König, nirgends vom Kaiser die Rede ist, dürfte die *Lex* zu einer Zeit abgefasst worden sein, als Rätien nicht unter einem Kaiser, sondern nur unter einem König stand."

Also see J. W. Thompson, *Feudal Germany*, pp. 468–469: "In 789 Charlemagne began the long and relentless war between the races [Teuton and Slav] which was to endure for centuries by attacking the Wilzi. In 806 he fixed the official frontier along the Elbe and Saale rivers, which was protected by a line of forts," and p. 468, n. 4 for the *Limes Saxoniae* and *Limes Sorabicus*. This excellent work on German eastward expansion establishes the geographical frontiers on an exact chronological basis. For the line of trading posts in 805 along the Slavonic frontier, cf. *ibid.*, p. 531, and the map facing p. 532. Professor Thompson (pp. 585–586) mentions the organization of the Ostmark at the diet of Regensburg in 803, the extension of the chain of marches southward along the eastern frontier to the head of the Adriatic, and the subjugation of the Avars (803 and 811). Since Rhaetia lay closer to the Avar and South Slavic frontiers than to the Saxons in the North, it seems probable that the references to paganism in the *Epitome S. Galli* may very well have arisen from conditions prevailing before the destruction of the Avar power. Also note Thompson (p. 619) on Charlemagne's contacts with Bohemia in 788 (erection of the Nordgau or Bohemian Mark), 791, 805 (invasion of Bohemia to "convert" the heathen Czechs), and 807. Cf. G. Seelinger, "Conquests and Imperial Coronation of Charles the Great," *Cambridge Medieval History* (Cambridge: Macmillan, 1913), II, 606–609 on Bavaria and the Avars; also *ibid.*, maps 26a and

such a time the basic meaning of the *maiestas* of Rome and her emperors must have been lost in the distant past or must have existed vaguely in the legendary background of imperial tradition that formed such a splendid portion of the mediaeval inheritance from Rome.[15] Legal ideas and legal influences operate in various subtle ways to modify the cast of thought and to give it a new direction during the Middle Ages, the ideas themselves often being altered or changed in the process of transmission. Grant Showerman has said "Rome is the epitome of occidental civilization";[16] and, it may be added, the memorial of the Roman Law is writ large therein.

If we turn back to the *Breviary* and the *Theodosian Code* for the *constitutio* of Arcadius and Honorius and especially for the subjoined *interpretatio* upon which this passage depends,[17] we discover that the important clause of "exception" reads "nisi forte dominum aut patronum de crimine maiestatis tractasse probaverit."[18] Nothing here suggests the idea of blaspheming the God of the Christians, nor does any other legislation in the *Code*, as far as I am aware, indicate specifically that such blasphemy could be construed as *laesa maiestas*.[19] Nevertheless, this

---

26b by F. Peisker, showing the Western Front of Slavdom in the seventh and eighth centuries A.D. Also see J. W. Thompson, *Middle Ages*, Ch. X.

[15] Law, as well as poetry, aided in creating the imperial tradition, and the conception of "majesty" in some hazy misty form was very possibly as potent as Vergil's songs celebrating "the glories and greatness of eternal Rome." In a general way, it conveyed the idea of the power and grandeur of the past. Cf. C. H. Haskins, *The Renaissance of the Twelfth Century* (Cambridge: Harvard University Press, 1927), pp. 105–106 and quotation from D. Comparetti, *Vergil in the Middle Ages* (reprint, New York: Stechert, 1929), p. 74. Note Comparetti's further remark that Vergil's fame "as interpreter of that Roman sentiment which survived the downfall of the Empire" was preserved by Justinian "in the most perfect monument of the practical wisdom of the Romans which has survived" (p. 74, n. 78 referring to the *Institutes* and *Digest*). He might have added that the entire *Corpus* of the Roman Law served in manifold ways as an interpreter of Roman sentiment and wisdom for later ages, perhaps a more pervasive symbol of pagan antiquity than the poet himself.

[16] Showerman, *Eternal Rome* (New Haven: Yale University Press, 1924), II, 586.

[17] C. Th. 9, 6, 3 (*L. R. V., C. 9, 3, 2*) *Impp. Arcadius et Honorius AA. Eutychiano Praefecto Praetorio* (8 November, 397).

[18] In the criminal law of the Roman codes and of the Roman jurists, the "great exception" relates primarily to accusations by slaves or freedmen and to the interrogation and torturing of slaves or freedmen in cases involving the infliction of capital punishment on their masters or patrons. See essay on *"Crimen Laesae Maiestatis* in the *Lex Romana Wisigothorum."*

[19] See Mommsen, *Römisches Strafrecht* (Leipzig: S. Hirzel, 1899), p. 598 for *blasphemia*; also pp. 579–580 for the related pagan conception of *iniuria*; and p. 580, n. 1, citing the interesting passage from *Codex Justinianus* 4, 1, 2 *De Rebus*

was the age that saw the concluding scenes of the dramatic struggle between paganism and Christianity for the official sanction and support of the State.[20] Mommsen points out that religious freedom was definitely ended by the famous decree of 379, which commanded that all heresies forbidden by divine laws and the imperial constitutions should cease and be laid at rest forever;[21] henceforth Catholic Christianity should be orthodox and universal. In 384 and 385 sacrilege, perhaps in the sense of heresy, had been enumerated among the unpardonable capital crimes.[22] Similarly the tables were turned against paganism, and the Christian emperors now forbade their pagan subjects all public exercise of their cult, including sacrifices and meetings, and pronounced the penalty of death with confiscation of goods upon those who refused to forsake their pagan deities.[23] And in 392 all such offenders were declared guilty of *laesa maiestas*.[24] It should be noted that as time went on and as paganism fell farther into its decline, heresy acquired importance as

---

Creditis et de Iureiurando which reads: "Iurisiurandi contempta religio satis deum ultorem habet." Observe that this phrase is taken from a *constitutio* of the pagan emperor, Severus Alexander, and was retained by Justinian's compilers. However, one can hardly determine whether Justinian meant to approve the pagan principle of *iniuria* and transfer it into the *Code* for Christian practice and application.

[20] For a detailed discussion of the laws against paganism and heresy in the *Theodosian Code*, see W. K. Boyd, *The Ecclesiastical Edicts of the Theodosian Code* (New York: Columbia University Press, 1905), Vol. XXIV, No. 2 in *Columbia Studies in History, Economics and Public Law*, pp. 15–70. For the contest with paganism, see Thompson, *Middle Ages*, I, 42–46.

[21] *C. Th.* 16, 5, 5 *De Haereticis; C. Just.* 1, 5, 2 *De Haereticis et Manichaeis et Samaritis*: "omnes vetitae legibus et divinis et imperialibus constitutionibus haereses perpetuo conquiescant," quoted in Mommsen, *Strafrecht*, pp. 595–596, and p. 596, n. 1. For the subsequent legislation on heresy, see Boyd, *Ecclesiastical Edicts*, pp. 44–50.

[22] Mommsen, *Strafrecht*, p. 600, n. 4, referring to *C. Th.* 9, 38, 7–8 *De Indulgentiis Criminum. C. Th.* 9, 38, 8 = *L. R. V.* 9, 28, 1, which is carried over into the *Epitome S. Galli*. However, the words *reus maiestatis* disappear in the *Epitome*. Mommsen argues from the expression *sacrilegus in maiestate* in *C. Th.* 9, 38, 3 that the term sacrilege can here relate only to heresy. But in *C. Th.* 8, 38, 7 the context leads me to believe the word may be used technically, referring to violation of a church or sacred place. Cf. *C. Th.* 16, 2, 25 *De Episcopis, Ecclesiis, et Clericis*: "Qui divinae legis sanctitatem aut nesciendo confundunt aut neglegendo violant et offendunt, sacrilegium committunt" (A.D. 380), quoted by Boyd in *Ecclesiastical Edicts* (p. 51).

[23] Cf. Daremberg et Saglio, *Dictionnaire des antiquités grècques et romaines*, article "Maiestas" by G. Humbert and Ch. Lécrivain (Graz, Austria: Akademische Druck-u. Verlagsanstalt, 1963), III (2), 1559.

[24] *C. Th.* 16, 10, 12 *De Paganis, Sacrificiis, et Templis*: "Quod si quispiam immolare hostiam sacrificaturus audebit et spirantia exta consulere, ad exemplum maiestatis reus licita cunctis accusatione delatus excipiat sententiam competentem, etiamsi nihil contra salutem principum aut de salute quaesierit."

the chief form of *laesa religio;* the heretic became more dangerous than the pagan.[25] James Westfall Thompson points out that "by 400 the Church had nearly extirpated paganism in the cities and begun the so-called 'evangelization of the fields'," but owing to the conservative attachment of the peasantry for the ancient rites, paganism was not proscribed in the rural districts until 407.[26] Despite severe repression the old cults still remained respectable in certain quarters and were not destroyed suddenly or at once. "For a long time [they] continued to claim the most distinguished families in the city of Rome and all the circles that represented literature and philosophy in such cities as Alexandria and Athens."[27] The spirit of Julian lived on in pagan hearts.[28] In any case, we find that certain *constitutiones* of the *Theodosian Code* declare definitely that adherence to paganism was a violation of majesty, but the problem raised by blasphemy is even more involved.

How are we to account for the fact that the compiler wrote what he did under this particular caption of *L. R. V., C.* 9, 3, 2 *Interpretatio*? In the first place, it may be best to note the relation of blasphemy (*blasphemare*) to malediction (*maledicere*) in mediaeval Latin usage. Du-Cange, following Casaubon, says that the term "malediction" was taken

[25] Mommsen, *Strafrecht*, p. 607; also note *ibid.*, p. 599, n. 1, showing that delicts against Christianity cease to be considered as treason, although *lèse-majesté* and heresy are united by ties of origin. Cf. Boyd, *Ecclesiastical Edicts*, p. 31, n. 3.

[26] J. W. Thompson, *An Economic and Social History of the Middle Ages* (New York: Century, 1928), p. 82. See *C. Th.* 16, 10, 19 *De Paganis, Sacrificiis et Templis*: "Simulacra, si qua etiam nunc in templis fanisque consistunt et quae alicubi ritum vel acceperunt vel accipiunt paganorum, suis sedibus evellantur, cum hoc repetita sciamus saepius sanctione decretum. Aedificia ipse templorum, quae in civitatibus vel oppidis vel extra oppida sunt, ad usum publicum vindicentur. Arae locis omnibus destruantur omniaque templa in possessionibus nostris ad usus adcommodos transferantur; domini destruere cogantur. Non liceat omnino in honorem sacrilegi ritus funestioribus locis exercere convivia vel quicquam sollemnitatis agitare." This decree was issued by Arcadius, Honorius, and Theodosius, and is dated 15 November, 408 (407), at Rome. Cf. original meaning of word *paganus*, as peasant or countryman in Mommsen, *Strafrecht*, p. 605, n. 4.

[27] E. M. Hulme, *The Middle Ages* (New York: Holt, 1929), pp. 36–37.

[28] Cf. E. K. Rand, *Founders of the Middle Ages* (Cambridge: Harvard University Press, 1928), pp. 137–138, for capital punishment inflicted on pagans a century later (*ca.* 525). Professor Rand's citation from *Edictum Theoderici Regis*, c. 108, is highly significant, for while it does not classify the offering of "sacrifice according to the pagan rite" (*pagano ritu sacrificare*) as *crimen laesae maiestatis*, nevertheless such acts are associated with sorcery, divination, and magical practices (*arioli, umbrarii, malefici*) and bring the death penalty. See "*Crimen Laesae Maiestatis* in the *Lex Romana Wisigothorum*" on the relation of *lèse majesté* to *mathematici, harioli, haruspices, vaticinatores*. Also Cf. Mommsen, *Strafrecht*, p. 584 with nn. 4–5.

over by the Christians from the pagans,[29] while he points out that "blasphemy" is used in the Scriptures and among ecclesiastical writers to designate impious speech and malediction against God.[30] At any rate, *maledicere* is found frequently in classical Latin writings and becomes technically a special offense in Roman Law involving the utterance of curses and reproaches, and the casting of foul or abusive words against the emperors,[31] whereas *blasphemare*, as here used, is an ecclesiastical Latin word derived from the Greek βλασφημεῖν, meaning to speak profanely, and thence transferred to Latin in the Vulgate and in the writings of the Church Fathers. The *New English Dictionary on Historical Principles* states that the word "blaspheme" became popular in late Latin in the sense of "revile, reproach"; in its transitive form it has evolved into the common modern sense, "To speak irreverently of or utter impiety against God or anything sacred."[32] Harper's *New Latin Dictionary* indicates that both words are synonymous, meaning "to revile," and cites examples of their usage in ecclesiastical Latin.[33] It is difficult to draw a clear-cut line between the usage of each, though *blasphemare*, unlike *maledicere*, is not classical Latin. However, in my opinion, if any line of distinction is to be drawn, malediction refers most typically to execrations or curses cast upon the divine emperor, the pagan deities, or even individuals, while blasphemy relates more particularly to profanity directed against the Christian God or other features of worship held especially sacred and holy among Christians. Nevertheless, one must bear in mind their similar or synonymous usage in ecclesiastical Latin.

---

[29] DuCange, *Glossarium Mediae et Infimae Latinitatis* (Paris: Firmin Didot Fratres, 1840–1850), IV, 202 quotes Papias: "*Imprecari mala, quod vulgo dicitur Maledicere*," and adds further: "Hinc *maledictus* vox Christianorum, pro ἐπικατάρατος, gliscente Christianismo sensim usurpata a Paganis, ut observat Casaubonus ad Spartianum in Geta."

[30] *Ibid.*, I, 700, comments on *Blasphemare*: "Occurrit etiam passim in Scripturis sacris et apud Scriptores Ecclesiasticos pro Maledicere Deo, impie loqui," and "Utraque etiam notione, pro vituperare scilicet et impie in Deum vel Sanctos loqui suum βλασφημεῖν sumunt Graeci."

[31] Cf. Paulus *Sententiae* 5, 29, 1. The text of the *Sentences* may be found in the first fascicule of the second volume of P. E. Huschke, *Iurisprudentia anteiustiniana* (6th ed. by E. Seckel and B. Kübler; Leipzig: Teubner, 1911). Also note that malediction involves legal principles similar to those applied in counterfeiting, and possibly sorcery and the consulting of *haruspices*.

[32] See *A New English Dictionary on Historical Principles*, edited by J. A. H. Murray (Oxford: Clarendon, 1888), I (2) 904 for *blaspheme; ibid.* (1908), VI (2) 81 for *malediction*.

[33] See Appendix A at the end of this article.

Next we must consider that the compiler of the *Epitome Sancti Galli* was an ecclesiastic or other person well educated for his time and locality, and so acquainted with the Vulgate and some Roman Law from the *Breviary.* Is it not reasonable to suppose that, given these two closely synonymous terms, he might employ the ecclesiastical Latin word *blasphemare* in his reconstruction of the law, although *maledicere* is the word employed in the older codes? The passage in question, *C. Th.* 9, 6, 3 (*L. R. V., C.* 9, 3, 2) with its *Interpretatio*, does not deal with malediction as a phase of *crimen laesae maiestatis*, but *C. Th.* 9, 4, 1 *Si Quis Imperatori Maledixerit*, which is found near at hand in the same Book Nine and would presumably be still in the mind of an excerptor when he reached *C. Th.* 9, 6, 3, treats specifically of the matter of cursing the divine emperor. However, *C. Th.* 9, 4, 1 is not found in the *Breviary*, and, as we have no reason for supposing the compiler of the *Epitome Sancti Galli* to have had the original *Theodosian Code* before him, we cannot assert that our passage was influenced by *C. Th.* 9, 4, 1.

Let us now turn to Paulus *Sententiae* 5, 29, 1 (*L. R. V., Paulus* 5, 31, 1) *Ad Legem Iuliam Maiestatis.* In this oft-quoted passage of Roman Law the crime of *laesa maiestas* is defined comprehensively, though concisely, and here Paulus mentions *verbis impiis ac maledictis*.[34] This passage is not found in the *Epitome Sancti Galli* since Book Five of the Sentences ends at *L. R. V., P.* 5, 7, 14 in our texts, but there is no necessary reason for supposing that the compiler of the *Epitome* was unaware of this provision in the *Breviary*.[35] Also *Lex Romana Curiensis* 27, 8, 1 uses *maledicere* in connection with cursing other people generally as follows: "Qui alterum hominem sine causa maledicit, in contumilio [*sic*] deputetur aut fustigetur."[36] The significance of this quotation resides in the fact that the word meaning malediction does actually appear in this compilation. This leads to the conclusion that while malediction appears nowhere in the *Epitome* in the accepted usage of the Roman Law as cursing or reviling a deified emperor, still there is no reason for dis-

---

[34] See "*Crimen Laesae Maiestatis* in the *Lex Romana Wisigothorum*" for translation and text of Paulus *Sent.* 5, 29, 1 (*L. R. V., P.* 5, 31, 1) and for *verbis impiis.* Cf. J. F. H. Abegg, "Zur Geschichte des römischen *crimen maiestatis,* im Verhaeltnis zu dem *crimen impietatis* und dem s.g. *crimen laesae venerationis,*" *Archiv des Criminalrechts* [*Neue Folge*] (Brunswick: Schwetschke, 1853), pp. 230–231.

[35] Vinogradoff's conclusion that the *Epitome S. Galli* is derived from a very imperfect abstract of the *Breviary* does not necessarily invalidate our assumption in this connection.

[36] This is based on Paulus *Sent.* 5, 4, 19: "Maledictum itemque convicium publice factum ad iniuriae vindictam revocatur; quo facto condemnatus infamis efficitur."

believing that the compiler knew that malediction was associated with
the *crimen laesae maiestatis.* Always bearing in mind that such negative
inferences as this fall far short of positive proof, we are now in the position to ask: What could be more natural for a Christian writer of this
frontier region in the later eighth century than to substitute the offense
of blaspheming the Christian God for the *crimen laesae maiestatis* in
which malediction against the divine emperors played an essential part,
and to employ the ecclesiastical Latin word *blasphemare,* which was
found in the Vulgate and was used by the Church Fathers, for *maledicere,* the expression common to the Roman Law in classical times?[37]
The Christian God seemed very close and very real; the pagan emperors were receding into the mist of the past and assuming the dim out-
lines that tradition wove for them. God sat mightily on his throne in
those days above holy men who labored where the heathen were always
close at hand. Cursing the mortal rulers of this world, long since passed
away, could not be mentioned in the same breath with blaspheming that
ruler in Eternity whom Sacred Writ made sovereign of the Kingdom of
Heaven and whom Augustine made master of his City of God.[38]

In the matter of adherence to paganism (*aut paganus eos probare
potuerit*), one must conclude that the *Epitome* relates to local conditions and does not represent a transfer of Roman Law.[39] It is true that
in 392 Arcadius declared persons guilty of *laesa maiestas* who refused
to forsake their pagan deities (*C. Th.* 16, 10, 12), but no part of the
Theodosian Code (particularly Book Sixteen) supporting this position
passed on into the *Breviary.* Hence one cannot assume that any such
provisions were accessible to the compiler of the *Lex Romana Curiensis.*

Finally if the problem be approached from the broader angle of political theory, any scholar familiar with the researches of Mommsen[40]

---

[37] The verb *blasphemare* and kindred forms do not appear in the *Theodosian
Code* within the limits of my observation. See Robert Mayr, *Vocabularium Codicis
Iustiniani, Pars prior* (*Pars Latina*), (Prague: Ceská Grafická Unie, 1923). He cites
forms of this word in *C. Just.* 3, 43, 1 and 3, 43, 2, 2 *De Aleae Lusu et Aleatoribus,*
but they are employed in unrelated contexts and belong to a later date (*ca.* 529).

[38] The Church Fathers display a tendency to associate the idea of "majesty," at
least in its highest sense, with God rather than with any earthly state or prince.

[39] This opinion receives further support from the clause "nisi si illus incredulus et
paganus probare potuerit," found in *Lex Rom. Cur.* 23, 14, 1 which is a revision of
Paulus *Sent.* 1, 12, 4 *De Iudiciis Omnibus.* This clause does not appear in the
Breviary and must have been added to the *Epitome* because of local considerations.

[40] Cf. Mommsen, *Strafrecht,* pp. 567–580, 595–611. Also see Daremberg et Saglio,
Dictionnaire, III, (2), 1559 and notes. A concise substantial survey with splendid
bibliography may be found in Pauly-Wissowa-Kroll, *Realencyclopädie der class-*

will recognize the close relation of *laesa maiestas* to *laesa religio*.[41] Indeed, it is an ancient subject, for one may find Ulpian quoted in the *Digest* to the effect that "the crime which is related most closely to sacrilege is that called the crime of majesty."[42] Not only the Roman lawyers but the Church Fathers perceived the intimate association between majesty and religion. Patristic, as well as juristic, literature supports this point of view. Thus, Tertullian in his *Apologeticus* defines vigorously the distinctions and connections between these two types of offenses.[43] We have a broad highway running from sedition (*seditio*) and treason against land and folk (*perduellio* or *Landesverrat*) through high treason (*Hochverrat*) and related crimes of majesty including counterfeiting, malediction, sorcery, and various injuries and insults to the imperial person, to sacrilege, impiety, blasphemy, and heresy.[44] This entire nexus

---

ischen Altertumswissenschaft, art. "Maiestas" by B. Kübler (Stuttgart: Metzler, 1928), XXVII, 542–559.

[41] See Mommsen, *Strafrecht*, pp. 569–570 on *crimen laesae romanae religionis*. Also Humbert observes in Daremberg et Saglio, *Dictionnaire*, III (2), 1558, that "the sacred character of the emperors contributed to transform every injury into the crime of *lesè-majesté*, making it an impiety." Cf. *ibid.*, III (2), 1559 and nn. 18–19, pointing out that Christians were considered ἄθεοί, declared guilty of *perduellio*, and treated as public enemies (*hostes publici*).

[42] *Digest* 48, 4, 1 *Ad Legem Iuliam Maiestatis*: "Proximum sacrilegio crimen est, quod maiestatis dicitur." Cf. Pollock and Maitland, *History of English Law before the Time of Edward I* (2d ed.; Cambridge: University Press, 1898) II, 505, n. 4: "The Roman idea of *maiestas* includes a religious element; falsifying Caesar's image is a kind of sacrilege"; also note the reference to *C. Just.* 9, 24, 2 *De Falsa Moneta*, which speaks of a *crimen obnoxii maiestatis*.

[43] Cf. Tertullian, *Apologeticus*, c. 10, 24, 27, 28, 35. These references are cited by Mommsen, *Strafrecht*, p. 569, n. 2, who remarks that "divinity and the imperial dignity always go hand in hand."

[44] Abegg has made an historical survey of the development and an analysis of the organic interrelations of these offenses in the Roman Law of the classical period in his previously cited study in *Archiv des Criminalrechts* (*Neue Folge*), pp. 205–238. He refers either to the common elements or to the distinctions between *crimen perduellionis*, *crimen imminutae maiestatis*, *crimen laesae maiestatis*; parricide against *pater patriae*, *crimen laesae pietatis*, or *crimen impietatis*; sacrilege and *crimen laesae venerationis*.
The views of the great commentators on the Roman Law in the sixteenth and seventeenth centuries need to be studied in this connection as well. Cf. Jacobus Gothofredus (Jacques Godefroi), *Opuscula varia; iuridica, politica, historica, critica* (Genevae: Ioannis Antonii et Samuelis de Tournes, 1654) who divides the crime of majesty into three categories in the *Discursus historicus, ad Legem Quisquis Cod. ad L. Iluliam Maiestatis*, c. vii. The second division of his classification is described briefly thus: "Secundum Maiestatis crimen voco, *laesae Venerationis*: 'quotiens videlicet, non hostili quidem in Rempubl. aut Imperium ipsum animo, salus aut securitas eius appetitur, verum debita tantum Principibus veneratio facto dictove aliquo atroci violatur, puta maledictis in eos iactatis, vel statuis eorum violatis'."

of crimes forms one organically correlated whole which holds as true for the ninth century as it had for the third century.[45] Hence, it was easy for the compiler of the *Epitome Sancti Galli* to substitute blasphemy against God, which is properly considered an aspect of *laesa religio*, for malediction or other *laesa maiestas* against a human emperor in the light of current political and religious conceptions. The legal theory supports the linguistic usage. But again our inference falls short of documented historical proof. Special local influences or individual cir-

---

(Owing to an error in pagination in the Geneva edition of 1654, whereby page numbers 31 and 32 are repeated, this reference may be located on the second p. 32.) Also contained in Jacobus Gothofredus (Jacques Godefroi), *Opera juridica minora* (Lugduni Batavorum: J. A. Langerak, 1733), in "Discursus hist., ad Leg. Quisquis," c. vii, p. 26. In addition, see Benedictus Carpzovius (Benedict Carpzov), *Practicae novae imperialis saxonicae rerum criminalium* (Frankfort: B. C. Wust, 1677); later edition (Frankfort: Franciscus Varrentrapp, 1758), (Pars I), pp. 245–325. Carpzov discusses *lèse-majesté*, heresy, blasphemy, sorcery, and witchcraft, and comments on each in its proper order. Cf. P. Bisoukides, *Der Hochverrath* (Berlin: Carl Heymanns Verlag, 1903), pp. 63–64 on the position of Carpzov. One must conclude that the *crimen laesae venerationis* against the pagan emperors links up indubitably with the Christian conception of a *crimen laesae maiestatis divinae*.

For the treatises of such writers as Bocerus, Bossius, Gentilis, and Gigas, consult Martinus Lipenius (Martin Lipen), *Bibliotheca realis iuridica*, post F. G. Struvii, with Supplement by G. A. Jenichen (Lipsiae: Wendler, 1743–1746), I, 354–355 under the topic "Maiestatis Laesae Crimen," and II, 268–269 in Supplement for Balduinus.

[45] In the third century *laesa maiestas* involved both religious and political factors since the ruler of the Roman world was god as well as emperor. By the close of the fifth century the Christian structure of human society made possible a differentiation between the spiritual (ecclesiastical) and temporal (imperial) spheres of government which could not have occurred in connection with pagan conceptions of "god-kingship." This tendency would have set a boundary between treason proper and the religious offenses of sacrilege, impiety, and heresy. Cf. R. W. and A. J. Carlyle, *A History of Mediaeval Political Theory in the West* (2d ed.; Edinburgh and London: Blackwood, 1927) Vol. I: The Second Century to the Ninth, pp. 190–192 on the Gelasian theory of the two spheres, *sacerdotium* and *regnum*; also p. 190 for Satan's device of the religious powers of the pagan emperors confounding the two spheres, Christ Himself being the only "true and perfect king and priest"; p. 256. See *ibid.*, Ch. XXI (The Relation of the Authorities of Church and State) for the invasion of the two "Vicars of God," king and bishop, upon each other's proper sphere in the ninth century. The logical consequence of this encroachment was a more organic correlation of *laesa religio* with *laesa maiestas*, a condition that flourished long and matured its choicest fruit under the "Godly Princes" of the sixteenth century in the identification of treason and heresy. Thus when Henry VIII became head of the English Church he did away with all competing authority and absorbed all obedience to himself, and it may be noted that still later the Presbyterians opposed the "Godly Prince" on the Gelasian principle of the spheres —spiritual and temporal. The subsequent development of the idea of the spheres has led finally to the modern attitude of government toward religion with the separa-

cumstances of which we have no record may hold the true key to the solution of this problem.[46] History is always filled with pitfalls when approached subjectively.

The results of this study may be summarized as follows: (1) This provision of the *Lex Romana Curiensis* provides evidence of the paganism that lingered long beyond the eastern marches and of the struggles of Christianity to advance among the heathen during the great German expansion at the expense of Slavdom. The reference to paganism cannot relate to the paganism of antiquity, but must apply to the heathen of the Avar and Slavic marches or possibly to unconverted Teutons. (2) It shows local customs and habits of thought under Christian and Germanic influences in the process of modifying an earlier system of universal statutes. (3) It reveals a conspicuous omission of the idea of *maiestas* in the usual sense of the Roman Law that is characteristic of many Germanic codes, but which, in this instance, can be interpreted only as a deliberately intended alteration, possessing genuine significance for the compiler. (4) It makes a curious and conscious substitution of *laesa religio* for *laesa maiestas;* injury to a human ruler is supplanted by insult to a divine ruler. Since these two types of offense are organically related in legal and political theory, this passage affords an interesting example of the interchange and transfer of ideas. Furthermore, in this respect the passage is quite unique throughout the entire range of Germanic customary law.

---

tion of Church and State. This would account for the vast gulf separating mediaeval from modern thought in the matter of the relation of treason to the religious offenses. The typical mediaeval conception represents a tendency toward integration of these offenses; the modern a strict differentiation. Cf. J. N. Figgis, *Studies of Political Thought from Gerson to Grotius (1414–1625),* (2d ed.; Cambridge: University Press, 1923), p. 55. He supports the same general point of view when he describes the Presbyterian theory of the *two distinct kingdoms* (Church and State), although he does not specifically associate this with the Gelasian principle of the spheres. Also see *ibid.,* pp. 64, 163. For a definitive analysis of this position, see the Introduction to *The Political Works of James I* (Cambridge: Harvard University Press, 1918), pp. xvii–xxiv, by Professor Charles H. McIlwain of Harvard University.

[46] Zeumer's description of the manuscript sources in *Praefatio,* pp. 291–296 suggests no clue to an answer that might be traced through external criticism of the codices, unless such examination might indicate why the Fifth Book of Paulus *Sentences* ends so abruptly at L. R. V., P. 5, 7, 14 in the *Epitome.* His definitive text is based on three separate MSS: (A1) *Codex bibliothecae monasterii* S. *Galli, No.* 722 (formerly *D. 184*), which dates from the ninth century and is, in large part, palimpsest, rewritten over S. *Hilarii expositio psalmorum* (*ca.* 6th cent.); (A2) *Codex bibliothecae universitatis Lipsiensis, No.* 3493 (9th–10th cent.); (B) *Codex archivi monasterii* S. *Galli xxx* (9th cent.). A1 and A2 derive from a common source and usually provide the sounder text.

Of course, one must recognize that the conclusions to which our special argument regarding the specific manner of interchange points would be still more convincing if we could assume that the compiler of the *Epitome* had access to the entire *Theodosian Code* rather than a garbled text of the *Breviary*, for the original *Code* did declare adherence to paganism a form of *laesa maiestas*, and the relation of malediction to the crimes against majesty is more intimate and apparent there.[47] However, without regard to the exact process of the compiler's thought or to the precise way in which the transfer occurred, the fact of the modified passage remains and attests a significant change in attitude toward the antique Roman conception of majesty. Finally, I would add that this study is largely suggestive to the end that legal materials be not neglected in reconstructing the intellectual activity of the Middle Ages.

A. Blasphemy in the Vulgate

An examination of the dictionary evidence based on the Vulgate, especially Lev. xxiv (*poena blasphemorum et talionis*) and Matt. xxvi, reveals a number of correspondences and similarities in usage. Several of the ensuing references are given in Harper's *A Latin Dictionary*, ed. by Lewis and Short (Oxford: Clarendon, 1955) without quotation.

Lev. xxiv, 11: Cumque *blasphemasset* nomen, et *maledixisset* ei, adductus est ad Moysen; xxiv, 14: Educ *blasphemum* extra castra; xxiv, 15–16: Homo, qui *maledixerit* Deo suo, portabit peccatum suum: et qui *blasphemaverit* nomen Domini, morte moriatur; xxiv, 23: qui *blasphemaverat*; Num. v, 23: Scribetque sacerdos in libello ista *maledicta*, et delebit ea aquis amarissimis, in quas *maledicta* congessit, et dabit ei bibere; xxii, 6: Veni igitur, et *maledic* populo huic, quia fortior me est: si quo modo possim percutere et eiicere eum de terra mea. novi enim quod benedictus sit cui benedixeris, et *maledictus* in quem *maledicta* congesseris; I Par. xx, 7: Hic *blasphemavit* Israel; Matt. ix, 3: Et ecce quidam de Scribis dixerunt intra se: Hic *blasphemat*; xii, 31: Ideo dico vobis: Omne peccatum et *blasphemia* remittetur hominibus, spiritus autem *blasphemia* non remittetur; xxvi, 65: Tunc princeps sacerdo-

---

[47] See Appendix B regarding the possible influence of Germanic customary law.

tum scidit vestimenta sua, dicens: *Blasphemavit*: quid adhuc egemus testibus? ecce nunc audistis *blasphemiam*: quid vobis videtur? Acta apost. xxiii, 4: Summum sacerdotum Dei *maledicis*? Acta apost. xxiii, 5: Principem populi tui non *maledices*. Also cf. Exod. xxii, 28: *Diis non detrahes,* et principi populi tui non maledices; Matt. xxvi, 74: Tunc coepit *detestari* et *iurare* quia non novisset hominem; Marc. xiv, 71: Ille autem coepit *anathematizare, et iurare*.

The italicized words are rendered as follows in the Oxford revision of the King James version (Oxford: University Press, 1885): Lev. xxiv, 11: blasphemed, cursed; xxiv, 14: him that hath cursed; xxiv, 15–16: curseth, blasphemeth; xxiv, 23: him that had cursed; Num. v, 23: curses, water of bitterness that causeth the curse; xxii, 6: curse me this people, he whom thou cursest is cursed (cf. the antonyms, *benedictus* and *maledictus*: he whom thou blessest is blessed); I Chr. xx, 7: defied (or reproached); Matt. ix, 3: blasphemeth; xii, 31: blasphemy, blasphemy; xxvi, 65: he hath spoken blasphemy, the blasphemy (cf. Mark xiv, 64: the blasphemy); Acts xxii, 4: Revilest thou; Acts xxiii, 5: thou shalt not speak evil of. Cf. Exod. xxii, 28: revile, curse; Matt. xxvi, 74: to curse, to swear; Mark xiv, 71: to curse, to swear.

These citations tend to prove clearly that any original distinctions in meaning between these two words have been quite lost in the Latin of the Vulgate.

Also it is my impression, based on limited observation, that these parallels in usage hold true in the writings of the more important Latin Fathers.

B. Blasphemy in Germanic Customary Law

Father A. K. Ziegler's *Church and State in Visigothic Spain* (Washington: Catholic University of America, 1930) directs attention to the close relation of the Alamannic and Bavarian Laws with the *Code of Euric,* a problem that had particularly interested Zeumer (cf. Ziegler, p. 57, n. 2). Since the two former compilations applied to regions adjoining Rhaetia and since Euric's *Code* had a widely diffused influence, the idea is suggested that the entire closely correlated group of *leges barbarorum* be examined with a view to determining whether any possible explanation of the reference to blasphemy in *Lex. Rom. Cur.* 9, 3 might be derived from some source in Germanic customary law.

Lex Wisigothorum 12, 3, 2 De *blasphematoribus sancti Trinitatis* appears to be the only specific reference to blasphemy in any sense in Visigothic legislation, and here the context has no bearing on the current problem. Neither is any light added by *L. Vis.* 2, 1, 9 *De non criminando principe nec maledicendo illi*, nor by *Leges Alamannorum*, c. 36, 2 *De conventu* (*nec maledicant duce*). There are no pertinent passages whatsoever in the *Lex Baiuvariorum* that mention either blasphemy or malediction. The only expressions concerning blasphemy that I have found in the Frankish and Lombard legislation are used in entirely unrelated contexts and also conflict with the chronological limits set by H. Brunner, *Rechtsgeschichte*, I, 520. Note the following instances: *Capitulare duplex in Theodonis villa* (a. 805)), c. 8: "qui nec iuditium scabinorum adquiescere nec blasfemare volunt"; *Ansegisi Capitularium* (a. 827) 1, 61 *De nimium blasphemis latronibus; Hlotharii I Constitutiones Papienses* (a. 832), c. 5, repeating *Cap. in Theod. villa, supra*. Certain features of the *Capitulare Paderbrunnense* or *Capitulatio de partibus Saxoniae* (a. 785) are suggestive, though it makes no specific use of the term *blasphemia*. Furthermore, in these codes any direct reference to the Roman Law of *laesa maiestas* is most exceptional, as in the *Capitulare Ticinense* (a. 801), c. 3 *De desertoribus*. Therefore, in my judgment no evidence of the Germanic codes invalidates the conclusions reached previously in this study.

Also, among the *leges romanae*, note the interesting passage in *Lex Romana Burgundionum* 7, 5–6, repeating the "great exception" and compare with *L. R. V., C.* 9, 3, 1–2, *L. R. V., P.* 9, 31, 1, and *Digest* 48, 4, 11. This citation from Ulpian in the *Digest* applies the principle of the "great exception" so as to involve attainder in accusations of majesty (*maiestatis reus*) made in cases of *perduellio* and high treason. Here the liberal general principle of the Roman Law that *extinguitur enim crimen mortalitate* is abandoned *hoc crimine nisi a successoribus purgetur*.

VIII

Treason and Related Offenses
in the Anglo-Saxon Dooms*

It has long been the accepted practice to begin the broader outline of British history with the Anglo-Saxon period, both in the textbooks and general histories. Although the treatment is frequently all too brief, this difficult epoch is dealt with competently in most of its major aspects despite the relative paucity of the sources. Monographs on the Anglo-Saxon era are fewer than one might expect, though some of the more recent are notably good, and a few of the older have become almost classic even when modified by subsequent research. Still the primary emphasis has been social, economic, or literary. There are significant studies on parliamentary origins, the beginning of feudalism, the village community, the class structure, and the transmission of the classical and Christian heritages.[1] But in legal history the field is narrowed down

---

* Reprinted from *The Rice Institute Pamphlet*, XXXVII (1950), 1–20.

[1] Among the most useful background books I should recommend F. M. Stenton, *Anglo-Saxon England* (Oxford: Clarendon, 1943), and R. H. Hodgkin, *A History of the Anglo-Saxons*, 2 vols. (Oxford: Clarendon, 1935). For valuable older studies on the Anglo-Saxon period, see H. M. Chadwick, *Studies on Anglo-Saxon Institutions* (Cambridge: University Press, 1905); F. W. Maitland, *Domesday Book and Beyond* (Cambridge: University Press, 1897); F. Seebohm, *The English Village Community* (4th ed.; London: Longmans, Green, 1915), and *Tribal Custom in Anglo-Saxon Law* (London: Longmans, Green, 1911); Sir Paul Vinogradoff, *The Growth of the Manor* (London: Macmillan, 1911); *English Society in the Eleventh Century* (Oxford: Clarendon, 1908); and *Villainage in England* (Oxford: Clarendon, 1892); Edward A. Freeman, *The Growth of the English Constitution* (London: Macmillan, 1872); and *The History of the Norman Conquest of England*, 6

markedly save for a few most distinguished contributions, despite the existence of a very considerable body of documentary sources of unusual richness and variety contained in the Anglo-Saxon Dooms.[2]

The Anglo-Saxon Dooms represent a unique development in Germanic legal history and are unlike the continental folk laws in many important respects. They are composed in the native tongue, Anglo-Saxon, for the most part, instead of in Vulgar Latin. They contain relatively few traces of the direct influence of Roman Law, although Roman ideas have been conveyed indirectly through ecclesiastical channels. They are not the completed work of a single legislator, but a series of enactments made by various kings from the seventh to the eleventh centuries. And, while they are unsystematic on the whole, they nevertheless constitute a fair representation of Germanic legal thought in a comparatively unadulterated form. It will not be the purpose of this study to analyze all matter relating to public law since, despite the admitted limitations in Anglo-Saxon studies, the Dooms have been investigated more adequately than most of the other *leges barbarorum*.[3] Such gen-

---

vols. (Oxford: Clarendon, 1867–1879). On Anglo-Saxon letters, see E. S. Duckett, *Anglo-Saxon Saints and Scholars* (New York: Macmillan, 1948) and G. K. Anderson, *The Literature of the Anglo-Saxons* (Princeton: Princeton University Press, 1949).

[2] The standard indispensable treatises on English law are F. Pollock and F. W. Maitland, *History of English Law before the Time of Edward I*, 2 vols. (2nd ed.; Cambridge: University Press, 1923), especially I, 25–63 on Anglo-Saxon Law; Sir William Holdsworth, *A History of English Law* (4th ed.; London: Methuen, 1936), II, 3–118, on Anglo-Saxon Antiquities (449–1066); Sir James Fitzjames Stephen, *A History of the Criminal Law of England*, 3 vols. (London: Macmillan, 1883), especially I, 51–74; Bishop William Stubbs, *The Constitutional History of England* (5th ed.; Oxford: Clarendon, 1891), I, 39–314.

[3] The most nearly definitive text of the Anglo-Saxon Dooms may be found in F. Lieberman, *Die Gesetze der Angelsachsen*, 3 vols. (Halle: Max Niemeyer, 1903–1916) with the Anglo-Saxon texts, German translation, and Glossary. There is also the older, but still useful, *Die Gesetze der Angelsachsen* by Dr. Reinhold Schmid (2nd ed.; Leipzig: F. A. Brockhaus, 1858) with Anglo-Saxon and Latin texts and German translation, and *Ancient Laws and Institutes of England* by B. Thorpe (folio, Public Records Commission, 1840) with the Anglo-Saxon and Latin texts, English translation, and Glossary. Thorpe's rendering into English is inadequate in many respects and is now generally supplanted by two very useful recent works: F. L. Attenborough, *The Laws of the Earliest English Kings* (Cambridge: University Press, 1922), and A. J. Robertson, *The Laws of the Kings of England from Edmund to Henry I* (Cambridge: University Press, 1925), which contain the edited Anglo-Saxon texts, an adequate English translation, and extensive notes in commentary upon the specific laws. Also see *English Historical Documents*, edited by Dorothy Whitelock (London: Eyre and Spottiswoode, 1955) Vol. I: c. 500–1042, 351–439, including the laws of Ethelbert of Kent, Ine, Alfred, and Cnut.

eral considerations as the theory of a special royal interest and the king's peace are tentatively accepted without an extended analytical examination.[4] The idea of a scandal, committed in violation of the royal peace, appears as early as the Dooms of Aethelberht (d. 617),[5] where one reads that "if the king summons his freemen [leode] before him and anyone there does evil to them, let the offender make double compensation [bot] and fifty shillings besides to the king,"[6] and "if the king feasts in a man's home and anyone there commits a wrong, let the offender make a double compensation."[7] The royal protection extends not only over certain places, but over certain property and persons as well. "If a freeman steals from the king, let him restore it ninefold,"[8] and "if anyone kills a man on the king's properties [tun], let him pay fifty shillings as compensation."[9] Later in the century this same general principle is evident in the laws of Ine, which probably fall between 688 and 694. "If anyone fights in the king's house, let him forfeit his property and be at the mercy of the king to decide whether he shall live or not."[10] A special ecclesiastical peace is also recognized,[11] together with the right of sanctuary, so that whoever is guilty of killing and flees to a church may keep his life and amend his crime according to law.[12]

Although high treason is not specifically mentioned in this legislation,[13] the laws of Ine mark a distinct step in the development of the

[4] The position of the king in his relation to the peace of the land is succinctly stated by Stubbs, *Constitutional History*, I, 200: "When the king becomes the lord, patron and *mundborh* of his whole people, they pass from the ancient national peace of which he is the guardian into the closer personal or territorial relation of which he is the source. The peace is now the king's peace," although this concept of a "national peace" is rejected by J. Goebel, *Felony and Misdemeanor* (New York: Commonwealth Fund, 1937), I, 7-25, 37-38, 327-335, 423-440. Also cf. Stubbs, *Constitutional History*, I, 193-206, on power of the king and special royal peace, and *Aethelberht*, c. 1, on ecclesiastical peace.

[5] Cf. *Leges Visigothorum*, ed. by Zeumer in *Monumenta Germaniae Historica, Leges* (Hanover and Leipzig: Hahn, 1902), Sectio I, Tomus I, 2, 1, 8 and 9, 2, 8; *Edictus Rothari*, ed. by Bluhme in *M. G. H.* (1889), Legum Tomus V, 35-40.

[6] *Aethelberht*, c. 2. The *leode* are comparable to the Frankish *leudes* and the later *barones* of the feudal age.

[7] *Aethelberht*, c. 3.

[8] *Aethelberht*, c. 4.

[9] *Aethelberht*, c. 5. *Tun* may mean a hamlet or small village.

[10] *Ine*, c. 6.

[11] *Ine*, c. 6, 1.

[12] *Ine*, c. 5.

[13] In general, for treason and related public offenses in early English law, see Pollock and Maitland, *History of English Law*, II, 462-511, on "Felony and Treason," which is an almost definitive treatment of the subject within the range under consideration; also Stephen, *Criminal Law*, I, 53-59. In addition, see Liber-

idea in Anglo-Saxon law. The earlier enactments of Aethelberht indicate plainly that royal displeasure was incurred by unruly conduct in the king's presence or by actions interfering with the royal business. All these crimes were repressed by very heavy fines. Nevertheless, they were amendable and may have been regarded as acts harmful to the general welfare quite as much as insults to the king. However, the idea was clearly emerging that certain crimes are unamendable and should be dealt with only by the king because they are in contempt (*oferhiernes, overseunessa*) of the king.[14] Thus, the royal peace came to include a class of crimes which were insulting to or in contempt of the king, and was no longer limited to specified persons, property, or places. The next stage in its evolution attaches obviously to the time when breaches of the peace become injuries to the person of the king, who personifies public authority. At that point insult and scandal shade into typical high treason. Little may be found in this early Anglo-Saxon legislation comparable to the provisions of the folk laws of the Germanic peoples on the continent for repressing offenses against the land and folk (*Landesverrat*). Ine declares that a man who has been accused of participation in a marauding expedition or raid (*hereteam*) may redeem himself only upon payment of his wergeld.[15] Another law states that an attack upon a fortified residence must be compensated by a payment to the king, bishop, or other holder of the property thus assailed.[16] Such laws indicate how offenses against the peace of king or bishop may be settled in the interest of the general welfare; and it is matters of this sort which become violations of the peace of the land and treason to land and folk when they are unregulated and perpetrated irresponsibly without restraint at the whim of individuals. In this connection one law commands:

If a *gesithcundman,* who possesses land, absents himself from military services on a campaign, he shall pay 120 shillings and lose his land; a nobleman,

---

mann, *Gesetze,* Glossary in Vol. II (first half) on *hlafordswice* (p. 116); Vol. II (second half) on *Hochverrat* (pp. 510–511); also notes on particular laws in Vol. III; and Schmid, *Gesetze,* on *hlafordsearo* (p. 612) and on *fyrd* (p. 587).

[14] Holdsworth, *English Law,* II, 48–49. The expression *oferhirness, ofer-hyrnes* "contempt," in the Anglo-Saxon Dooms corresponds to *overseunessa* (*ofer-seweness*) in the *Leges Henrici Primi.* The term, *overseunessa,* is very probably a corrupt rendering by an Anglo-Norman scribe. Numerous similar corrupt Norman renderings of Anglo-Saxon terms appear in the Latin text of the *Laws of Henry I.*

[15] *Ine,* c. 15.

[16] *Ine,* c. 45. Attack upon or breaking into a fortified post, residence, or premises is termed *burg-bryce.*

who holds no land, shall pay sixty shillings; and a churl, thirty shillings as fine for not accompanying the host.[17]

When one comes to the so-called Introduction to the Dooms of Alfred (871–900), treason is definitely recognized as an unamendable crime. Ecclesiastical influences evidently did much to give direction to the evolution of the crime and to give shape to the matured idea which was set forth as follows:

> They, then, ordained, out of the mercy which Christ had taught, that secular lords, with their leave, might, without sin, take for almost every misdeed for the first offence, the money bot which they established; except in cases of treason against a lord, to which they dared not assign any mercy, because God Almighty adjudged none of them that despised Him, nor did Christ, the son of God, adjudge any to him who sold Him to death.[18]

It should be noted, however, that high and petty treason are not differentiated here, and that treason is not associated with the king's peace. In the main code of Alfred's Dooms the more purely Germanic ideas are evident, and the law establishes that it is necessary before all else that each man be faithful to his oath and pledge and respect his contract.[19] But, if anyone is compelled to do anything wrong thereby, be it the betrayal of his lord or aid in an unlawful undertaking, it is better that he break such an oath than fulfill it.[20] The old Germanic principles of fidelity are maintained in their complete integrity. Broken troth is the supreme offense, and is justified only in cases where keeping the oath leads to a greater injustice or treason. The first detailed definition of treason in Anglo-Saxon law is contained in a famous enactment of Alfred:

> If anyone plots against the king's life, of himself, or by harboring outlaws or faithless men in the king's service, let him be liable in his life and in all that he has. 1. If he wishes to prove himself true, let him do so according to the king's wergeld [i.e., by an oath equal to the king's wergeld]. 2. So, also, we ordain for all degrees, whether *ceorl* or *eorl*. He, who plots against his lord's life, shall be liable in his life to his lord, as well as in all that he has, or he shall prove himself true according to his lord's *wer*.[21]

Here high treason is specifically distinguished from petty treason, and the idea of conspiracy is emphasized over actual killing, as has been

---

[17] *Ine*, c. 51. Such a fine is designated *fyrd-wite*.
[18] *Alfred*, Introd., 49. Cf. Thorpe, *Ancient Laws*, p. 26.
[19] *Alfred*, c. 1.
[20] *Alfred*, c. 1, 1.
[21] *Alfred*, c. 4; 4, 1, 2. Cf. Hodgkin, *Anglo-Saxons*, II, 604.

observed in many continental codes.[22] The view advanced in this study is consistent with the position of Pollock and Maitland, who hold that conspiracy is not based on any original Germanic tradition, but is borrowed from the Roman law of *maiestas,* especially the provisions which relate to plotting against the lives of the republican magistrates and later of the emperors.[23] Further they consider that no aspect of Roman Law was more likely to be adopted by the Germanic invaders of the Empire and the barbarian conquerors of the *provinciales* than this material concerning the crime of majesty. Hence, when the idea of conspiracy is first encountered in England in the legislation of Alfred it may be presumed to have been imported from the continent, although one should not infer that the rulers of the barbarian kingdoms needed the formal example of the *lex Julia maiestatis* to impress upon them the importance of repressing plots and machinations against their lives. But, on the other hand, these authors hold rightly that "the close association of treason against the king with treason against one's personal lord who is not the king is eminently Germanic. This was preserved in the 'petty treason' of mediaeval and modern criminal law."[24] And it is precisely this bond of personal faith and troth between a king and his *fideles* and between a lord and his vassals, this element of a contractual allegiance, that is not discernible in Roman Law where the relation between emperor and subjects rests upon a basis of deference and veneration.[25]

An additional feature appears in this law which may be made the subject of dispute. This is the matter of a royal wergeld after the fashion of the ducal wergeld in Bavarian law.[26] As has been noted, the Introduction to Alfred's Dooms designates treason very definitely to be an

---

[22] Cf. *Ed. Roth* 1; *Leges Saxonum* 24; *Leges Baiuwariorum* 2, 1; *Leges Alamannorum* 23. See Pollock and Maitland (*History of English Law,* II, 503, 504), who, in speaking of the contrast between Roman Law and early English Law, observe that "the crime was in this case [treason] found, not in a harmful result, but in the endeavour to produce it, in machination, 'compassing,' 'imagining.' The strong feudal sentiment claimed as its own this new idea; the lord's life, as well as the king's, is to be sacred against plots or 'imaginations' "; also Brunner-von Schwerin, *Deutsche Rechtsgeschichte* (2nd ed.; Duncker and Humblot, Leipzig: 1928), II, 884, n. 26; *Codex Justinianus* 9, 8, 5 *Ad Legem Iuliam Maiestatis,* and *Codex Theodosianus* 9, 14, 3 *Ad Legem Corneliam de Sicariis,* for the principles of the *Lex Quisquis.*

[23] Cf. *Digest* 48, 4, 1, 1 *Ad Legem Iuliam Maiestatis;* Paulus *Sententiae* 5, 29, 1–2 *Ad Legem Iuliam Maiestatis;* Glanvill, 14, 1.

[24] Pollock and Maitland, *History of English Law,* I, 51–52.

[25] In general, on the problem of allegiance in barbarian law, see the essay on "Contractual Allegiance *vs.* Deferential Allegiance in Visigothic Law."

[26] Cf. *Lex Baiuvariorum* 2, 20, 1–5.

unamendable crime, and this precludes the possibility of a wergeld payment, such as is suggested in *Alfred*, c. 4, 1. The result is an apparent contradiction. Wilda pointed out in his *Strafrecht der Germanen* more than a century ago that a special wergeld was attached to the king, partly because of his descent from the first family of the land and partly because of the royal office vested in him. He then drew the distinction between the real wergeld belonging to the king through the circumstances of his exalted position and birth and payable to his relatives, and the *cynebot* or *cynegyld*, which pertains to the kingdom and is paid to the folk.[27] But Wilda acknowledged that treason is an inexpiable offense, and he attempted to reconcile the situation by suggesting that such a *wergeld* could not be paid in cases where the king was struck down premeditatedly, but only where he was struck down in the heat of anger. In the latter instance the offense cannot be construed as real treason. Thus, Wilda seemed to discriminate here much along the line of the difference that distinguishes murder (*morth*) from ordinary homicides in Germanic law. Also clearly he differentiated the person of the king from the office of king. This would make the determination of treason very much a matter of intent, and this is a most dangerous rule to apply to a crime whose scope tends to widen constantly, as well as a very awkward precedent to attach to the foundations of the English Common Law. Wilda further suggested that in cases of acknowledged treason it is possible that the people or the king's successor might allow the offender to redeem himself by paying the royal *wer* which, however, would be so large an amount that very few could pay it. Hence, the crime would be virtually unamendable in practice. The higher wergeld, he continued, was not so much the basis as the consequence of a higher law and a higher fine attached to the king, and this higher law partook of the nature of a special peace.[28] All crimes committed against the king must be amended by a heavier fine than in the case of anyone else, and were punished in a higher degree without being regarded as high treason.[29] This argument establishes some validity for the wergeld and

[27] W. E. Wilda, *Geschichte des deutschen Strafrechts* (Halle: C. A. Schwetschke, 1842), I: Das Strafrecht der Germanen, pp. 990–991; Brunner-von Schwerin, *D. R.*, II, 884–885.

[28] Cf. Wilda, *Strafrecht*, I, 258–264; 460–472.

[29] *Ibid.*, 991: "Das höhere wergeld war nicht sowohl der Grund, als vielmehr die Folge des höheren Rechtes und der höheren Busse, die dem König eigen waren, welches höhere Recht den Charakter eines besonderen Friedens annahm. . . . Alle Missethaten gegen den König begangen, mussten daher schwerer gebüsst werden,

proves equally that such a wergeld could not be offered ordinarily in restitution for plotting against the king's life, as set forth in *Alfred*, c. 4. Furthermore, a careful reading of the law shows that nothing is said to the effect that a man may redeem himself upon payment of the royal wergeld. It states merely that if a man wishes to clear himself, prove that he has been faithful, and is wrongfully charged with the crime, he must do so in accordance with some weighty method of proof equated to and corresponding with the scale of the royal wergeld. In other words, the defendant must have more compurgators or successfully pass a more difficult ordeal. It is not at all a question of allowing a guilty man to escape with the payment of "blood-money" or a fine.[30]

Very little additional legislation on treason appears in Alfred's Dooms. Scandals in the royal palace are repressed by a law stating that if anyone fights or draws his weapon in the king's house the king may kill him or let him live, provided he wants to forgive him.[31] The culprit is thus placed completely at the king's mercy. Similar special ecclesiastical peaces are established[32] which prohibit stealing from churches[33] and which maintain the right of asylum and sanctuary.[34] There are no laws specifically directed against *Landesverrat* although penalties are provided for attacks on fortified posts (*burgbryce*),[35] and an enactment in the Introduction establishes the death penalty for parricide.[36]

Additional legislation relating to treason appears in the laws of Aethelstan, Edmund, and Edgar of the early tenth century. Aethelstan (*ca.* 925–939) commands that those accused of plotting against their

---

als gegen irgend einen andern, waren in einem höhern Grade strafbar, ohne dass sie als Hochverrath angesehen wurden."

[30] Pollock and Maitland, *History of English Law*, I, 52: "The crime of treason was unatonable, and the charge had to be repelled by an oath adequate in number of oath-helpers, and perhaps in solemnity, to the wergild of the king or other lord as the case might be. If the accused could not clear himself by oath, and was driven to ordeal, he had to submit to the threefold ordeal." Cf. *ibid.*, II, 503, n. 6: "In old times the king had a wergild, but before we draw inferences from this we must remember both that a wergild was exacted when the slaying was unintentional, and that the price set on the king was no less than £ 240. Hardly in any case could such a sum be raised, except when the death of the king of one folk could be charged against another folk, as when Ine obtained a heavy sum from the men of Kent for the death of Mul."

[31] *Alfred*, c. 7.

[32] *Alfred*, c. 5.

[33] *Alfred*, c. 6.

[34] *Alfred*, c. 2 and 5.

[35] *Alfred*, c. 40.

[36] *Alfred*, Introd., c. 14.

lords shall hold their lives forfeit if they cannot purge themselves or come clean from the triple ordeal.[37] Punishment is also prescribed for breaches of the ecclesiastical peace.[38] And for the first time in Anglo-Saxon law, penalties are provided for the crimes of moneyers, a fact which would indicate the increasing influence of the Roman law. Aethelstan demands that "there be one money in the whole realm, and let no one mint money except in a town."[39] Furthermore, if a moneyer is found guilty he shall lose the hand with which he fashioned the illegal coin, but if he wants to clear himself he must submit to the ordeal of the hot iron and redeem the hand with which he is charged with having wrought the false money.[40] This crime is not associated with treason by Aethelstan, but it was to resume the connection, which it formerly possessed with that crime in the Roman law, in the later compilations of Glanvill and Bracton.[41] In a law of Edmund the special peace and rights of sanctuary of churches and certain royal forts are affirmed.[42] Edgar commands that the lives of those who have plotted the death of their lords shall never find safety in any refuge unless the king grants them protection.[43] He, too, ordains that there shall be but one money throughout the realm, and no one shall refuse it.[44]

The Dooms of Aethelred develop more fully the laws concerning the coinage. Thus, one reads:

Let every moneyer, who shall be accused that he has wrought false after it has been forbidden, go to the triple ordeal, and, if guilty, let him die. And no one shall have a moneyer save the king.[45]

And moneyers, who make counterfeit in the forests shall forfeit their lives unless the king show them mercy.[46]

The laws reiterate the necessity for "improving the coinage, so that there shall be one money throughout the land without counterfeit."[47] The seriousness of these crimes becomes evident when one notes that the penalty is death and that the accused has to clear himself through the

[37] *Aethelstan*, c. 2, 4.
[38] *Aethelstan*, c. 2, 5.
[39] *Aethelstan*, c. 2, 14.
[40] *Aethelstan*, c. 2, 14, 1.
[41] Cf. Glanvill, 14, 7; Bracton, f. 119b; Britton, I, 41; Fleta, p. 42. Also cf. *Codex Justinianus* 9, 24, 2 *De Falsa Moneta*.
[42] *Edmund*, c. 2, 2.
[43] *Edgar*, c. 3, 7.
[44] *Edgar*, c. 3, 8.
[45] *Aethelred*, c. 3, 8.
[46] *Aethelred*, c. 3, 16.
[47] *Aethelred*, c. 5, 26; 6, 32, 1.

triple ordeal.[48] It will be observed that these are practically the same
regulations prescribed for cases of high treason, so that crimes of falsification and treason are now associated through identical procedure and
penalties.

> If any one plots against the life of the king, let him forfeit his life, and if he
> will purge himself, let him do so according to the king's wergeld and with the
> triple ordeal following the English law.[49]
> And, if any one plots against the life of the king, let him forfeit his life and
> everything he has if it be proved against him, and if he will and can purge
> himself, let him do so with the hardest oath or with the triple ordeal accord-
> ing to the law of the English, or according to the law of the Danes, as the
> case may be.[50]

But in general, little is added to the definition of high treason established in Alfred, c. 4. Besides the matter of counterfeiting mentioned
above, other features of Aethelred's Dooms are certain distinct references to folk treason. The general principle is stated that the king's subjects should willingly undertake the repair of fortified posts and bridges,
and provide for the equipment of the royal navy and perform the duties
of military service, since those are matters promoting the general welfare (*for gemaenelicre neode*).[51] Military crimes detrimental to the
common weal are punished as follows:

> If anyone leaves the army without permission, when the king is with the
> army, let it be at peril of his life and all his estate; and whoever deserts the
> army when the king is not present shall be fined 120 shillings.[52]
> If anyone leaves the army without permission, when the king is with it, he
> shall imperil his estate.[53]

Desertion at a time when the king is accompanying the host is plainly
designated a more serious offense than desertion under other circumstances. Perhaps this may be explained on the ground that desertion in
the former instance might imperil the king's life, and therefore could
be construed as a sort of high treason. Finally, a law is established protecting the navy, which states that any one harming a public warship
must pay a fine, and if he destroys it so that it cannot be used he must

---

[48] Cf. *Edgar*, c. 1, 9: "the iron, for the triple ordeal, three pounds weight, and for
the single ordeal, one pound weight."
[49] *Aethelred*, c. 5, 30.
[50] *Aethelred*, c. 6, 37.
[51] *Aethelred*, c. 5, 26–27; 6, 32, 3 (*trinoda necessitas*).
[52] *Aethelred*, c. 5, 28.
[53] *Aethelred*, c. 6, 35. Here mention of the death penalty is conspicuously omitted.

recompense the damage in full.[54] In addition, he must pay the *mund-bryce* to the king for breaking the peace. The entire realm is considered to be in the royal *mundium* or under the king's protection, and since the king personifies public authority he is responsible for the maintenance of the general welfare. Thus, in a large measure, the king's peace and the peace of the land are identified. But traces of the original distinction remain in the compensation to the people which is kept separate from the special fine to the king.

The Dooms of Cnut of the eleventh century constitute, perhaps, the most fully developed body of Anglo-Saxon law. High treason is punished by death and confiscation of property: "If anyone shall plot the death of the king or of his lord in any way, let him forfeit his life and all that he has, unless he purge himself by the triple ordeal."[55] The idea of scandal emerges in a law stating that "if anyone fights in the king's household, he shall lose his life, unless the king shows him mercy."[56] Other laws are directed against the more general, undifferentiated type of treason, which may be either high treason against the king or petty treason against a lesser lord. Thus, one reads that "Whoever plots the death of his lord shall ever be in danger of his life."[57] And in another place, the ancient Germanic idea of "infidelity" is stressed instead of the Roman idea of conspiracy or plotting that becomes so common in the later Anglo-Saxon Dooms. "Infidelity toward one's lord (*hlafordswice*) is unamendable (*botleas*) according to the secular law," and is associated with the crimes of housebreaking (*husbryce*), arson (*baernet*), open theft (*open thyfth*), and manifest killing (*aebere morth*) which is undeniable. [58] Another enactment prescribes penalties for a crime resembling the Frankish *herisliz*.

The man who flees from his lord, or from his comrade, by reason of his cowardice, be it in the *ship-fyrd* or in the *land-fyrd*, shall forfeit all that he possesses and his life as well; and let his lord seize the property and the land that he [the lord] previously gave him; and, if he have *bocland*, let that pass into the hands of the king.[59]

[54] *Aethelred*, c. 6, 34.
[55] *Cnut* 2, 57.
[56] *Cnut* 2, 59; *Leges Henrici Primi* 13, 7; 80, 1–2; 80, 7.
[57] *Cnut* 2, 26; *L. H. P.* 75, 1–2.
[58] *Cnut*, 2, 64. Cf. *L. H. P.* 12, 1: "Quedam non possunt emendare, quae sunt: husbryce et baernet et open ðyfð et aebere mor et hlafordswice et infraccio pacis ecclesie vel manus regis per homicidium." It should be noted that these crimes are related through common characteristics, being alike unfaithful, treacherous, dishonorable, and deceitful.
[59] *Cnut* 2, 77; *L. H. P.* 13, 12; 43, 7.

But the *heriots* of the man, who falls in battle before his lord, be it within the land or abroad, shall be remitted; and his heirs may inherit his land and property, and justly divide it among themselves.[60]

Folk treason is not as carefully defined. The general principle is stated that one should willingly participate in the repair of forts and bridges and in the mobilization of the navy and army as often as the general welfare or common need requires it.[61] But, if any one neglects the performance of these duties he shall pay a fine of 120 shillings to the king, or he may clear himself.[62] However, if any one causes a capital breach of the peace (probably homicide) in the king's army he must lose his life or redeem it by the payment of his wergeld, but if he merely makes a minor breach of the peace (less than a homicide) he shall be fined according to what he has done.[63] Finally, those who become outlaws shall be at the king's mercy, and if they possess *bocland* (i.e., held by title-deed) it shall pass into the hands of the king regardless of whose vassal they are.[64] A special law states the penalities for counterfeiting:

Whoever makes counterfeit shall lose the hand with which he did the crime, and he may not redeem it with silver or gold or in any way. If he claims that the reeve gave him leave to commit the crime, let the reeve clear himself by a threefold oath [probably requiring 76 compurgators], and let him suffer the same doom as he who wrought the false "money."[65]

This extension of the law is clearly intended to prevent the connivance of public officers with counterfeiters, and shows how vital the king considered his policy of maintaining a single coinage throughout the realm. The introductory portion of Cnut's Dooms consists of ecclesiastical regulations supporting the special peace attached to churches and clergymen. One enactment possesses unusual interest because it seems to define what the relation should be between ecclesiastics and their lords, and suggests a considerable trend toward feudalism as reflected in the personal relation between lord and vassal.

We [ecclesiastics] believe that we should always be faithful and true to our lords, and that we should exalt their glory among all men and do as they wish us to do, because, whatever we do in just fidelity to our lords, may redound to our great advantage; and, surely, God is true to him who is rightly

[60] *Cnut* 2, 78. One might use "be it on land or at sea" as a possible alternative reading for "be it within the land or abroad."
[61] *Cnut* 2, 10.
[62] *Cnut* 2, 65; *L. H. P.* 13, 9.
[63] *Cnut* 2, 61; *L. H. P.* 13, 8.
[64] *Cnut* 2, 13.
[65] *Cnut* 2, 8, 1–2. Cf. *L. H. P.* 1, 5; 13, 3.

true to his lord. And, likewise, every lord has the very great duty that he treat his men justly.[66]

Finally, as the Anglo-Saxon period drew to its close, the tendency becomes apparent that the royal power is drawing a wide variety of offenses relating to public order and the general welfare into the special area of the king's peace. A brief summary of such crimes is contained in the *Leges Henrici Primi*, a late compilation, probably of the earlier twelfth century, based on the Dooms of Cnut and other similar materials.[67] Among the pleas placing a man at the mercy of the king are listed: breach of the peace established by the king; contempt for the royal writ; whatever is done to injure the king's person or whatever is done in contempt of his commands; the killing of royal servants or agents in a city, or in a castle, or wheresoever they happen to be; infidelity and treason; disrespect to the king; holding a castle without royal permission; outlawry. Whoever does these things shall be held accountable to the king's law, and if he have *bocland*, it shall pass into the king's hands; theft, if proved, shall merit death.[68] And, again, among the criminal or capital cases are named: theft, murder, treason to one's lord, robbery, outlawry, housebreaking, arson, and counterfeiting.[69] But securing control over whole classes of crimes was a slow process, and the royal peace long remained an attribute peculiar to specially designated and limited geographical areas or to specially designated persons and property. The tenor of the following laws will substantiate this assertion:

If anyone shall commit homicide in a house, or in a courtyard, or in a town, or in a castle, or in the army, or in the host of the king, let him be at the king's mercy in life, limb, and property.[70]

And if anyone shall assault another on the king's highway, which is the crime called *forestel*, let him pay one hundred shillings to the king.[71]

Besides, this code continues that "Whoever fights in the king's house shall pay with his life,"[72] and "whoever breaks the peace in the host shall lose his life and compound with his wergeld."[73] In addition, "Let coun-

---

[66] *Cnut* 1, 20.
[67] See Stephen, *Criminal Law*, I, 51–52, on the authenticity and significance of the *Leges Henrici Primi*.
[68] *L. H. P.* 13, 1.
[69] *L. H. P.* 47.
[70] *L. H. P.* 80, 1.
[71] *L. H. P.* 80, 2.
[72] *L. H. P.* 13, 7.
[73] *L. H. P.* 13, 8.

terfeiters lose a hand and redeem it in no wise";[74] "Whoever shall flee because of cowardice from his lord or companion in arms, whether in war by land or by sea, shall lose all that he has and his life besides, and his lord shall take back for his own the land and property which he gave him, and if it be *bocland,* it shall rightfully fall to the king."[75]

In conclusion, one cannot fail to be struck by the fact that the Anglo-Saxon Dooms, although written in a native Teutonic tongue and filled with purely Germanic legal ideas, contribute little to the general conception of treason and related offenses that has not already been encountered in the continental folk laws. The peculiar royal wergeld is only incidental to the study of treason and finds a close parallel in Bavarian law. The penalty for deserting the host, heavier when the king accompanies it than when he is absent, creates an interesting situation associating typical high treason and typical folk treason in a single crime; yet it has a modified counterpart in the Frankish *herisliz.* The strictly Germanic idea of *infidelitas* persists in Anglo-Saxon law, even in the most recent legislation, as the Dooms of Cnut attest, but the early definition of high treason in the laws of Alfred considers the essence of the crime to be conspiracy. The bond of fealty is always respected despite the incorporation of Roman concepts. However, as Pollock and Maitland assert, "A Roman element entered when men began to hear a little of the *crimen laesae maiestatis.* Less emphasis was thrown upon the idea of betrayal, though such terms as *traditio, proditio, seditio* are always pointing back to this—and plotting against the king's life or the lord's life became prominent."[76] Nevertheless, the term *maiestas* is not used, and there seems to be no reason to believe that the Anglo-Saxons understood that Roman conception better than their continental neighbors.[77] It is true that high treason consists of plotting the death of an individual who is the bearer of public authority, a king with executive powers far stronger than the ancient Germanic royalty that "ruled but did not govern." But the Anglo-Saxon king can hardly be considered to personify governmental authority in a regularly constituted state, for it was an age "becoming feudal," in which a ruler tended to be *dominus* as well as *rex.* The ruler's constitutional position was gravitating away

---

[74] *L. H. P.* 13, 3.

[75] *L. H. P.* 13, 12. Cf. *L. H. P.* 43, 7.

[76] Pollock and Maitland, *History of English Law,* II, 503.

[77] Regarding the absence and omission of the expression *maiestas* from the barbarian codes, see essay on "Blasphemy in the *Lex Romana Curiensis.*" Further consideration is given to this problem in the essay on "The Public Law of the Visigothic Code."

from the pole of sovereign majesty, which, of course, no Anglo-Saxon
king had ever attained, toward the opposite pole of mere *dominium.* It
is difficult to allocate his position exactly, or measure his progress along
this course with precision in the Anglo-Saxon period. The uncertain,
even precarious, condition of the state is evident when one observes
that it was still a time of outlawry and special peaces (*paces*). In an effort to secure the general welfare the king was endeavoring to attract
all particularly destructive and disruptive offenses into his special interest and special field of competence. Therefore, it must be given as a
final opinion that the Anglo-Saxon Dooms differ in no essential respect
as regards the sphere of public criminal law from the Germanic legislation on the continent, despite considerable evidence of Roman influence
and Christian purpose.

IX

The Public Law of the Ripuarian, Alamannic, and Bavarian Codes*

Any estimate of the legal contribution of those Germanic peoples who did not fully penetrate the boundaries of the Roman Empire, but, instead, remained mostly within their native lands beyond the Rhine and Danube rivers, must recognize that the legal matter of the North is, in general, later in point of time and more strictly Germanic with respect to content. It is true, also, that the chronology of some of the codes is by no means certainly established and that Roman influences are markedly present, though subordinate, in many instances. The Teutonic quality of any particular code of the *leges barbarorum* may not be assumed solely on the basis of chronological and geographical considerations, with the largest number of Germanic traits apparent in those codes which are oldest and intended for use in regions farthest from the Roman provinces. Each set of laws must be regarded independently and analyzed for its own specific content. And for the purpose of this study, only such matter as relates to public law and offenses against the state can be deemed relevant. Thus, the Salic Code, which is perhaps the oldest of the barbarian folk laws and the most widely removed from Roman influences, contains little material relating directly to public criminal law and need not be examined here. However, the Ripuarian kinsmen of the

* Reprinted by special permission of the Editor from *Medievalia et Humanistica*, 2 (1944), pp. 3–27. Read in part before the Southern Classical Association at Charleston, S. C., on November 29, 1940.

Salian Franks did possess a closely related body of law that provides several highly significant legal concepts.

The Ripuarian Franks were established along the middle Rhine frontier and were thus located at the very portals of the Roman Empire. Their tribal authority seems to have been surrendered gradually under Salian domination. Allied with Clovis even before the battle of Vouillé in 507, they were induced by that crafty chieftain to rid themselves of their own royal house by a typical scheme of Salian duplicity and to elevate him to the vacant throne as the ruler of the united Frankish nation. Certainly the tribal independence of the Ripuarians and a measure of their tribal identity must have been lost before the middle of the sixth century.[1] However, it is commonly agreed that the formulation of the *Lex Ribuaria* can hardly be attributed to a period earlier than this, and it is unlikely that it attained its final form until some time in the course of the eighth century. Maitland observes that it is uncertain whether the Ripuarian Franks possessed a written law in the time of the eastern emperor, Justinian, but suggests that the main part of the *Lex Ribuaria* may be older than A.D. 596.[2] To what degree their close association with the related Salian tribe affected this legislation one cannot conjecture with assurance. However, the common Frankish characteristics must have tended under these conditions to eliminate tribal differences and peculiarities. Maitland, assuming the great antiquity of the Salic Law, states that "Though there are notable variations, it [*Lex Ribuaria*] is in part a modernized edition of the *Salica,* showing the influence of the clergy and of Roman Law."[3] Such an interpretation really makes the *Lex Ribuaria* that step in the evolution of Frankish Law at which the process of incorporating ecclesiastical and Roman elements begins, while the *Lex Salica* is considered the primitive, thoroughly Germanic archetype.[4]

---

[1] Cf. Gregory of Tours, *History of the Franks,* ed. by O. M. Dalton (Oxford: University Press, 1927), I (Introduction), 94–95; *ibid.,* II, 29 (40); Fredegar, *Monumenta Germaniae Historica, SS Rerum Meroving.,* ed. by B. Krusch (Hanover: Hahn, 1888), II, 103 (iii, #25).

[2] Maitland, *Select Essays in Anglo-American Legal History* (Boston: Little, Brown, 1907), I, 14; also H. Brunner, *Deutsche Rechtsgeschichte* (2nd ed.; Leipzig: Duncker and Humblot, 1906), I, 444–448; Schröder-von Künssberg, *Lehrbuch der deutschen Rechtsgeschichte* (6th ed.; Berlin and Leipzig: De Gruyter, 1922), pp. 264–265.

[3] Maitland, *Select Essays,* I, 14.

[4] The entire question of the chronology of the *Lex Salica* and *Lex Ribuaria* offers peculiar difficulties, especially since the dating of the *Salica* has been a matter of grave dispute among authorities. Cf. series of controversial articles in *Neues Archiv*

A direct examination of the *Lex Ribuaria* reveals a situation still Germanic in its most essential features.[5] The long series of wergeld tariffs, usually found in the *leges barbarorum*, appears covering a wide variety of crimes, distinguishing every manner of social station, and establishing penalties suited to the offense and to the rank of the parties concerned. The Ripuarian tribal bias or identity is preserved in this wergeld system, since the killing of a Frank (presumably Salian) is regulated by a provision quite separate from that dealing with the homicide of a native Ripuarian.[6] It is noteworthy, however, that the composition is on an equal basis in both cases, a payment of two hundred *solidi* being levied alike in the case of a *Francus* or *ingenuus Ribuarius*. Likewise, the

---

der Gesellschaft für ältere deutsche Geschichtskunde: Mario Krammer, "Forschungen zur Lex Salica," XXXIX (1914), 601–691; Bruno Krusch, "Der Umsturz der kritischen Grundlagen der Lex Salica. Eine textkritische Studie aus der alten Schule," XL (1915–1916), 497–579; Claudius Freiherr von Schwerin, "Zur Textgeschichte der Lex Salica," XL (1915–1916), 581–637; Mario Krammer, "Zum Textproblem der Lex Salica. Ein Erwiderung," XLI (1917–1919), 103–156; "Gutachtliche Aeusserungen über Krammer's Ausgabe der Lex Salica" (a critical symposium), XLI (1917–1919), 375–418; Ernst Heymann, "Zur Textkritik der Lex Salica," XLI (1917–1919), 419–524. For a sound exposition of the older views regarding the Salic Law, see Brunner, *D. R.*, I, 427–442.

A good survey of the recent literature on this subject, representing German research under the National Socialists, may be found in a paper by Claudius Freiherr von Schwerin, entitled "Germanische Rechtsgeschichte" and published in *Forschungen und Fortschritte* (20 May 1941), 165–168. Baron von Schwerin points out that H. K. Claussen ("Ueber die Beziehungen der Lex Salica zu den Volksrechten der Alemannen, Bayern und Ribuarier," *Zeitschrift für Rechtsgeschichte* [2], LVI [1936], 359 seq.) attributes the *Lex Ribuaria* to the eighth century, whereas K. Beyerle establishes it in the time of Dagobert I and concludes that it was not primarily legislation for the Ripuarian folk but for a political district (*Z R. G.* [2], LV [1935], 1 seq.). Furthermore, G. Baesecke relates this Ripuarian legal material to the Burgundian *Gundobaba* on the basis of a list of counts contained in the MSS (*Z. R. G.* (2), LXIX (1939), 233 seq.). Also see Baesecke, "Die deutschen Worte der germanischen Gesetze," *Beiträge zur Geschichte der deutschen Sprache und Literatur*, LXIX (1935), 1–101, for additional information on the dating of these laws based on the philological evidence. The most comprehensive work of textual criticism on the *Lex Ribuaria* is by R. Buchner who has evaluated the MS materials by a sound textual method in *Textkritische Untersuchungen zur Lex Ribuaria* (Leipzig: K. W. Hiersemann, 1940).

[5] The best text of the *Lex Ribuaria* is still that of R. Sohm in *Monumenta Germaniae Historica, Leges* (Hanover: Hahn, 1883), Tomus V, pp. 185–268, with glossary on pp. 277–288 by K. Zeumer.

[6] *Lex Ribuaria* (ed. by Sohm) 36, 1: "Si quis Ribuarius advenam Francum interficerit, 200 solidos culpabilis iudicetur." Cf. *L. Rib.* 7: "Si quis homo ingenuum Ribuarium interficerit, 200 solidos culpabilis iudicetur." These enactments govern ordinary homicides by violence. See *L. Rib.* 15 for special heinousness of murder with triple composition of 600 *solidi*.

tribal identity is maintained against Burgundian, Roman, Alamannian, Frisian, and Saxon as well, through discriminatory wergelds for homicides varying in amount for different nationalities.[7] The ecclesiastical influence is marked, as evinced in wergeld tariffs regulating the homicides of clergymen from simple priest to bishop.[8] Also, the church appears as a privileged special interest, not only because a special wergeld was attached to its officials, but because its merest menial, as well, could be compounded for only at a higher rate than in the case of similar menials in the service of private individuals.[9] The same sort of privileged special interest pertained to the crown, since royal servants of various types were protected by higher wergelds,[10] usually following the scale prescribed for ecclesiastical servants.[11] Thus, the homicide of a count could be compounded only at the high rate of six hundred *solidi* (*ter ducenus solidus*), the wergeld of a presbyter.[12] Yet the royal interest was concerned not only with its officers and servants, but with other persons who were taken under its special protection and placed *in truste regia*.[13] The lives of such men could be compounded only at the rate of six hundred *solidi* set for counts, and all injuries done them must be compensated according to a triple wergeld. The king's special private interest in his servants and familiars was extended in the case of these men until it became a veritable "king's peace." The execution of public authority was in the process of being delegated to or assumed by an individual, but the royal peace did not yet reach out over all men and all places at all times. In ordinary procedure, the same difficulty that had appeared earlier in the Salic Code is experienced in getting offenders into court and forcing them to submit to the law.[14] The king could declare a man to be *wargus, expulsus, forbannitus*, that is, *utlagatus* or outlaw,[15] but he might be of little positive assistance in securing redress for an individual. Much must still have depended on private action,

---

[7] *L. Rib.* 36, 2–4.

[8] *L. Rib.*, 36, 5–9 (*clericum ingenuum, subdiaconum, diaconum, presbyterum, episcopum*).

[9] *L. Rib.* 10, 1–2; 11, 3; 14, 1. Note that *L. Rib.* 65, 2 and 87 seem to provide a special mitigation of punishment in the case of ecclesiastical servants.

[10] *L. Rib.* 9; 10, 2; 11, 1–3; 14, 1; also with special mitigation of penalty for royal servants in 65, 2 and 87.

[11] Cf. *L. Rib.* 9 and 10, where homicide of either an ecclesiastical or a royal servant is amendable at 100 *solidi*.

[12] *L. Rib.* 53, 1–2.

[13] *L. Rib.* 11, 1.

[14] *L. Rib.* 32, 1–4; cf. *Lex Salica*, 1, 1–5; 56.

[15] *L. Rib.* 85, 2; 87.

though revenge was probably tempered by the legal regulations. The *Lex* does not indicate whether the *Sippe* or expanded kinship group formally retained its earlier public authority.[16] It still existed as a corporate entity that could receive inheritances in lack of nearer heirs, and still consisted of those who would have received the wergeld of the deceased, had he been killed.[17] Perhaps one may assume that the *Sippe* had lost most of its earlier public functions and was now primarily a private agent, but an agent that actively maintained the right of revenging the injuries of its members when the authority of the state proved inadequate. Indeed, one derives a general impression that the Ripuarian Code represents a transitional era in which the chief instruments of social control embodied in state powers are only in the "process of becoming public."

Despite these limitations, the royal office presents a well-defined public character, already attaching particular interests to itself. Hence injuries done the king constitute high treason. On the other hand, the supreme treason among the Germanic peoples was private in its essence, being a breach of faith pledged by man to man; it was broken troth, *Treubruch, infidelitas.* This situation is neither contradictory nor paradoxical, since the royal office was a public position rendered secure through the medium of personal contract with the subjects. The result is that high treason is defined thus in the *Lex Ribuaria:* "If any man shall be unfaithful [*infidelis*] to his king, let him pay with his life and let all

---

[16] The relation of the *Sippe, Geschlecht* or family-clan group (Anglo-Saxon *maegth*), to the incipient state is a highly controversial subject that transcends the limits of this study. Brunner, *D. R.,* I, 119, presents the traditional views. "Das Geschlecht hatte gewisse öffentlichrechtliche Funktionen, die bei entwickelteren Verhältnissen als Aufgaben der Staatsgewalt erscheinen." However, one must remember that the *Sippe* like the Greek *polis* was a "life" which was not limited to political activity, but which embraced the economic, military, religious, and legal aspects of society. Thus, the *Geschlecht* or *Sippe* becomes the *fara, fyrd,* when considered as a division of the host or army, and it seems likely that, considered as an area of residence, it becomes the *Dorf* or *vicus.* Also, the burden of authority must be regarded as passing successively from one social grouping to another wider, superior group by a natural evolutionary process. Cf. Sir Paul Vinogradoff, *Historical Jurisprudence* (London: Humphrey Milford, 1920), I, 351–353. Thus, the household and family (*Hausgemeinschaft, Familie, Geschlecht*) expand into wider circles of relatives (*Sippschaften, Verwandtschaften*), which become communities of persons not necessarily related (*Gemeinde*), and these, in turn, merge into tribes which combine to form an entire people (*Volk*). Finally, the stage of social development represented by the folk laws indicates the transition from *Volk* to *Staat,* from an ethnic group to a political organ.

[17] *L. Rib.* 67, 1: "cui weregildum eius, si interfectus fuisset, legitimi obvenibat."

his property be forfeit to the treasury."[18] The king is elevated distinctly above his fellows, and no wergeld is allowed in his case. But there is no trace of Roman *laesa maiestas* here—even the expression *maiestas* does not appear—it is all Germanic breach of faith or *infidelitas*.[19] One may not allege the absence of Roman influences, but certainly they are organically integrated with the Germanic custom in this code. Rather, ecclesiastical and Roman expressions are employed where the Germanic law is extended to cover the cases of ecclesiastics and Romans. The ideas of the Roman law are not incorporated so that they alter Germanic legal conceptions. Following the enactment concerning high treason one reads: "Moreover, if anyone shall kill a near relative, or shall commit incest, let him suffer exile and let all his property be forfeit to the treasury."[20] This close association of parricide with high treason and of crimes of infamy with crimes of infidelity was already an ancient feature of Germanic customary law which had been observed by Tacitus in his *Germania*.[21] Treason against land and folk (*Landesverrat, perduellio*) does not appear conspicuously in this legislation and is mentioned only by implication in its relation to military offenses. Thus, one finds that "If anyone shall kill a man or steal from a man in the host or army, let him compound for the act in accordance with a triple wergeld";[22] that "If anyone shall have been summoned according to law into the king's service or into the host or for any other purpose, and if he shall not have answered the summons, unless detained by sickness, let him be fined in the sum of sixty *solidi*."[23] Hence, in general, the *Lex Ribuaria* conveys the impression that it is genuinely Germanic in spirit and content, that it refers to a condition of increasing royal authority and centralization of power, and that offenses against the state are primarily breaches of faith, *Treubruch, infidelitas*.

[18] *L. Rib.* 69, 1: "Si quis homo regi infidelis exsteterit, de vita conponat, et omnes res suas fisco censeantur."

[19] See essays on "The Idea of Majesty in Roman Political Thought" and "Contractual Allegiance vs. Deferential Allegiance."

[20] *L. Rib.* 29, 2: "Si autem quis proximum sanguinis interficerit, vel incestum commiserit, exilio susteniat, et omnes res suas fisco censeantur."

[21] Cf. Tacitus *Germania*, c. 12: "Licet apud concilium accusare quoque et discrimen capitis intendere. Distinctio poenarum ex delicto. Proditores et transfugas arboribus suspendunt; ignavos et imbelles et corpore infames caeno ac palude, iniecta insuper crate, mergunt. Diversitas supplicii illuc respicit, tanquam scelera ostendi oporteat, dum puniuntur, flagitia abscondi."

[22] *L. Rib.* 63, 1-2. Cf. *Leges Visigothorum*, ed. by Zeumer in *Monumenta Germaniae Historica, Leges* (Hanover and Leipzig: Hahn, 1902), Sectio I, Tomus I, 2, 1, 7; 2, 1, 33.

[23] *L. Rib.* 65, 1. Cf. *L. Vis.* (ed. by Zeumer) 2, 1, 7; 2, 1, 33.

Another closely related people from the point of view of racial affinity and of geographical propinquity are the Alamanni. This tribe was located above the Ripuarian Franks along the upper waters of the Rhine and possessed a body of customary law, portions of which may be of little later date than the *Lex Ribuaria*. The early contacts between the Franks and Alamanni were not amicable and resulted in an attack by the Alamanni upon the Ripuarians, whose king Sigebert was injured seriously at the ensuing battle of Tolbiacum or Zülpich. As a consequence, Clovis, King of the Salian Franks on the lower Rhine, was called to the aid of his kinsmen and helped them win a decisive victory in a second engagement fought in 495 or 496 in Alsace, probably near Strasbourg.[24] The Alamanni were driven southward into Baden, Württemberg, and eastern Switzerland. Many were compelled to become Frankish vassals and were included later within the duchy of Swabia, while a small remnant took refuge beyond the Rhine in Rhaetia under the protection of the Ostrogothic king, Theodoric, forming a buffer state between the Ostrogoths and the Franks.[25] Meanwhile, the Ripuarian Franks occupied the territory on the upper Rhine vacated by the Alamanni and converted it into the Frankish duchy of Franconia or East Francia. Later Clovis persuaded the Ripuarian prince Chloderic to assassinate his father, Sigebert; then, posing as Sigebert's avenger, Clovis devised the assassination of Chloderic and brought about the union of all the Franks, Salian and Ripuarian, situated in the Rhine valley.[26] The subsequent history of the Alamanni can hardly be considered apart from the rise of the great Frankish power which had defeated and dispersed them.[27]

The earliest body of Alamannic law is made up of five fragments, known collectively as the *Pactus Alamannorum*, which may date from

---

[24] Cf. J. B. Bury, *The Invasion of Europe by the Barbarians* (London: Macmillan, 1928), pp. 238–239. Note *Hist. Fran.*, ii, 27 (37), on Sigebert at Zülpich; ii, 21 (30), on battle of Strasbourg and conversion of Clovis; also Dalton, *History of the Franks*, I (Introd.), 171; Fredegar, iii, 21, in *M. G. H., SS. rer. Merov.*, II, 101. See note by Dalton, II, 498 [21 (30)], on possibility that the battle of Zülpich may be identified with the so-called battle of Strasbourg—a view not sustained by Bury.

[25] See Dalton, I (Introd.), 171, n. 3; J. B. Bury, *History of the Later Roman Empire* (2nd ed.; London: Macmillan, 1923), I, 461; F. Dahn, *Die Könige der Germanen* (Leipzig: Breitkopf and Härtel, 1902), IX (1), 64–65; G. Waitz, *Deutsche Verfassungsgeschichte* (3rd ed.; Berlin: Weidmann, 1882), II (1), 56–57.

[26] Dalton, *Hist. Fran.*, II, 29 (40).

[27] Cf. C. Pfister, "Franks," *Encyclopaedia Britannica* (11th ed.; Cambridge: University Press, 1910–1911), XI, 36.

the beginning of the seventh century.[28] The *Pactus* is not commonly regarded as a private compilation but was probably drafted by an official commission of the Frankish king. Its content is chiefly private law, criminal as well as civil, and it contains numerous peculiar Teutonic expressions, emphasizing its fundamentally Germanic character. Many of these expressions seem to be derived from the Salian Franks and do not appear in later Alamannic legislation. Furthermore, it should be noted that many early Teutonic words contained in the *Pactus* belong to the period of transition from the Old Germanic tongue (*Altgermanisch*) to Old High German (*Althochdeutsch*), which occurred toward the beginning of the seventh century.[29] This philological evidence adds weight to the view that the *Pactus* belongs to the early seventh century, having been published possibly during the reign of the Merovingian king, Dagobert I. However, like the Salic Law, little may be found in it that casts light on the nature of the state and of public authority. Approximately a century later (*ca.* 720) a second body of Alamannic law was issued, called the *Lex Alamannorum* or *Leges Alamannorum*.[30] One tradition maintains that this compilation originated in an agreement between the great Alamannic barons and Duke Landfrid who governed Swabia from 709 to 730, while an alternative tradition holds that the *Lex* was promulgated under the Merovingian king, Clothar I (717–719), the only Frankish ruler of the period bearing that name who was contemporary with Duke Landfrid.[31] These two traditions are not entirely inconsistent when one considers the weakness of the Frankish kings and the strength of the Swabian dukes at that time. Thus one may assume that the *Lex* was promulgated while Clothar was king of Austrasia but is essentially the result of a local arrangement between the Swabian duke and his barons. The sovereign

[28] The best edition of the *Pactus Alamannorum* is by K. Lehmann in *M. G. H.*, *Leges* (Hanover: Hahn, 1888), Sectio I, Tomus V, Pars 1, pp. 21–33. The definitive edition of the *Lex Alamannorum* is, likewise, by Lehmann in this same volume, pp. 35–159. The Latin index and Germanic glossary on pp. 60–70 are most valuable.

[29] Schröder-von Künssberg, *Lehrbuch*, p. 269.

[30] For the historical background and textual tradition of the Alamannic laws, see H. Brunner, *D. R.*, I, 448–454 and the Latin preface of Lehmann's edition, pp. 3–19.

[31] The first tradition is derived from the *A* group of codices, containing twelve different MSS of which the codex Sangallensis is regarded by Lehmann as the primary codex. The Prologue of the *Lex* in the *A* group reads: "In Christi nomine incipit textus lex Allamannorum, qui temporibus Lanfrido filio Godofrido renovata est." The *B* group of codices, which are more numerous and include thirty-eight MSS and three additional variants, substitutes the name of King Clothar for Duke Lanfrid in the Prologue which reads: "Incipit lex Alamannorum quae temporibus Hlodharii regis—constituta est."

power of the Frankish king is acknowledged in theory by the duke of
the Alamanni; yet throughout the law the duke appears to possess decisive political power within his duchy.

These later laws differ in several respects from the early custom of
the *Pactus* inasmuch as they are permeated with Roman and ecclesiastical influences. Their codification seems to have been performed under
the supervision of persons who were acquainted with the systematic
arrangement of the Roman Law. A formal and regular separation of
the laws into suitable categories and classifications is evident. In addition, much that is obviously Roman has been incorporated into the
content of the law. However, the question of whether Roman expressions, terminology, and ideas have been assimilated organically in their
Roman sense and spirit must be answered negatively from general
considerations to be investigated shortly. The *leges* are divided topically
into three sections: cases relating to ecclesiastics,[32] cases pertaining to
the duke,[33] and cases settled customarily among the people.[34] Thus, the
existence of three separate groups within the state is recognized, each
of which possesses its own special private or possibly corporate interests. First of all, the church secures recognition of its own peculiar
property-holding rights[35] and of the idea of sanctuary.[36] Next, it secures
protection by law for its officers and servants.[37] Finally, a special peace
is established under specified conditions, as set forth in the law *De eo,
qui in presbiteri curtem armatus ingreditur*,[38] and *De eo, qui in curte
episcopi armatus ingreditur*.[39] The second of these laws states: "If anyone shall enter a bishop's courtyard, armed, contrary to law, an offense

[32] *Leges Alamannorum* (ed. by Lehmann) 1–22 (codex *A*).

[33] *L. Alam.* 23–43: "De causis, qui ad duce pertinent" (codex *A*).

[34] *L. Alam.* 44–91: "De rixis, quae saepe fieri solent in populo" (codex *A*).

[35] *L. Alam.* 1, 1–2: "De liberis, qui res suas ad ecclesiam Dei tradunt" (codex
B); 2, 1–2: "De liberis, qui res suas ad ecclesiam Dei tradunt et in beneficium sub
usufructuario accipiunt"; 18: "Ut nullus laicus rem ecclesiae absque carta praesu-
mat possidere."
Unless otherwise stated, the captions cited for particular laws will be derived
from codex *B*, since they are omitted frequently in codex *A*. The notation of the
laws is based on the arrangement of codex *A*, as the differences between *A* and *B*,
though slight, are confusing.

[36] *L. Alam.* 3, 1–3: "De liberis vel servis, qui ad ecclesiam confugiunt"; 4: "De
liberis, qui infra ianuas ecclesiae interfecti fuerint."

[37] *L. Alam.* 11–15, which deal with injuries to church officers: *episcopus,
presbiter, diaconus, monachus, clericus*. Cf. *L. Alam.* 8: "De colonis ecclesiae
occisis"; 16: "De liberis, qui ad ecclesiam dimissi sunt, si occidantur."

[38] *L. Alam.* 10.

[39] *L. Alam.* 9.

called by the Alamanni *aisstera anti* [*manu violenta*], let him pay eighteen *solidi*. If he shall enter the house, let him pay thirty-six *solidi*." The double composition required for entering the house forcibly under arms indicates that a breach of the *Heimfrieden* has occurred in addition to the breach of the special ecclesiastical peace.[40] This curious sanctity of a man's private dwelling will be alluded to again later. One may not venture to call breaches of these special "peaces" (*Frieden*), treason; yet they occupy a peculiar intermediate position between purely private offenses against individuals and treasonable attacks against public authority or a body politic. As a matter of political theory, an element of treason enters into such breaches in the exact degree to which public authority has been delegated to the special interest and is involved in the special peace.[41]

The cases recognized as falling under the duke's personal jurisdiction relate to infringements of special ducal interests. Among these cases one finds high treason (*Hochverrat*), treason against land and folk (*Landesverrat*), breaches of the ducal peace (analogous to the king's peace), and other related offenses.[42] Heading the list, high treason is referred to under the caption *De eo, qui mortem ducis consiliatus fuerit* as follows:

If anyone shall have plotted the death of the duke and it shall have been proved against him, let him forfeit his life or redeem it in such manner as the duke or the leaders of the people[43] shall consider suitable; if he shall wish to redeem himself under oath, let him swear with twelve *nominati*[44] in the church in the presence of the duke or his representative.[45]

[40] The special sanctity of the home and the notion that "a man's house is his castle" may possibly revert to a very early time when the *Sippe* was an agent for enforcing authority of a public nature. It is notable that forcible entry in a man's house or burning a man's house is a most heinous crime throughout the folk laws. Also, killing or injuring a man within his own house is a far graver matter than committing the same offense elsewhere. Cf. W. E. Wilda, *Geschichte des deutschen Strafrechts* (Halle: C. A. Schwetschke, 1842), I: Das Strafrecht der Germanen, pp. 241–245.

[41] See essay on "Contractual vs. Deferential Allegiance" for references to this difficult problem of the Germanic *paces* or *Frieden*.

[42] Cf. Dahn, *Die Könige der Germanen*, IX (1), 343–344 for a brief survey of treason among the Alamanni.

[43] Cf. Waitz, *D. V.*, II (2), 182, n. 1, concerning *principes populi*.

[44] Cf. K. Lehmann in *M. G. H., Leges*, Sectio I, Tom. V, Pars 1, p. 84. n. 5: " 'Nominati' Legis in Pacto 'electi' nominantur." However, the distinction between the *nominati* and the *electi*, mentioned in several barbarian codes, remains ambiguous in most cases. Possibly the *nominati* represent appointive selections by a judge or other official, while the *electi* are chosen by the people in some sort of elective procedure.

[45] *L. Alam.* 23.

Three peculiar features distinguish this law, which is perplexing in many respects. In the first place, apparently the offender might redeem his life if the duke felt disposed to allow redemption in lieu of the death penalty. Thus, he was completely at the duke's mercy in this regard. Such redemption, if permitted by the duke, implies the payment of a composition, and the terms were presumably to be set at the discretion of the duke. But it would seem that the defendant might claim, as a right, the opportunity to establish his innocence through compurgation. This ceremony, however, must be conducted in the duke's presence, and the oaths must be taken by twelve appointed or chosen men in a church, thus adding to the gravity of the occasion. Every effort is made to safeguard the duke's interests. Hence, one may state in general that the duke has a right to insist on the death penalty or he may accept a composition on his own terms, provided the accused does not demand that he be given a chance to clear himself by a most difficult compurgation. Secondly, the entire law refers to a duke and not to a king. The duke of the Alamanni was unquestionably a bearer of public authority of a kind essentially the same as that possessed by the Frankish kings, although it was a delegated authority. The matter of subordination does not enter here to the extent that it does in Roman legal theory, where one finds a hierarchy of officials possessing delegated powers of a carefully restricted nature. Nevertheless, this distinction in title makes it impossible to say that this is a provision for a "royal" wergeld: it is a "ducal" wergeld, if the composition paid by the offender can be considered in the light of a wergeld at all. It seems more probable that, when the duke allowed composition, the payment should be viewed in the light of an arbitrarily assessed fine. In any case, the offense is high treason because it is directed against the administrator of public authority. Finally, this law refers specifically to plotting the death of the duke (*in mortem duci consiliatus fuerit*). And the use of the expression *in mortem consiliatus fuerit* instead of *infidelis fuerit* must signify that this provision was constructed on the basis of the Roman law dealing with *laesa maiestas* and that it is no unadulterated case of Germanic *Treubruch.*[46] The theoretical conception of majesty is probably lacking

[46] Cf. *Digest* 48, 4, 1–3 *Ad Legem Iuliam Maiestatis*, which indicates the idea of conspiracy under the formula *cuius opera dolo malo consilium initum erit*; R. de Glanville, *Tractatus de Legibus* 14, 1. Also see *Edictus Rothari*, ed. by Bluhme in *M. G. H.* (1889), Legum Tomus V, 1: "Si quis contra animam regis cogitaverit aut consiliaverit"; *Leges Visigothorum*, ed. by Zeumer, 2, 1, 7: "Quicunque . . . in necem vel abiectionem nostram sive subsequentium regum intendere vel intendisse proditus videtur esse vel fuerit"; also 6, 2, 1; *Lex Baiuvariorum*, ed. by Walter

here; yet the form and content of the Roman Law are clearly apparent. Despite this, the Roman spirit resists amalgamation with specifically Germanic phenomena such as compurgation and wergelds, and the incompatibility of the two legal tempers insures a solid Germanic foundation in the *leges barbarorum*.

A subsequent law has a more truly Germanic ring of the sort that was to sound at frequent intervals during the ensuing centuries: *De filio ducis, qui contra patrem suum surrexerit.*[47] This law states:

1. If any duke has a son so rebellious and evil, that he attempts to revolt against his father either because of his own folly or because of the counsels of evil men who desire to despoil the province [Alamannia], and if the son rises up with hostile design against his father, while his father is yet competent to perform his duties, to lead his army, to ride his horse and to be useful to his king, and if his son wishes to dishonor him or to possess his realm [*aut per raptum regnum eius possedere*][48] through forcible seizure [*raptum*], may that son not obtain that which he attempts to secure. And if his father should conquer him and be able to capture him, let him be in his father's power to exile from the province or send away whithersoever he pleases, or at the mercy of his lord, the king; and let no more of his father's inheritance pertain to him, because he has committed an unlawful act against his father.

2. And if he has brothers, let them divide their father's property among themselves according to the king's wishes; but to him who rebelled against his father, let them give no part. And if he who rebelled shall be the only heir, let the property which that duke possessed come, after his death, into the hands of the king to be given to whomsoever the king pleases, or even to that son of the duke who rebelled if he casts himself at the king's feet to secure this favor, but if the king wishes to give it to someone else, it is in his power to do so.

(Berlin: Reimer, 1824), 2, 1; *Leges Saxonum*, ed. by von Schwerin (Leipzig: Hansche Buchhandlung, 1918), 24; Alfred, ed. by Liebermann, (Halle: Max Niemeyer, 1903), 4, 1–2, and other Anglo-Saxon Dooms.

Note Pollock and Maitland, *The History of English Law before the Time of Edward I* (2nd ed.; Cambridge: University Press, 1923), I, 51–52, which states that the idea of conspiracy probably "does not represent any original Germanic tradition, but is borrowed from the Roman law of *maiestas*"; II, 502, which observes that in later English law of the feudal period the crime of treason encompasses not merely "the harmful result, but the endeavor to produce it, in machination, 'compassing,' 'imagining' "; Brunner-von Schwerin, *Deutsche Rechtsgeschichte* (2nd ed.; Munich and Leipzig: Duncker and Humblot, 1928), II, 884, with n. 25. I do not consider that the validity of this theory is impaired by the presence of the idea of "plotting" in the Icelandic *Egils-saga* (ca. A.D. 970), c. 13, which is a strictly Germanic source and could hardly reflect Roman influence.

[47] *L. Alam.* 35, 1–2; cf. *L. Baiuv.* 2, 9.

[48] The expression *per raptum regnum* implies more than mere forcible seizure of the land of the realm and includes the illegal seizure of the office of duke and the functions of public authority associated with that office.

These provisions are infused with an eminently Germanic spirit and portray a situation that arose again and again during the barbarian period and in later feudal times as well. The personal bias of Germanic legal thought is reflected in such breaches of fidelity. When the son becomes able and mature enough to cope with his father with any chance of success, he assumes public authority in contempt of his father and, in a very real sense, steals (*raptus*) it and makes off with it. Clearly this is no *maiestas*, resting on a substantial basis of territoriality and associated with state sovereignty, that may be thus seized. Another regulation probably derived from Roman Law and closely related to high treason is entitled *De eo, qui sigillum aut mandatum ducis neglexerit.*[49] Similar provisions, dealing with insubordination and negligence, may be noted in the Visigothic Code.[50] Such insulting disregard for the duke's commands was associated naturally with this general category of crime.

In the Alamannic Law *Landesverrat* is included among the cases wherein prosecution falls within the province of the ducal interest, although originally it must have been the most important type of case that could come before the people. When the duke came to assume public authority in increasing measure he seems to have set aside such cases that he might investigate and judge the matter in person. One very significant law appears, entitled *De homine, qui gentem extraneam infra provinciam invitaverit.* It states:

> If any man shall invite a foreign people to enter the province that they may devastate the land after the manner of an enemy or burn houses, and if this fact shall be proved against him, let that man either lose his life or go into exile, wheresoever the duke may send him, and let his property be confiscated to the public treasury.[51]

This is a clear-cut instance of external treason or *Landesverrat an den äusseren Feind*. Other regulations follow dealing with various violations of the special ducal interest and various infractions of the ducal peace, some of which are related closely to high treason while others are seditious in nature and correspond more nearly to internal treason or *Landesverrat aus dem inneren Feind*. Of the latter type, one finds a

---

[49] *L. Alam.* 27, 1–3.

[50] Cf. *L. Vis.* 2, 1, 33 *De his, qui regiam contemserint iussionem*; 2, 1, 19 *De his, qui admoniti iudicis epistula vel sigillo ad iudicium venire contemnunt.*

[51] *L. Alam.* 24. Cf. Wilda, *Strafrechts*, I, 984 seq.; E. Osenbrüggen, *Das alamannische Strafrecht im deutschen Mittelalter* (Schaffhausen: Hurter, 1860), pp. 394 seq.

law punishing those who stir up riots within the army or host with death or exile, and confiscation of property to the public treasury.[52] The old peace of the host or *Heerfrieden* is identified with the peace of the duke and is enforced by a triple wergeld.[53] Thefts within the army are punished with a ninefold fine.[54] Other provisions deal with acts in contempt of the ducal peace that resemble the Visigothic *scandalum*:[55] they point plainly to the fact that certain persons and certain places have received a special protection which may not be violated without payment of a triple wergeld. For instance, the law *De eo, qui in curte ducis hominem occiderit* reads as follows:

1. Whoever shall kill a man either at the duke's court or going thither or returning thence must redeem himself with a triple wergeld, for he has transgressed the duke's command that every man shall have peace and safety in coming to his lord and returning to his home.
2. Let no one presume to disturb a man coming from the duke or journeying to him, even though he be guilty of a crime; and if any one shall so presume, either to do anything to such a man or to kill him, or if the man escapes alive and may be placated, let the offender always compound triply.[56]

Theft at the duke's court shall be compounded doubly,[57] while even heavier penalties atone for the great scandal caused by a fight at the court with its accompanying noise (*clamor orta fuerit*) and mob (*concursio populi*) struggling excitedly to see what is going on.[58] In such cases all damage caused by the tumult shall be recompensed triply by those responsible for it, and the man who started the trouble shall pay a fine of sixty *solidi* to the treasury. Composition for the inflicted injury is made through a wergeld payment to the aggrieved party, while something additional in the way of an arbitrary fine (*fredus*) must be given

---

[52] *L. Alam.* 25, 1 *De his, qui in exercitu litem commiserint.*

[53] *L. Alam.*, 25, 2: *"tripliciter solvat."* Cf. Wilda, *Strafrechts*, I, 238–241.

[54] *L. Alam.*, 26, 1–2: *"novem vicibus novigildos solvat."*

[55] Cf. *L. Vis.* 2, 1, 8 *De his, qui contra principem vel gentem aut patriam refugi sive insulentes existunt;* 9, 2, 8 *Quid debeat observari, si scandalum infra fines Spanie exsurrexerit;* also *Ed. Roth.* 35–40, in the Lombard law.

[56] *L. Alam.* 28, 1–2. Cf. *Pact. Alam.* 2, 50; Wilda, *Strafrechts*, I, 780, and 258 seq. on *Königsfriede;* K. Lehmann, *Der Königsfriede der Nordgermanen* (Berlin and Leipzig: J. Guttentag [D. Collin], 1886), on the general subject of the "king's peace" in Germanic law. Also note *L. Alam.* 58 *De eo, qui alteri viam contradixerit,* which indicates that a special peace had long extended over the highways in accordance with ancient popular custom. Cf. *Ed. Roth.* 16–17, 26–28 *De wegworin, id est hor-bitariam.*

[57] *L. Alam.* 30 *De eo, qui in curte regis furtum commiserit.* The reading *regis* is probably in error as alternative texts give *ducis.*

[58] *L. Alam.* 33 *De eo, qui in curte ducis pugnam commiserit.*

as a payment for breach of the peace in alleviation of the insult offered the duke by such scandalous conduct on his premises. Indeed, two distinct factors seem to underlie the payment of the *fredus*: there has been a violation of the special ducal interest involved (1) in the duke's personal guarantee of his ducal peace, and (2) in the authority to maintain public order that has been delegated to the duke by his people. The duke's person has been insulted by the flouting of his pledged guarantee, and his public authority has been challenged by an unlawful act. In addition, certain individuals are protected by a special ducal peace. Whoever kills a messenger within the province must compound triply for his deed.[59] Injuries done to the maidservants connected with the duke's household must be triply compounded.[60] The property of the duke received special protection, and whoever steals any of it must compound *ter novigildus*.[61] The presence of a special ducal interest possessing both personal or private and public characteristics is, thus, confirmed at every hand.

Finally near the end of the list of cases pertaining to the duke one finds laws prohibiting incestuous marriages[62] and stating the punishments for parricide and fratricide.[63] Christian influence has affected the latter law markedly, so that the old fierce revenge disappears and the offender is warned "se contra Deum egisse et secundum iussionem Dei fraternitatem non custodisse, in Deum graviter deliquisse." Wilda believes that the writings of the Old Testament and the Roman Law introduced along with Christianity have been chiefly responsible for the formulation of laws directed specifically against parricide and incest. He upholds the views that these crimes were relatively infrequent among the primitive Germans, and appear to such an extent as to make

---

[59] L. Alam. 29 *De eo, qui missum ducis infra provinciam occiderit.*

[60] L. Alam. 32 *De feminis, qui in ministerio ducis sunt.*

[61] L. Alam. 31 *De eo, qui res ducis furaverit.* Cf. L. Alam. 34, 1–2 *De eo, qui praesumpserit infra provinciam res ducis hostiliter invadere.*

[62] L. Alam. 39 *De inlicitis nuptiis.*

[63] L. Alam. 40 *De parricidiis et fraticidiis.* Cf. L. Rib. 29, 2. See Osenbrüggen, *Das alamannische Strafrecht,* p. 225; Wilda, *Strafrechts,* I, 714–718. Wilda notes that parricide in Germanic law did not include the killing of wives or husbands, but was limited to the homicide of "blood relatives." The wife was bound to her husband by special pledges and was dependent upon him. In general, husbands might kill wives who broke their pledges without liability to punishment, although some laws required that the woman's family be consulted before any action was taken. Wives who killed their husbands, proved, by the act, unfaithful to their pledges. This was *Ehebruch* and, therefore. *Treubruch*, and a basis for the later petty treason of feudal times in which it was equally treasonable for the wife to kill her husband or for a vassal to kill his lord.

legislation necessary only with the loosening of family bonds and the increasing demoralization of the Germanic peoples.[64] It is significant that these crimes of infamy are still associated with treason and its related offenses, so that the old connection of the crimes of infamy and infidelity is maintained as in the time of Tacitus. Like *Landesverrat,* these crimes must be old causes which had once belonged to the people, but owing to their heinous nature have since been attached to the list of crimes under the duke's jurisdiction.

The third subdivision of the *Lex Alamannorum* includes those cases settled habitually by the people. A great variety of subjects may be found here, mostly in the sphere of private law, such as selling a free man or woman into slavery outside the land[65] or within the province, murder,[66] betrothal, divorce and matrimonial problems, inheritance, homicide,[67] and arson.[68] Finally one finds an interesting law dealing with *Landesverrat* of the *herisliz* type: *De eo, qui in pugna parem suum dereliquit et fugit,*[69] which states that if any man in the host flees from his comrade once battle has been joined, leaving him to fight alone, and if that comrade stays out the fight, he who fled must pay composition of eighty *solidi* to the other upon his return from the battle. This provision seems strangely out of place among the *rixae populorum,* since it belongs clearly to the general category of public offenses pertaining to the duke. One cannot escape the conviction that the codifiers of the Alamannic law, in their efforts to systematize and organize, have transferred many offenses from the list of *rixae populorum* to the *causae ducis.* Possibly this law may have been overlooked in the transfer. However, it seems more likely that the process of withdrawing causes from the people and resting them with the duke may have been gradual and was accomplished law after law as the necessity for such change be-

[64] Cf. Wilda, *Strafrechts,* I, 714–718. One cannot assume positively that Wilda intended to leave the impression that the introduction of Christianity caused the demoralization of Germanic pagan character. On the other hand, a certain sentimental dedication to early Teutonic ideals is hinted in many places in his *Strafrechts.* Thus, the current cult, devoted to these primitive Germanic ideals and stressed by some leaders of modern National Socialism, follows an historical tradition advocated by members of the Germanist school among German constitutionalists of the nineteenth century, a movement which also received considerable support from British scholars.

[65] *L. Alam.* 45–47: "*extra terminos, extra marcam, infra provinciam.*"

[66] *L. Alam.* 48 *De eo, qui hominem occiderit et eum morttodum fecerit.*

[67] *L. Alam.* 60; 69; 72; 86.

[68] *L. Alam.* 76, 1–2; 77, 1–3.

[69] *L. Alam.* 90. Cf. Wilda, *Strafrechts,* I, 986–988.

came apparent in particular instances. Thus, the people were shorn slowly of their public authority, and the systematic arrangement of the Alamannic Code with its three categories of cases made an orderly transfer very easy. The general impression evoked by a study of the *rixae populorum* indicates that they constitute a residue of mixed private-law materials left after the removal of public matter. How far Roman influence has played a part in effecting this change would be difficult to estimate. The formal systematization is suggested by the Roman example. As has been noted, certain expressions and ideas relative to treason have been taken from Roman law, and the entire ecclesiastical subdivision is certainly not Germanic. Still one cannot assert safely that the Roman law was primarily responsible for this concentration of public authority in the hands of a single individual. One may be certain that Roman ideas did not impede such a tendency, however it may have started. In its general character the Alamannic Code remains dominantly Germanic with all the usual phenomena of wergeld and compurgation, special *paces, herisliz,* and scandals.

The Bavarian laws are closely related to the Alamannic Code.[70] The Bavarians occupied an interior district of Germany east of the Alamanni along the upper Danube River, where Roman influences may have been less strongly defined, although the legislation recognizes the episcopal organization of the Catholic church in Bavaria, introduced by St. Boniface in 739. Historically, the Bavarian dukes had the misfortune to encounter the rising fortunes of the great Frankish Carolingian dynasty. Charles Martel, who became sole *major domus* of the Franks, abolished the duchy of Alamannia and intervened in the affairs of Bavaria, compelling the Alamanni to render assistance against the Bavarians and slaying the Swabian duke, Landfrid, who rebelled because of his alarm at the subjugation of Bavaria.[71] Later, in the time of Pepin the Short, Duke Odilo of Bavaria formed an alliance with Aquitania, Swabia, Saxony, and the Slavonic peoples in the east to resist the Frankish advance, but was defeated at the Lech River so that Bavaria was restored to Frankish control.[72] Again, under Charlemagne, the powerful Duke

---

[70] Cf. K. Beyerle, *Lex Baiuvariorum* (Munich: Hueber, 1926), pp. xxviii–xxxviii, lxx–lxxv, on the relation of the Bavarian Code to the Alamannic, Visigothic, Lombard, and other barbarian legislation.

[71] C. Pfister, "Gaul under the Merovingian Franks," *Cambridge Medieval History* (New York: Macmillan, 1913), II, 129.

[72] See *Annales Mettenses* (a. 742–746) in *M. G. H., Scriptores*, ed. by Pertz (Hanover: Hahn, 1826), I, 327–329; *Annales Laurissenses et Einhardi* (a. 742–

Tassilo III, whose wife was a daughter of the Lombard king, Desiderius, urged on by the Bavarian clergy, broke the peace between Bavaria and the Franks.[73] Hostilities ensued, but Tassilo was compelled to sue for peace and to accept conditions requiring him to renew his vassalage and surrender his duchy to the Franks. This implied the end of independent sovereignty in Bavaria. Thereafter, that he might destroy utterly the long-established reputation and influence of the Agilolfing ducal dynasty, Charlemagne revived an old charge against Tassilo, accusing him of the crime of *herisliz* for desertion in battle.[74] Tassilo was condemned to death, but his great opponent mitigated the penalty to confinement in a monastery. Bavaria was declared part of the Frankish kingdom and was governed by Frankish counts.

Although the Bavarian Code is based on various older sources, including a large accumulation of ancient custom, it appears to be the result of a single enactment. And, since there is strong presumption that the *Lex Alamannorum* was employed in the redaction of the *Lex Baiuvariorum*, one may conclude that the Bavarian Code must be later than *ca.* A.D. 720. Furthermore, evidence from the period of Duke Tassilo (748–788) indicates that the Code was then a finished compilation. It is referred to in the decretals of ecclesiastical synods for the years 756, 770, and 772, as *Baivariorum lex atque pactus*, while at the Synod of Ascheim in 756 the Bavarian bishops describe it to Duke Tassilo as *precessorum vestrorum depicta*. If the Code was published under the predecessor of Tassilo (i.e., *ante* 749) its date may be established between 739 and 749, because the episcopal organization mentioned in the Code derives from the former year, as has been noted above. Also the failure of the Bavarian law to make reference to ducal powers such as were exercised in Swabia indicates that Bavaria did not enjoy an independence comparable to that of the Alamanni under Duke Landfrid. In fact, the *Lex Baiuvariorum* shows that the code was made under strong Frankish influence since it refers to the royal authority exercised in Bavaria. This excludes the years 739–743 as the time of compilation, for Odilo's rebellion occupied that interval preceding the

---

744) in *M. G. H.*, S S., I, 134–135; *Einhardi Fuldensis Annales* (a. 742–746) in *M. G. H.*, S S., I, 345–346.

[73] Cf. C. R. L. Fletcher, *The Making of Western Europe* (London: J. Murray, 1912), I, 249–250. He suggests that the insurrections of Tassilo were instigated by his Lombard wife.

[74] See *Annales Laurissenses et Einhardi* (a. 787–788) in *M. G. H.*, S S., I, 168–174.

restoration of Frankish control in 743 or 744. Finally, since the Synod of Ascheim attributed these laws to the predecessors of Tassilo, the period most closely fulfilling the conditions of this legislation are the years between 744 and 749.[75]

Thus it may be accepted that both the Alamanni and the Bavarians promulgated their codes of law during the first half of the eighth century with the *Lex Alamannorum* somewhat earlier than the *Lex Baiuvariorum*.[76] Both codes exhibit marked Roman influences in form and content; both retain numerous Germanic expressions which afford much interest to philologists and legal scholars alike.[77] The same threefold classification of cases (*causae*) appearing in the Alamannic Code characterizes the *Lex Baiuvariorum*. Thus one finds, first, the ecclesiastical cases,[78] then the cases pertaining to the duke;[79] and lastly the cases relating to the people.[80] In the ecclesiastical matter several provisions appear which establish a *Kirchenfrieden* or *pax ecclesiae* for the preser-

[75] This discussion of the historical background of the *Lex Baiuvariorum* is derived from the orthodox interpretation of Brunner, *D. R.*, I, 454–464; Schröder-von Künssberg, *Lehrbuch*, pp. 269–272; and Maitland in *Select Essays*, I, 19, n. 5. More recently, Bruno Krusch, in *Die Lex Bajuvariorum* (Berlin: Weidmann, 1924), advanced an alternative view that the *Lex* was imposed on the Bavarians about A.D. 728 by Charles Martel in the name of the Merovingian *roi fainéant*, Theuderich IV. Also see E. von Schwind, "Kritische Studien zur Lex Baiuvariorum," *Neues Archiv*, XXXI (1906), 399–453; XXXIII (1908), 605–694; XXXVIII (1912), 415–451; Franz Beyerle's review of Krusch study, *Zeitschrift der Savigny-Stiftung für Rechtsgeschichte (Germanistische Abtheilung)*, 45 (1925), 416–457.

[76] The best edition of the *Lex Baiuvariorum* is that of Konrad Beyerle (Munich: Max Hueber Verlag, 1926), based on the Ingolstadt MS. This is a splendid work of recent German scholarship, including text, German translation, historical survey of the MSS traditions and previous editions, critical analysis of the laws, glossary of old Germanic terms, and photographic reproductions of the entire Ingolstadt MS. The edition of J. Merkel in *M. G. H.*, *Leges* (Hanover: Hahn, 1863), Tomus III, gives three alternative texts with seventeen *additiones*. The old edition of F. Walter in his *Corpus iuris germanici antiqui* (Berlin: Reimer, 1824), I, 237–298, is still useful and authentic, being based in part on Mederer's collation of 1793 which employed the Ingolstadt MS. Because of its easier use for reference purposes, I am giving Walter's notation in citations from the *Lex Baiuvariorum*.

[77] Cf. Dietrich von Kralik, "Die deutschen Bestandteile der Lex Baiuvariorum," *Neues Archiv*, XXXVIII (1913), 13–55, 401–449, 581–624. Constant reference must be made to the glossaries of Merkel and Beyerle, as well as to Lehmann's annotations of the Alamannic laws, since many Germanic terms are not defined in the original Latin texts and provide formidable riddles for competent linguistic scholars. On the Latinity of the *Lex Baiuvariorum*, see K. Beyerle, *Lex Baiuvariorum*, pp. xx–xxii.

[78] *L. Baiuv.* Titulus 1 *De ecclesiasticis rebus, de libris legis institutionum, quae ad clerum pertinent, seu de ecclesiarum iure.*

[79] *Ibid.*, Titulus 2 *De ducibus et eorum causis, quae ad eos pertinent.*

[80] All the remaining titles from 3 to 21 inclusive relate to popular cases.

vation and protection of church property: slaves, real estate, or other possessions.[81] Next comes a specific recognition of the rights of sanctuary,[82] and finally, a long wergeld tariff is set forth, providing special protection for the clergy according to their rank and the nature of the injury done them.[83] Little that is really new can be discovered in this section of the laws. The chief contribution seems to be the evidence given regarding the existence of a special ecclesiastical interest whose legal support depends in great measure on scriptural ideas and Roman law.

The cases falling under the jurisdiction of the duke contain much information bearing on treason and other public offenses.[84] The first case on the list deals with high treason under the caption *Si quis de morte ducis consiliatus fuerit.*[85] It reads as follows:

1. If anyone shall plot the death of his duke, whom the king has set over the province or the people have chosen, and cannot disprove the charge, let that man be in the power of the duke, his life at the duke's mercy, and his property confiscated to the public treasury.

2. And that the matter may be settled fairly and the truth ascertained, let the proof rest not on a single witness but on three witnesses of equal rank with the persons accused. Moreover, if one witness disagrees with another, let God decide between them. Let them go out upon a field, and, there, let him be believed to whom God shall grant victory. And let this be done in the presence of the people, that no one may perish through unfair play.

3. Let no free Bavarian be deprived of his freehold [*alodem*] or his life unless he has committed a capital crime, that is, if he has plotted the death of the duke, or has invited enemies into the province, or has schemed to take possession of the state through an attack from without. But, if these things be proved against him, then let his life and all his property and his patrimony be at the duke's disposal.

Although the presumption holds that treasonable acts are unamendable crimes, there is evidence that under certain circumstances a ducal wergeld might be paid by the offender.[86] The general rule is followed

---

[81] *L. Baiuv.* 1, 1–6.

[82] *L. Baiuv.* 1, 7, 1–4. Cf. *L. Baiuv.* 1, 7, 3: "Nulla sit culpa tam gravis ut vita non concedatur propter timorem Dei et reverentiam sanctorum quia Dominus dixit: Qui dimiserit, dimittetur ei. Qui non dimiserit, nec ei dimittetur."

[83] *L. Baiuv.* 1, 8–12, setting wergelds for *ministri (subdiaconum, lectorem, exorcistam, acolytum, ostiarium), monachi, presbyteri, diacones, episcopi, sanctimoniales.*

[84] Cf. Dahn, *Könige,* IX (2), 279–280 for a brief summary concerning treason in Bavarian law; Waitz, *D. V.,* II (2), 369–373 on ducal powers.

[85] *L. Baiuv.* 2, 1, 1–5. Cf. *L. Alam.* 23–24.

[86] Cf. *L. Alam.* 23, regarding redemption of life by a traitor under the conditions established by the duke or *principes populi. L. Baiuv.* 2, 20, 2, provides that the ducal family of the Agilolfingi may be compounded for by a quadruple payment,

that the composition for any offense against the duke shall be one-third higher than for the same offense against any other member of the ducal house. In the case of homicide, it shall be six hundred *solidi* for the duke's relative, nine hundred *solidi* for the duke himself. Doubtless, killing the duke or plotting his death was an unamendable crime if treasonable intent could be proved, and, of course, conspiracy was an indication of such intent. On the other hand, mere homicide without malice and without the premeditation implied in murder (*murdrida*) might permit composition under the higher rates stated above in *L. Baiuv.* 2, 20, 2, although *L. Baiuv.* 2, 2 *Si quis ducem suum occiderit* seems contradictory, declaring that "If any one shall kill his duke, let his life be rendered up in payment for the life he took, and let his property be forever confiscated to the public treasury." In any case, such subjective questions of intent and malice aforethought must have been as difficult to establish in barbarian law as the crime of "imagining the king's death" in the literal sense in the later Middle Ages or some modern criminal cases involving circumstantial evidence. At any rate, the barbarian could settle many knotty points with dispatch by committing the decision to wager of battle. Furthermore, it is apparent that the Bavarian law of treason coincides very closely with its counterpart in the Alamannic Code.[87] Both treason laws contain evidence indicating popular participation in the government; in both codes the idea appears that popular authority, in theory at least, has not been superseded entirely by ducal control. *L. Baiuv.* 2, 1, 1, speaks of the duke "whom the king has set over the province or the people have chosen" (*aut populus sibi elegerit ducem*). Thus the idea is retained that the people have the right to select their duke, although the appointive power of the Frankish king may be considered as exercising a prior right. The popular right is the older but it is not disregarded despite the recognition of the new royal authority. *L. Alam.* 23, grants the *principes populi* a co-ordinate

---

while *L. Baiuv.* 2, 20, 4, states: "Et pro eo quia dux est, addatur ei maior honor quam ceteris parentibus eius, sic ut tertia pars addatur super hoc quod parentes eius componutur. Si vita parentorum eius aufertur, cum sexcentis solidis componuntur. Dux vero dum nongentis solidis componitur parentibus, aut regi, si parentes non habuerit."

[87] Note that treason may be committed according to both the Alamannic and Bavarian codes by plotting the duke's death (*in mortem consiliare*). This Roman influence may have penetrated by way of the *Leges Visigothorum* (cf. note 46 *supra*). Also the crime of *scandalum* is common to the Bavarian and Visigothic, as well as the Lombard, laws. See Dahn, *Könige*, IX (2), 280 with n. 3; F. Dahn, *Westgothische Studien* (Würzburg: Stahel, 1874), pp. 236–237.

right with the duke in determining whether a traitor shall be permitted to redeem his life (*sicut dux aut principes populi iudicaverint*). Regulations fixing the discipline for the rebellious sons of a duke observe the general tenor of the Alamannic law.[88]

1. If any son of a duke shall be so haughty or foolish as to wish to depose his father following the advice of evil men [*ut patrem suum dehonestare voluerit per consilium malignorum*], or because of a sense of his own strength, and to take his realm from him, while his father is neither deaf nor blind but still able to contend in the wager of battle, to ride into conflict, to judge his people, to mount his horse in manly fashion, to fight a strenuous battle at arms [*arma sua vivaciter baiulare*], let that son know that he has acted contrary to law, and let him be cut off from his inheritance, let no more of his father's authority pertain to him, and let him be in the power of the king or of his father that they may exile him if they wish.
2. Let him have no authority except what the king or his father, out of mercy, choose to give him.
3. And if he shall survive his father and have other brothers, let them give him no portion, since he has sinned against his father contrary to law.
4. And if he, alone of the heirs, should survive his father, it shall be within the power of the king to give the inheritance to whomsoever he wishes: either to that son or to someone else.

Likewise, the duke himself must render proper obedience and allegiance to his king and not hold royal commands in contempt. The subordinate position of the duke is more positively emphasized than in the Alamannic Code, as may be noted from the following law which is directed against rebellious and treasonable actions on the part of the dukes, that is, high treason in its most heinous aspect:

If any duke, whom the king has placed over the province, shall be so bold or disrespectful, or fired with foolhardiness, or impudent and conceited, or haughty and rebellious, as to hold the king's command in contempt, let him be deprived of the gift of the office of his dukedom [*dignitatis ipsius ducati*], and furthermore let him know that his hope of the contemplation of Heaven is condemned and denied him, and let him lose the power of his salvation.[89]

And this same principle is extended, also, to those who hold the commands of the duke in contempt:

If any one shall hold in contempt the orders of the duke or his mark [signature] which is used in transmitting orders or his signet or his seal, and if

---

[88] *L. Baiuv.* 2, 10, 1–4 *De filiis ducum si protervi fuerint.* An interesting study of the chief differences in the spirit characterizing these two codes may be made by comparing *L. Alam.* 35, 1–2, with *L. Baiuv.* 2, 10, 1–4, in the original texts.

[89] *L. Baiuv.* 2, 9 *De duce si protervus et elatus, vel superbus atque rebellis fuerit, et decretum regis contempserit.*

any one shall fail to come or to act accordingly as he has been ordered, let him pay fifteen *solidi* into the public treasury for his negligence and let him carry out the order.[90]

Landesverrat is closely associated with high treason in the law which relates to plotting the duke's death, and remains intimately connected with that crime throughout the code. The impression is created that the popular interest in public authority has, in large measure, become identified with the ducal interest, so that crimes subversive of the welfare of the people become treason against the duke. A law concerning sedition appears near the head of the list of cases pertaining to the duke and prescribes the following heavy fines:

1. If anyone shall stir up sedition against his duke, a crime called by the Bavarians *carmulum*, let him who first raised the sedition, pay the duke six hundred *solidi*.
2. Let every other man, who followed him and took counsel with him, compound with two hundred *solidi*.
3. Let lesser folk, who followed him and who are freemen, compound with forty *solidi*, that such scandal may not arise in the province.[91]

This is followed by several regulations establishing a special peace within the host (*Heerfrieden*). First comes the law *Si quis in exercitu scandalum excitaverit*, in which the chief provision states:

If anyone in the army, which the king or the duke has assembled together, shall create a scandal [or riot] within the host, and if men shall be killed as a result of it, let him pay a composition of six hundred *solidi* into the public treasury.[92]

Another enactment penalizes those soldiers who ravage the province without the explicit command of their duke, and thus exhibits a marked similarity to certain provisions of the *Corpus Juris Civilis*.[93] Finally, one finds an extension of the special peace of the army covering cases of stolen property.[94] The distinction between treason against land and folk and high treason is, to a degree, bridged by various breaches of a

---

[90] *L. Baiuv.* 2, 14 *De his qui iussionem ducis contempserint.* Cf. *L. Alam.* 27, 1–3; *L. Vis.* 2, 1, 19; 2, 1, 33.

[91] *L. Baiuv.* 2, 3, 1–3 *Si quis seditionem excitaverit contra ducem suum.* Note that *seditio* is identified with *scandalum* in this law, or is possibly regarded as an aspect of *scandalum*.

[92] *L. Baiuv.* 2, 4, 1. Cf. *L. Alam.* 25, 1–2; *L. Baiuv.* 2, 4, 2–6.

[93] *L. Baiuv.* 2, 5, 1–7 *Si quis infra provinciam, ubi dux exercitum ordinaverit, sine ducis iussione aliquid praedaverit.* Cf. *Codex Justinianus* 12, 35, 15–16 *De Re Militari; Codex Theodosianus* 7, 1 *De re militari.*

[94] *L. Baiuv.* 2, 6 *Si quis in exercitu aliquid furaverit.* Cf. *L. Alam.* 26, 1–2.

special ducal peace comprehending specified persons and places. Special rules are established concerning the killing of persons in the service of their duke or lord.[95] A special immunity protects and attaches to those who commit a homicide at the express command of their king or duke.[96] Scandals committed at the duke's court are punished appropriately:

1. If anyone shall cause a scandal at the duke's court, either by fighting there through sheer haughtiness or because of drunkenness, whatever he shall do there, let him compound for it all according to law, and, on account of his folly, let him pay the sum of forty *solidi* into the public treasury.
2. If anyone's slave performs such actions, let him lose a hand.
3. Let no one ever have the presumption to create a scandal at the duke's court.[97]

Furthermore, no one at the duke's court shall fight duels (*campiones*) without permission, for this creates scandals.[98] If a freeman breaks this rule, he must compound forty *solidi* to the public treasury, while a slave must lose his right hand unless his master redeems him with twenty *solidi*. If any freeman steals anything at the duke's court, let him compound for it *trimniungeldum, hoc est, ter novem,* because the duke's house is a public place (*quia domus ducis domus publica est*); and, if a slave steals, let him lose his hands.[99] If any one finds anything about the duke's court, even though it be left through neglect, and he carries it off, stealing away by night, let him be reputed a thief and pay fifteen *solidi* into the public treasury.[100] Despite the presence of much that is Roman in form and somewhat less that is Roman in content, the general spirit of this legislation is Germanic in much the same proportion as the Alamannic Code. The resemblances between the two sets of laws are marked, although the *Lex Baiuvariorum* is the more complete and applies to a wider variety of offenses.

The titles which do not relate specifically to ecclesiastical and ducal concerns constitute the greatest part of the Bavarian Code and correspond generally to the *rixae populorum* of the Alamannic laws. They deal with all sorts of civil and criminal matters, chiefly of a primitive nature, such as woundings (*plotruns*), theft, rape, arson, marriage, in-

[95] *L. Baiuv.* 2, 7, 1–2 *Si quis in utilitate ducis vel domini sui mortuus fuerit.* Cf. *L. Alam.* 29.
[96] *L. Baiuv.* 2, 8, 1–2 *Si quis regis vel ducis sui iussione hominem interfecerit.*
[97] *L. Baiuv.* 2, 11, 1–3 *De eo qui scandalum in curte ducis commiserit.* Cf. *L. Alam.* 28, 1–3; 33.
[98] *L. Baiuv.* 2, 12, 1–2 *Ut nullus in campiones sine iussu manus iniiciat.*
[99] *L. Baiuv.* 2, 13, 1 *De his qui in curte ducis aliquid furaverint.* Cf. *L. Alam.* 30.
[100] *L. Baiuv.* 2, 13, 2.

heritance, and sales. One gains the same impression that he derived from the *Lex Alamannorum*: these popular causes seem to be the residue left after important public matters have been collected in a separate list of cases pertaining to the duke. The ecclesiastical cases, on the other hand, are something new and recent, added in a separate category but devised along the lines of the older special peaces. The church was a strange institution which had to be clothed in Germanic guise as regards its legal relationships. Likewise, a few actions based on Roman law were added to the duke's causes to provide for matters not specifically treated in Germanic law, such as the plotting of the duke's death or the marauding activity of soldiers in the province. Since the Bavarian Code is a more complete and extensive body of law, the balance remaining after the duke's cases had been subtracted from the whole is substantially larger than in the case of the Alamannic Code. The addition of new materials and the reclassification of old materials in new categories went on in a generally parallel fashion in both bodies of law. However, it is a curious fact that certain offenses listed among the ducal cases in the Alamannic law still remain among the popular causes in the Bavarian law. This difference involves important considerations in the study of public law since it indicates in what manner treasonable actions of great public significance were gradually attracted into the ducal causes. This transfer from the popular to the ducal category did not proceed synchronously in both codes; otherwise the difference could not have occurred. And the fact that the absorption into the duke's list did not proceed at an equal rate in both codes adds proof, for the benefit of those who may question the entire theory of a transfer, that such a transfer actually took place. Thus, since the Germanic peoples had no dukes bearing full public authority in the earlier period of the migrations, there was no popular cause relating to high treason in the *rixae populorum*. Legal protection for the duke's person as a symbol of public authority had to rest on such an innovation from the Roman Law as may be found in the rule: *Si quis de morte ducis consiliatus fuerit*. But *Landesverrat* was an ancient crime against land and folk. Now that the duke's interests coincided theoretically with the welfare of the people *Landesverrat* was logically the first crime to be transferred to the causes pertaining to the duke. On the lists it follows directly after the laws against high treason. The people had depended upon an army for protection; hence they established the *Heerfrieden*. But now the army was the duke's army, and breaches of the special peace of the army became causes pertaining to the duke. Such breaches were equally treason, however, whether they were popular or ducal causes. Hence, military offenses occupy a prominent position near the top of the list of ducal causes. After the analogy of these special *paces* of *Frieden* the duke establishes his own special private ducal peaces protecting his court and servants. Naturally these never belonged to the *rixae populorum*, for they were created after public authority had passed from the people, but they were patterned after earlier models found in the popular causes.

Perhaps the earliest peace of all was the peace of the home (*Heim-frieden*), which laid down the principle that "a man's house is his castle." The home was the capital from whence public authority proceeded when the *Sippe* or family group was the state. But the home had long since become a private institution, and, unlike the army, had few public functions. Hence, one finds the *Heimfrieden* still included in the *rixae populorum*, where it had been from the beginning of the evolution of the state as the primary agent of public authority. Breaches of this peace of the home are punishable according to the terms of the law *De violentia*: "If anyone shall enter another's courtyard by force contrary to law, let him pay the sum of three *solidi*."[101] This is followed by other similar enactments: "1. If anyone shall enter a house by force, which is called *Huspruch*—let him compound six *solidi*. 2. No one shall enter another's home forcibly, since such actions create scandals."[102] Setting fire to a man's house, particularly by night, was an atrocious breach of the *Heimfrieden* and was punished severely,[103] while property stolen from a burning home had to be restored fourfold (*in quadrup-lum*).[104] Also, from a very early time a need was felt to keep the highways open freely to all men, and a special peace was extended over them which proved difficult to maintain. Later, when the duke became the primary agent in the exercise of public authority among the Al-amanni, he, too, saw the necessity for protecting the highways along which people must pass, to and fro, in attendance upon his court.[105] Vestiges of the old peace of the folk were still retained among the popular causes in a law entitled *De eo, qui alteri viam contradixerit*, and any

---

[101] *L. Baiuv.* 10, 1 *De curte.* Cf. *L. Baiuv.* 9, 10 *De curtis dissipatione*, which reads: "Si curtem dissipaverit aut inruperit liber liberi, cum tribus solidis componat, et restituat damnum." Destruction of property in another's courtyard involves not only the payment of composition but also the restoration of damages.

[102] Cf. *L. Baiuv.* 10, 2, 1–3.

[103] *L. Baiuv.* 9, 1, 1–4.

[104] *L. Baiuv.* 14, 3, 1–2.

[105] Cf. *L. Alam.* 28, 1–2.

violator was compelled to make composition in the sum of six *solidi*.[106] This same offense was noted in the ancient *Pactus Alamannorum: De wegalaugem (insidiatio, viae contradictio) sex solidos solvat*.[107] In the Bavarian Code the special protection accorded the highways is found only among the ancient popular laws, such as *De via publica*: "If anyone shall close a public road along which the king or duke passes, or the road of any other person contrary to law, let him compound with twelve *solidi*—and if he wishes to deny the charge, let him swear with twelve oath-takers [*sacramentalibus*],"[108] and *De peregrinis transeuntibus viam*,[109] which forbids injuring or killing strangers on the highways since *una pax omnibus necessaria est*.

Finally, it may be recalled that Tacitus associated crimes of infamy very closely with crimes of infidelity. Perhaps this was because incest, adultery, and parricide were considered the grossest kind of *Treubruch* in the family-state, and the traditional relation had been perpetuated until the time when it came to the attention of Tacitus. Thus, the two offenses of gravest public significance in the age of government through kinship groups were (a) breaches of the *Heimfrieden* developing into *Landesverrat in dem äusseren, sowohl dem inneren Feind*, with internal treason exemplified commonly by sedition, scandal, and military crimes, and (b) the crimes of infamy, incest, and parricide. However, when dukes appear later to assume the burdens of public authority, the crimes of infamy, being associated most often with family concerns, were in process of relegation to the realm of private law. Hence, it is not surprising to find the law *De nuptiis et operationibus inlicitis prohibendis* still remaining among the popular causes in the Bavarian Code.[110] But in the *Lex Alamannorum* the laws *De nuptiis inlicitis*[111] and *De patricidiis, fratricidiis*[112] have been added near the very end of the list of ducal cases. Also, it should be noted that in the earlier and more primitive Ripuarian laws the ancient union of the crimes of infamy and infidelity was maintained since the penalties for parricide and incest and for high treason are specified together in the same section of the law.[113]

---

[106] *L. Alam.* 58, which is listed among the *rixae populorum*. Cf. Wilda, *Strafrechts*, I, 780.

[107] *Pactus Alamannorum* 2, 50.

[108] *L. Baiuv.* 9, 13.

[109] *L. Baiuv.* 3, 14, 1–3.

[110] *L. Baiuv.* 6, 1, 1–3.

[111] *L. Alam.* 39.

[112] *L. Alam.* 40.

[113] *L. Rib.* 69, 1–2. In the Ripuarian Law all three crimes, treason, parricide and

And, as late as the *Capitulare missorum generale* (*ca.* 802) of Charlemagne, parricide and incest are listed side by side in the catalogue of penalties.[114] It is difficult to resist the conclusion that this traditional association of the crimes of infidelity and infamy still persisted since both were grave public offenses, and that the duke took cognizance of the fact, adding these crimes to his list after he had absorbed all the treasonable actions. This study of the ducal *causae* in the light of the various *paces* or *Frieden* adds force to the theory that treason, the primary offense in public criminal law, has evolved parallel with the evolution of the state and differs in its characteristic expression from age to age according to the nature of public authority at any given time. One can see the duke beginning with a definition of treason suited to his own day, and, then, reaching back and attaching the treasons of earlier days which still remain treason to the ducal *causae* until only a residue is left, little of which relates to public matters or to public law. In the case of breaches of the *Heimfrieden* an ancient and extinct treason remains buried in private law. The crimes of infamy emerge in the *Lex Alamannorum*, possibly because they had been treasonable in the rudimentary state and still retained a public character owing to their heinous nature, possibly because the tradition of their connection with infidelity was not yet dead.

In conclusion, it may be repeated that the process indicated in this legislation evidences an increasing centralization of authority in the person of the duke with the consequent absorption of various special interests and the legal areas over which their peace extended into a comprehensive ducal peace. This evidence is, on the whole, inconclusive regarding Brunner's orthodox theory of a pre-existing archetypal general or folk peace; yet it does bring some support to the recent view of Goebel that Brunner failed to demonstrate the existence of such a peace.[115] Rather, these Germanic codes reveal the primitive origins of

---

incest, are associated together. In the somewhat more recent Alamannic Code the same three crimes are mentioned, but in a less organic union. In the Bavarian Law, which is the most recent of the three codes, only treason and incest appear, the former as a "ducal" cause, the latter as a "popular" cause. It would seem that the relationship of these crimes becomes closer, as one reaches back to the time of Tacitus and on into deepest antiquity when the crimes of infamy may be acts of infidelity to the family-state or kinship group (*Sippe*).

[114] *Capitulare missorum generale* (*ca.* 802), c. 37–38.

[115] See J. Goebel, *Felony and Misdemeanor* (New York: 1937), I, 7–25, 37–38, 327–335, 423–440. This is a significant criticism of the older Wilda-Waitz-Brunner theory. Cf. suggestions in my review of Goebel in *Illinois Law Review*, XXXII (1937), 386–388.

these "pacific" areas in the circumscribed sphere of the individual household, expressed in the opinion that "a man's house is his castle" and
doubtless supported by religious considerations of the sanctity of hearth
and home. Later there emerges the peace of the host which may well
be the clan or expanded kinship group (*Sippe*) at arms, and the further
extension of this principle into wider areas such as the public assembly
of freemen (*Ding, thing, gemot, moot*), seasons and times of special
significance, places enjoyed in a common utility and need (including
highways and streams), and even the immunities of individuals in
specially recognized services.[116] Finally, in the laws examined in this
study one reaches the phase in the evolution of the peace where the
duke and the church have enclosed a vast legal area within their domain
of special interest. Also the expanding pacific areas, perceived in the
succession of special *paces*, keep pace with the "process of becoming
public," until in the ducal peace and, to some extent, in the ecclesiastical
peace one discovers a special jurisdiction so comprehensive as to approach a true general peace or public order. Some conscious recognition
of this tendency was already evident in that enactment of the Bavarian
Law which prohibited the malicious injury and homicide of strangers
on the highways because "one peace is needful for all," and from such
ideas must develop a common law extending uniformly throughout the
entire public order.[117] The transition from a ducal peace to a royal peace
is largely a matter of degree, such as one encounters in passing from
the ducal interest in Swabia or Bavaria to the more inclusive imperial
authority of Charlemagne. However, if it be regarded as a public order,
which some would deny, it must be observed that the public element is
asserted as a personal right, ducal, royal, or imperial, for these lesser
pacific areas and special interests have been concentrated into a nucleus
of personal right. It is a "king's peace" because the king has identified
his rights with the rights of all and to that extent the royal peace, con-

---

There is considerable literature on the *Landfrieden*, but nearly all relates to a
later period, twelfth and thirteenth centuries. Wilda in his "Strafrecht der
Germanen" (*Strafrechts*) does not discuss it in connection with the earlier *Frieden*,
such as the *Heimfrieden* and *Heerfrieden*. I am convinced that these *Frieden* are all
interrelated and that perhaps the *Landfrieden* emerges later as a development from
these earlier ideas. I have not entered into the controversy in this paper whereby
Goebel in his *Felony and Misdemeanor*, Vol. I, undertook to overthrow Brunner's
theory of an original general Germanic peace of the land and folk. This is a subject
that will bear investigation.

[116] See Wilda, *Strafrechts*, I, 224–264.
[117] *L. Baiuv*. 3, 14, 1.

ceived in the Germanic personal sense, becomes a general peace of the land and a basis of public order, if one may speak of public in an order where rights remain personal.

One additional reflection should be made in the light of Kern's view that the Germanic idea of customary law regards that custom as a totality of individual rights or what were later designated liberties. Indeed, he would assert that the objective legal order is "the sum total of all the subjective rights of individuals" and that even "the king's right to rule was but his private right, a mere parcel of the law itself."[118] He would say further that king and people are not bound as partners by any legal bond of contract but are mutually bound only in their common obligation to the objective legal order. This can only mean that the objective legal order prevails over or is efficient within all pacific areas, and when king or duke have absorbed the more limited special *paces* into the royal or ducal peace they become responsible personally for the guarantee of all subjective individual rights contained within those special areas. The objective legal order remains constant, regardless of what individual rights are enclosed in any given pacific area, but if the "king's peace" should attract all lesser *paces* within its orbit, and so all subjective individual rights, it would become the sole agency for maintaining custom and the rights guaranteed by custom. In effect, the royal peace would become a general peace embracing land and folk and would be identified with support of the entire subjective legal order. It should be noted, also, that within each pacific area individual rights divide sharply into rights involving life, liberty, and property, as if these distinctions were reflecting some basic moral principle inherent in natural law. Historically it is a point of interest in view of our recent sesquicentennial anniversary of the American Bill of Rights to find these conceptions of individual rights grounded in the ancient framework of the custom of our Germanic forebears. These individual rights were preserved with little change in feudal law, and even the vestiges of the older special interests recur in the distinct and separate liberties guaranteed to the feudal estates of clergy, barons, and townsmen in the Magna Charta. By the time we reach the British Bill of Rights and the first ten

[118] See F. Kern, *Kingship and Law in the Middle Ages*, trans. with Introd. by S. B. Chrimes (Oxford: Blackwell, 1939), pp. xx–xxi. These studies by Professor Kern represent a fresh approach in recent German scholarship to such problems as the relation of contract to custom, and the nature and sources of royal authority in Germanic custom. It is an invaluable corrective and check upon the earlier views of Wilda and Brunner. These references are simplified statements taken from Chrimes' introductory commentary.

amendments of our American constitution, the basic rights of life, liberty, and property have become functions of the individual citizen rather than of members of limited areas of special interest. The modern State appears as a public agent to replace the personal or private agency of the mediaeval duke and king, and with the State emerges a true public order and general peace. Modern doctrines of sovereignty have modified profoundly the relation of the State to Law; yet there inheres still a final irreducible remnant of the ancient view of personal individual liberties in our Bill of Rights, to which some of us cling today amid the rising tide of socialistic and totalitarian theories because it constitutes a legal bulwark, protecting individuals and minorities, which even states cannot remove and obliterate save by an act of force. These rights of life, liberty, and property are unamendable and unchanging in their intrinsic qualities by the very conditions of their nature. Assuredly this truth, which has survived across two thousand years from the very origins of Germanic custom, demonstrates that the Law will hold its hallowed place above transient states and the ephemeral opinions of men.

X

Notes on Public Law: Ostrogothic, Burgundian, Lombard, North German*

The material contained in the notes forming this study either supplements or adds confirmatory evidence to the ideas developed in the preceding essays. Thus the Ostrogothic *Edict* provides an example of the mingling of Roman and Germanic elements at a level of fusion far lower than in the Visigothic law, but nevertheless reveals an attempt to adjust the more sophisticated Roman ideas to the simpler intellectual resources of a people emerging from barbarism. The Burgundian codes involve similar problems although differing in detail. Neither Burgundian nor Ostrogothic law provides clear evidence of a complete grasp of the majesty concept although both set forth the rule regarding accusations of majesty which was so significant in the *Breviary* and later in the *Lex Romana Curiensis*. The Lombard legislation contains much that is strictly Germanic such as military offenses of the *herisliz* type, many aspects of folk treason, and a wide variety of *paces*. The North German codes are especially valuable for their extensive enumeration of the various *paces* and for their elaboration of data relating to the peace principle together with the penalties attaching to violations of the peace. It is also significant that the Lombard and North German laws are generally more purely Germanic in spirit although later in point of time than many of the other codes.

* Section III on Lombard Law consists of a revision of a paper on "Treason and Related Offenses in Lombard Law," which was given at a meeting of the Southern Classical Association in Birmingham, Alabama, on November 27, 1947.

I

The legal monuments of the Ostrogoths are far less extensive and their enduring contributions to legal history much fewer than those of their Visigothic kinsmen. The period of their independent exercise of public authority was brief, and their legal activity constitutes a mere episode in the long history of the law in Italy, isolated and detached from the main current. Their chief legal monument is the *Edict of Theodoric* (493–526), which was issued about A.D. 512 and is, thus, contemporary with the *Breviary* of Alaric and the Burgundian *Papian.*[1] This body of law was promulgated in pursuance of Theodoric's policy of amalgamating Goths and Romans; hence it contains much that is typical of the legal and social systems of both peoples. *Coloni* and *curiales* are somewhat incongruously mentioned side by side with the *Sippe* and are incorporated into wergeld tariffs. The two kinds of law are not fused in any organic fashion but are combined arbitrarily. In general the Germanic influence is the more prominent despite the prevalence of Roman terms and expressions. The sources are substantially the same as for the *Breviary,* save that Gaius was not used, but the discriminating selection from the Roman law and the careful quotation of that law verbatim in the *Breviary* are superseded in the *Edict* by an awkward restatement which deals largely with criminal matters. Homicides, woundings, theft of women (*raptus*), theft of property (*furtus*), adultery, and arson occupy a conspicuous place in this legislation as is commonly the case in the *leges barbarorum.*

The number of laws which deal with treason is very small. One clearcut statement defines the crime and the penalty for treason against land

---

[1] See text of F. Bluhme, *Edictum Theodorici regis* in *Monumenta Germaniae Historica* (Hanover: Hahn, 1889), Legum Tomas V, pp. 145–179; also Ferd. Walter, *Corpus iuris germanici antiqui* (Berlin: Reimer, 1824), I, 391–414; and recently Riccobono, *Fontes iuris romani antejustiniani* (Florence: Barbèra, 1941), II, 681–710. Cf. H. Brunner, *Deutsche Rechtsgeschichte* (2nd ed.; Leipzig: Duncker and Humblot, 1906), I, 525–529; Schröder-von Künssberg, *Lehrbuch der deutschen Rechtsgeschichte* (6th ed.; Berlin and Leipzig: De Gruyter, 1922), pp. 255–256. F. Dahn, *Die Könige der Germanen* (Würzburg: Breitkopf and Härtel, 1866), IV: Edictum des Theoderichs.

A relatively brief account of the Germanic kingdoms and their legislation, based on recent work in the field and accompanied with substantial current bibliography, may be found in H. Conrad, *Deutsche Rechtsgeschichte* (Karlsruhe: Müller, 1954), Vol. I: Frühzeit und Mittelalter, pp. 73–111. There is also a great deal of reference material based on contemporary literature dealing with barbarian legislation in J. M. Wallace-Hadrill, *The Long-Haired Kings and Other Studies in Frankish History* (London: Methuen, 1962), but it touches the problem of treason only tangentially. This material is scattered in footnotes since there is no formal bibliography.

and folk: "Whosoever shall instigate sedition either among the people
or in the army shall be destroyed with fire."[2] This is followed by regulations against impious rites, pagan worships, the practice of evil arts,
and sacrilege.[3] Another provision regulates the punishment in instances
where a man is expelled forcibly from his home and property, and
where a riot, sedition, or fire is caused incidentally in the commission of
that crime.[4] However, mere rioting cannot be construed as treasonable
as long as no malicious intentions are exhibited against public authority.
If public agencies are resisted when they are defending private property, no treason can well be alleged so long as the rioters direct their evil
designs against the property alone and display no intent to destroy the
state. Still the line between mere rioting and treasonable sedition is a
narrow one at times, since, in such cases as this where the state under-
takes to protect private property, the protected private interest tends to
identify itself with the public interest. Such an identification of interests
is difficult to establish strictly on the basis of the political theory of
treason. However, if actual insubordination and overt resentment against
the state as such appear, the complexion of the matter is altered. That
the Ostrogothic law intended no such confusion of rioting with folk
treason seems certain when the punishments are considered. In the case
of sedition *honestiores* shall lose a third of their property and suffer exile
for five years, whereas *humiliores* shall be beaten to death or perpetually
exiled. But treason is distinguished from this crime since the traitor shall
be burned to death. Nevertheless these are closely related offenses. The
crime and the penalties are defined in no part of the edict. The phrases
crimine maiestatis and *causa maiestatis* appear but in no case is a definition of *maiestas* given. One law repeats the old Roman principle that
familiar and household servants (*cuiuslibet familiaritati vel domui in-
haerentes*) shall not inform or make accusations against their masters
save when the master is implicated in *laesa maiestas*.[5] Another provision,
illustrating the same exceptional nature of *maiestas*, states: "If any condemned *curialis* have sons, they shall receive all the property he leaves;
if he have no sons, the property shall revert to the *curia*, save in cases of
laesa maiestas, under which circumstances all property of the condemned man shall pass not to his sons, if he have any, but to the treasury

[2] *Ed. Theod.* 107.
[3] *Ed. Theod.* 108, 110.
[4] *Ed. Theod.* 75.
[5] *Ed. Theod.* 49, and cf. 48.

following established custom."[6] It is clear that in the *Edict* the same restrictions which had been set forth in the *Theodosian Code* are retained in cases of accusations of *maiestas*. The influence of the Roman law is apparent in Theodoric's compilation. The concept of *maiestas* is recognized, and presumably violations of *maiestas* constituted the crime of high treason.

A brief survey of the Ostrogothic kingship suggests that high treason must have been the most serious offense known to this people. Before the time of Theodoric the power of the king seems to have been limited by popular custom (*Freiheistsrechte*), which preserved much of the ancient Germanic idea of personal freedom.[7] Nevertheless even before the time of Tacitus certain obscure forces which tended to the increase of royal authority appear in operation. A certain propensity for strong leadership distinguished the Ostrogoths from their western kinsmen, who sought constantly to limit and decentralize. In addition, the numerous migrations and wars and the powerful personalities of many of the chieftains paved the way for absolutism when the time came for the final settlement in Italy amid a people filled with the ideas of Roman imperialism. Just as the emperors before him, Theodoric exercised legislative powers without limitation or association with his nobles or popular assembly.[8] Real legislation had been practically unknown among the ancient Germans with their customary conception of law, in which the slightest alteration or change in interpretation had required the consent of both nobles and common folk. Hence great indeed was the change to a situation where a Germanic king could promulgate a general edict for both Roman and German subjects and could attempt the unification of two legal systems which by no means harmonized in many respects. The general outline suggests a monarch who approached the Roman conception of absolutism, who personified public authority, and who held himself above his subjects, noble and ignoble alike, much as the Roman emperors whom he succeeded had done not so many years earlier.

II

The Burgundian laws are among the oldest of the Germanic folk laws and are peculiarly interesting both on account of their age and the fact that they were compiled in an old Roman province amid Roman sur-

---

[6] *Ed. Theod.* 113.

[7] Dahn, *Könige* (2nd ed.; Leipzig: Breitkopf and Härtel, 1911), II, 105.

[8] Dahn, *Könige* (1866), III, 135.

roundings. The presence of so many Roman *provinciales* in the newly occupied region made it essential that two separate codes be devised, since the Burgundians were not inclined to impose their tribal custom upon strange peoples and consistently practiced their Germanic legal principle of personality by permitting the conquered to retain their own law. Thus there was created a *Lex Romana Burgundionum*, the so-called *Papian*,[9] which was based on Roman law and was used among Roman subjects, while a separate compilation of *constitutiones* was prepared for the Germanic ruling people which seems to contain somewhat more typically German materials. Both works were prepared at the behest of King Gundobad (474–516): the Germanic *constitutiones* appearing perhaps as early as A.D. 502 and the *Lex Romana* somewhat later.[10] Since the *Lex Romana* was based very largely on the *Theodosian Code* and the *Sentences* of Paulus, one might expect here a certain amount of general information concerning the *crimen laesae maiestatis* which could be contrasted with similar Germanic ideas in the *Liber constitutionum*, thereby affording a valuable study of two different legal systems and their distinguishing concepts at a relatively early period before either had had opportunity to influence or alter the form of the other to any great extent. However, the results are disappointing. The *Liber constitutionum* gives no information concerning *maiestas* but is taken up with the usual lists of wergeld tariffs covering ordinary breaches of criminal law: homicides, theft of women (*raptus*), and adultery, together with laws concerning succession and inheritance of property. It gives the general impression of being more Roman than Germanic in

[9] The tradition associated with the word *Papian(us)* holds that it is a corruption of the name of the Roman jurist Papinian. A scribe is believed to have omitted the letters *in* in transcribing the word which divided at consecutive pages of a codex.

[10] See texts of L. R. de Salis, *Lex Romana Burgundionum or Papian*, and *Leges Burgundionum or Lex Gundobada*, in M. G. H., Legum Sectio I, Tomus II, Pars I. See the recently edited text of *Lex Romana* in Riccobono, *Fontes*, II, 711–750. For the *Gundobada* see the translation of K. M. Fischer, *The Burgundian Code* (Philadelphia: The University of Pennsylvania Press, 1949), Translations and Reprints, Third Series, Vol. V, with bibliography, pp. 97–102; also German translation by F. Beyerle in *Germanenrechte* (Weimar: Böhlaus, 1936), Vol. 10, entitled *Gesetze der Burgunden*; Walter, *Corpus*, I, 299–350. For the *Lex Romana* see Wilfried Roels, *Onderzoek naar het Gebruik van de aangehaalde Bronnen van Romeins Recht in de Lex Romana Burgundionum* (Antwerp: de Sikkel, 1958) with bibliography, pp. 1–4. Cf. Brunner, *D. R.*, I, 506–510 (*Lex Romana Burgundionum*) and I, 497–506 (*Lex Burgundionum*); Schröder-von Künssberg, *Lehrbuch*, pp. 256–257. F. Dahn, *Könige* (Leipzig: Breitkopf and Härtel, 1908), XI (Die Burgunden).

form and perhaps in content. It indicates the existence of a special royal
peace with added protection in the form of a higher wergeld for those
serving the king's personal interest.[11]

The *Lex Romana* has the general appearance of a combined textbook
and code of ordinary private law derived from Roman sources for the
use of the Roman subjects of the Burgundian king. Dahn notes that one
does not find the Germanic idea of infidelity (*Untreue*) here,[12] but there
is a brief definition of *maiestas* in the code: "Crimine vero maiestatis
haec sunt, quae legibus designantur, id est: salus principis, traditio
regionis aut adeptio tyrannidis."[13] Thus while one is unable to compare
the conceptions of treason in two different legal systems, he does find an
interesting statement of what the Burgundians believed were the chief
components of the Roman law of *maiestas*. The safety of the prince,
insuring against attacks on his life, refers clearly to high treason while
the betrayal or surrender of the land as plainly denotes treason against
land and folk. But the *adeptio tyrannidis*, or attainment of tyranny, embraces a conception which cannot be found in any other barbarian code
so far as my experience extends in the study of these materials. Wilfried
Roels renders this expression as high treason (*hoogverraad*), which it
may well be in the sense of usurpation of authority.[14] However, the
appearance of this Greek word in a barbarian text is an anomaly, and it
would probably be unsafe to jump to any conclusion as to what these
people understood it to mean. It is not impossible that it may be used in
the usual Greek context as unconstitutional rule or the illegal seizure of
authority. The violent overthrow of rulers was not exceptional in the
barbarian kingdoms. There is the alternative possibility that it might
apply to a ruler who has failed to observe his contractual obligations to
his people. Such a ruler is false to his office and no true ruler but a

---

[11] *Liber Constitutionum* (*Lex Gundobada*) 2, 2; 50, 1, 2, 4.

[12] Dahn, *Könige*, II, 250.

[13] *L. R. B.* 7, 6. Cf. Paulus *Sententiae* 5, 29, 1; *Digest* 48, 4, 10–11.

[14] Roels (*Onderzoek*, p. 54) says the source of *L. R. B.* 6 is unknown. The threefold definition of the idea of *maiestas*—attack on the life of the *princeps* (*salus
princeps*), folk treason (*traditio regionis, landverraad*), high treason (*adeptio
tyrannidis, hoogverraad*)—agrees with the content of the idea in the Roman-law
sources but not in the form found here. The possibility that it derives from lost texts
cannot be precluded, and the author may have included it for that reason. Perhaps
the definition is not derived in its entirety from Roman sources but simply follows
the custom that attaches to the word *maiestas* in legal practice, that is, in the
Vulgärrecht. This is the explanation advanced by Roels for this peculiar provision
of the *lex*. *Dahn* seems to imply here the usurpation of authority by the Burgundians
at the expense of Roman power (*Staatsgewalt*).

tyrant and traitor in Germanic thinking.[15] In any case the association of
tyranny with high treason and folk treason is a decidedly curious circumstance in Germanic folk law. It tends to prove that while the Germans took over the forms of Roman law including the term *maiestas*
they did not fully grasp the meaning of the word, since the Roman law
hardly considers tyranny a form of the *crimen laesae maiestatis* save
possibly in the sense of usurpation.

Immediately preceding this provision relating to *maiestas* one finds
a law reflecting some ideas embodied in the petty treason of later times.
This law is based on the old Roman enactment concerning accusation,
which states that no slave may accuse his master and no freedman or
servant his patron except for the crime of majesty.[16] This right of accusation was probably not extended to slaves since a discontented servile class might raise much malicious mischief to the great danger and
inconvenience of their masters. Further, the personal relationship between client and patron possessed a certain sanctity in the eyes of the
law which was inferior only to majesty itself. In either case slave or
client formed part of the lord's familiar household. Hence it was a kind
of petty treason for the bondsman to accuse his master in any case save
where the master was guilty of *laesa maiestas* and where the bondsman
would incriminate himself likewise if he remained silent. Another law,
De violentiis, indicates that slaves who created tumults on their master's
property or destroyed it without his knowledge should be put to death.[17]
Also, a general law existed which stated that any one who collected a
mob for the purpose of destroying property by violence should be
punished capitally.[18] Rioting is seditious when directed against public
authority but can hardly be construed as treasonable when directed
against private property only, although the situation may be somewhat
different in the case of slaves. Nearly all this material is based directly
upon Roman law, and it is possible that the Burgundian occupation of
this Roman land would have led to these adaptations eventually even
if the invaders had not directly taken over Roman ideas of the state and
public authority. Dahn sees a Roman absolutism arising among the

[15] Cf. *Frostuthingslög*, trans. by Larson (New York: Columbia University Press, 1935), 287.
[16] *L. R. B.* 7, 5. Cf, *Codex Theodosianus* 9, 6 *Rubric*: "Ne praeter crimen maiestatis servus dominum vel patronum libertus seu familiaris accuset." This pro-vision is only a paraphrased copy derived from the title *Rubric* of *C. Th.* 9, 6, without essential change.
[17] *L. R. B.* 8, 3. Cf. *C. Th.* 9, 10, 4.
[18] *L. R. B.* 8, 1. Cf. *C. Th.* 9, 10, 1–3, and *L. R. B.* 8, 5.

Burgundians and quotes Avitus: "tu enim es caput populi, non populus caput tuum." He notes the extravagant titles in both sets of Burgundian laws: *dominus noster, gloriosissimus praecellentissimus dominus noster, dominantes, vir gloriosissimus, clarissimus, venerabilis,*[19] and finally he describes the Burgundian state as a German kingdom built into an old Roman land, forming a picture of varied contrasts and contradictions.[20] The general impression conveyed by the Burgundian laws is that of a more vital appropriation of Roman legal and political ideas than occurred among the Franks farther north in Gaul in the Salic and Ripuarian codes; yet even here Romanization was scarcely more than half accomplished.

III

The Lombard laws constitute an integral part of the Germanic folk laws or *leges barbarorum,*[21] but deserve special consideration owing to their unique character. Brunner asserted that the Lombard folk laws occupy a peculiar position relative to the other Germanic laws, and insisted that they form a distinctive narrow group together with the laws of the old Saxons and Anglo-Saxons with whom they shared in common certain characteristic legal concepts and experiences. However, aside from the *Edict of Theodoric,* they are the only barbarian laws promulgated in Italy. It is doubtful whether they were influenced to any extent by the Ostrogothic legislation, which ceased to be effective about A.D. 552. The period of the reconquest of Italy by Justinian (552–568) was marked by the temporary introduction of the *Corpus Juris Civilis.* Then the Lombards under Alboin entered Italy (A.D. 568), although the first Lombard Laws do not appear until Rothar's *Edict* was issued in 643. There was, thus, a long tradition of the Roman Law

[19] F. Dahn, *Könige* (1908), XI, 251.

[20] *Ibid.,* XI, 250.

[21] See text of F. Bluhme, *Leges Langobardorum,* in *M. G. H.* (Hanover: Hahn, 1869), Legum Tomus IV, and of Guido Padeletti, *Edictum regum langobardorum,* in *Fontes juris italici medii aevi* (Turin: Loescher, 1877), Vol. I; also the revised Bluhme text with translation in German by F. Beyerle, *Die Gesetze der Langobarden* (Weimar: Böhlaus, 1947), and Walter, *Corpus,* I, 670–838. There is an unpublished English translation of the Lombard laws in the doctoral dissertation of Katherine M. Fischer, entitled *A Study of the Lombard Laws* (Cornell University, 1950).

Important secondary analyses and interpretations of this Lombard material may be found in F. Dahn, *Könige* (Leipzig: Breitkopf and Härtel, 1909), XII (Die Langobarden), T. Hodgkin, *Italy and Her Invaders* (Oxford: Clarendon, 1896), VI, 183–238 (Ch. V on "The Legislation of Rothari"); H. Brunner, *D. R.,* I, 529–539; Schröder-von Künssberg, *Lehrbuch,* pp. 265–268.

in Italy, continuing on down from the time of the *Theodosian Code* (A.D. 438), but growing more and more faded and broken in the later centuries. During the period A.D. 568–643, the Lombards were becoming settled in northern Italy and associating with *Romani*, among whom Roman legal knowledge must have persisted. Hence it is only natural to expect to find a very considerable admixture of Roman Law in their legislation. In general, an organic consolidation and amalgamation of Germanic and Roman elements have occurred; yet the Teutonic note dominates the whole in spirit, content, and form. In point of time, these laws are practically contemporary with the Visigothic *Forum Judicum*, and about a century earlier than the Bavarian Code. In many respects, these two codes bear close resemblance to the Lombard Laws; nevertheless, the Lombard Code lacks the Roman formal systematization of the Bavarian Code, while it is more concise than the *Leges Visigothorum*. Also, it would hardly be correct to look upon the Lombard legislation as an intermediate code bridging the gap between the Visigothic and Bavarian laws, despite the presence of certain common factors in all three codes, such as the conception of *scandalum* and the idea of conspiracy as high treason. The similarity is not altogether to be accounted for by a common history or by any historical continuity, connecting and running through all three sets of laws. Rather it would seem to be due to the fact that when a Germanic people attempts to incorporate or reconcile Roman legal ideas with its native custom the resultant product assumes certain common, typical forms. Furthermore, tribal peculiarities are marked in Lombard legislation and accentuate its distinctive individuality. In any case, "it is accounted to be one of the best statements of ancient German usages."[22]

Thus, the earliest and largest body of written Lombard Law is contained in Rothar's *Edict* of A.D. 643, enacted seventy-five years after the arrival of this people in Italy. At this time King Rothar prepared a comprehensive statement and record of their law which is designated as the *Edict*—the same expression applied by King Theodoric to his promulgation of the Ostrogothic laws. In a Prologue, which contains pointed reference to one of Justinian's Novels, Rothar declares that his work is a revision of the existing law—presumably the immemorial custom of the Lombard folk. Later he appends a statement that the source of his legislation is the law of his forefathers, which had been used from of old

[22] *Select Essays in Anglo-American Legal History*, compiled and edited by a Committee of the Association of American Law Schools (Boston: Little, Brown, 1907), I, 19.

but which had long remained unwritten. After he drafted the *Edict* with the advice and consent of his chieftains and the people it was confirmed through formal action of the general assembly, or host at arms (*gaire thinx*), in accordance with established practice.

Some have suggested with just cause that the *Edict of Rothar* is the most distinguished legislative product of the age of folk law. Despite borrowings from foreign sources, it possesses an organic consistency quite different from the artificial, mosaiclike structure of most barbarian codes. Brunner states:

It appears to be a spontaneous piece of work. The statements of law are formulated concisely and sharply. The material is arranged according to a definite plan. In the text which is written in the Vulgar Latin of the period one finds numerous technical expressions which seem to be legal terms peculiar to the Lombards. Most are demonstrably German, and indeed are related to High German speech, but many have long defied any satisfactory linguistic classification. (Brunner, *D.R.*, I, 531)

The older Visigothic legislation was undoubtedly used in the compilation of the *Edict* in its present form as revealed by the wording and phraseology. Occasional instances are derived from the Bible, while Roman legal sources were not unknown to the authors of the *Edict*. Much that suggests the precedent of Roman Law was transmitted through Visigothic sources or oral Latin popular custom; yet some places betray a knowledge of the *Code* and *Novels* of Justinian. Furthermore, Brunner notes emphatically that, viewed in the light of Ostrogothic, Visigothic, and Burgundian legislation, the *Edict* has maintained a large measure of independence of the Roman Law in its legal opinions, and, although Roman legal terminology is not lacking, the number of legal concepts derived from Roman Law is comparatively small. As far as may be determined, the Roman population was subjected to the provisions of the *Edict* in all matters of public law and in all legal business with the Lombards, and the use of the Roman Law was permitted only in the mutual legal relations among Romans alone (Brunner, *D. R.*, I, 532–533).

Attention must now be turned to this earliest body of Lombard Law contained in Rothar's *Edict* (A.D. 643).[23] As regards treason and related public offenses the *Edict* opens with a provision against high treason: "If any man shall plan in his own mind or plot with others against the

---

[23] For a brief summary regarding treason in Lombard Law, see E. Osenbrüggen, *Das Strafrecht der Langobarden* (Schaffhausen: Hurter, 1863), pp. 52–55; F. Dahn, *Könige*, XII, 178–182.

life of the king [*contra animam regis cogitaverit aut consiliaverit*], he shall be in peril of his life and his property shall be confiscated."[24] The idea of plotting or conspiracy is foremost rather than the idea of infidelity, and plotting seems to be emphasized over actual killing, although one must not infer too much because of the absence of specific words directed against the killing of the king. The only new conception is contained in the verb *cogitaverit*; this makes mere "cogitating" high treason, merely thinking about or planning the king's death in the mind of the accused, and suggests the development which culminated in mediaeval English law with the establishment of "imagining the king's death" as high treason.[25]

In this law the chief weight is laid ostensibly upon the intent rather than the overt act; this would suggest a Roman basis. However, neither *cogitaverit* nor *consiliaverit* preclude the possibility that the plot was actually executed or attempted by some overt act. It seems probable that "imagining or compassing the king's death" were punished alike by Lombard law. In addition to this law, various elements relating to high treason are given appropriate penalties in the regulations punishing infractions of the royal "peace." A special royal interest is clearly defined in this legislation, possessing special rights, privileges, and immunities not enjoyed by ordinary freemen. Thus, one reads:

> If a man joins with the king in plotting the death of another, or kills a man in accordance with a royal command, such a man is, in no sense, liable to punishment, and neither he nor his heirs shall suffer any molestation by the victim or his heirs; because since we believe that the hearts of kings rest in the hand of God, it is not possible that a man can clear himself [*eduniare*] whom the king has ordered to die.[26]

This last clause is significant and suggestive of a sort of "divine right" theory. The king is represented as a special agent of God, not bound by the ordinary restrictions of society and placed above or outside the law

---

[24] *Edictum Rothari* 1. Cf. C. Calisse, *A History of Italian Law*, trans. by L. B. Register, Continental Legal Series, Vol. VIII (London: John Murray, 1928), p. 89. Calisse observes that Lombard law imposed penalties in the king's name for public offenses such as "an attempt upon the king's life, conspiracy against the State, desertion from the army, betrayal to the enemy, falsehood by an official, and similar offenses."

[25] P. Bisoukides, *Der Hochverrat* (Berlin: Carl Heymanns Verlag, 1903), p. 43: "Der Gegensatz des 'cogitare' zum 'consiliare' besteht offenbar darin, dass das erstere die von einer einzelnen Person ausgehenden, das letztere dagegen die von mehreren geplanten Angriffe gegen das Leben des Königs umfasst."

[26] *Ed. Roth.* 2: "quia postquam corda regum in manum dei credimus esse, non est possibile ut homo possit eduniare quam rex occidere iusserit."

so that he may act in ways ordinarily forbidden to other men.[27] The
idea is also present that since kings are especially favored by God no
man may question their motives or right to do things which would
appear wrong if done by anyone else. This spirit is similar to the spirit
of Roman *maiestas* with added overtones from Christian theology. However, one cannot safely assert that the entire tenor of Lombard law is
colored by such a theory of royal rights. Indeed, a careful survey of the
entire code leads one to believe that this clause may be merely an
appendage added by a pious legist to an enactment which offended the
entire spirit of Germanic law and needed some religious sanction to give
it respectable appearance. As in Frankish law, one seems to be dealing
with despotism, and despotism could not be justified in Germanic custom. Also it must be remembered that despotism is inconsistent with the
constitutional aspects of Roman *maiestas*. Nevertheless, this passage has
a spirit reminiscent of later Roman practice where allegiance had become an act of deference to authority and no longer a matter of contract
and mutual obligation.

With certain exceptions all royal causes (*regales causas, quae ad
manum regis perteneunt*) could be compounded only by a twofold payment.[28] Various agents and officials in the king's service, such as *scul-
dahis*, were protected by an extra fine of eighty *solidi* payable to the
king in addition to the customary composition to their relatives in case
of death or injury occasioned through violence.[29] The royal peace is
extended over the highways as is notably the case in many barbarian
laws:

> If any one of our freemen wishes to come to us, he shall come in safety and
> return unharmed to his home; none of his enemies shall do him any injury
> or presume to molest him on his journey. It is ordered thus so that each man
> who hastens to come to his king may come in safety and in good faith,[30] and
> receive no injury or loss on this journey coming to or returning from the royal
> court; and, if harm is done him, it shall be compounded as this edict
> establishes.[31]

The *Edict* then goes on to state that such violence will be punished by
a fine of nine hundred *solidi*, half going to the king and half to the in-

---

[27] Cf. *Ed. Roth.* 10–11, where ordinary plotting is punishable by a fine of twenty
solidi and homicide requires full payment of the victim's wergeld.
[28] *Ed. Roth.* 369.
[29] *Ed. Roth.* 374.
[30] Good faith (*honeste*), that is, believing that he can depend on the king's
assurance of safe-conduct.
[31] *Ed. Roth.* 17.

jured person.[32] Vicious attacks along the highways and obstruction of the highways are made punishable by heavy fines which vary in amount according to the condition of the individual who has been waylaid or held up.[33] The fine in the case of free women and girls was set at nine hundred *solidi*, payable half to the king and half to the injured party or her guardian (*mundius*) to whom her *mundium* belongs, while a composition of twenty *solidi* was paid to the master where slaves, servingmaids and thralls (*haldii*) or freedmen were concerned. Opposition to public authority in the maintenance of a special peace established to promote the general welfare comes very near to treason against land and folk. When the special peace is also a royal peace attached to the special interest of an individual personifying public authority elements of high treason may be considered present. Also, high treason and folk treason are one and the same to the degree that the special royal interest and the general welfare are identical. The conception of *scandalum* also appears in the Lombard laws and retains its characteristic features, that is, it seems to be a type of high treason in which the element of personal insult to the king dominates over the idea of some more vital injury to the monarch or general welfare. Thus, one reads: "If any one presumes to create a scandal in the royal palace in the presence of the king, he shall be in peril of his life or redeem it if he can from the king."[34] If one may judge from the capital penalties prescribed in either case, the most aggravated scandals were considered essentially as serious as plotting against the king's life. Just what sort of conduct constituted such scandal is not always definitely set forth, but, in general, brawling and fighting in the king's presence were common offenses, considered as belonging to this category. Occasionally *scandalum* appears to refer to rioting and seditious tumults on the part of mobs, in which case it would seem to fall within that type of folk treason designated *seditio*. However, it is the unseemly breaches of royal etiquette that are deemed most scandalous in the *Edict of Rothar*. For instance:

If any free man presumes to create a scandal in a city where the king is found to be present at that time, that is, if he incites the trouble and does not strike a blow, he shall pay a fine of twelve *solidi* to the king. But if he continues the disturbance and strikes a blow in it, he shall pay twenty-four *solidi* to the king, and in addition he shall make composition for any blows and strikes he may have given as the law requires.[35]

[32] *Ed. Roth.* 18.
[33] *Ed. Roth.* 26–28 *De wegworin, id est hor-bitariam.*
[34] *Ed. Roth.* 36.
[35] *Ed. Roth.* 37.

If a slave acts in this manner he shall be fined either six or twelve *solidi* according to the degree of his participation.[36] If the trouble occurs in any other city than that in which the king is present a free man shall pay a fine of either six or twelve *solidi* according to the degree of his participation, and a slave shall pay half that amount.[37] This indicates clearly that the scandal is the disorderly act, and the proximity of the king is not essential to the crime. However, if the king is near at hand when the offense occurs its seriousness is magnified greatly. The treasonable nature of the scandal evidently depends upon the degree of insult or affront offered the king. It is interesting to note that the crime is amended by a smaller fine in the case of a slave. Very possibly this may have been occasioned by the fact that little was expected of slaves and their actions were considered less significant. On the other hand, masters may have been unwilling to pay more, and the king had to be content with levying the highest rate the situation permitted. Crimes of falsification and counterfeiting are penalized under this code, but are not specifically named high treason as in the Roman law. The law reads: "If any one mints gold or counterfeits money without the authorization of the king, his hands shall be cut off."[38] "If any one writes a false charter or any similar document, his hands shall be cut off."[39]

Folk treason or *Landesverrat* appears in a variety of its typical Germanic forms. In common with Frankish law, any one who attempts to flee outside the province shall be in peril of his life and have his property confiscated in the treasury.[40] Restrictions were also placed on freedom of movement within the realm; even free men apparently had to secure royal permission to move about.[41] External and internal treason (*Verrat an den aüsseren, als an den inneren Feind*) are similarly punished:

If any one invites or introduces enemies within the province, he shall be in peril of his life and his property shall be confiscated;[42] if any one conceals spies (*escamaras*) within the province or gives them food, he shall be in peril of his life and compound 900 *solidi* to the king;[43] if any one causes sedition outside the province in the army against his duke or him whom the king has given authority over the army, or if any one alienates the army and leads it away into another place, he shall be in peril of his life;[44] and if any one commits any scandal in the council or any assemblage, he shall pay 900 *solidi* to the king.[45]

---

[36] *Ed. Roth.* 38.
[37] *Ed. Roth.* 39–40.
[38] *Ed. Roth.* 242.
[39] *Ed. Roth.* 243.
[40] *Ed. Roth.* 3.

[41] *Ed. Roth.* 177.
[42] *Ed. Roth.* 4.
[43] *Ed. Roth.* 5.
[44] *Ed. Roth.* 6.
[45] *Ed. Roth.* 8.

Penalties are provided for other seditious acts. If slaves plot together through ill advice in armed bands and enter a village with some evil purpose in view each one shall compound forty *solidi* as a fine to the king and the injured parties; if a free man has placed himself at their head he shall be in peril of his life unless he compounds nine hundred *solidi*, half to the king and half to the victim of the crime.[46] And, if for any reason bands of country folk (*rusticani*) assemble together, presume to make plots and create sedition, and attack or annoy people, their leader shall be killed or redeem his life according to his wergeld, while other members of the band shall compound twelve *solidi* each, half to the king and half to the party whom they attacked or injured.[47]

If any one shall gather together an armed band and attack someone to avenge an injury or shall enter a village, the leader shall die for his presumption or compound 900 *solidi* to the king and the injured party. But the accessories shall compound eighty *solidi* each in the same way, with the exception that if they shall burn any huts in the village or kill a man, they shall compound according to the worth of the burned huts, of the station of the dead man's relatives or the value of the dead slave.[48]

Provision is made against various military offenses, some of which resemble the Frankish *herisliz*. Thus, "if any one deserts his comrade who still remains fighting the enemy or acts faithlessly (*astalin fecerit*), that is, if he runs away from his comrade and does not fight at his side, he shall be in peril of his life."[49] This law is clearly directed against the type of infidelity associated with breaches of the *comitatus* relationship. Another regulation applies to insubordination and states that soldiers who are disobedient to their duke are commonly fined twenty *solidi*.[50] In addition to the peace of the land other special interests receive protection. Thus, if any one creates a scandal within a church, he is required to pay a fine of forty *solidi* to the injured ecclesiastical corporation.[51] Among the regulations relating to the peace of the home are laws providing that if a free man or a slave enters another man's courtyard by night without signalling his approach, he should be fined eighty or forty *solidi* according to his station; and, if he is killed, the relatives or master can demand no compensation.[52] And this law is established thus, "be-

[46] *Ed. Roth.* 279.
[47] *Ed. Roth.* 280.
[48] *Ed. Roth.* 19.
[49] *Ed. Roth.* 7: *astalin = deceptio, fraus.*
[50] *Ed. Roth.* 20–22.
[51] *Ed. Roth.* 35.
[52] *Ed. Roth.* 32–33.

cause it is not reasonable that a man should enter another's courtyard silently and secretly by night, but, if he has any business there, he must shout before he enters."[53] Also if any one, having been angered, shoots arrows or hurls lances or from without does any damage within another man's courtyard he shall compound twenty *solidi*.[54] And if any one enters another man's courtyard in anger (i.e., *haistan*) he shall pay that man twenty *solidi*.[55] Some of this material corresponds in a measure with the Roman legal tradition coming down from the *Theodosian Code*, but the general spirit of this legislation is dominantly Germanic.

A number of laws may be found relating to the crime later known as petty treason. Thus:

> If any one kills his lord, he shall be killed also; but if the man who kills his lord wishes to amend this homicide, he shall pay 900 *solidi* to the king and the relatives of the dead man.[56]
> And if a woman plots the death of her husband, either through her own act or through the act of another, her husband shall have the power to do with her and her property as he wishes. If she deny the act, her relatives may prove her innocence either by oath or by wager of battle.[57]

But if the woman kills her husband she shall be killed and her husband's relatives shall possess her property if there be no children.[58] These provisions against the killing of a lord by his man and of a husband by his wife constitute the chief content of the later English laws concerning petty treason. Parricide, which is also a violent breach of a special personal bond, is punished in this *Edict* as follows: "We hereby establish that these are just causes for disinheriting a son: if a son plots or schemes against his father's life or if he strikes his father voluntarily or if he commits incest with his step-mother (*matrinia*), he may be justly disinherited by his father."[59]

Unquestionably many of the elements contained in this *Edict* have some foundation in Roman law, but it is almost impossible to dissociate the Roman element, so organically has the whole been correlated. Nothing illustrates this situation better than Rothar's law of accusations, which treats of the general Roman idea of accusation but handles it in such typically Germanic fashion that one can find little or nothing Roman except the basic idea. This law states:

---

[53] *Ed. Roth.* 32.
[54] *Ed. Roth.* 34.
[55] *Ed. Roth.* 277.
[56] *Ed. Roth.* 13.
[57] *Ed. Roth.* 202.
[58] *Ed. Roth.* 203.
[59] *Ed. Roth.* 169.

If any one accuses a man before the king so that he is in danger of his life, the accused shall be permitted to clear himself by oath. And if such a case arises and the man accused of the crime is present, he may clear himself of the charge by wager of battle if he can. And if the proof goes against him, he shall pay with his life or compound as the king pleases. But if the crime cannot be proved against him, then the man who made the charge but could not prove it shall compound his wergeld as a fine to the king and to the man he accused.[60]

Attempts to entangle enemies in legal difficulties by accusing them falsely before the emperor were peculiarly characteristic of the later Roman period and exhibit much the same spirit as the practice of delation. The tradition of such habits seems to have been maintained among the German invaders, ruled as they often were by despotic princes, and legislation was still required to curb such vicious practices. However, the general spirit and the concrete detail of procedure remain quite Germanic, and this condition prevails throughout the *Edict of Rothar*. This Lombard code is decidedly unusual, not because it is so different from all other Germanic legislation but because it is, perhaps, more typical of Germanic law than any other code in the *leges barbarorum*. It contains Roman elements from the law of accusations to counterfeiting, but they are not organically assimilated. It is concise, though not brief, lacking the exaggerated detail of the *Leges Visigothorum* but not fragmentary like the North German legislation. It is very inclusive as to subject matter, dealing with crimes ranging from the Bavarian and Visigothic *scandalum* to the Frankish *herisliz*. And finally, it possesses an individuality of its own, marked by curious Lombard expressions and procedure.

There still remain three groups of Lombard laws belonging to a later period that may be mentioned. A law of Liutprand (*ca.* A.D. 723) provides penalties for sedition. If any one in any district (*civitas*) raises up sedition against the local judge contrary to the will of the king, or does any evil or expels the judge without royal permission, or if men from other districts seek to commit such crimes, the leader of the sedition shall be in peril of his life and all his property shall be confiscated to the people; the accomplices shall compound their wergeld.[61] An enactment of Ratchis (*ca.* A.D. 746) regulates the matter of spies hidden about

---

[60] *Ed. Roth.* 9.
[61] *Liutprandi Leges* (a. 723), 35, VI.

the royal palace who reveal the king's plans to his foreign enemies. The law runs:

> But it seems to us that the man who presumes to do such things is not right and true in his faith but rests under the suspicion of evil. Wherefore we decree that whoever attempts a thing of this sort, giving or receiving information, shall be in peril of his life, and his property shall be confiscated, because according to the Scriptures: While it is honorable to reveal the works of God, it is well to conceal the secrets of a king.[62]

This is a type of high treason, corresponding to the folk treason committed by concealing spies within a province, and is, perhaps, merely an extension of the principle laid down in that connection in Rothar's *Edict*. Finally another law of Ratchis is directed against any *iudex*, or man, who seeks to go away into another land or among another people. Death and confiscation of property are threatened as penalties to those who presume to go into these places: "Roma, Ravenna, Spoleti, Benevento, Francia, Baioaria, Alamannia, Ritias aut in Avaria," without royal permission.[63] This tendency to prohibit departure from the land resembles the Frankish practice and must be considered a type of folk treason (*Landesverrat*).

IV

Among the Germanic peoples who dwelt in areas adjacent to the lands occupied at one time by the Lombards but who did not leave their homes in the more extreme regions of northern Germany were the Frisians, Saxons, Thuringians, and Franks of Hamaland. Their laws constitute a body of interrelated legislation probably representing a Carolingian influence that dates from the close of the Saxon wars. The laws of the Frisians are among the oldest deriving from this group of peoples, since they date from the latter part of the eighth century (A.D. 785).[64] The Frisian Code opens with an unusually complex list of wer-

---

[62] *Ratchis Leges* (a. 746) 12, VIII. Cf. *Ed. Roth.* 5; also E. Osenbrüggen, *Strafrecht der Langobarden*, p. 52: "Mit den Worten '*non est in fide sua rectus*' ist auf den Fundamentalbegriff der Infidelität hingewissen."

[63] *Ratchis Leges* 9, V. Cf. E. Osenbrüggen, *Strafrecht*, p. 53; also *Ed. Roth.* 244.

[64] For text of the Frisian laws, see *Lex Frisionum*, edited by Karl Freiherr von Richthofen (Leeuwarden: Haag, Nijhoff, 1866), and in *M. G. H.*, Legum Tomus III (Hanover: Hahn, 1863), also Walter, *Corpus*, I, 351–374. In addition, see R. His, *Das Strafrecht der Friesen im Mittelalter* (Leipzig: Dieterich, 1901), and P. Heck, *Die Entstehung der Lex Frisionum* (Stuttgart: W. Kohlhammer, 1927), including the *Lex Frisionum* according to the Herold text, pp. 139–156; Brunner, *D. R.*, I, 475–481; Schröder-von Künssberg, *Lehrbuch*, pp. 275–277. For the later influence of Frisian law, see W. J. Buma and Wilhelm Ebel, *Das Rüstringer Recht* in *Altfriesische Rechtsquellen*, Band 1 (Göttingen: Musterschmidt, 1963).

gelds, providing penalties for all classes of people according to their social station and determining how compositions shall be divided among the recipients. One common rule in the case of homicides was that two parts of the fine (*mulcta*) should go to the heirs of the deceased and a third part to the near relatives. Thus the *Sippe* still existed as a party interested in the settlement of hereditable property. The various *Frieden* are designated in the Frisian law in much the same manner as in the other Germanic codes. The ancient *Heimfrieden* is set forth in the provision *De brand*, which states that if any one burns another's home he must compound doubly for the loss, and that if any one fires another's house and kills the owner as he emerges from his burning house the offender must compound ninefold according to his station.[65] A number of special peaces are established under the law entitled *Hic bannus est*:

1. If any one shall create trouble in the army, he must compound ninefold for the damage he has caused, and pay a nine-fold *freda* to his lord. 2. Whoever shall kill a man at the duke's court or in a church must compound his wergeld nine-fold, and pay a nine-fold *freda* to his lord. 3. If any one shall kill an officer of the king or duke, he must compound likewise nine-fold for the victim and pay a similar nine-fold *freda* to his lord. 4. Whoever shall collect a band with hostile intent and surround another's villa or house must compound his wergeld to the king, and his followers must each pay a fine of twelve *solidi*, and the victim, if he has suffered loss, must be compensated doubly.[66]

No set of laws contains a more concise statement regarding these breaches of special *paces* than the example cited above. An organic relationship clearly exists among these *Frieden*; public authority, personified in king or duke, is interested in their maintenance because they are essential to public peace. Hence breaches are treasonable inasmuch as they attack public safety and the state which upholds that safety. Seditious violations of the *Heerfrieden* constitute folk treason (*Landesverrat*); the commission of violence at the duke's court is a scandal; the killing of royal officers verges upon high treason.[67]

An ensuing law deals with parricide but prescribes a most lenient penalty: "If any one shall kill his father, he shall lose the inheritance which he would have received otherwise."[68] Fratricide is regulated by a separate provision.[69] Treachery and treason have the same philosophical

[65] *L. Fris.* 7, 1–2.
[66] *L. Fris.* 19, 2 (17, 1–4 Herold).
[67] Cf. His, *Strafrecht*, pp. 191–196, on *Landesverrat*.
[68] *L. Fris.* 19, 1 (14, 1 Herold).
[69] *L. Fris.* 19, 2 (14, 2 Herold).

background but are not necessarily identified at law; however, the Frisian law offers a curious suggestion of their relationship. Under the caption *De mordrito*, dealing ostensibly with murder (secret homicide), that offense, considered so repulsive and heinous by the early Germanic peoples, is associated with the killing of a hostage and the killing of a master by his slave or leet (*litus*).[70] All three are treacherous acts, but only the last can be related to treason in its commonly accepted connotation. The killing of masters by their slaves was severely punished in the Roman law and may be connected with the origins of petty treason. Finally in the *Additio sapientium* of Wulemar one finds a confirmation of the earlier laws concerning breaches of the peace. Under the caption *De pace faidosi* it is provided that the faithful man (*faidosus*) shall have peace in the church, in his home, on his way to and from the church, and on his way to and from the court (*placitum*), and that whoever shall break this peace and kill a man must compound 270 *solidi*, while if the man is wounded only, 108 *solidi* (*novies XII solidos*) must be paid as the king's portion.[71] That the king profits from breaches of his peace is clear. Under such circumstances it is difficult to tell how far such violations are considered as attacks upon the general welfare, public authority, and the state, and how far they are considered as mere trespasses upon certain private interests of the king which may be settled on the practical basis of business concern without regard for the just claims of the injured party. In the first case the king personifies public authority and protects his subjects by punishing their wrongs with justice and equity. But in the second instance he is merely a shrewd bargainer, making an advantageous arrangement with offenders but not interested in the intrinsic merits of the case. It is difficult to tell when violation of the king's peace becomes a mere article of commerce and a matter for traffic and sale. The intrusion of the royal interest into the area of the *paces* paves the way for situations where the rights of the folk could be turned to the personal gain and advantage of the king.

Among the neighbors of the Frisians were the continental Saxons of Old Saxony, whose laws contain a somewhat larger amount of material relating to treason. In general the codes of these north German peoples are similar, possessing some characteristics common to Carolingian legislation. The *Capitulatio de partibus Saxoniae* (a. 775–790) established an ecclesiastical peace and special wergelds for the clergy,[72] and

---

[70] L. Fris. 20, 1–3.

[71] L. Fris., *Additio sapientium Wulmaris* 1, 1 (*De pace faidosi*).

[72] *Capitulatio de partibus Saxoniae* (a. 775–790), c. 2–5. See *Leges Saxonum et*

provided capital penalties for treasonable acts of infidelity against the king or royal officers.[73] Also petty treason against one's lord was made punishable by death.[74] In addition folk treason is conjoined with acts hostile to Christendom so that "whoever plots with pagans and with them persists in his opposition against Christians shall suffer death, and whoever consents to such disloyalty [*fraude*] against the king or Christian people shall suffer death."[75] The *Capitulare saxonicum* (a. 787) established the "Peace of God" over churches and over weak and helpless persons; it prohibited presumptuous acts of violence throughout the land; it punished those who failed to heed the king's summons to arms.[76] Next it levied a fine against such nobles as failed to obey the summons to court.[77] Royal officers (*missi*) and their subordinates were protected against death or injury by a triple wergeld.[78] Finally a provision in the *Fragments of Ansegisus* states that whoever shall destroy another's house or steal anything therefrom must compound the damage triply (*infracta et spoliata in triplum componat*).[79]

The main body of Saxon law is contained in the *Leges Saxonum* (a. A.D. 802).[80] A long introductory tariff of wergelds, covering a great variety of private criminal actions and including every station of society, precedes the law dealing with criminal acts of public significance. An ecclesiastical peace is established by the law providing capital penalties in cases where any one kills a man, steals anything, destroys anything,

---

Lex Thuringorum, ed. by v. Schwerin, in *Fontes iuris germanici antiqui* (Hanover and Leipzig: Hansche Buchhandlung, 1918), pp. 35–49, for the Saxon capitularies, and p. 50 for the *Fragments of Ansegisus*.

[73] *Cap. de part. Sax.*, c. 11, 12, 30. Cf. G. Waitz, *Deutsche Verfassungsgeschichte* (2nd ed.; Berlin: Weidmann, 1883), III, pp. 132–135.

[74] *Cap. de part. Sax.*, 13. This may refer only to the royal *dominus*.

[75] *Cap. de part. Sax.*, c. 10.

[76] *Capitulare Saxonicum* (a. 787), c. 1.

[77] *Cap. Sax.*, c. 5.

[78] *Cap. Sax.*, c. 7.

[79] *Fragmenta Ansegisi* 3, 65.

[80] For text of the Saxon laws, see *Leges Saxonum et Lex Thuringorum*, edited by Claudius Freiherr von Schwerin, in *Fontes iuris germanici antiqui*, pp. 7–34; also the older edition, *Leges Saxonum* and *Lex Angliorum et Werinorum, hoc est Thuringorum*, by K. von Richthofen and K. R. von Richthofen in *M. G. H., Legum Tomus V* (Hanover: Hahn, 1875–1889), pp. 1–102, including *Capitula de partibus Saxoniae, Lex Saxonum*, and *Capitulare saxonicum*; Walter, *Corpus*, I, 382–390. In addition, see Karl Freiherr von Richthofen, *Zur Lex Saxonum* (Berlin: W. Hertz, 1868); H. Brunner, *D. R.*, I, 464–469; Schröder-von Künssberg, *Lehrbuch*, pp. 272–274. The most fundamental and comprehensive recent work on the Saxons is Martin Lintzel, *Ausgewählte Schriften* (Berlin: Akademie-Verlag, 1961), Vol. I, especially pp. 309–416.

or knowingly perjures himself in a church.[81] Folk treason and high treason are made capital offenses by an ensuing law which states: "Whoever shall plot against the realm, or whoever shall plot against the king of the Franks or his sons shall be punished capitally."[82] This law is significant in three respects. First it exhibits a close association and little discrimination between high treason and folk treason since both are mentioned side by side in the same provision. One may infer that the interests of the folk and of the king are regarded as identical; hence violations of either are made punishable under the same enactment. Secondly high treason is not merely an offense against the person of the king but extends as well to his sons, who are his prospective heirs. Finally the use of *consiliatus* rather than *infidelis* suggests Roman or Visigothic influence, and does not represent typically Frankish and native Germanic conceptions of treason. Next one finds two laws proclaiming that the man who kills his lord shall be punished capitally, and that the man who kills his lord's son or violates his lord's daughter, wife, or mother shall be killed according to the lord's desire.[83] These laws apparently cover cases of either high treason or petty treason depending upon whether the *dominus* to whom the law refers is also *rex*. This extension of treason to crimes committed against various members of the lord's family is obviously not common to all Germanic legislation; yet it is quite in keeping with Teutonic conceptions of *Treubruch*. Surely such acts constituted the gravest infidelity and the worst sort of broken troth.[84] The close connection of breaches of the *Heimfrieden* with treason is indicated by the circumstance that they are listed with the one following the other in this code. The very next law, following the provisions against treason, commands: "The man shall be punished capitally who kills another in his own home and thus breaks the peace of the home (*propter faidam*)."[85] Two additional laws protect this sanctity of the home and the general principle that "a man's house is his castle" as follows:

The man shall be punished capitally who enters another's home by night and breaks or destroys anything there, and who carries away property valued

[81] *Leges Saxonum* 21, and cf. 23.
[82] L. *Sax.* 24.
[83] L. *Sax.* 25–26. Cf. v. Richthofen, *Zur Lex Sax.*, pp. 273–275, and Waitz, *D. V.*, III, 132, n. 3.
[84] It should be noted that these are the same type of offenses that appeared in the definitive definition of treason in Statute 5, 25 Edward III (1352).
[85] L. *Sax.* 27.

at two *solidi*; if the criminal shall be killed there, no compensation shall be made for his death.[86]

The man shall be punished capitally who, by premeditation and of his own accord, burns another's home either by night or by day.[87]

Sanctuary is denied to traitors and to other criminals who have incurred capital penalties: "Let him who has been condemned to capital punishment never have peace; if he shall take refuge in a church, he shall be returned."[88] The remainder of this code is taken up for the most part with laws concerning inheritance. Thus, the *Leges Saxonum* contain considerable additional material dealing with treason despite their brevity; still it is not at all easy to establish how much of this represents native Germanic custom and how much is of Roman importation. The general spirit is unquestionably Germanic with its wergelds and special peaces, but such matters as conspiracy and the extension of treason to crimes against certain members of the royal family may very well be of Roman origin although they harmonize with Germanic views concerning infidelity.

The short code of the Franks of Hamaland known as the *Lex Francorum Chamavorum* (*ca.* A.D. 802) contains a few references to treasonable offenses.[89] The homicides of counts and *missi dominici* must be compounded triply.[90] Strangers (*wargengus*) are protected by a special royal peace, and their deaths can be settled only upon payment of a fine of six hundred *solidi* to the lord's treasury.[91] A number of offenses are designated that appear to relate closely to folk treason. Those who are summoned to come with arms or with a horse but fail to appear must compound four *solidi* to the lord.[92] Whoever fails to perform watch and ward (*wactam aut wardam*) after the count has requested it must pay four *solidi*.[93] Whoever hears the sound of arms and does not respond to the occasion must pay a similar fine.[94] If any one abandons the sluices

---

[86] *L. Sax.* 32.   [87] *L. Sax.* 38.   [88] *L. Sax.* 28.

[89] For text of *Lex Francorum Chamavorum* by Sohm, see *M. G. H.* Legum Tomus V, 269–288; also see Brunner, *D. R.*, I, 473–475 for *Ewa Chamavorum*; Schröder-von Künssberg, *Lehrbuch*, pp. 277–278.

This brief code is also known as the *Notitia vel commemoratio de illa Euua, quae se ad Amorem habet*. It is associated with the region of Hamaland (Amore), located north of the Ripuarians and belonging to the Chamavi, and seems to be influenced by the Ripuarian, Frisian, and Saxon codes.

[90] *L. Fran. Cham.* 7–8.

[91] *L. Fran. Cham.* 9.

[92] *L. Fran. Cham.* 34–35.

[93] *L. Fran. Cham.* 36.

[94] *L. Fran. Cham.* 37.

(*sclusae*) when his count has commanded him to guard them, he shall pay with four *solidi*; also he shall pay the same amount if he breaks the sluices and does not wish to repair them.[95] This same fine holds for those who fail to answer the summons to protect a public bridge or attend a count's court,[96] and for those who obstruct a public highway.[97] All these breaches of royal *paces*, established in the interest of the public, are in a measure treasonable attacks upon the general welfare and constitute varying degrees of folk treason.

Finally, the Thuringian laws (*Lex Thuringorum aut Lex Angliorum et Werinorum, ca.* 802) contain little relating to treason save a few regulations against *Hausfriedensbruch*.[98] Whoever burns another's home by night must compensate the loss threefold and pay sixty *solidi* for breaking the peace (*in fredo*); or if he denies the crime he shall swear with eleven men or decide the issue by wager of battle.[99] If any man kills another man within the latter's home (enclosure-*septa*) he shall compound a triple wergeld, and whatever damage he shall cause there, he shall restore threefold.[100] If a band shall be assembled with hostile intent and shall surround a man's home each of the three leaders shall compound sixty *solidi* and a like amount for breaking the king's ban, while each of the remaining members of the band shall compound ten *solidi* and pay sixty *solidi* to the king for breaking the ban.[101] No direct references are made to high treason or to the common forms of folk treason. The code consists almost solely of private civil and criminal law.

In conclusion it should be pointed out that no entirely satisfactory classification of the *leges barbarorum* can be devised for the purposes of legal analysis. A study of the laws pursued in their chronological sequence will be misleading since little can be inferred about their character from the date of compilation. If it be thought that the earliest laws should be the most purely Germanic, one will find support for his supposition in the Salic law, which may contain materials reaching back as far as the late fifth century, or in the Ripuarian laws, some of which

---

[95] *L. Fran. Cham.* 38.

[96] *L. Fran. Cham.* 39–40.

[97] *L. Fran. Cham.* 41.

[98] See text of *Leges Thuringorum*, edited by Claudius Freiherr von Schwerin, in *Fontes iuris germanici antiqui*, pp. 51–66; also Brunner, *D. R.*, I, 469–473, for *Lex Angliorum et Werinorum* (Thuringorum).

[99] *Leges Thuringorum* 41.

[100] *L. Thur.* 48.

[101] *L. Thur.* 54–55.

date from the early sixth century, but he will also discover that much which is strictly Germanic is found in the Lombard laws of the seventh and eighth centuries. On the other hand if any one expects to find Roman influences becoming stronger as he goes back toward the Roman period, he will find this true in the case of the barbarized *leges romanae* of the Visigoths and Burgundians (*Breviary and Papian*), both of which belong to the first decade of the sixth century, but the Salic law, which is probably earlier than either, is quite entirely Germanic. Furthermore the Roman influence appears strongly in such late codifications as the *Leges Alamannorum* and *Leges Baiuvariorum*. No golden rule may be found which is based on chronology alone. If a classification on a geographical basis is attempted the result will be disappointing. One might expect to find that those people who entered the Roman Empire would exhibit the most marked influence of the Roman law in their codes. This is true in the case of the Visigoths and Burgundians, but the Lombard codes in Italy itself were very Germanic. One would hardly anticipate extensive Roman influences in Germany; yet the law of the Bavarians exhibits much that is Roman both in form and content. Therefore hardly any method of classification can be suggested that will be logical in all respects. The barbarian codes are as individual in nature as the barbarians themselves and must be studied individually.

XI

Review of Ernst Levy, *West Roman Vulgar Law:*
*The Law of Property**

A good many years ago a scholar whom my memory no longer serves to identify remarked that it is impossible to integrate the law with the history of ideas because the study of the law is not an activity of the intellect. I have never been willing to concede the validity of this somewhat cynical observation but have rather lived in the hope that more might be done to bring basic legal concepts within the larger context of the intellectual climate of their appropriate historical era. The tendency to distrust and dismiss these legal concepts as mere esoteric technical expressions, desiccated and irrelevant, emerges all too frequently in casual converse with scholars in other disciplines. This unsatisfactory situation occasions genuine concern to the reviewer of a study such as this masterly legal analysis based on the late Roman vulgar law. The difficulty of the evaluation of the source materials on the one hand and of the interpretation of the legal concepts on the other makes this an extremely hard book to represent adequately for the advantage of scholars not specialists in this field.

Professor Levy's mastery of the dim legal area lying midway between the classical jurists and the Justinian legislation is unchallenged. Valuable background for the treatise under review may be gained by consulting two previous studies by Dr. Levy: "Reflections on the First

* *Memoirs of the American Philosophical Society*, Vol. 29. Philadelphia: The Society, 1951. Reprinted by special permission of the Editors of *Speculum* and the Mediaeval Academy of America from *Speculum*, XXVIII, No. 3 (1953), 586–591.

'Reception' of Roman Law in Germanic States," *American Historical Review*, XLVIII (1942), 20–29, and "Vulgarization of Roman Law in the Early Middle Ages," *Medievalia et Humanistica*, I (1943), 14–40. These articles familiarize the reader with the nature and significance of the vulgar law, based on selection and adaptation from the three codices—Gregorian, Hermogenian, and Theodosian—and on abridgements and modifications of classical juristic sources such as the *Sentences* of Paulus and the *Institutiones* of Gaius. These materials emerge in the Romano-Germanic West in such compilations as the *Lex Romana Visigothorum* or *Breviarium Alarici*, the *Lex Romana Burgundionum* or *Papian*, and the Ostrogothic *Edictum Theodorici*. In addition there are the vulgar *interpretationes* of the *Codex Theodosianus* and of the *Pauli Sententiae* as preserved in the *Breviary* and further modified in such epitomes and glosses as the eighth-century *Lex Romana Curiensis* derived from the *Breviary*. And beyond this is the pervasive influence of the *Breviary* and its Roman vulgar law upon the Germanic *leges barbarorum*, Visigothic, Burgundian, Frankish, Bavarian, Lombard. The chronological interval of this postclassical development is largely comprehended within the period from *circa* A.D. 240 to the compilation of the *Corpus Juris* (*c.* A.D. 530) with some projections as late as the eighth century or beyond. A central point at which we may discover the principles of the West Roman Vulgar Law defined in their mature form may be established in the reign of Constantine.

The introduction to this book (pp. 1–18) constitutes an extremely valuable historical survey of the evolution of this West Roman Vulgar Law. Levy points out that about seventy-five years ago it became evident "that not all the texts found under the name of a classical jurist were actually of classical origin," whereupon it was presumed that Justinian had introduced changes to bring these texts into conformity with the needs of his time. But this resulted in the incorrect assumption that the *Digest* must perforce contain only classical law and Justinian law, leaving the intervening period from A.D. 240 to 530 unaccounted for. Also, it was often possible to show that a given rule of law could be neither classical nor Justinian law. Hence, Levy notes, "for the last forty or fifty years, the existence of pre-Justinian interpolations has been taken into consideration. . . . This process went so far that according to the notion rightly prevailing today most non-classical norms were not created but already found by Justinian" (p. 1). However, he goes on to say that modern research in this field has been chiefly interested in showing how the classical system of law developed into that of Jus-

tinian, whereas it is his purpose to investigate this previously un-
charted middle region of the vulgar law, sometimes designated "postclassical" and again "pre-Justinian." As the title of his book indicates,
it is the author's purpose to examine this process of legal development
in the Roman West, although he does not disregard Hellenistic influences, which have a demonstrable bearing on Western law, and he
makes a very close study of numerous points of contact between Germanic custom and the vulgar law. In general he suggests that the vulgar
law "comprises all those rules or concepts appearing on Roman soil,
especially in [this] intervening period, which differ from the classical
system and yet cannot be traced to some positive enactment," regardless
of whether these provisions and ideas originated in statutes of limited
application, in peregrine usage, or entirely apart from non-Roman
thought (p. 6). In an age of cultural decline the average man became
less and less capable of comprehending the highly refined and intricate
concepts of the classical system as well as becoming more and more
insistent upon the simple and readily understood definitions and statements of empirical practices, "governed by social and economic rather
than legal considerations." In this intellectual milieu the classical models
are distorted and the classical principles twisted to produce almost un-
recognizable new meanings.

Since this present volume deals with those aspects of the West Roman
Vulgar Law comprehended under the law of property, this is primarily
a study in the private civil law, although public considerations are dealt
with fully when germane to the subject. The reviewer has found his
greatest interest in the skillful manner whereby Dr. Levy has indicated
the fluctuating content of meaning ascribed to certain basic legal concepts. It is the terminology rather than the technique of law toward
which my attention has been chiefly directed, for it is here that legal
history is most clearly brought into conjunction with the broader history
of ideas, and the long, closely reasoned first chapter (pp. 19–99) is significantly entitled "Concepts." Here the analysis narrows down to a close
examination of the basic concepts of *dominium* and *possessio,* translated
commonly as "ownership" and "possession." Levy begins by noting that
the great classical jurists stressed in these terms the distinction "between
the right and fact of control over a thing" (p. 19). *Dominium* designated
legal proprietary rights; *possessio,* physical control or occupation. The
distinction between *proprietas* and *possessio* is sharply defined. But
when we pass to the age of Constantine and enter the post classical era
interesting semantic questions arise. The legal terminology remains un-

changed, but the thought content is no longer the same. Indeed, the vulgarization of the classical law produces a strange "sea change" whereby at its most extreme point each term approximates its opposite (p. 61); *possessio* simulates ownership and *dominium* becomes hardly more than possession.

In the early phases of this process *possessio* may signify *dominium* or a *ius in re aliena* (p. 21), or, as Levy concludes from a *constitutio* of Constantine in *C. Just.* 7, 32, 10 *De Acquirenda et Retinenda Possessione*, "one type of *possessio* 'consisted' in the right to possess and the other in the mere corporeal holding" (p. 27). Again he observes that a gulf separates postclassical from classical diction. "It is the language of laymen who at all times have taken factual holding as the visible expression of legal control" (p. 26). By the late fourth and the fifth centuries *possessio* is more and more regarded as ownership, that is, it comes to imply title, while *dominium* indicates what would have been *possessio* to a classical jurist (p. 32). Next he goes on to illustrate how *dominium*, as the "essentially total right of control," ceases to be sharply distinguished from limited rights which others might have in the property (*iura in re aliena*), such as *ususfructus* (pp. 34–40), *ius perpetuum* and *emphyteusis* (pp. 43–49), *superficies* (pp. 49–55), *servitus* (pp. 55–59), and *pignus* (pp. 59–61). All these types of property right come to assume in varying degrees the aspect of full rights of *dominium in re sua*, while the term *possessio* comes "to designate all real rights normally combined with factual holding, whether ownership or usufruct, perpetual lease or building rights. But this very usage, not conceivable on the part of a classical jurist, demonstrates that *possidere* offered the general term suitable to express ownership and any right of real control" (pp. 61–62). For the practitioners of the vulgar law it mattered little that the antithesis between *factum* and *ius* was obscured. Complications arise, however, when the true nature of these limited *iura in re aliena* is no longer understood or, as Levy says, when the concept becomes extinct. All are now regarded as varieties of *dominium* and none operates as an exclusive *dominium*. Thus lands of the imperial domain let out in *emphyteusis* are also owned by the emperor, so that two ownerships, domainial and emphyteutic, differing in scope and duration, appear to coexist resulting in a *dominium* (*possessio?*) *duorum in solidum* (pp. 67–69). Space forbids an examination of the reverse process whereby the Justinian law rejects the dual *dominium* and restores, for the most part, the sharp distinction between *dominium* and *iura in re aliena* (see pp. 72–83).

Another long chapter is the third, entitled "Acquisition of *Dominium*" (pp. 127–201), the greater part of which deals with transfer of ownership. Here the same forces of cultural denigration may be seen at work modifying the precise classical concepts into vulgar forms more comprehensible to unlearned lawyers, laymen, and barbarians. Much as it seems to a modern layman, a sale appeared to be an exchange of land or goods for money; it bore the aspect of a cash transaction and meant only conveyance and transfer (p. 127). But as Levy states concisely in *A. H. R.*, XLVIII (1942), 24:

In Roman law at its peak a sale was solely a contract to sell. The seller agreed to transfer the land or the article sold; the buyer agreed to pay the price. It follows that neither transfer nor payment was part of the sale. These effects were attained rather by separate transactions designed to perform what in the contract of sale had merely been promised. Hence failure to transfer the title or pay the price could plainly not affect the validity and binding force of the contract.

Again one encounters the complete confusion of meaning and misunderstanding of basic concepts that has been noted in *dominium* and *possessio*. Thus, *traditio* means in some instances the actual transfer or real surrender of the land, but in others, the agreement or contract without surrender (p. 136). Then later, with the Justinian restoration, we discover "a definite attempt to resume the forgotten distinction between the *contractus* as engendering mere obligations and the transaction producing a change in ownership" (p. 148). Other important conceptual changes are indicated in the second chapter, "*Dominium* and Public Interest" (pp. 100–126), and the fourth and final chapter, "Remedies," proprietary and possessory (pp. 202–276), which are of somewhat more specialized and technical interest. Of special value to the research scholar in working through these materials are an adequate index of subjects and an extensive table of sources. Since very many references are made to the *Codex Theodosianus*, the recent translation of *The Theodosian Code* by Clyde Pharr and associates (Princeton: Princeton University Press, 1952) is an invaluable aid to a further understanding of these problems of the vulgar law.

For the student of Germanic law and institutions an extremely valuable feature of the book is the portion devoted to the impact of the Roman vulgar law upon the Romano-Germanic kingdoms in the West as illustrated in such sources as the Visigothic *antiquae* and the Burgundian *Lex Gundobada* (cf. pp. 84–99; 122–126; 156–168; 240–242). The dual character of *possessio* noted in the vulgar law is retained in the Germanic codes. For example, Levy shows how *possidere* and its derivatives come to include a wide range of concepts extending from factual control to actual *dominium* in the sense of legal right. "They could connote factual control as in connection with long possession or with actions for recovery. Normally, however, they implied the right of one in control. What particular right they meant to denote was often left to the context to tell" (p. 87). Thus, a usufructuary right appeared as a sort of *proprietas*, "as a right *in re sua* rather than *aliena* and distinguished from a full *proprietas* not in structure but only in scope and duration" (p. 89). An extremely interesting example involving the right of *superficies* is cited from the Lombard *Edictum Rothari*, c. 151, which states: "If anyone builds a mill on another's land (*molinum in terram alienam*) and cannot prove the mill his own (*suum probare non potuerit*), let him lose the mill and all his investment, and let him have it who is found to own the land or riverbank because everyone should be able to distinguish his own property from another's [*quia omnes scire debent quod suum, non alienum est*]." Thus, the excuse of ignorance as to the ownership of the land is ruled out from the beginning, but the rule is qualified and would not apply if the builder can prove the mill his own. As Levy observes, it would be a contradiction of terms in classical law that a builder *in terra aliena* should prove the building his, but the classical concept was unknown to the seventh-century jurist, for whom the alternative was solely which one owned the mill as indicated in the clause *suum probare non potuerit*. How easy it is to mistake the meaning of the Germanic codes is evident from F. Beyerle's translation in *Gesetze der Langobarden* (Weimar: Böhlans, 1947), p. 49, which follows Del Giudice and reads as if the text were *suam probare*. Levy holds rightly that "if the *terra* is *aliena*, it cannot be *sua*" (p. 95, n. 447), and the builder's superficial right is here regarded as a sort of *proprietas in re sua* although the land under it remained *aliena*. Under classical law "even the landowner's consent could at best have resulted in the grant of a *ius in re aliena*."

In general Levy supports with heavy documentation the point of view expressed by Professor C. H. McIlwain in *The Growth of Political Thought in the West* (New York: Macmillan, 1936), p. 176, where he states that Germanic ideas of property, especially landed property, were based on the protection of use and enjoyment rather than ownership, and that "Interests in land were much like personal status in that both had more the character of rights *in personam* than of rights *in rem*." Therefore, Germanic *seisin* (*Gewere*) involved no superiority of the rights of ownership over other types of property rights, or as Levy says, "the right to possess, ordinarily underlying both *possessio* and *Gewere*, did not have to be ownership" (p. 97). *Gewere*, like *possessio*, required a factual holding *suo nomine*, and, although not a real right, was its typical outward appearance. Just as *dominium* at times hardly meant more than lawful possession, so the right to possess, underlying both *possessio* and *Gewere*, did not have to be ownership (*proprietas, dominium*) but might be usufruct, perpetual lease, or some other real right. There is no sharp distinction among these rights, between *proprietas* and *ius in re aliena*, but "Since they were mere varieties or degrees of the same legal power, the term *Gewere* was no better apt to identify them unequivocally than was *possessio* or *dominium*" (cf. pp. 96–97).

In conclusion I would point out that the semantic confusion occasioned by the fluctuating concept of *dominium* remains undiminished to the present day. When, partly under the influence of Germanic ideas of landholding, the notion became fixed that there could be a variety of rights and interests in the same piece of land the way was paved for those feudal concepts wherein "ideas of proprietary right and governmental authority" are commingled (McIlwain, *Political Thought*, p. 177). This led to a confusion of the concepts of *dominium* and *imperium* as significant in the sphere of public law as the confusion of *dominium* and *possessio* in the sphere of private law. One has only to read Dean Roscoe Pound's devastating "Critique on the Texas Tidelands Case" in the Symposium contained in the *Baylor Law Review*, III (1951), 120–129, to see that our contemporary jurists are as much at sea over the distinction between ownership and sovereignty as any feudal lawyer could have been over the distinction between ownership and possession. The entire nexus of ideas is correlated, because when a debased vulgar sense of the law fails to perceive the refinement that distinguishes legal right from factual control it is only a step to the larger confusion of physical control with the power of government, or of governmental authority with ownership. As Dean Pound concludes, "It is a startling proposition to tell Americans that sovereignty, which we have thought of as political, must be proprietary as well—must include ownership of the soil." Yet no more startling than it would have appeared to a classical Roman jurist when the Lombard builder of the mill considered that he had a proprietary right in the structure erected upon land which was not in his *dominium*. Dr. Levy's book is a fundamental work that sets our feet on paths that have no ending, because it deals with ideas that endure.

Note: Some of the problems involved in the interpretation of the Roman Vulgar Law which are associated with the law of property are considered in this review, and it is hoped that these references will help to bring into clearer perspective parallel problems in the public law raised in Essay VII dealing with the *Lex Romana Curiensis*.

XII

The Literature on Treason
in Roman Public Law*

The two concluding bibliographical essays are intended as a general
survey of the literature relevant to these studies in Roman and Germanic
public law. Descriptive and interpretative works in the English language which deal with such aspects of political and legal theory are not
numerous. Furthermore, the most readily available textbooks on the
Roman law are devoted to an examination of the private civil law.
Offenses against the state and the public criminal law generally are
either treated cursorily and neglected, or entirely ignored, save in a
very small number of special studies which will be noted shortly. On the
other hand, continental European scholars, chiefly German and French
with some Italian contributors, have produced an extensive literature
in this field. For the comparable area in Germanic customary law there
is almost a complete lacuna in American and British scholarship which
is fortunately corrected by important works of continental scholars.
However, these European materials are often highly specialized and
not well known in this country. Also they are in large measure works
of the nineteenth century which tend to be disregarded by contemporary scholars or considered obsolete. This position is ordinarily not
well taken since these studies, for the most part, represent fundamental
research in the primary sources and have proved substantial in high
degree. The present century, however, has not supplemented these

* Reprinted with additions from *The Rice Institute Pamphlet*, XLII (1955),
79–89.

investigations with comparable advances in constitutional and legal history. Therefore, it has seemed desirable to collect in short monographic studies some of the fundamental data of these fields with rather heavy documentation. Much of the evidence is controversial and the facts alleged not altogether easy to substantiate. The author lays claim to no special originality in the presentation of this factual data although he does believe that the interpretation represents an independent approach.

The history of treason is much easier to investigate in the Roman law than among the highly complex and confusing Greek and Germanic materials. In the first place, a great treatise of widely accepted authority is available in the monumental *Römisches Strafrecht* of Theodor Mommsen (Leipzig: S. Hirzel, 1899). Secondly, numerous Roman legal remains have been preserved and have been carefully studied by generations of scholars, analyzed and classified in an orderly manner, and made accessible to the modern investigator. The most serious exception to this generally fortunate situation relates to the early Republican and so-called Regal periods of Roman history. Even here some legal materials are available, but questions concerning their precise authenticity involve great difficulties of interpretation and application. These very early legal sources are the *Leges Regiae* and the fragments of the *Laws of the Twelve Tables*. They throw some light upon the relation of the family to the early state, upon parricide as a form of treason, and upon the early history of *perduellio*. Well-edited texts of these laws may be found in C. G. Bruns, *Fontes iuris romani antiqui*, ed. by Otto Gradenwitz (7th ed.; Tübingen: Mohr, 1909), Part I: *Leges et Negotia;* Paul F. Girard, *Textes de droit romain* (3rd ed.; Paris: A. Rousseau, 1903); P. E. Huschke, *Iurisprudentia anteiustiniana*, ed. by E. Seckel and B. Kübler (6th ed.; Leipzig: Teubner, 1911). More recently an excellent collection of pre-Justinian legislation has been assembled in the Riccobono, Baviera, Ferrini, Furlani, Arangio-Ruiz editor under the title *Fontes iuris romani antejustiniani*, 3 vols. (Florence: Barbèra, 1940–1943). A number of these sources are translated by A. C. Johnson, Paul R. Coleman-Norton and Frank C. Bourne in *Ancient Roman Statutes* (Austin: University of Texas Press, 1961). Among the earlier materials here translated which are relevant to these studies are the *Leges Regiae* and Fragments of the *XII Tables*, and of the later legislation the *Senatus Consultum de Bacchanalibus* and the *Lex de imperio Vespasiani*. In addition to Mommsen's *Strafrecht*, two secondary treatises should be noted which are extremely useful in the study of this early period. These are E. C.

Clark, *History of Roman Private Law* (Cambridge: University Press, 1919), Part III: Regal Period, and A. H. J. Greenidge, *Roman Public Life* (London: Macmillan, 1911). Clark is valuable for his discussion of the relation of parricide to *perduellio,* while Greenidge indicates the constitutional significance of many legal concepts. Mommsen is indispensable for his presentation of an important theory concerning the origin of the idea of *maiestas.* To these may be added several papers in the *Studi in onore di Salvatore Riccobono* (Palermo: Arti grafiche G. Castiglia, 1936), Vol. II: especially "Imperium," by M. Radin; "Zur Infamie in Römischen Strafrecht," E. Levy; and "Paricidas esto," by F. Leifer.

As a rule, the legal ideas of the later Republic have been transmitted to modern times in two ways. Either extracts from republican legislation were incorporated in the great codes and the juristic literature of the late Empire, or the prevailing legal practice of the Republic has been set forth in the orations of Cicero. A very complete account of treason in the late Republic could be written from the speeches of Cicero alone. Other literary sources are less valuable although Livy, Diodorus Siculus, and Dionysius of Halicarnassus should be examined closely. The accounts of these historians extend into the regal and republican eras and must be used with care for the earliest times, in connection with which they narrate much traditional and legendary matter. A great convenience in the use of classical literature, lacking a generation ago, is the Loeb Classical Library in Greek or Latin text with English translation, published in London by William Heinemann, Ltd. and in this country by the Harvard University Press. The orations of Cicero most relevant to this subject are the *De Re Publica* and *De Legibus,* trans. by C. W. Keyes (1928); *De Oratore,* trans. by E. W. Sutton (1942); *De Inventione,* trans. by H. M. Hubbell (1949); *Pro Cluentio* and *Pro Rabirio Perduellionis,* trans. by H. G. Hodge (1927); *In Prisonem,* trans. by N. H. Watts (1931); *Brutus,* trans. by G. L. Hendrickson (1939). Livy has been translated: Books 1–22 by B. O. Foster (1919–1929), Books 23–30 by F. G. Moore (1940–1947), and Books 31–42 by E. T. Sage and A. C. Schlesinger (1935–1938); Dionysius by E. Cary on the basis of Edmund Spellman (1937–1950); and Diodorus: Books I–XV. 19 by C. H. Oldfather (1933–1954), and continued currently through Book XX by Russel M. Geer of Tulane University (1947–1954).

Good secondary works are available to expedite investigations in this field. In addition to Mommsen there is a very substantial article on

maiestas by Humbert and Lécrivain in Vol. III (Part II) of Daremberg
and Saglio, *Dictionnaire des antiquités grècques et romaines* (Graz,
Austria: Akademische Druck-u. Verlagsanstalt, 1963), which has been
followed at many points in this study. This article is documented with
numerous citations that serve as a useful guide to the literature of the
subject but they must be verified with extreme care. In many respects
Humbert's study is a résumé of Mommsen's discussion in the *Strafrecht*,
but it adds some new material and, at times, criticizes Mommsen. It
may be noted that, for those preferring to read French, a translation of
the *Strafrecht* has been prepared under the title *Le droit pénal romain*
and is published as Volume XVIII in the *Manuel des antiquités romains*,
edited by Mommsen, Marquardt, and Krüger (Paris: E. Thorin [A.
Fontemoing], 1907). In addition, Lécrivain has a short article on *perduellio* in Vol. IV (*Part I*) of Daremberg and Saglio's *Dictionnaire*.
Finally both Mommsen and Humbert must be reconsidered and compared with the more recent independent study, "Maiestas," by B.
Kübler in Pauly-Wissowa-Kroll, *Realencyclopädie der classichen Altertumswissenschaft* (Stuttgart: Metzler, 1928), XXVII, 542–559, which
cites many less obvious sources and contains an extended analysis of
the *lex Quisquis*. Two additional monographic studies should be mentioned that deserve careful attention. The first is J. L. Strachan-Davidson, *Problems of the Roman Criminal Law*, 2 vols. (Oxford: Clarendon,
1912), which presents important views relating to *perduellio* and the
senatus consultum ultimum. It also examines in some detail the relation
of religion to law, including the problems associated with *sacratio,
sacrilegium*, and the *aquae et ignis interdictio*. The second of these
works is P. M. Schisas, *Offences against the State in Roman Law* (London: University of London Press, 1926) of which Part I, pp. 3–15,
provides a brief analysis of *perduellio* and *maiestas*. The balance of the
book is a detailed procedural study, heavily documented and not dupli-
cated elsewhere. It is one of the few distinguished contributions in this
field in English. Another significant recent study is C. H. Brecht, *Perduellio: Eine Studie zu ihrer begrifflichen Abgrenzung im römischen
Strafrecht bis zum Ausgang der Republik* (Munich: C. H. Beck, 1938).
The older secondary works have been supplanted largely by Mommsen's
Strafrecht. Nevertheless, the pre-Mommsen treatises should not be entirely overlooked. G. Geib, *Geschichte des römischen Criminalprocesses
bis zum Tode Justinian's* (Leipzig: Weidmann, 1842), pp. 50–66, contains an especially good study of *perduellio*. In addition, there are W.
Rein, *Das Kriminalrecht der Römer von Romulus bis auf Justinianus*

(Leipzig: K. F. Köhler, 1844), pp. 504–597, and A. W. Zumpt, *Das Criminalrecht der römischen Republik* (Berlin: F. Dümmler, 1865–1869), I (2), 324–338, on *perduellio*; II (1), 226–264, 376–392, on *perduellio* and *maiestas*. P. E. Huschke, *Die Multa und das Sacramentum* (Leipzig: Teubner, 1874), should be noted in its relation to public offenses.

As their titles indicate, many of the secondary works mentioned above deal with the legislation of the Imperial period. However, the large quantity of legal materials readily accessible in the great codes makes it both feasible and desirable to gain fresh impressions directly from the sources in the investigation of treason under the emperors. This task is rendered the more easy because Mommsen has classified the various aspects of treasonable offenses in the *Strafrecht* and provided invaluable documentation for the different categories, directing his reader to the appropriate sections of the *Corpus Juris Civilis, Codex Theodosianus,* and *Sententiae* of Paulus. In the *Corpus Juris* the *Code* and *Digest* are fundamental. The best modern edition is that of Mommsen-Krüger-Schöll-Kroll, recently reissued for the entire *Corpus* (Berlin: Weidmann, 1954). However, interesting and often valuable suggestions may be obtained by comparing recently edited texts with early editions representing late Renaissance scholarship. In many respects the work of Dionysius Gothofredus (Denis Godefroi, 1549–1621) has never been surpassed. In this study the *Corpus Juris* of Gothofredus has been used in the Geneva edition of 1619 and the Amsterdam edition of 1663. The marginal notes in these older editions commonly constitute a running commentary upon the text and give sixteenth- and seventeenth-century interpretations of the Roman law. Such notes afford points of view and angles of approach to the subject that would be missed entirely if one confined himself to modern studies. The early writers, also, have prepared many special treatises dealing with limited fields or particular aspects of the Roman law. Among these special topics *maiestas* has not been slighted, for a column of goodly length containing the names of writers on majesty and related crimes may be found in the *Bibliotheca realis iuridica* of M. Lipenius (Leipzig: Wendler, 1746), I, 354–355, with the *Supplement* of G. A. Jenichen, II, 268–269. However, research should be pursued, in the main, in the most recent and best authenticated texts, using the old editions for occasional comparison and for the suggestions they contain. A notable aid for expediting research in the *Code* is a product of contemporary scholarship entitled *Vocabularium Codicis Iustiniani* Pars prior (Pars Latina) (Prague: Ceská Grafická

Unie, 1923), by Robert Mayr. This lists a large number of references relating to treason under the word *maiestas*. The *Theodosian Code* should be used in the Mommsen-Meyer edition (Berlin: Weidmann, 1905), reprinted 1954, although the older edition of G. Haenel (Bonn: A. Marcus, 1842), including the *Gregorian* and *Hermogenian Codes*, may be used for purposes of comparison. The Mommsen edition contains in the Introduction (pp. xiii–xxvii) a most serviceable list of cross references that relate titles in the *Codex Theodosianus* to the appropriate parallel title in the *Codex Iustinianus*, while similar cross references that are printed with the text may be found relating the *Theodosian Code* to the *Breviary* of Alaric. As in the case of the Justinian legislation, valuable reference may be made to the old texts of the *Codex Theodosianus*, edited by Jacobus Cujacius (Jacques Cujas, 1522–1590) and Jacobus Gothofredus (Jacques Godefroi, 1587–1652) with commentaries. A convenient text of the *Sentences* of Paulus is available in the Huschke-Seckel-Kübler, *Iurisprudentia anteiustiniana* (Leipzig: Teubner, 1911), II (1), Girard's *Textes*, pp. 356–431, and Riccobono, *et al, Fontes*, II, 317–417.

In no respect has modern scholarship advanced the opportunities for research more than by the production of accurate translations of the source materials of the classical period. As the nineteenth century advanced the establishment of definitive texts through competent collation and textual criticism, so the twentieth century is providing scholarly translations of many of these texts. However, this work has proceeded rather more slowly with the juristic literature than with the classical belles-lettres. Nevertheless, one great achievement completed recently has been the translation into English of the entire *Theodosian Code and Novels and Sirmondian Constitutions*, with commentary, glossary, and bibliography (Princeton: Princeton University Press, 1952) by Clyde Pharr, now research professor of classical languages at the University of Texas, and associates. The author of this monograph can testify from his own experience how greatly the investigation of these recondite legal sources has been facilitated by the work of Dr. Pharr, when he recalls the slow process of dredging through the massive Mommsen text of the *Codex Theodosianus* in the preparation of his doctoral dissertation forty years ago. *The Ecclesiastical Edicts of the Theodosian Code* by William K. Boyd (New York: Columbia University Press, 1905) was one of the few studies completed in this country making use of this legal material which was also relevant to the study of treason. Book Sixteen of the Code, covering the religious offenses, supplements in many ways

Book Nine, dealing with offenses against the state. The Justinian material is now available in a translation by S. P. Scott, but will be supplanted by the work of Clyde Pharr now in progress. The Scott translation, entitled *The Civil Law*, includes the *Twelve Tables*, the *Institutes* of Gaius, the *Rules* of Ulpian, the *Opinions* of Paulus, the *Enactments* of Justinian, and the *Constitutions* of Leo, in 17 vols. (Cincinnati: Central Trust Co., 1937). Scott's rendering is not altogether satisfactory and should be checked critically for the treason legislation in the *Code, Digest,* and *Opinions (Sententiae)* of Paulus. Many of Scott's long essay-type notes accompanying the translated text are useful historical summaries containing information not readily obtained elsewhere.

The historical literature of the Imperial period supplements the juristic literature in many important respects and must not be neglected. For the problem of *maiestas* the indispensable works are the *Annals* of Tacitus and the *Lives of the Caesars* by Suetonius among Latin authors, and the *Roman History* of Cassius Dio in Greek. These works fill in gaps left by the theoretical expositions of the jurists and the pragmatic statements of the imperial constitutions by providing specific cases that may be used to illustrate the prevailing situation. For these historical materials the text and translations of the Loeb Classical Library may again be recommended, although the older translations of Tacitus and Suetonius in Bohn's Classical Library are also useful. The Latin text of the *Annals* by Henry Furneaux, 2 vols. (2nd ed.; Oxford: Clarendon, 1896) with voluminous notes is excellent. The Greek text of Cassius Dio, trans. by E. Cary (Loeb, Vols. IV–IX, [1916–1927]), is invaluable for the closing years of the Republic and supplements the accounts of Tacitus and Suetonius for the early Empire with much additional material. These literary materials of the Empire are filled with numerous cases of violated majesty, so that an independent study of treason could be based on them alone, as, indeed, has been done in considerable measure for the reign of Tiberius. Here mention should be made of R. S. Rogers, *Criminal Trials and Criminal Legislation under Tiberius*, Philological Monographs Published by the American Philological Association, No. VI (Middletown, Conn.: The Association, 1935), and C. E. Smith, *Tiberius and the Roman Empire* (Baton Rouge: Louisiana State University Press, 1942), especially Ch. VIII on the *Lèse-Majesté* Prosecutions. Various articles and studies by the distinguished Italian scholar E. Ciaceri, dealing with the problem of *maiestas* under Tiberius, should also be consulted. Other important treatments of *maiestas* dealing with special areas within the late Republican and Imperial periods may be found in various chapters of the *Cambridge Ancient History* (Cambridge: University Press), notably Ch. VI (Sulla) in Vol. IX (1932) by Hugh Last and Ch. XIX (Tiberius) in Vol. X (1934) by M. P. Charlesworth. Standing in a class by itself is the monograph by the late Frederick H. Cramer, entitled *Astrology in Roman Law and Politics,* Memoirs of the American Philosophical Society, Vol. 37 (Philadelphia: The Society, 1954), together with his article on "Bookburning and Censorship in Ancient Rome," *Journal of the History of Ideas,* VI (1945), 157–196. An important complementary study, dealing with the subject of magic, is Clyde Pharr, "The Interdiction of Magic in Roman Law," *Transactions of the American Philological Association,* LXIII (1932), 269–295. Among more extensive interpretive works none gives more adequate attention to the place of *maiestas* in the general framework of Roman thought than the recent *Civilization and the Caesars* by C. G. Starr (Ithaca: Cornell University Press, 1954). For the correlative concepts of *libertas* and *auctoritas,* the chapters on Liberty and Authority in Fritz Schulz, *Principles of Roman Law* (Oxford: Clarendon, 1936) are essential, as is also Ch. Wirszubski, *Libertas as a Political Idea at Rome during the Late Republic and Early Principate* (Cambridge: University Press, 1950). For Hellenistic theories of kingship and their impact on Roman political theory, the documentary extracts and commentary in Ernest Barker, *From Alexander to Constantine* (Oxford: Clarendon, 1956) are invaluable. For an analysis of imperial power and its exemptions, the definitive treatment may be found in Mason Hammond, *The Augustan Principate in Theory and Practice during the Julio-Claudian Period* (Cambridge: Harvard University Press, 1933) and *The Antonine Monarchy* (American Academy in Rome, 1959), both with comprehensive bibliographical data.

Finally, a number of highly specialized monographic studies by German scholars should be noted: P. J. A. Feuerbach, *Philosophisch-juridische Untersuchung über das Verbrechen des Hochverraths* (Erfurt: Henningschen Buchhandlung, 1798); J. Weiske, *Hochverrath und Majestätsverbrechen, das* CRIMEN MAJESTATIS *der Römer* (Leipzig: Verlag von Georg Joachim Göschen, 1836); J. Zirkler, *Die gemeinrechtliche Lehre vom Majestätsverbrechen, und Hochverrath* (Stuttgart: Franz Heinrich Köhler, 1836); J. F. H. Abegg, "Zur Geschichte des römischen *crimen majestatis," Archiv des Criminalrechts* (Neue Folge), 1853 (Zweites Stück), pp. 205–238; W. E. Knitschky, *Das Verbrechen des Hochverraths* (Jena: Mauke's Verlag, 1874), pp. 17–41, on "Das römische *crimen majestatis";* P. Bisoukides, *Der Hochverrat: eine his-*

torische und dogmatische Studie (Berlin: Carl Heymanns Verlag, 1903), pp. 6–33, on the Roman Law; and Erich Pollack, *Der Majestäts-gedanke im römischen Recht: eine Studie auf dem Gebiet des römischen Staatsrechts* (Leipzig: Verlag von Veit, 1908); Ernst Meents, *Die Idee der Majestätsbeleidigung* (Berlin: R. V. Decker, 1895). The greater part of this material has been used and, to some extent, synthesized in the essay on "The Idea of Majesty in Roman Political Thought."

XIII

The Literature on Public Law
in Germanic Custom*

The study of treason in Germanic Law is more difficult than in the case of the Roman law since the Germanic materials have not been classified and arranged in a systematic, accessible manner. With the single exception of G. A. Davoud-Oghlou, *Histoire de la législation des anciens germains*, 2 vols. (Berlin: Reimer, 1845), no extensive commentaries and few bibliographical aids are available to expedite research in the barbarian codes. Moreover, the compilation of Davoud-Oghlou is not only old but its value is impaired by a complex arrangement which makes the process of locating references to the codes both slow and difficult. Nevertheless, it contains many shrewd observations and close definitions not readily discovered elsewhere and should not be neglected. It must be emphasized that the only certain method to follow in investigating the *leges barbarorum* involves a careful examination of every law, so that no matters relevant to the subject at hand may be overlooked. This means that many hours must be spent in a research that yields all too often a very slight return. However, one cannot satisfy himself with a mere reading of the titles or captions of these laws. Many suggestions concerning treason may be found incidentally under topics that have little direct relation to public offenses. Thus, if one scans superficially or is guided by outward appearances alone, he will neglect or lose sight of many significant details. A number of good accounts and

* Reprinted with revisions from *The Rice Institute Pamphlet*, XLII (1955), 90–110.

descriptions of the chief Germanic legal sources have been prepared, of which the most satisfactory may be found in F. C. von Savigny, *Geschichte des römischen Rechts im Mittelalter* (2nd ed.; Heidelberg: J. C. B. Mohr, 1834), especially Vols. I and II; Max Conrat, *Geschichte der Quellen und Literatur des römischen Rechts im früheren Mittelalter*, (Leipzig: J. Hinrichs, 1891), Vol. I; Paul Krüger, *Geschichte der Quellen und Literatur des römischen Rechts* (Leipzig: Duncker and Humblot, 1888), in *Systematisches Handbuch der deutschen Rechtswissenschaft*; Heinrich Brunner, *Deutsche Rechtsgeschichte* (2nd ed.; Leipzig: Duncker and Humblot, 1906), Vol. I, pp. 417–563; Schröder-von Künssberg, *Lehrbuch der deutschen Rechtsgeschichte* (6th ed.; Berlin and Leipzig: DeGruyter, 1922; 7th ed.; Berlin: DeGruyter, 1932), pp. 252–280 on "Die Volksrechte und die Leges Romanae," and 280–287 on "Die fränkischen Reichsgesetze"; and *Select Essays in Anglo-American Legal History* (Boston: Little, Brown, 1907), Vol. I, compiled and edited by a Committee of the Association of American Law Schools. This last-mentioned work contains "A Prologue to a History of English Law" by F. W. Maitland (Ch. I), and "The Development of Teutonic Law" by Edward Jenks (Ch. II), with a most convenient synoptic table of the Germanic legal sources (pp. 69–87). It is also worthwhile to dip into the curious old book by A. F. Gfrörer, *Zur Geschichte deutscher Volksrechte im Mittelalter*, 2 vols. (Schaffhausen: F. Hunter, 1865–1866).

The most satisfactory general treatise on Germanic legal history is Brunner's well-known *Rechtsgeschichte*, using Volume I in the second edition and the revised and expanded Brunner-von Schwerin, Volume II (Leipzig: Duncker and Humblot, 1928), while Schröder's *Lehrbuch* in the revised and enlarged Schröder-von Künssberg sixth and seventh editions affords a concise survey for reference purposes within this field. Both these works provide good starting points from which one may begin a study of treason in the Germanic family group (*Sippe*) and an investigation of the nature of public authority in the incipient state, but they should be compared with the views presented in Volume One of the *Deutsche Verfassungsgeschichte* (3rd ed.; Berlin: Weidmann, 1880) by George Waitz and Volume Three of the *Deutsche Rechtsgeschichte* (Brunswick: F. Wreden, 1872) by Heinrich Zoepfl. Contemporary sources dealing with treason and the state in this early time are limited to a few references in Caesar's *Commentaries on the Gallic Wars* and to certain parts of the *Germania* of Tacitus. Special difficulties of interpretation are encountered here, arising from the use of the Latin language in the description of Germanic institutions. However, for Tacitus an indispensable aid may be found in the analytical commentary of Rudolf Much, *Die Germania des Tacitus* (Heidelberg: C. Winter, 1937), together with the Loeb Series text (trans. by William Peterson, 1914). For the period of settling-down following the great migrations Brunner and Schröder are standard authorities, and in this study the writer inclines to accept their theory of the "ducal king" and to view him as the agent for exercising public authority that is most characteristic of this age. However, their treatment of this period should be supplemented by reading Fustel de Coulanges, *Histoire des institutions politiques de l'ancienne France (La Monarchie franque)*, 6 vols. (5th ed.; Paris: Hachette, 1926), especially Vol. II entitled "L'invasion germanique et la fin de l'empire." Also one should consult G. von Below, *Der deutsche Staat des Mittelalters* (2nd ed.; Quelle and Meyer, Leipzig: 1925), Vol. I, and Karl von Amira, *Grundriss des germanischen Rechts* (Part 5 in Paul's *Grundriss der germanischen Philologie*) (3rd ed.; Strassburg: Trübner, 1913). Felix Dahn's *Die Könige der Germanen*, 12 vols. (Munich, Würzburg and Leipzig: Breitkopf and Härtel, 1861–1909) provides an invaluable series of special studies, treating each of the different Germanic tribes and kingdoms separately. A. von Halban, *Das römische Recht in den germanischen Volksstaaten*, 3 vols. (Breslau: Marcus, 1899) is more valuable on matters of national origins and social background than for public law, but may be consulted with advantage on many points of interpretation. A considerable amount of material relating to the early family and the origins of the state that is equally applicable to all the Germanic peoples may be found in the first two volumes of Sir William Holdsworth, *A History of English Law* (4th ed.; London: 1936), while portions of Pollock and Maitland's *The History of English Law before the Time of Edward I*, 2 vols. (2nd ed.; Cambridge: University Press, 1923) possess even greater general value because of the stimulating suggestions regarding broad questions of legal theory and the historical development of legal institutions. Also much of Bishop William Stubbs' *Constitutional History of England* (5th ed.; Oxford: 1903), Vol. I, is helpful in a general study of Germanic political and legal institutions. Finally attention must be directed to the first three chapters of Julius Goebel, Jr., *Felony and Misdemeanor* (New York: The Commonwealth Fund, 1937), Vol I, which reflects views, on the whole critical, of the established positions of Wilda, Waitz, Brunner, and Beyerle regarding the problem of the Germanic "peace." It is an excellent corrective, discouraging sole reliance on these earlier works although by no means refuting them. Probably the most comprehensive bibliographical survey is found in the *Cambridge Mediaeval History* (Cambridge: Macmillan, 1926), V, 921–936, in connection with the splendid article by H. D. Hazeltine in Ch. XXI ("Roman and Canon Law in the Middle Ages"), pp. 697–764.

Only a few brief general studies have been made concerning treason in Germanic law. Of these, although old, one of the best is still that of W. E. Wilda, *Das Strafrecht der Germanen*, Vol. I of the uncompleted *Geschichte des deutschen Strafrechts* (Halle: Schwetschke, 1842), pp. 984–992, entitled "Missethaten gegen das Gemeinwesen und den König als Haupt desselben." Next in value one must rate the section on "Landes–und Hochverrat" in Brunner-von Schwerin, II, 881–886. Wilda emphasizes throughout the essentially Germanic character of the concept of *Treubruch* and supplies, in addition, a most valuable compendium of source materials. Brunner inclines to stress Roman contributions to Germanic law, including the transmission of the Roman idea of *maiestas*. He has the advantage of giving an extremely clear and readable account. Waitz, likewise, leans toward a Roman interpretation of treason in his *Verfassungsgeschichte*, Vol. 2 (I), 185 *et seq.*, and Vol. 2 (II), 291. Pollock and Maitland's *History of English Law* contains some general considerations of treason in Germanic Law in connection with the specific treatment of treason in Anglo-Saxon law. They, too, indicate the influence of the Roman concept of *maiestas* upon the legal principles expressed in the Dooms. Dahn's *Könige* has a few short notes on treason or related public offenses for each of the different Germanic tribal groups. An extremely good and relatively recent analysis of the various types of treason in Germanic law may be found in Rudolf His, *Geschichte des deutschen Strafrechts bis zur Karolina* (Munich and Berlin: R. Oldenbourg, 1928), pp. 113–118. Additional remarks concerning treason among the primitive Germans and in the *leges barbarorum* may be found in the monographs of Knitschky and Bisoukides previously noted in the essay on "The Literature on Treason in Roman Public Law." Several doctoral dissertations in German universities have dealt with this subject also. Among these may be noted M. Haidlen, *Der Hochverrat und Landesverrat nach altdeutschem Recht* (Stuttgart: Tübingen Diss., 1896), which contains a fairly extended summary of treasonable offenses in the various barbarian codes; Otto Kellner, *Das Majestätsverbrechen im deutschen Reich bis zur Mitte des 14. Jahrhunderts* (Halle a.S.: Halle-Wittenberg Diss., 1911), which leans rather heavily on Waitz but with considerable added documentation; Albert

Caflisch, *Der Landfriedensbruch* (Bern: Bern Diss., 1923), treating briefly the Germanic peace and feud, based largely on Wilda and Waitz; and Hans Nelson, *Der Landesverrat* (Cologne: Cologne Diss., 1929), touching on the Germanic concept of infidelity and its relation to the Roman idea of majesty. In general, however, these dissertations are slender and disappointing, adding little to the great legal and constitutional histories of the Germanic peoples by Wilda, Waitz, Brunner, and Schröder.

The chief collection of sources for the study of treason in Germanic law is contained in the section of the *Monumenta Germaniae Historica* devoted to *Leges*. The folk laws of nearly all the continental Germanic tribes have been edited for this great compilation. It is a truly monumental demonstration of the talent of the nineteenth century for the critical editing and establishment of texts. Most of these laws are also available in the same texts but in a more convenient format, in the *Fontes iuris germanici antiqui . . . ex monumentis Germaniae historicis.* Another useful, although older and less accurate, text of the *leges barbarorum* may be obtained in Ferdinand Walter's *Corpus juris germanici antiqui* (Berlin: Reimer, 1824), Vol. I. If Walter's text is used for any matter of significance, it should be checked carefully against the text in the *Monumenta* or another comparable text of recent scholarship. In addition to these more general collections of source materials, there are some special collections relating to particular Germanic tribes. Also Wilda's *Strafrecht* should be mentioned in this connection, because it cites important selections from a number of obscure and inaccessible sources, particularly Scandinavian materials. The value of Wilda's work is not limited to its excellence as a secondary work by any means, for, since it is based directly on the original sources and quotes them extensively, it serves, in a measure, to remedy the lack of a systematic reference book in this field, which is almost complete save for the compilation of Davoud-Oghlou.

It is not the purpose of this bibliographical sketch to survey in detail the literature (especially the secondary works) relating to each of the several Germanic folk laws. However, it may be useful to point out certain facts regarding the primary texts. The two chief legal monuments of the Visigoths are the *Lex Romana Visigothorum* or *Breviary of Alaric* and the *Leges Visigothorum* or *Forum Judicum.* The best available text of the *Breviary* is in the old edition of Gustav Haenel (Leipzig: Teubner, 1849). To facilitate research in the *Breviary* it is well to follow the cross references in the Mommsen edition of the *Theo-*

dosian Code which relate the titles in the *Breviary* to the corresponding titles in the *Codex Theodosianus*. Another aid to research is Max Conrat, *Breviarium Alaricianum: Römisches Recht im fränkischen Reich im systematischer darstellung* (Leipzig: J. C. Hinrichs, 1903), which provides a systematic topical arrangement of the material in the *Breviary*. The best text of the *Leges Visigothorum* is found in the magnificent edition of Karl Zeumer in the *Monumenta* (Hanover and Leipzig: Hahn, 1902), Legum Sectio I, Tomus I, which also includes the reconstructed text of the *Code of Euric*. A Zeumer text (*Leges Visigothorum antiquiores*) is also contained in the *Fontes* (1894), while an older text is available in Walter's *Corpus*. Both these sources contain much material relevant to treason, *maiestas, infidelitas, scandalum,* and related offenses, and must be worked through very carefully. Another source, containing a few significant definitions bearing on treason, is the *Etymologies* of St. Isidore of Seville, edited by W. M. Lindsay in the *Scriptores Classicorum Bibliotheca Oxoniensis,* 2 vols. (Oxford: Clarendon, 1911). Among secondary works deserving special mention are F. Dahn, *Könige* (Würzburg: Breitkopf and Härtel, 1871), Vol. VI: "Die Verfassung des Westgothen"; F. Dahn, *Westgothische Studien* (Würzburg: Stahel, 1874); the articles by K. Zeumer in *Neues Archiv der Gesellschaft für ältere deutsche Geschichtskunde,* entitled "Geschichte der westgothischen Gesetzgebung," XXIII (1898), 419–516; XXIV (1889), 39–122, for analysis of Section II of the *Leges,* 571–630, on Section III; and XXVI (1901), 91–149, on Section IV; R. de Ureña y Smenjaud, *La Legislación góticohispaña* (Madrid: I. Moreno, 1905) for criticism of the texts; E. de Hinojosa, "Das germanische Element im spanischen Rechte," *Zeitschrift der Savigny-Stiftung für Rechtsgeschichte (Germanistische Abtheilung),* XXXI (1910), 282–359; D. Antonio Ballesteros y Beretta, *Historia de España y su influencia en la historia universal* (Barcelona: P. Salvat, 1918), Tomo I, 55–59 with notes; Ramón Menéndez Pidal, *Historia de España* (Madrid: Espasa-Calpe, 1940), Tomo III, 202–264 with notes (Part II, chs. IV–VI by Manuel Torres and Ramón Prieto Bances); Rafael Altamira y Crevea, *Historia general del derecho español* (Madrid: V. Suárez, 1908); Theophil Melicher, *Der Kampf zwicshen Gesetzes- und Gewohnheitsrecht im Westgotenreiche* (Weimar: Böhlaus, 1930), and Paulo Meréa, *Estudos de direito visigótico* (Coimbra: Por Ordem da Universidade, 1948); and the important treatment of Visigothic institutions in Claudio Sánchez-Albornoz y Menduiña, *En torno a los orígines del feudalismo,* 3 vols. (Mendoza, Argentina: Universidad Nacional de Cuyo, 1942), especially the chapter "Los Fideles

Regis Visigodos" (I, 41–76). The most important sources for the parallel Burgundian legislation are the *Lex Romana Burgundionum* or *Papianus* and the *Leges Burgundionum* or *Lex Gundobada*. Both these laws have been edited by L. R. de Salis in the *Monumenta* (Hanover: Hahn, 1892); Legum Sectio I. Tomus II, Pars I. More recently the *Lex Romana* has been edited by J. Baviera in Riccobono *et al.*, *Fontes iuris romani antejustiniani* (Florence: Barbéra, 1940), II, 711–750. However, little material relating directly to treason may be discovered in these codes, and only a few notes dealing with public offenses are contained in Dahn's *Könige* (Leipzig: Breitkopf and Härtel, 1908), Vol. XI: "Die Burgunden." Special treatises on the Burgundians and their legislation may be found in the bibliography of K. M. Fischer, *The Burgundian Code* (Philadelphia: The University of Pennsylvania Press, 1949), Translations and Reprints, Third Series, Vol. V, pp. 97–102.

Little material is available for the later Vulgar Roman or Romance legislation of which the most important example is the *Lex Romana Raetica Curiensis* or *Epitome Sancti Galli*. The text of this compilation is edited by Karl Zeumer in the *Monumenta* (Hanover: Hahn, 1889), Legum Tomus V. Unfortunately the general significance of this material in public law is touched only tangentially in the exhaustive treatises of Ernst Levy, *West Roman Vulgar Law: The Law of Property*, published by the American Philosophical Society at Philadelphia in 1951, and *Weströmisches Vulgarrecht: Das Obligationenrecht* (Weimar: Hermann Böhlaus, 1956).

The Swabian-Bavarian area of Germanic custom is illustrated by the Alamannic and Bavarian codes. The *Leges Alamannorum* are an important source for the study of treason and infidelity in Germanic law, but, save for Davoud-Oghlou, no systematic guide exists to expedite research in this legislation. Fortunately this code is arranged in an orderly fashion so that the general topic sought can usually be found without great difficulty, although it is often necessary to read through a considerable quantity of irrelevant matter in establishing details. The best text of the Alamannic Code is edited by Karl Lehmann in the *Monumenta* (Hanover: Hahn, 1888), Legum Sectio I, Tomus V, Pars I. An older text is contained in Walter's *Corpus*, and in the original folio edition of the *Monumenta*, Legum Tomus III, by J. Merkel (1863). The Bavarian laws are closely related to the Alamannic, which they resemble both in form and content. However, the Bavarian laws are more extensive and at the same time less systematic than the Alamannic. As a result, they are correspondingly more difficult for research purposes.

Nevertheless, they contain much material relating to the entire problem of treason and infidelity in Germanic law and must be read with care. Many valuable suggestions and ideas may be derived through comparing those provisions in both laws that deal with similar subjects. The old *Monumenta* edition of the *Lex Baiwariorum* by J. Merkel (Hanover: Hahn, 1863), Legum Tomus III, has been supplanted by the new *Monumenta* edition of Baron Ernst von Schwind (Hanover: Hahn, 1926), Legum Sectio I, Tomus V, Pars II. Both these editions, however, are inferior to the splendid text of Konrad Beyerle (Munich: Max Hueber Verlag, 1926), which is accompanied with a translation, historical survey of the manuscript traditions and previous editions, critical analysis of the laws, glossary of old Germanic terms, and photographic reproductions of the entire Ingolstadt MS upon which this text is based. This is one of the finest examples of recent German scholarship in the field of Germanic law. The old edition in Walter's *Corpus* is still useful and relatively authentic since it is based in part on Mederer's collation of 1793, which employed the Ingolstadt MS. Any scholar working in this area should check his conclusions with the discussion of public offenses in Dahn's *Könige* (Leipzig: Breitkopf and Härtel, 1905), Vol. IX, Part I: "Die Alamannen" and Vol. IX, Part II: "Die Baiern". Eduard Osenbrüggen's *Das alamannische Strafrecht im deutschen Mittelalter* (Schaffhausen: Hurter, 1860) has a few references to treason in early Alamannic law, but is chiefly devoted to a later period and the origins of Swiss law. For critical comment on the Bavarian legislation one should consult E. von Schwind, "Kritische Studien zur Lex Bajuvariorum," *Neues Archiv*, XXXI (1906), 399–453; XXXIII (1908), 605–694; XXXVII (1912), 415–451; Bruno Krusch, *Die Lex Bajuvariorum* (Berlin: Weidmann, 1924); and the review of the Krusch study by Franz Beyerle, *Zeitschrift der Savigny-Stiftung für Rechtsgeschichte (Germanistische Abtheilung)*, 45 (1925), 416–457. The laws of the Ripuarian Franks, which have many significant resemblances to the Alamannic and Bavarian codes, contain few important references to public offenses. The *Lex Ribuaria* has been edited, together with the *Lex Francorum Chamavorum*, by Rudolf Sohm in the *Fontes* and the *Monumenta* (Hanover: Hahn, 1882), Legum Tomus V, pp. 185–268, with glossary on pp. 277–288 by K. Zeumer.

In addition to the Ripuarian laws, the most important Frankish materials are in the highly controversial *Salic Law*, which may be as early as the fifth century, and the later *Capitularies* of the Merovingian and Carolingian periods. Unfortunately, Frankish law contains little material bearing directly on treason, although in the *Capitularies* some important references are made to such offenses as *herisliz* and *scandalum*, and significant inferences may be drawn concerning allegiance and sovereignty. These are questions that center about the transmission of the concept of *maiestas* from Roman to Frankish law and the impact of *maiestas* upon Germanic ideas of fidelity. No specific provisions concerning treason and very little that may be described as public law can be found in the *Salic Law*. The chief importance of the *Salic Law* for contemporary scholarship revolves about extremely difficult and highly controverted problems of chronology, authenticity, and textual criticism. These matters are discussed in an extensive symposium contained in the *Neues Archiv* for the years 1914–1919 and including such specialists on Germanic law as Mario Krammer, Bruno Krusch, Claudius Freiherr von Schwerin, and Ernst Heymann. A further survey of literature of the Salic and Ripuarian problem is found in a paper by Baron von Schwerin entitled "Germanische Rechtsgeschichte" and published in *Forschungen und Fortschritte* (20 May 1941), 165–168. A still later phase of the Salic question is developed in a long study entitled "Lex Salica, I and II," by Simon Stein in *Speculum*, XXII (1947), 118–134; 395–418. Here Stein asserts that the *Salic Law* is presumably a forgery of the ninth century and reflects certain legal norms of the period in which it was constructed. He alleges further that the Ripuarian, Alamannic, and Bavarian codes may also be Carolingian forgeries. These articles constitute an interesting piece of detective work in historical and textual criticism, taking the reader behind the scenes into the editorial sanctum of the legal section of the *Monumenta Germaniae Historica*. They reveal the technical difficulties and deficiencies of this editorial work but are far from convincing in their generally critical attitude toward the *Leges* as edited in the *Monumenta*. More conventional comment and discussion of the *Salic Law* may be found in the *Rechtsgeschichte* of Brunner and Schröder and the standard histories of Frankish political institutions. The only secondary work treating the matter of treason in the *Salic Law* in any detail is the somewhat old and little known *L'organisation judiciare, le droit pénal et la procédure pénale de la Loi Salique* (2nd ed.; Brussels and Paris: Bruylant-Christophe, 1882), by J. J. Thonissen. A useful text is the *Lex Salica*, edited by Heinrich Geffcken (Leipzig: Velt, 1898). The earlier capitularies are collected in the *Capitularia regum Francorum*, edited by Alfred Boretius in the *Monumenta* (Hanover: Hahn, 1883), Legum Sectio II, Tomus I. The older *Monumenta* edition of 1835 in folio (Legum Tomus

I) was reprinted in 1925, together with the supplementary enactments, *Tomi primi supplementa constitutiones et acta Regum Germanicorum* (1837) in *Monumenta* (Legum Tomus II, Pars I). Most of these sources are also available in Walter's *Corpus*. Some valuable suggestions concerning treason among the Franks may be obtained in Dahn's *Könige* (Leipzig: Breitkopf and Härtel, 1894–1895), Vol. VII: "Die Franken unter den Merovinger" and (Leipzig: Breitkopf and Härtel, 1897–1900), Vol. VIII: "Die Franken unter den Karolinger." Special attention must be directed to the article by M. Lemosse, entitled "La Lèse-Majesté dans la Monarchie Franque," in *Revue du Moyen Âge Latin*, II (1946), 5–24. This study analyzes the problem of *maiestas* in the capitularies and its reception into Frankish law. There is one respect in which the Frankish sources differ materially from those of the other Germanic groups. The reason for this is the existence of an important literary source, the *Historia Francorum* of Gregory of Tours. An accurate evaluation of this work relative to treasonable offenses can be made only on the basis of a detailed examination of the entire text with special reference to *maiestas, scandalum,* and various descriptive features. The old work of Paul Roth, *Geschichte des Beneficialwesens* (Erlangen: Palm and Enke, 1850), contains a discussion, which is based heavily on Gregory, of several cases of treason occurring in the Frankish kingdom during the Merovingian period. Also one must not overlook another old book, J. W. Loebell, *Gregor von Tours und seine Zeit* (2nd ed., with additions by F. Bernhardt; Leipzig: Brockhaus, 1869), for matters of interpretation. The standard text with introduction, English translation, and bibliography is that of O. M. Dalton, 2 vols. (Oxford: Clarendon, 1927).

The Frisian and Saxon laws are less important for their direct contributions in the study of treason than for certain more general provisions relating to public law, notably the special *paces*. The most acceptable text of the *Lex Frisionum* has been edited by Karl Freiherr von Richthofen (Leeuwarden: Haag, Nijhoff, 1866); also by von Richthofen in *Monumenta* (Hanover: Hahn, 1863), Legum Tomus III. Some discussion of treasonable offenses among the Frisians may be found in R. His, *Das Strafrecht der Friesen im Mittelalter* (Leipzig: Dieterich, 1901). A good recent text of the Saxon laws, together with the Thuringian laws, is available in the *Fontes* in the *Leges Saxonum et Lex Thuringorum*, edited by Baron von Schwerin (Hanover and Leipzig: Hansche Buchhandlung, 1918). These laws are much more carefully annotated than the texts of the other *leges barbarorum* in earlier editions, published previously in the *Monumenta* and *Fontes*. In fact, von Schwerin's notes constitute the only set of cross references, aside from Davoud-Oghlou, available for these Germanic legal codes. He has seen fit fortunately to prepare notes for his text which relate many titles in the Saxon and Thuringian laws to the corresponding titles in the other *leges barbarorum*. These references are incidental to other purposes of the editor and are necessarily incomplete, but they do provide one of the few aids yet devised to facilitate and expedite research in the tangled mazes of the folk laws. The main secondary work touching upon treason in the Saxon laws is Baron von Richthofen's old treatise, *Zur Lex Saxonum* (Berlin: W. Hertz, 1868), while for the Thuringian law one may use Dahn's *Könige* (Leipzig: Breitkopf and Härtel, 1907), Vol. X: "Die Thüringe." There is also an earlier text of these codes, *Leges Saxonum* and *Lex Angliorum et Werinorum, hoc est Thuringorum*, by K. de Richthofen and K. F. de Richthofen in the *Monumenta*, Legum Tomus V.

The most important legal materials of early mediaeval Italy are the *Edict of Theodoric* and the so-called Lombard laws. These have been edited in Walter's *Corpus* and in the *Monumenta*. Very few provisions of the *Edict* have any relation to treason, but its broader significance for public law generally has not been explored sufficiently. The best texts are those of F. Bluhme in the *Monumenta* (Hanover: Hahn, 1875), Legum Tomus V, and of J. Baviera in Riccobono, *Fontes*, II, 681–710. The only secondary work of importance dealing with crimes against public authority in the *Edict of Theodoric* and Ostrogothic law is Dahn's *Könige* (Würzburg: Breitkopf and Härtel, 1866), Vol. IV: "Edictum des Theoderichs." The Lombard legislation represents a very important and, in many respects, unique area of Germanic custom. Important evidence concerning treason and the related offense of *scandalum* is contained in the *Edict of Rothair* with some supplementary data in the laws of Liutprand and Ratchis. For years the standard text of the *Leges Langobardorum* has been the edition of F. Bluhme in the *Fontes* and *Monumenta* (Hanover: Hahn, 1868), Legum Tomus IV, although many scholars consider the preferable text to be that of Guido Padeletti in the *Fontes juris italici medii aevi* (Turin: Loescher, 1877), Vol. I, published under the title *Edictum regum langobardorum*. Recently the Lombard legislation has been republished on the basis of the Bluhme text, revised with translation in German, topical summary of the contents, and glossary by Franz Beyerle under the title *Die Gesetze der Langobarden* (Weimar: Böhlaus, 1947). Eduard Osenbrüggen, *Das Strafrecht der Langobarden* (Schaffhausen: Hurter, 1863), should be consulted on the subject of treason in the Lombard laws. Additional suggestions may be obtained in Dahn's *Könige* (Leipzig: Breitkopf and Härtel, 1909), Vol. XII: "Die Langobarden," and T. Hodgkin, *Italy and Her Invaders* (Oxford: Clarendon, 1896), especially Vol. VI, 194–238, (Ch. V, "The Legislation of Rothari"). Scattered references of considerable value relating to treason, *lèse-majesté,* and public law in general may be found in C. Calisse, *A History of Italian Law,* trans. by L. B. Register, Continental Legal Series, Vol. VIII (London: John Murray, 1928).

The Anglo-Saxon legislation contains much material relevant to the study of treason, including provisions relating to petty treason and the royal wergeld. The most nearly definitive text of the Anglo-Saxon Dooms may be found in F. Liebermann, *Die Gesetze der Angelsachsen,* 3 vols. (Halle: Max Niemeyer, 1903–1916). This work makes these texts in the Anglo-Saxon tongue accessible by providing an excellent German translation, and, in addition, supplies a most valuable and convenient glossary of Anglo-Saxon terms that are commonly encountered in these laws. There is also the older, but still useful, *Die Gesetze der Angelsachsen* by Dr. Reinhold Schmid (2nd ed.; Leipzig: F. A. Brockhaus, 1858) with Anglo-Saxon and Latin texts and German translation; also *Ancient Laws and Institutes of England* by B. Thorpe, published by the Public Records Commission in 1840 with the Anglo-Saxon and Latin texts, English translation, and glossary. Thorpe's rendering into English is inadequate in many respects and is now generally supplanted by two useful recent works: F. L. Attenborough, *The Laws of the Earliest English Kings* (Cambridge: University Press, 1922) and A. J. Robertson, *The Laws of the Kings of England from Edmund to Henry I* (Cambridge: University Press, 1925), which contain the edited Anglo-Saxon texts, an adequate English translation, and extensive notes in commentary upon the various specific laws. A valuable discussion of treason in Anglo-Saxon law may be found in Pollock and Maitland's *History of English Law* to which may be added scattered references in Holdsworth and Stubbs.

The Scandinavian laws have been the most inaccessible of all Germanic legal sources to students not versed in the archaic tongues of the North countries. A generation ago Wilda's *Strafrecht* and *Das altnorwegische Vollstreckungsverfahren* (Munich: I. Ackermann, 1874) by Karl von Amira were practically indispensable as guides to research in this material. They are still extremely useful as foundation studies. In these works a large number of provisions from the various Scandinavian laws dealing with treason and public offenses are cited in German translation. The most important of these laws are the Norwegian *Gulathings-lög*, and *Frostuthingslög*, the Swedish *Westgötalag* and *Ostgötalag,* and the Danish laws of King Erik. Additional secondary works of value, treating the general field of offenses against public authority in Scandinavian law including outlawry and "peacelessness," are F. P. Brandt, *Forelaes-ninger over den norske Retshistorie* (Kristiania [Oslö]: N. W. Damm, 1883), Vol. II, Konrad von Maurer, *Altisläandisches Strafrecht und Gerichtswesen, Vorlesungen über altnordische Rechtsgeschichte* (Leipzig: A. Deichert, 1910), Vol. V, and Andreas Heusler *Das Strafrecht der Isländersagas* (Leipzig: Duncker and Humblot, 1911). More recently a work has appeared which facilitates the study of these materials very greatly. This is a translation into English of the Norse Gulathing law and Frostathing law found in L. M. Larson, *The Earliest Norwegian Laws,* Columbia Records of Civilization Series, No. XX (New York: Columbia University Press, 1935). Another more extensive series of aids has been made available through the translation into German of a wider range of Scandinavia legal material in the *Germanenrechte: Schriften der Akademie für deutsches Recht.* This series contains not only renderings into German by Rudolf Meissner of the Frostathing law (Weimar: H. Böhlaus, 1939), Vol. 4, and the Gulathing law (Weimar: H. Böhlaus, 1935), Vol. 6, but also the old Norwegian Law of the Following (Hirthskrá) by Meissner (Weimar: H. Böhlaus, 1938), Vol. 5, the Swedish *Westgötalag* and *Uplandslag* by Baron von Schwerin (Weimar: H. Böhlaus, 1935), Vol. 7; the Danish laws including Erichs *seeländisches Recht* by Baron von Schwerin (Weimar: H. Böhlaus, 1938), Vol. 8; and the Icelandic laws by Andreas Heusler (Weimar: H. Böhlaus, 1937), Vol. 10. Also it should be noted that one can hardly obtain a complete grasp of the problems of public law among the early Scandinavian peoples without having recourse to the Saga literature. A valuable source for this material is the *Fagrskinna-Kortfattet norsk Konge-saga,* edited by P. A. Munch and C. R. Unger (Christiania [Oslö]: Kongelige Norske Fredericks-Universitet, 1847). Among the various sagas, the *Egils-saga* is particularly significant because of its reference to conspiracy as a form of treason. This has been translated from the Icelandic by the Reverend W. C. Green (London: Elliott Stock, 1893) under the title of *The Story of Egil Skallagrimsson,* and by Gwyn Jones in *Egil's-saga* (Syracuse: Syracuse University Press, 1960).

A few concluding remarks should be written concerning English translations of the Latin texts of the *leges barbarorum.* Here no project is in progress nor, indeed, has ever been made in the way of a comprehensive plan for turning into English the entire corpus of Germanic law. In this field there is nothing comparable to the Pharr translations of the Roman law material, or even Scott's translation of the *Corpus Juris Civilis*. Nevertheless, some work has been completed in this direction. The Visigothic *Forum Judicum* has been translated under the title of *The Visigothic Code* (Boston: Boston Book Company, 1910) by S. P. Scott. As is the case with his work in the Roman law, Scott's Visigothic translation is inadequate and should be checked independently against Zeumer's text in any matter of importance. However, his annotation often contains valuable historical and interpretive matter that is very difficult to uncover elsewhere. The work should not be discarded but should be used with caution. Selections from the Visigothic laws may also be found in the *Germanenrechte* (Weimar: Böhlaus, 1936), Vol. 11; in the Zeumer text with German translation by E. Wohlhaupter under the title *Gesetze der Westgoten*. It is unfortunate that most of these extracts are from the *Antiqua*, which is relatively easy to read, whereas the highly complex and difficult royal enactments are omitted. The old Spanish and Latin texts of the *Fueros* and *Fazañas* of Leon, Castile, Navarre, Aragon, and Catalonia are contained in *Germanenrechte* (Weimar: Böhlaus, 1936), Vol. 12; with German translation by E. Wohlhaupter, under the title *Altspanisch-gotische Rechte*. The Burgundian *Lex Gundobada* is translated by Katherine Fischer and published by the University of Pennsylvania Press in the Third Series of Translations and Reprints (1949), Vol. V. The same code was published in the de Salis text with German translation by Franz Beyerle in the *Germanenrechte* (Weimar: Böhlaus, 1936), Vol. 10; under the title *Gesetze der Burgunden*. The Lombard legislation has been translated with an exhaustive introduction, commentary, and bibliography by Katherine Fischer in her unpublished Cornell University dissertation (1950), entitled *A Study of the Lombard Laws*. This work is particularly useful since the Lombard material is central in any detailed consideration of the barbarian codes. These laws are available in the Bluhme text with German translation and glossary by Franz Beyerle under the title *Die Gesetze der Langobarden* (Weimar: Böhlaus, 1947). The Alamannic and Bavarian group of laws have been translated with an introductory sketch in the unpublished Rice Institute master's thesis (1941) of Floy King Rogde. There is no other work in English dealing with this legislation, within my knowledge. An excellent German translation of the Bavarian law is contained in the previously mentioned work *Lex*

Baiuvariorum (Munich: Max Hueber Verlag, 1926) by Franz Beyerle. The minor codes remain untranslated into English, save for extracts from the Salic Law in E. F. Henderson, *Select Historical Documents of the Middle Ages* (London: Bell, 1921), pp. 176–189, and O. J. Thatcher and E. H. McNeal, *A Source Book for Mediaeval History* (New York: Scribner's, 1914), pp. 14–26. The related codes of Vulgar Roman Law, such as the *Breviary, Papianus,* and *Lex Romana Curiensis,* also are not translated, save for the citations contained in them from such translated sources as the *Theodosian Code* and *Sentences* of Paulus. However, additional texts with German translation by K. A. Eckhardt may be found in the *Germanenrechte* for the *Pactus Legis Salicae,* the Salic *Extravagantes* and *Novellae,* and the *Pactus Alamannorum* (Weimer: Böhlaus, 1935), Vol. 1; the *Lex Salica* and *Lex Ribuaria* (Weimar: Böhlaus, 1934), Vol. 2 [I]; and *Lex Alamannorum* and *Lex Baivariorum* (Weimar: Böhlaus, 1934), Vol. 2 [II]. The results of this literary survey show that the large constructive research projects in Germanic customary law belong to the era of the establishment of texts and the pursuit of constitutional history. There still remains a vast reservoir of social and economic data that has never been adequately assessed but which will require the most discriminating judgment to interpret and evaluate. The philological and linguistic difficulties are very considerable in the utilization of this material, but the most baffling questions are those which arise from the intellectual climate itself within which the barbarian mind functioned and had its being.

Since 1953 a very considerable increase in the range of published texts of Germanic law with accompanying translations into the German language has appeared in the two series of the *Germanenrechte*: the simplified editions of the *Texte und Übersetzungen* and the critical editions of the *Neue Folge (Westgermanisches Recht)*. Much of this advance in textual criticism and careful translation is the result of the studies of Karl August Eckhardt, beginning with his *Lex Salica: 100-Titel Text Westgermanisches Recht* (Weimar: Böhlaus, 1953). This has been followed by the texts *(Neue Folge),* usually accompanied with German translation of the *Pactus Legis Salicae* I(1) *80-Titel Text* with introduction (Göttingen: Musterschmidt-Verlag, 1954); I(2) *Systematisches Text,* including text and translation of the Italian Fragment (1957); II(1) *65-Titel Text* with translation (1958); II(2) *Kapitularien und 70-Titel Text* with translation (1956). Also see *Texte und Übersetzungen,* edited by K. A. Eckhardt, *Die Gesetze des Merowingerreiches, 481–714* (Frankfort: Musterschmidt, 1955), 1(I) *Pactus Legis Salicae:*

Recensiones Merovingicae, and *Die Gesetze des Karolingerreiches, 714–911* (Weimar: Böhlaus, 1953), 2(I) *Lex Salica: Recensio Pippina.*

In addition to this extensive collection of material on the Salic Law much new textual and translation work has been directed to the other barbarian codes, as follows by K. A. Eckhardt: *Neue Folge,* Vol. IV, *Leges Anglo-Saxonum, 601–925,* Anglo-Saxon text and German translation (Göttingen: Musterschmidt, 1958) [Cf. Vol. XIII *(Texte und Über.), Gesetze der Angelsachsen, 601–925* (Göttingen: Musterschmidt, 1958).]; Vol. V., *Leges Alamannorum,* I: Introduction and *Recensio Chlothariana (Pactus)* (Göttingen: Musterschmidt, 1958), and II: *Recensio Landfridana (Lex)* (Witzenhausen: Deutschrechtlicher Instituts-Verlag, 1962); Vol. VI *Lex Ribuaria,* I: *Austrasisches Recht im 7 Jahrhundert* (Göttingen: Musterschmidt, 1959). See also by Frank Beyerle, *Neue Folge,* Vol. IX, *Leges Langobardorum, 643–866,* Latin text with Glossary (Witzenhausen: Deutschrechtlicher Instituts-Verlag, 1962), and *Texte und Über.,* Vol. III, *Die Gesetze der Langobarden,* I: *Edictus Rothari,* and II: *Novellen,* 2nd revised ed., translation only (Witzenhausen: Deutschrechtlicher Instituts-Verlag, 1962).

Among other recent works are Rudolf Buchner, *Die Rechtsquellen* [Beiheft to Wattenbach-Levison] *Deutschlands Geschrichtsquellen im Mittelalter: Vorzeit und Karolinger* (Weimar: Böhlaus, 1953), with review by Luitpold Wallach in *Speculum,* XXX (1955), 92–96, which includes additional bibliographical information; H. Conrad, *Deutsche Rechtsgeschichte,* (Karlsruhe: Verlag C. F. Müller, 1954), Band I: *Frühzeit und Mittelalter;* the new edition of the *Lex Ribuaria* by Franz Beyerle and Rudolf Buchner in the *Monumenta, Leges Nationum Germanicarum* (Hanover: Hahn, 1954), Tomus II, Pars II, supplementing the old edition of Rudolf Sohm. There is still a great dearth of translated and/or interpreted material in the English language in this field. However, the *Lex Ripuaria* has been translated into English by James P. Barefield in his unpublished Rice Institute master's thesis (1958), and Book II of the *Leges Visigothorum* by Ralph Ewton in his unpublished Rice University master's thesis (1961).

INDEX

absolutism: in Rome, 21, 23–24, 25, 93–94, 133; and majesty, 24, 64–66, 67, 238; among Germanic tribes, 230, 233–234, 238. SEE ALSO tyranny

accusation, right of: nature of, 33, 151 n.; in Germanic law, 37–38, 151, 233, 242–243; in Roman law, 115; and petty treason, 121, 129

Additio sapientium: 246

adultery: as treason, xv, 81, 150, 151, 222; in Germanic law, 228, 231

Aegidius, *Epitome* of: 116, 166 n.

Aethelberht, Dooms of: 183, 184

Aethelred, Dooms of: 189–190

Aethelstan, laws of: 188–189

Agilolfing dynasty: 213, 215 n.

Aire, assembly at: and *Breviary*, 110

Alamanni: history of, 80, 202, 203

Alamannic laws: and other Germanic codes, 125 n., 179–180, 208, 212, 213, 214, 216–217, 220

—, contents of: blasphemy, 180; public law, 202–212; special peaces, 204–205, 209, 210, 221–222, 227; *Heimfrieden*, 205; wergeld, 206, 209, 212; Treubruch, 206–207; majesty, 206–207; conspiracy, 207 n.; *Landesverrat*, 208, 211–212; treason, 208–209, 212, 216, 223 n.; theft, 209; *scandalum*, 209–210, 212; compurgation, 212; infamy, 223

—, influences on: Roman, 40, 41, 204, 206–207, 208, 210, 212, 214, 216 n., 251; Germanic, 203, 206–207, 208, 212, 214; ecclesiastical, 204–205, 210, 212

—, text of: 203 and n., 214 n.

Alaric, King: power of, 75, 84

Alaric II, King: *Breviary* by, 110, 126–127, 128; and Visigothic laws, 137

Alboin, King: 234

Alexander the Great: 24, 66, 74

Alfonso the Wise: 139

Alfred, Dooms of: 185–186, 188, 190, 194

allegiance: in Germanic law, 38–43, 123, 128; and majesty, 49, 60 n., 83, 121 n.; nature of, 87–89, 105, 146, 162; in Roman law, 123, 128

—, contractual: nature of, 83, 87, 129–130, 132, 134, 146, 149, 186; and feudalism, 88, 121 n., 130 n., 164; and deferential allegiance, 83, 123–135, 157, 186, 238; in Visigothic society, 142, 143–144, 162; in Germanic law, 153, 200–201

—, deferential: and contractual allegiance, 83, 123–135, 157, 186, 238; and concept of majesty, 130; nature of, 132

Anglo-Saxon Dooms. SEE Dooms, Anglo-Saxon

Animate Law: 24

Annals of Tacitus. SEE Tacitus

Ansegisus, Fragments of: 247

Antonine Monarchy: on absolutism, 23

Antonines, the: 23, 65

Apollinaris Sidonius: 127

Appius Claudius: 15

Arator of Liguria: 155 n.

Arcadius, Emperor: on treason, 32, 36, 72; on majesty, 44–45, 169; on paganism, 174

Arian Christianity: 32, 138

Aristotle: on nature of the state, 9

arson: as treason, 81, 96, 219, 221, 241, 245, 249, 250; in Germanic codes, 193, 228, 241, 245, 249, 250

Ascheim, Synod of: 213, 214

Asconius Pedianus: on majesty, 51, 63

assemblies, popular: 82, 85

asylum, right of. SEE sanctuary, right of

attainder, concept of: and treason, 45; and majesty, 70, 116, 180; in Visigothic law, 153–154, 157

Augustine, Saint: 174

Augustine Principate: 23, 24, 68. SEE ALSO Augustus Caesar; Principate, the

Augustus Caesar: and majesty, 22, 23, 64–65, 67, 69–70; and treason, 19, 34; allegiance to, 74; mention of, 43 n., 44 n. SEE ALSO Augustine Principate; Principate, the

Aurelian, Emperor: 21, 24, 65

authority, patriarchal: treason under, xiv–xv, 13; among Romans, 4, 22; in Germanic tribes, 77–78

Ingram Content Group UK Ltd.
Milton Keynes UK
UKHW042249260323
418963UK00011B/190